Blackstone's

Handbook of Youths in the Criminal Courts

Blackstone's

Handbook of Youths in the Criminal Courts

Mark Ashford
Gareth Branston
Naomi Redhouse

Consultant Editor
Anthony Edwards

OXFORD
UNIVERSITY PRESS

OXFORD
UNIVERSITY PRESS

Great Clarendon Street, Oxford, OX2 6DP,
United Kingdom

Oxford University Press is a department of the University of Oxford. It furthers the University's objective of excellence in research, scholarship, and education by publishing worldwide. Oxford is a registered trade mark of Oxford University Press in the UK and in certain other countries

First Edition published in 2013
Second Edition published in 2018
Third Edition published in 2024

Published in the United States of America by Oxford University Press
198 Madison Avenue, New York, NY 10016, United States of America

British Library Cataloguing in Publication Data

Data available

Library of Congress Control Number: 2023951453

ISBN 978–0–19–891314–6

DOI: 10.1093/oso/9780198913146.001.0001

Printed and bound by CPI Group (UK) Ltd, Croydon, CR0 4YY

Preface

We have written this third edition of the book with the busy practitioner in mind. We hope that this includes solicitors, barristers, youth justice service staff and other professionals working in the criminal justice system. We know from our experience that it is also useful to District Judges (Magistrates' Courts) and legal advisers. This edition is intended to be of use in the Crown Court as well.

Dealing with cases involving children and young people (referred to through the text as youths) presents a number of challenges and our aim is to provide, in accessible form, all that is immediately necessary to deal with the day-to-day practice of the criminal courts where those defendants appear.

Since the second edition in 2018, there have been very significant changes in the law, procedural rules, and practice directions applicable to youth defendants. This edition follows the layout of the previous edition but has been fully updated to reflect those important changes. It is hoped that there will now be more regular updates to keep on top of an ever-changing legal landscape. The aim is also to provide a more substantial revision to the layout of the book for a 2025 edition.

We are particularly grateful to Anthony Edwards: without his continuing determination, this edition would not have come about.

We would also like to thank our colleagues who have contributed their ideas to this work. Good ideas which have not been incorporated this time should be found in future editions. Any mistakes are entirely our own.

We have stated the law as at 18 October 2023.

Gareth Branston
Naomi Redhouse

Contents

Icons List

The following icon is use in this book:

Cross reference to *Blackstone's Criminal Practice 2024*

Table of Cases

Table of Primary Legislation

Table of Secondary Legislation

Children (Secure Accommodation) Regulations 1991 (SI 1991/1505)
- reg 4 . . . . H13.1
- reg 5(2)(a) H13.1
- reg 5A H13.1
- reg 6 . . . . H13.4
- reg 10 . . . . H13.4
- reg 13 . . . . H13.3

Civil Procedure Rules 1998 (SI 1998/3132) N1.2
- r 2.1(1) N1.2
- Pt 31 . . . . N1.2, N1.3

Criminal Legal Aid (Financial Resources) Regulations 2013 (SI 2013/471)
- reg 22 . . . . H4.5

Criminal Justice Act 2003 (Commencement No 14 and Transitional Provision) Order 2006 (SI 2006/3217) H3.4.1

Criminal Procedure Rules 2020 (SI 2020/759) I1, I1.2, M2, N1.2
- Pt 3 . . . . I3.7
  - r 3.5(3) K2.3
  - r 3.8(3)(b) I2.2
  - r 3.10 . . . . I2.7, J9.2, J16.3
- Pt 7
  - r 7.4 . . . . M2
  - r 7.4(8) M2
- Pt 9
  - r 9.13 . . . . H2.4.1
- Pt 14
  - r 14.8 . . . . H3.11.1
- Pt 18 . . . . I3.7
  - r 18.4 . . . . I3.7
  - r 18.4(a) I3.7
  - r 18.4(b) I3.7
  - rr 18.8–18.10 . . . . I3.7
  - r 18.10(a)–(i) I3.7
  - rr 18.11–18.13 . . . . I3.7
  - r 18.23 . . . . I1.2
  - r 18.23(1)–(6) I1.2
  - r 18.24 . . . . I1.2
  - r 18.24(1)–(2) I1.2
  - r 18.25 . . . . I1.2
  - r 18.25(1)–(3) I1.2
  - rr 18.26–18.28 . . . . I1.2, I3.8.5
- Pt 24
  - r 24.11 . . . . J18
  - r 24.11(3), (4) J18
  - r 24.11(7) J18
  - r 24.11(9) J18
  - r 24.12 . . . . H8.2
- Pt 25
  - r 25.10 . . . . I2.7, J9.2, J16.3
- Pt 28
  - r 28.8 . . . . I2.7, J9.2, J16.3
- Pt 31 . . . . J3.2, N1.2
  - r 31.3 . . . . J2.1
  - rr 31.10–31.11 . . . . J3.2
- Pt 34 . . . . K5.1

Family Procedure Rules 2010 (SI 2010/2955)
- Pt 12 . . . . H13.3

Justices of the Peace Rules 2016 (SI 2016/709) H5
- r 19 . . . . H5
- r 30 . . . . H5

Magistrates' Courts Rules 1981 (SI 1981/552) N1.2, N1.5
- r 3A N1.3
- r 3A(1)–(3) N1.3
- r 14 . . . . N1.5
- r 14(1)–(6) N1.5

Magistrates' Courts (Children and Young Persons) Rules 1992 (SI 1992/2071)
- Pt III H13.3
- r 14 . . . . H13.3

Magistrates' Courts (Hearsay Evidence in Civil Proceedings) Rules 1999 . . . . N1.4.1
- r 3 . . . . N1.4.1

Table of Conventions

International conventions

International standards and rules

Table of Practice Directions

Abbreviations

ABCPA 2014	Anti-social Behaviour, Crime and Policing Act 2104
ADHD	attention deficit hyperactivity disorder
ASBI	anti-social behaviour injunction
ASBO	anti-social behaviour order
BA 1976	Bail Act 1976
CBO	criminal behaviour order
CDA 1998	Crime and Disorder Act 1998
Civ PR	Civil Procedure Rules
CJA 2003	Criminal Justice Act 2003
CJIA 2008	Criminal Justice and Immigration Act 2008
CPIA 1996	Criminal Procedure and Investigations Act 1996
CPDs	Criminal Practice Directions
CPS	Crown Prosecution Service
Crim PR	Criminal Procedure Rules
CYPA 1933	Children and Young Persons Act 1933
CYPA 1963	Children and Young Persons Act 1963
CYPA 1969	Children and Young Persons Act 1969
DAA 2021	Domestic Abuse Act 2021
DPP	Director of Public Prosecutions
DTO	detention and training order
ECHR	European Convention on Human Rights
ECtHR	European Court of Human Rights
ISS	intensive supervision and surveillance
ISSP	intensive supervision and surveillance programme
LAA	Legal Aid Agency
LASPO 2012	Legal Aid, Sentencing and Punishment of Offenders Act 2012
MCA 1980	Magistrates' Courts Act 1980
MDA 1971	Misuse of Drugs Act 1971
MHA 1983	Mental Health Act 1983
NPCC	National Police Chiefs' Council

PACE 1984	Police and Criminal Evidence Act 1984
PCCSA 2000	Powers of Criminal Courts (Sentencing) Act 2000
PCSCA 2022	Police Crime Sentencing and Courts Act 2022
POCA 2002	Proceeds of Crime Act 2002
PSR	pre-sentence report
RTA 1988	Road Traffic Act 1988
SC	Sentencing Code (Sentencing Act 2020)
SHPO	sexual harm prevention order
SOA 2003	Sexual Offences Act 2003
TA 1968	Theft Act 1968
TIC	taken into consideration
YJB	Youth Justice Board
YJCEA 1999	Youth Justice and Criminal Evidence Act 1999
YOI	young offender institution
YOT	youth offending team
YRO	youth rehabilitation order

Part E
Offences

E1 Offence Guidelines—Introduction

Most of the Sentencing Council's guidelines, both offence-specific and overarching principles, apply only to offenders who are aged 18 or older at the date of sentence. These guidelines appear in the Magistrates' Court Handbook. In this section, the three youth-specific offence sentencing guidelines are set out in full. The *Sentencing Children and Young People–Overarching Principles* definitive guideline is in Appendix Y1. These guidelines have a different format to those applicable to adults and provide the court with a wide discretion. In applying the *Sentencing Children and Young People–Overarching Principles* definitive guideline, which must be considered alongside any offence-specific guideline, the court is urged to make an individualistic decision based on a full assessment of the young person. The offence-specific guidelines relating to robbery and sexual offences were issued attached to the 2017 *Sentencing Children and Young People–Overarching Principles* definitive guideline and, perhaps for that reason, their existence is sometimes overlooked. In the digital applications now available and on relevant websites they rarely appear separately from the adult guideline for these offences in the index. Advocates should be aware that the court may not be aware of their existence and specific reference should be made to them.

The relationship of the youth-specific offence guideline to the equivalent adult guideline is dealt with in the text of each:

> Where a custodial sentence is unavoidable the length of custody imposed must be the shortest commensurate with the seriousness of the offence. The court may want to consider the equivalent adult guideline in order to determine the appropriate length of the sentence.
>
> If considering the adult guideline, the court may feel it appropriate to apply a sentence broadly within the region of half to two thirds of the appropriate adult sentence for those aged 15–17 and allow a greater reduction for those aged under 15. This is only a rough guide and must not be applied mechanistically. The individual factors relating to the offence and the child or young person are of the greatest importance and may present good reason to impose a sentence outside of this range.

This means that the adult guideline only becomes relevant to the courts' deliberations once the court has followed all of the steps set out in the youth-specific offence guideline and has decided that a custodial sentence is unavoidable.

Blackstone's Handbook of Youths in the Criminal Courts. Mark Ashford, Gareth Branston, and Naomi Redhouse, Oxford University Press.
 DOI: 10.1093/oso/9780198913146.003.0001

The role of the adult guideline where there is no youth-specific offence sentencing guideline is set out in paras 6.45 and 6.46 of the *Overarching Principles* definitive guideline:

> 6.45 Only if the court is satisfied that the offence crosses the custody threshold, and that no other sentence is appropriate, the court may, as a preliminary consideration, consult the equivalent adult guideline in order to decide upon the appropriate length of the sentence.
>
> 6.46 When considering the relevant adult guideline, the court may feel it appropriate to apply a sentence broadly within the region of half to two thirds of the adult sentence for those aged 15–17 and allow a greater reduction for those aged under 15. This is only a rough guide and must not be applied mechanistically. In most cases when considering the appropriate reduction from the adult sentence the emotional and developmental age and maturity of the child or young person is of at least equal importance as their chronological age.

It is important that the court does not go straight to these paragraphs and consult an adult guideline too early in the sentencing process. This would be to ignore the important principles applicable to youths and designed to emphasize the necessity for an individualistic approach for young defendants: *R v ZA* [2023] EWCA Crim 596.

The adult guidelines do contain factors which may affect the courts' assessment of the seriousness of the offence, which may assist a court where there is no youth-specific guideline for that offence.

E2 Bladed Articles and Offensive Weapons (Having in Public/ Education Premises and Threats)—Sentencing Children and Young People Guideline—effective from 1 June 2018

This guideline should be read alongside the *Sentencing Children and Young People – Overarching Principles definitive guideline* which provides comprehensive guidance on the sentencing principles and welfare considerations that the court should have in mind when sentencing children and young people.

This offence is subject to statutory minimum sentencing provisions. See STEP FIVE for further details.

The first step in determining the sentence is to assess the seriousness of the offence. This assessment is made by considering the nature of the offence and any aggravating and mitigating factors relating to the offence itself. The fact that a sentence threshold is crossed does not necessarily mean that that sentence should be imposed.

STEP 1
Offence Seriousness—Nature of the offence

The boxes below give examples of the type of culpability and harm factors that may indicate that a particular threshold of sentence has been crossed.

A non-custodial sentence* may be the most suitable disposal where one or more of the following factors apply:
Possession of weapon falls just short of reasonable excuse
No/minimal risk of weapon being used to threaten or cause harm
Fleeting incident and no/minimal distress

Blackstone's Handbook of Youths in the Criminal Courts. Mark Ashford, Gareth Branston, and Naomi Redhouse, Oxford University Press.
 DOI: 10.1093/oso/9780198913146.003.0002

A custodial sentence or youth rehabilitation order with intensive supervision and surveillance* or fostering* may be justified where one or more of the following factors apply:
Possession of a bladed article whether produced or not
Possession of a highly dangerous weapon† whether produced or not
Offence motivated by, or demonstrating hostility based on any of the following characteristics or presumed characteristics of the victim: religion, race, disability, sexual orientation or transgender identity
Prolonged incident and serious alarm/distress
Offence committed at a school or other place where vulnerable people may be present

* Where the child or young person appears in the magistrates' court, and the conditions for a compulsory referral order apply, a referral order must be imposed unless the court is considering imposing a discharge, hospital order or custody.

† NB an offensive weapon is defined in legislation as 'any article made or adapted for use for causing injury, or is intended by the person having it with him for such use'. A highly dangerous weapon is, therefore, a weapon, including a corrosive substance (such as acid), whose dangerous nature must be substantially above and beyond this. The court must determine whether the weapon is highly dangerous on the facts and circumstances of the case.

STEP 2
Offence Seriousness—Aggravating and mitigating factors

To complete the assessment of seriousness the court should consider the aggravating and mitigating factors relevant to the offence.

Aggravating factors
Statutory aggravating factors:
Previous findings of guilt, having regard to a) the nature of the offence to which the finding of guilt relates and its relevance to the current offence; and b) the time that has elapsed since the finding of guilt (unless the convictions will be relevant for the purposes of the statutory minimum sentencing provisions—see step five)
Offence committed whilst on bail
Other aggravating factors (non-exhaustive):
Significant degree of planning/premeditation

Deliberate humiliation of victim, including but not limited to filming of the offence, deliberately committing the offence before a group of peers with the intent of causing additional distress or circulating details/photos/videos etc. of the offence on social media or within peer groups
Victim is particularly vulnerable due to factors including but not limited to age, mental or physical disability
Offence was committed as part of a group or gang
Attempts to conceal identity
Steps taken to prevent reporting the incident/seeking assistance
Commission of offence whilst under the influence of alcohol or drugs
Offence committed against those working in the public sector or providing a service to the public

Mitigating factors (non-exhaustive)
No findings of guilt or no relevant/recent findings of guilt
Good character and/or exemplary conduct
Participated in offence due to bullying, peer pressure, coercion or manipulation
Little or no planning
Cooperation with the police

STEP 3
Personal mitigation

Having assessed the offence seriousness the court should then consider the mitigation personal to the child or young person to determine whether a custodial sentence or a community sentence is necessary. The effect of personal mitigation may reduce what would otherwise be a custodial sentence to a non-custodial one or a community sentence to a different means of disposal.

Personal mitigating factors (non-exhaustive)
Particularly young or immature child or young person (where it affects their responsibility)
Communication or learning disabilities or mental health concerns

Unstable upbringing including but not limited to: • time spent looked after • lack of familial presence or support • disrupted experiences in accommodation or education • exposure to drug/alcohol abuse, familial criminal behaviour or domestic abuse • victim of neglect or abuse, or exposure to neglect or abuse of others • experiences of trauma or loss
Determination and/or demonstration of steps taken to address offending behaviour
Child or young person in education, training, or employment

STEP 4
Reduction for guilty pleas

The court should take account of any potential reduction for a guilty plea in accordance with section 73 of the Sentencing Code and part one, section five of the *Sentencing Children and Young People – Overarching Principles* definitive guideline.

The reduction in sentence for a guilty plea can be taken into account by imposing one type of sentence rather than another; for example:

- by reducing a custodial sentence to a community sentence, or
- by reducing a community sentence to a different means of disposal.

Alternatively the court could reduce the length or severity of any punitive requirements attached to a community sentence.

See the *Sentencing Children and Young People – Overarching Principles* definitive guideline for details of other available sentences including Referral Orders and Reparation Orders.

STEP 5
Statutory minimum sentencing provisions

The following provisions apply to those young people who were aged 16 or over on the date of the offence:

Threatening with Bladed Articles or Offensive Weapons

When sentencing these offences a court must impose a sentence of at least 4 months Detention and Training Order **unless:**

- (if the offence was committed on or after 28 June 2022) **the court is of the opinion that there are exceptional circumstances which relate to the offence or to the young person, and justify not doing so**; or
- (if the offence was committed before 28 June 2022) **the court is of the opinion that there are particular circumstances relating to the offence or the young person which make it unjust to do so in all the circumstances.**

Possession of Bladed Articles or Offensive Weapons

When sentencing the offences of:

- possession of an offensive weapon in a public place;
- possession of an article with a blade/point in a public place;
- possession of an offensive weapon on school premises; and
- possession of an article with blade/point on school premises

a court must impose a sentence of at least 4 months' Detention and Training Order where this is a **second or further** relevant offence **unless:**

- **(if the offence was committed on or after 28 June 2022) the court is of the opinion that there are exceptional circumstances which relate to the offence or to the young person, and justify not doing so; or**
- **(if the offence was committed on or after 28 June 2022) the court is of the opinion that there are particular circumstances relating to the offence, the previous offence, or the young person which make it unjust to do so in all the circumstances.**

A 'relevant offence' includes those offences listed above and the following offences:

- threatening with an offensive weapon in a public place;
- threatening with an article with a blade/point in a public place;
- threatening with an article with a blade/point on school premises; and
- threatening with an offensive weapon on school premises.

Exceptional circumstances (offence committed on or after 28 June 2022):

In considering whether there are exceptional circumstances that would justify not imposing the minimum term the court must have regard to:

- the particular circumstances which relate to any of the offences **and**
- the particular circumstances of the offender.

either of which may give rise to exceptional circumstances.

Where the issue of exceptional circumstances has been raised the court should give a clear explanation as to why those circumstances have or have not been found.

Where the factual circumstances are disputed, the procedure should follow that of a Newton hearing: see Criminal Practice Directions 9.3.3.

Circumstances are exceptional if the imposition of the minimum term would result in an arbitrary and disproportionate sentence for that young person.

The offence

Having reached this stage of the guideline the court should have made a provisional assessment of the seriousness of the offence. Where the court has determined that the offence seriousness falls far below the custody threshold the court may consider that this gives rise to exceptional circumstances that justify not imposing the statutory minimum sentence. Where the court is considering a statutory minimum sentence as a result of a second or further relevant offence, consideration should be given to the seriousness of the previous offence(s) and the period of time that has elapsed between offending. Where the seriousness of the combined offences is such that it falls far below the custody threshold, or where there has been a significant period of time between the offences, the court may consider that this gives rise to exceptional circumstances that justify not imposing the statutory minimum sentence.

The young person

The statutory obligation to have regard to the welfare of a young person includes the obligation to secure proper provision for education and training, to remove the young person from undesirable surroundings where appropriate, and the need to choose the best option for the young person taking account of the circumstances of the offence. **In having regard to the welfare of the young person, a court should ensure that it considers:**

- any mental health problems or learning difficulties/disabilities;
- any experiences of brain injury or traumatic life experience (including exposure to drug and alcohol abuse) and the developmental impact this may have had;
- any speech and language difficulties and the effect this may have on the ability of the young person (or any accompanying adult) to communicate with the court, to understand the sanction imposed or to fulfil the obligations resulting from that sanction;

- the vulnerability of young people to self harm, particularly within a custodial environment; and
- the effect on young people of experiences of loss and neglect and/or abuse.

In certain cases the concerns about the welfare of the young person may be so significant that the court considers that this gives rise to exceptional circumstances that justify not imposing the statutory minimum sentence.

Where exceptional circumstances are found

If there are exceptional circumstances that justify not imposing the statutory minimum sentence then the court must impose an alternative sentence.

Unjust in all the circumstances (offence committed before 28 June 2022):

The guideline includes further assistance on this concept which has not been reproduced here given that it will now be very rare for the court to be dealing with a young defendant who has committed such an offence before 28 June 2022.

STEP 6
Review the sentence

The court must now review the sentence to ensure it is the most appropriate one for the child or young person. This will include an assessment of the likelihood of reoffending and the risk of causing serious harm. A report from the Youth Offending Team may assist.

See the *Sentencing Children and Young People – Overarching Principles* definitive guideline for comprehensive guidance on the sentencing principles and welfare considerations that the court should have in mind when sentencing children and young people, and for the full range of the sentences available to the court.

Referral orders

In cases where children or young people have offended for the first time and have pleaded guilty to committing an offence which is on the cusp of the custody threshold, youth offending teams (YOT) should be encouraged to convene a Youth Offender Panel prior to sentence (sometimes referred to as a 'pseudo-panel' or 'pre-panel') where the child or young person is asked to attend before a panel and agree an intensive contract. If that contract is placed before the sentencing youth court, the court can then decide whether it is sufficient to move below custody on this occasion.

The proposed contract is not something the court can alter in any way; the court will still have to make a decision between referral order and custody but can do so on the basis that if it makes a referral order it can have confidence in what that will entail in the particular case. The court determines the length of the order but a Referral Order Panel determines the requirements of the order.

Offence seriousness	Suggested length of referral order
Low	• 3–5 months
Medium	• 5–7 months
High	• 7–9 months
Very high	• 10–12 months

The YOT may propose certain requirements and the length of these requirements may not correspond to the above table; if the court feels these requirements will best achieve the aims of the youth justice system then they may still be imposed.

Youth Rehabilitation Order (YRO)

The following table sets out the different levels of intensity that are available under a Youth Rehabilitation Order. The level of intensity and the content of the order will depend upon the court's assessment of seriousness.

Requirements of order		
Standard	Low likelihood of re-offending **and** a low risk of serious harm	Primarily seek to repair harm caused through, for example: • reparation; • unpaid work; • supervision; and/or • attendance centre.
Enhanced	Medium likelihood of re-offending **or** a medium risk of serious harm	Seek to repair harm caused and to enable help or change through, for example: • supervision; • reparation; • requirement to address behaviour e.g. drug treatment, offending behaviour programme, education programme; and/or • a combination of the above.

Intensive	High likelihood of re-offending **or** a very high risk of serious harm	Seek to ensure the control of and enable help or change for the child or young person through, for example: • supervision; • reparation; • requirement to address behaviour; • requirement to monitor or restrict movement, e.g. prohibited activity, curfew, exclusion, or electronic monitoring; and/or • a combination of the above.

YRO with Intensive Supervision and Surveillance (ISS) or YRO with fostering

A YRO with an ISS or fostering requirement can only be imposed where the court is of the opinion that the offence has crossed the custody threshold, and custody is merited.

The YRO with ISS includes an extended activity requirement, a supervision requirement, and curfew.

The YRO with fostering requires the child or young person to reside with a local authority foster parent for a specified period of up to 12 months.

Custodial Sentences

If a custodial sentence is imposed, the court must state its reasons for being satisfied that the offence is so serious that no other sanction would be appropriate and, in particular, why a YRO with ISS or fostering could not be justified.

Where a custodial sentence is **unavoidable** the length of custody imposed must be the shortest commensurate with the seriousness of the offence. The court may want to consider the equivalent adult guideline in order to determine the appropriate length of the sentence.

If considering the adult guideline, the court may feel it appropriate to apply a sentence broadly within the region of half to two thirds of the appropriate adult sentence for those aged 15–17 and allow a greater reduction for those aged under 15. This is only a rough guide and must not be applied mechanistically. The individual factors relating to the offence and the child or young person are of the greatest importance and may present good reason to impose a sentence outside of this range.

E3 Robbery—Sentencing Children and Young People Guideline—effective from 1 June 2017

This guideline should be read alongside the *Sentencing Children and Young People – Overarching Principles* definitive guideline which provides comprehensive guidance on the sentencing principles and welfare considerations that the court should have in mind when sentencing children and young people.

The first step in determining the sentence is to assess the seriousness of the offence. This assessment is made by considering the nature of the offence and any aggravating and mitigating factors relating to the offence itself. **The fact that a sentence threshold is crossed does not necessarily mean that that sentence should be imposed.**

STEP 1
Offence Seriousness—Nature of the offence

The boxes below give **examples** of the type of culpability and harm factors that may indicate that a particular threshold of sentence has been crossed.

A non-custodial sentence* may be the most suitable disposal where one or more of the following factors apply:
Threat or use of minimal force
Little or no physical or psychological harm caused to the victim
Involved through coercion, intimidation or exploitation

A custodial sentence or youth rehabilitation order with intensive supervision and surveillance* or fostering* may be justified where one or more of the following factors apply:
Use of very significant force
Threat or use of a bladed article, firearm or imitation firearm (where produced)
Significant physical or psychological harm caused to the victim

Blackstone's Handbook of Youths in the Criminal Courts. Mark Ashford, Gareth Branston, and Naomi Redhouse, Oxford University Press.
 DOI: 10.1093/oso/9780198913146.003.0003

* Where the child or young person appears in the magistrates' court, and the conditions for a compulsory referral order apply, a referral order must be imposed unless the court is considering imposing a discharge, hospital order or custody.

STEP 2
Offence Seriousness—Aggravating and mitigating factors

To complete the assessment of seriousness the court should consider the aggravating and mitigating factors relevant to the offence.

Aggravating factors
Statutory aggravating factors:
Previous findings of guilt, having regard to a) the **nature** of the offence to which the finding of guilt relates and its **relevance** to the current offence; and b) the **time** that has elapsed since the finding of guilt
Offence committed whilst on bail
Offence motivated by, or demonstrating hostility based on any of the following characteristics or presumed
characteristics of the victim: religion, race, disability, sexual orientation or transgender identity
Other aggravating factors (non-exhaustive):
Significant degree of planning
Deliberate humiliation of victim, including but not limited to filming of the offence, deliberately committing the offence before a group of peers with the intention of causing additional distress or circulating details/photos/videos etc. of the offence on social media or within peer groups
Threat or use of a weapon other than a bladed article, firearm or imitation firearm (whether produced or not)
Threat to use a bladed article, firearm or imitation firearm (not produced)
Victim is particularly vulnerable due to factors including but not limited to age, mental or physical disability
A leading role where offending is part of a group
Attempt to conceal identity (for example, wearing a balaclava or hood)
Any steps taken to prevent reporting the incident/seeking assistance
High value goods or sums targeted or obtained (includes economic, personal or sentimental)
Restraint, detention or additional degradation of the victim

Mitigating factors (non-exhaustive)
No previous findings of guilt **or** no relevant/recent findings of guilt
Good character and/or exemplary conduct
Participated in offence due to bullying, peer pressure, coercion or manipulation
Remorse, particularly where evidenced by voluntary reparation to the victim
Little or no planning

STEP 3
Personal mitigation

Having assessed the offence seriousness, the court should then consider the mitigation personal to the child or young person to determine whether a custodial sentence or a community sentence is necessary. The effect of personal mitigation may reduce what would otherwise be a custodial sentence to a non-custodial one, or a community sentence to a different means of disposal.

Personal mitigating factors (non-exhaustive)
Particularly young or immature child or young person (where it affects their responsibility)
Communication or learning disabilities or mental health concerns
Unstable upbringing including but not limited to: • time spent looked after • lack of familial presence or support • disrupted experiences in accommodation or education • exposure to drug/alcohol abuse, familial criminal behaviour or domestic abuse • victim of neglect or abuse, or exposure to neglect or abuse of others • experiences of trauma or loss
Determination and/or demonstration of steps taken to address offending behaviour
Child or young person in education, training or employment

STEP 4

Reduction for guilty plea

The court should take account of any potential reduction for a guilty plea in accordance with section 73 of the Sentencing Code and part one, section five of the *Sentencing Children and Young People – Overarching Principles* definitive guideline.

The reduction in sentence for a guilty plea can be taken into account by imposing one type of sentence rather than another; for example:

- by reducing a custodial sentence to a community sentence; or
- by reducing a community sentence to a different means of disposal.

Alternatively the court could reduce the length or severity of any punitive requirements attached to a community sentence.

See the *Sentencing Children and Young People – Overarching Principles* definitive guideline for details of other available sentences including Referral Orders and Reparation Orders.

STEP 5

Review the sentence

The court must now review the sentence to ensure it is the most appropriate one for the child or young person. This will include an assessment of the likelihood of reoffending and the risk of causing serious harm. A report from the Youth Offending Team may assist.

See the *Sentencing Children and Young People – Overarching Principles* definitive guideline for comprehensive guidance on the sentencing principles and welfare considerations that the court should have in mind when sentencing children and young people, and for the full range of the sentences available to the court.

Referral Orders

In cases where children or young people have offended for the first time and have pleaded guilty to committing an offence which is on the cusp of the custody threshold, YOTs should be encouraged to convene a Youth Offender Panel prior to sentence (sometimes referred to as a 'pseudo-panel' or 'pre-panel') where the child or young person is asked to attend before a panel and agree an intensive contract. If that contract is placed before the sentencing youth court, the court can then decide whether it is sufficient to move below custody on this occasion. The proposed contract is not something the court can alter in any way; the court will still have to make a decision between referral order and custody but can do so on the basis that if it makes a referral order it can have confidence in what that will entail in the particular case. The court determines the length of the order but a Referral Order Panel determines the requirements of the order.

Offence seriousness	Suggested length of referral order
Low	• 3–5 months
Medium	• 5–7 months
High	• 7–9 months
Very high	• 10–12 months

The YOT may propose certain requirements and the length of these requirements may not correspond to the above table; if the court feels these requirements will best achieve the aims of the youth justice system then they may still be imposed.

Youth Rehabilitation Order (YRO)

The following table sets out the different levels of intensity that are available under a Youth Rehabilitation Order. The level of intensity and the content of the order will depend upon the court's assessment of seriousness.

Requirements of order		
Standard	Low likelihood of re-offending **and** a low risk of serious harm	Primarily seek to repair harm caused through, for example: • reparation; • unpaid work; • supervision; and/or • attendance centre.
Enhanced	Medium likelihood of re-offending **or** a medium risk of serious harm	Seek to repair harm caused and to enable help or change through, for example: • supervision; • reparation; • requirement to address behaviour e.g. drug treatment, offending behaviour programme, education programme; and/or • a combination of the above.

Intensive	High likelihood of re-offending **or** a very high risk of serious harm	Seek to ensure the control of and enable help or change for the child or young person through, for example: • supervision; • reparation; • requirement to address behaviour; • requirement to monitor or restrict movement, e.g. prohibited activity, curfew, exclusion or electronic monitoring; and/or • a combination of the above.

YRO with Intensive Supervision and Surveillance (ISS) or YRO with Fostering

A YRO with an ISS or fostering requirement can only be imposed where the court is of the opinion that the offence has crossed the custody threshold, and custody is merited.

The YRO with ISS includes an extended activity requirement, a supervision requirement and curfew.

The YRO with fostering requires the child or young person to reside with a local authority foster parent for a specified period of up to 12 months.

Custodial Sentences

If a custodial sentence is imposed, the court must state its reasons for being satisfied that the offence is so serious that no other sanction would be appropriate and, in particular, why a YRO with ISS or fostering could not be justified.

Where a custodial sentence is **unavoidable** the length of custody imposed must be the shortest commensurate with the seriousness of the offence. The court may want to consider the equivalent adult guideline in order to determine the appropriate length of the sentence.

If considering the adult guideline, the court may feel it appropriate to apply a sentence broadly within the region of half to two thirds of the appropriate adult sentence for those aged 15–17 and allow a greater reduction for those aged under 15. This is only a rough guide and must not be applied mechanistically. The individual factors relating to the offence and the child or young person are of the greatest importance and may present good reason to impose a sentence outside of this range.

E4 Sexual Offences—Sentencing Children and Young People Guideline—effective from 1 June 2017

This guideline should be read alongside *Sentencing Children and Young People – Overarching Principles* definitive guideline, which provides comprehensive guidance on the sentencing principles and welfare considerations that the court should have in mind when sentencing children and young people.

Sentencing a child or young person for sexual offences involves a number of different considerations from adults. The primary difference is the age and level of maturity. Children and young people are less emotionally developed than adults; offending can arise through inappropriate sexual experimentation; gang or peer group pressure to engage in sexual activity; or a lack of understanding regarding consent, exploitation, coercion, and appropriate sexual behaviour.

Below is a non-exhaustive list of factors that illustrate the type of background factors that may have played a part in leading a child or young person to commit an offence of this kind.

- Victim of neglect or abuse (sexual, physical or emotional) or has witnessed the neglect or abuse of another.
- Exposure to pornography or materials which are age inappropriate.
- Involvement in gangs.
- Associated with child sexual exploitation.
- Unstable living or educational arrangements.
- Communication or learning disabilities or mental health concerns.
- Part of a peer group, school, or neighbourhood where harmful sexual norms and attitudes go unchallenged.
- A trigger event such as the death of a close relative or a family breakdown.

The first step in determining the sentence is to assess the seriousness of the offence. This assessment is made by considering the nature of the offence and any aggravating and mitigating factors relating to the offence itself. **The fact that a sentence threshold**

Blackstone's Handbook of Youths in the Criminal Courts. Mark Ashford, Gareth Branston, and Naomi Redhouse, Oxford University Press.
 DOI: 10.1093/oso/9780198913146.003.0004

is crossed does not necessarily mean that that sentence should be imposed.

STEP 1
Offence Seriousness—Nature of the offence

The boxes below give **examples** of the type of culpability and harm factors that may indicate that a particular threshold of sentence has been crossed.

A non-custodial sentence* may be the most suitable disposal where one or more of the following factors apply:
Any form of non-penetrative sexual activity
Any form of sexual activity (including penetration) without coercion, exploitation or pressure except where there is a significant disparity in age or maturity
Minimal psychological or physical harm caused to the victim

A custodial sentence or youth rehabilitation order with intensive supervision and surveillance* or fostering* may be justified where one or more of the following factors apply:
Any penetrative activity involving coercion, exploitation or pressure
Use or threats of violence against the victim or someone known to the victim
Prolonged detention/sustained incident
Severe psychological or physical harm caused to the victim

* Where the child or young person appears in the magistrates' court, and the conditions for a compulsory referral order apply, a referral order must be imposed unless the court is considering imposing a discharge, hospital order or custody.

STEP 2
Offence Seriousness—Aggravating and mitigating factors

To complete the assessment of seriousness the court should consider the aggravating and mitigating factors relevant to the offence.

Aggravating factors
Statutory aggravating factors:
Previous findings of guilt, having regard to a) the **nature** of the offence to which the finding of guilt relates and its relevance to the current offence; and b) the time that has elapsed since the finding of guilt
Offence committed whilst on bail
Offence motivated by, or demonstrating hostility based on any of the following characteristics or presumed characteristics of the victim: religion, race, disability, sexual orientation or transgender identity
Other aggravating factors (non-exhaustive):
Significant degree of planning
Child or young person acts together with others to commit the offence
Use of alcohol/drugs on victim to facilitate the offence
Abuse of trust
Deliberate humiliation of victim, including but not limited to filming of the offence, deliberately committing the offence before a group of peers with the intention of causing additional distress or circulating details/photos/videos etc. of the offence on social media or within peer groups
Grooming
Significant disparity of age between the child or young person and the victim (measured chronologically or with reference to level of maturity) (where not taken into account at step one)
Victim is particularly vulnerable due to factors including but not limited to age, mental or physical disability
Any steps taken to prevent reporting the incident/seeking assistance
Pregnancy or STI as a consequence of offence
Blackmail
Use of weapon

Mitigating factors (non-exhaustive)
No previous findings of guilt **or** no relevant/recent findings of guilt
Good character and/or exemplary conduct
Participated in offence due to bullying, peer pressure, coercion or manipulation
Genuine belief that activity was lawful

STEP 3
Personal mitigation

Having assessed the offence seriousness, the court should then consider the mitigation personal to the child or young person to determine whether a custodial sentence or a community sentence is necessary. The effect of personal mitigation may reduce what would otherwise be a custodial sentence to a non-custodial one, or a community sentence to a different means of disposal.

Personal mitigating factors (non-exhaustive)
Particularly young or immature child or young person (where it affects their responsibility)
Communication or learning disabilities or mental health concerns
Unstable upbringing including but not limited to: • time spent looked after • lack of familial presence or support • disrupted experiences in accommodation or education • exposure to drug/alcohol abuse, familial criminal behaviour or domestic abuse • exposure by others to pornography or sexually explicit materials • victim of neglect or abuse, or exposure to neglect or abuse of others • experiences of trauma or loss
Determination and/or demonstration of steps taken to address offending behaviour
Strong prospect of rehabilitation
Child or young person in education, training or employment

STEP 4
Reduction for guilty plea

The court should take account of any potential reduction for a guilty plea in accordance with section 73 of the Sentencing Code and part one, section five of the *Sentencing Children and Young People – Overarching Principles* definitive guideline.

The reduction in sentence for a guilty plea can be taken into account by imposing one type of sentence rather than another; for example:

- by reducing a custodial sentence to a community sentence; or
- by reducing a community sentence to a different means of disposal.

Alternatively the court could reduce the length or severity of any punitive requirements attached to a community sentence.

See the *Sentencing Children and Young People – Overarching Principles* definitive guideline for details of other available sentences including Referral Orders and Reparation Orders.

STEP 5
Review the sentence

The court must now review the sentence to ensure it is the most appropriate one for the child or young person. This will include an assessment of the likelihood of re-offending and the risk of causing serious harm. A report from the Youth Offending Team may assist.

See the *Sentencing Children and Young People – Overarching Principles* definitive guideline for comprehensive guidance on the sentencing principles and welfare considerations that the court should have in mind when sentencing children and young people, and for the full range of the sentences available to the court.

Referral Orders

In cases where children or young people have offended for the first time and have pleaded guilty to committing an offence which is on the cusp of the custody threshold, YOTs should be encouraged to convene a Youth Offender Panel prior to sentence (sometimes referred to as a 'pseudo-panel' or 'pre-panel') where the child or young person is asked to attend before a panel and agree an intensive contract. If that contract is placed before the sentencing youth court, the court can then decide whether it is sufficient to move below custody on this occasion. The proposed contract is not something the court can alter in any way; the court will still have to make a decision between referral order and custody but can do so on the basis that if it makes a referral order it can have confidence in what that will entail in the particular case.

The court determines the length of the order but a Referral Order Panel determines the requirements of the order.

Offence seriousness	Suggested length of referral order
Low	• 3–5 months
Medium	• 5–7 months
High	• 7–9 months
Very high	• 10–12 months

The YOT may propose certain requirements and the length of these requirements may not correspond to the above table; if the court feels these requirements will best achieve the aims of the youth justice system then they may still be imposed.

Youth Rehabilitation Order (YRO)

The following table sets out the different levels of intensity that are available under a Youth Rehabilitation Order. The level of intensity and the content of the order will depend upon the court's assessment of seriousness.

Requirements of order		
Standard	Low likelihood of re-offending **and** a low risk of serious harm	Primarily seek to repair harm caused through, for example: • reparation; • unpaid work; • supervision; and/or • attendance centre.
Enhanced	Medium likelihood of re-offending **or** a medium risk of serious harm	Seek to repair harm caused and to enable help or change through, for example: • supervision; • reparation; • requirement to address behaviour e.g. drug treatment, offending behaviour programme, education programme; and/or • a combination of the above.
Intensive	High likelihood of re-offending **or** a very high risk of serious harm	Seek to ensure the control of and enable help or change for the child or young person through, for example: • supervision; • reparation; • requirement to address behaviour; • requirement to monitor or restrict movement, e.g. prohibited activity, curfew, exclusion or electronic monitoring; and/or • a combination of the above.

YRO with Intensive Supervision and Surveillance (ISS) or YRO with Fostering

A YRO with an ISS or fostering requirement can only be imposed where the court is of the opinion that the offence has crossed the custody threshold and custody is merited.

The YRO with ISS includes an extended activity requirement, a supervision requirement, and curfew. The YRO with fostering requires the child or young person to reside with a local authority foster parent for a specified period of up to 12 months.

Custodial Sentences

If a custodial sentence is imposed, the court must state its reasons for being satisfied that the offence is so serious that no other sanction would be appropriate and, in particular, why a YRO with ISS or fostering could not be justified.

Where a custodial sentence is **unavoidable** the length of custody imposed must be the shortest commensurate with the seriousness of the offence. The court may want to consider the equivalent adult guideline in order to determine the appropriate length of the sentence.

If considering the adult guideline, the court may feel it appropriate to apply a sentence broadly within the region of half to two thirds of the appropriate adult sentence for those aged 15–17 and allow a greater reduction for those aged under 15. This is only a rough guide and must not be applied mechanistically. The individual factors relating to the offence and the child or young person are of the greatest importance and may present good reason to impose a sentence outside of this range.

Part F
Youth Justice System

F1 Aim of the Youth Justice System

The legislation relating to children and young persons is contained in many different statutes and is unlikely to be fully codified in the near future (save that sentencing provisions are now mainly found in the SC). The Crime and Disorder Act (CDA) 1998 defined the youth justice system and set up some of its current structure. The CDA 1998, s 42(1) provides:

Crime and Disorder Act 1998

42 Supplementary provisions

(1) In the foregoing provisions of this Part. . .'youth justice system' means the system of criminal justice in so far as it relates to children and young persons.

It also established the principal aim of the youth justice system. The CDA 1998, s 37 provides:

Crime and Disorder Act 1998

37 Aim of the youth justice system

(1) It shall be the principal aim of the youth justice system to prevent offending by children and young persons.

(2) In addition to any other duty to which they are subject, it shall be the duty of all persons and bodies carrying out functions in relation to the youth justice system to have regard to that aim.

The Sentencing Council's *Sentencing Children and Young People – Overarching Principles* definitive guideline is essential reading for all those who work in the youth court or who deal with youths in any other criminal court.

Blackstone's Handbook of Youths in the Criminal Courts. Mark Ashford, Gareth Branston, and Naomi Redhouse, Oxford University Press.
 DOI: 10.1093/oso/9780198913146.003.0005

F2 European Convention on Human Rights

The European Convention on Human Rights (ECHR) is embodied in domestic legislation through the Human Rights Act 1998. The most relevant principles applicable to the youth justice system are:

- Article 3 Protection from inhuman degrading treatment
- Article 5 Guarantee of the right to liberty and the security of the person
- Article 6 Guarantee of due process (fair trial, impartial and independent tribunal, etc.)
- Article 8 Right to privacy and family life.

The guarantees of Article 6 apply with equal force to juveniles as they do to adults, as was stated in *Nortier v Netherlands* (1993) 17 EHRR 273:

> That minors are as entitled to the same protection of their fundamental rights as adults . . . but the developing state of their personality—and consequently their limited social responsibility—should be taken into account in applying Article 6 of the Convention . . .

The European Court of Human Rights (ECtHR) rules on Convention Rights when domestic remedies are exhausted. The position of children and young people in relation to Article 6 was extensively discussed, prior to the implementation of the Human Rights Act 1998, in *T v United Kingdom, V v United Kingdom* (2000) 30 EHRR 121 and is important in consideration of issues concerning effective participation by children in the criminal process. In *T v United Kingdom,* neither the attribution of criminal responsibility to a 10-year-old, nor the three-week trial in public, were thought to constitute inhuman or degrading treatment or punishment in breach of Article 3. However, the appellants were unable to participate effectively in the criminal proceedings and were therefore denied a fair hearing, in breach of Article 6(1). They had a right to hear and follow the proceedings.

In *SC v UK* (2005) 40 EHRR 226 there was a breach of Article 6(1) where an 11-year-old defendant with limited intellectual ability was tried in the Crown Court. The ECtHR held that it was essential in such circumstances that a specialist tribunal should be the trial court.

See *Blackstone's Handbook of Youths in the Criminal Courts 2024 Criminal Practice 2024* **A7**.

Blackstone's Handbook of Youths in the Criminal Courts. Mark Ashford, Gareth Branston, and Naomi Redhouse, Oxford University Press.
 DOI: 10.1093/oso/9780198913146.003.0006

F3 UN Convention on the Rights of the Child

F3.1 UN Convention on Human Rights of the Child 1989

The United Kingdom is a signatory to this Convention although it is not part of domestic law. The standards established in the Convention have been increasingly accepted as relevant to decisions regarding the rights of children and young persons under the ECHR. Examples can be seen in the international courts in *V v UK and T v UK*, (2000) 30 EHRR 121 and in the domestic courts in *McKerry v Teesdale & Wear Valley Justices* [2000] All ER (D) 140 QBD.

F3.2 Other international standards

The United Nations has adopted detailed standards for children and young persons involved in the youth justice system and they are contained in:

- The UN Standard Minimum Rules for the administration of juvenile justice 1985 ('The Beijing Rules')
- The UN Rules for the protection of juveniles deprived of their liberty 1990 ('The Havana Rules')
- The UN guidelines for the administration of juvenile delinquency 1990 ('The Riyadh Guidelines').

Although not binding in the United Kingdom, they form part of the international standards that would be relevant to considering any human rights question relating to a child or young person.

The need for a court to consider these provisions is referred to in the *Sentencing Children and Young People – Overarching Principles definitive guideline*, paras 1.3 and 1.4, which state:

> 1.3 Domestic and international laws dictate that a custodial sentence should always be a measure of last resort for children and young people and statute provides that a custodial sentence may only be imposed when the offence is so serious that no other sanction is appropriate . . .
>
> 1.4 It is important to avoid 'criminalising' children and young people unnecessarily; the primary purpose of the youth justice system is to encourage children and young people to take responsibility for their own actions and promote re-integration into society rather than to punish. Restorative justice disposals may be of particular value for children and young people as they can encourage them to take responsibility for their actions and understand the impact their offence may have had on others.

Blackstone's Handbook of Youths in the Criminal Courts. Mark Ashford, Gareth Branston, and Naomi Redhouse, Oxford University Press.
 DOI: 10.1093/oso/9780198913146.003.0007

F4 Welfare Principle

F4.1 Welfare of the child or young person

The introduction of the principal aim of the youth justice system did not lead to any lessening in importance of the welfare principal which is set out in the CYPA 1933, s 44 as:

Children and Young Persons Act 1933

44 General considerations

Every court in dealing with a child or young person who is brought before it, either as an offender or otherwise, shall have regard to the welfare of the child or young person and shall in proper cases take steps for removing him from undesirable surroundings and for securing that proper provision is made for his education and training.

There is no statutory definition of 'welfare' but assistance can be found in the *Sentencing Children and Young People–Overarching Principles* definitive guideline, para 1.12:

In having regard to the 'welfare' of the child or young person, a court should ensure that it is alert to:

- any mental health problems or learning difficulties/disabilities;
- any experiences of brain injury or traumatic life experience (including exposure to drug and alcohol abuse) and the developmental impact this may have had;
- any speech and language difficulties and the effect this may have on the ability of the child or young person (or any accompanying adult) to communicate with the court, to understand the sanction imposed or to fulfil the obligations resulting from that sanction;
- the vulnerability of children and young people to self harm, particularly within a custodial environment; and
- the effect on children and young people of experiences of loss and neglect and/or abuse.

In making any decision involving a child or young person, the court will have regard to the principal aim and the welfare principle. The welfare principle, for example, is not only relevant to a sentencing decision but is also relevant when considering bail: *R(B) v Brent Youth Court* [2010] EWHC 1893 (Admin).

Blackstone's Handbook of Youths in the Criminal Courts. Mark Ashford, Gareth Branston, and Naomi Redhouse, Oxford University Press.
 DOI: 10.1093/oso/9780198913146.003.0008

F5 Youth Offending Team/Youth Justice Service

The CDA 1998, s 39 places a duty on local authorities, in consultation with the police, probation, and health authority to establish one or more YOTs in its area. It is possible for neighbouring local authorities to establish a joint YOT.

The YOT must consist of at least one of each of the following:

- a probation officer
- a social worker of a local authority social services department
- a police officer
- a person nominated by a health authority
- a person nominated by the Chief Education Officer.

It is the duty of the YOT to coordinate the provision of the youth justice services 'for all those in the authority's area who need them' and carry out the functions set out in the Youth Justice Plan which sets out how the local authority intends to fulfil its duties in relation to the provision of youth justice services.

The CDA 1998, ss 38–39 place a duty on every local authority with responsibility for education and social services to ensure the availability of appropriate youth justice services within their area. A duty to cooperate with the local authority in the discharge of this obligation is placed on the police, probation committees, and health authorities. These services include:

- Prevention and early intervention work
- Provision of persons to act as appropriate adults
- Assessment and intervention work in support of a final warning
- Support for young persons whilst on bail
- The placement in local authority accommodation of children and young people remanded to such accommodation
- Provision of reports or other information required by the court
- Provision of responsible officers in relation to Parenting Orders and other orders of the court
- Supervision of community sentences and DTOs
- Post-release supervision of children and young persons released from custody
- Management of referral orders.

Recently, many YOTs have rebranded themselves as the youth justice service, thereby placing an emphasis on justice rather than on offending. The statutory definition remains 'youth offending team'.

Blackstone's Handbook of Youths in the Criminal Courts. Mark Ashford, Gareth Branston, and Naomi Redhouse, Oxford University Press.
 DOI: 10.1093/oso/9780198913146.003.0009

F5.1 Asset and AssetPlus

All YOTs use a standardized assessment tool. Originally called Asset, it was described by the Youth Justice Board for England and Wales (YJB):

> Asset is a structured assessment tool to be used by YOTs in England and Wales on all young offenders who come into contact with the criminal justice system. It aims to look at the young person's offence or offences and identify a multitude of factors or circumstances—ranging from lack of educational attainment to mental health problems—which may have contributed to such behaviour. The information gathered from Asset can be used to inform court reports so that appropriate intervention programmes can be drawn up. It will also highlight any particular needs or difficulties the young person has, so that these may also be addressed. Asset will also help to measure changes in needs and risk of reoffending over time.

Since 2015, the YJB has introduced a new assessment tool to all YOTs, known as AssetPlus, which is said to improve on the Asset and other tools and provide a single tool to be used for assessing the needs of the young person and is used to inform decisions on bail, sentencing, and management of court orders.

Part G
Decision to Prosecute and Diversion

G1 Introduction

The key factors which will be relevant in deciding whether to caution, conditionally caution, or charge a youth for an offence are:

- do they admit the offence?
- the seriousness of the offence;
- the age of the person arrested;
- their previous offending history;
- does the proposed disposal adequately address, support, and reduce the risk of re-offending?
- is it in the public interest to prosecute?
- the welfare of the person arrested.

Blackstone's Handbook of Youths in the Criminal Courts. Mark Ashford, Gareth Branston, and Naomi Redhouse, Oxford University Press.
 DOI: 10.1093/oso/9780198913146.003.0010

G2 Caution

G2.1 Youth caution

The CDA 1998, ss 66ZA and 66ZB give the police the power to administer a youth caution.

Youth cautions have replaced the earlier system of reprimands and warnings. The Ministry of Justice and the YJB have issued a document entitled *Youth Cautions: Guidance for Police and Youth Offending Teams.* It is available on government websites.

The police may administer a youth caution of their own initiative or on the direction of the Crown Prosecution Service (CPS). The police are permitted to make the decision to offer a simple youth caution for any offence triable summarily or either way in the case of an adult. Authorization from a Crown Prosecutor should be sought before offering a youth caution for an indictable-only offence.

The decision whether to give an out-of-court disposal or to charge will depend in part on the seriousness of the offence. To help the police assess the seriousness of an offence, the National Police Chiefs' Council (NPCC) has published, in September 2023, a *Child Gravity Matrix* (replacing the March 2013 *Youth Gravity Factor Matrix)* under which offences are given a gravity 'score' based on the offence itself and any mitigating or aggravating factors. The gravity score will be used to assess whether a young person should be charged for an offence or given an out-of-court disposal. The *Child Gravity Matrix* is available online.

A youth caution may be given whether or not the youth has a previous youth caution or conviction.

All young people made subject of a youth caution will be referred to a YOT. The *Guidance* suggests that the first out-of-court disposal for a youth may be a decision for the police but the decision to offer a second such disposal will be taken jointly by the police and YOT after YOT assessment.

Following a youth caution, the young person must be assessed by the YOT. The YOT has a duty to assess the young person and put in place a rehabilitation programme unless deemed inappropriate. A 'rehabilitation programme' means a programme with the purpose of rehabilitating participants and preventing them from re-offending.

Blackstone's Handbook of Youths in the Criminal Courts. Mark Ashford, Gareth Branston, and Naomi Redhouse, Oxford University Press.
 DOI: 10.1093/oso/9780198913146.003.0011

The offender may be made subject to the sexual offences notification requirements if a caution is administered for a relevant sexual offence. See **J21**.

A youth caution is spent as soon as it is given: Rehabilitation of Offenders Act 1974, s 8A and Schedule 2.

Where a defendant, who has been made subject of two youth cautions or a youth conditional caution followed by a youth caution, is prosecuted for an offence committed within two years of the last caution, a sentencing court may not impose a conditional discharge unless it is satisfied that there are exceptional circumstances which justify it doing so.

A youth caution and a report on any failure to comply with a rehabilitation programme may be cited in criminal proceedings in the same way as a conviction.

Persons under the age of 18 years cannot be given penalty notices for disorder.

G2.2 **Cautions and the *CPS Code for Crown Prosecutors***

The *CPS Code for Crown Prosecutors* states:

> Out-of-Court Disposals
>
> 7.1 An out-of-court disposal may take the place of a prosecution if it is an appropriate response to the offender and/or the seriousness and consequences of the offending.
>
> 7.2 Prosecutors must follow any relevant guidance when asked to advise on or authorise an out-of-court disposal, including any appropriate regulatory proceedings, a punitive or civil penalty, or other disposal. They should ensure that the appropriate evidential standard for the specific out-of-court disposal is met including, where required, a clear admission of guilt, and that the public interest would be properly served by such a disposal.

G3 **Conditional Caution**

The CDA 1998, ss 66A to 66G provide for youth conditional cautions. The statute requires that guidance be issued by the Secretary of State and by the Director of Public Prosecutions (DPP). The *Code of Practice for Youth Conditional Cautions* is available on the government website. *The Director's Guidance on Youth Conditional Cautions* is available on the CPS website. The Ministry of Justice and the YJB have issued non-statutory guidance entitled *Youth Cautions: Guidance for Police and Youth Offending Teams.* It is available on the government website.

A youth conditional caution may be administered whether or not the youth has a previous youth caution, youth conditional caution, or conviction.

In any case where an authorized person or prosecutor is considering offering a youth conditional caution, the local YOT must be consulted to ensure that the youth understands the nature of the proposed caution, is suitable to undertake the required conditions, and that the conditions are likely to have a positive impact on offending behaviour. The YOT will also ascertain whether the offender accepts responsibility for the offending behaviour and is willing to admit the offence and to be cautioned. The YOT may also carry out a risk assessment, ascertain the views of the victim, and recommend specific conditions for inclusion.

A police officer of the rank of sergeant or above is permitted to make the decision to offer a youth conditional caution for any offence which for an adult would be triable summary only or either way. For offences which involve domestic violence or hate crime, a conditional caution is considered to be generally inappropriate and will only be given in exceptional circumstances with the authority of a CPS prosecutor.

The decision whether to give an out-of-court disposal or to charge will depend in part on the seriousness of the offence. To help the police assess the seriousness of an offence, the NPCC has published, in September 2023, a *Child Gravity Matrix* (replacing the March 2013 *Youth Gravity Factor Matrix)* under which offences are given a gravity 'score' based on the offence itself and any mitigating or aggravating factors. The gravity score will be used to assess whether a young person should be charged for an offence or given an out-of-court disposal. The *Child Gravity Matrix* is available online.

Blackstone's Handbook of Youths in the Criminal Courts. Mark Ashford, Gareth Branston, and Naomi Redhouse, Oxford University Press.
 DOI: 10.1093/oso/9780198913146.003.0012

Authorization from a Crown Prosecutor must be sought before offering a youth conditional caution for an indictable-only offence. Only in the most exceptional circumstances will a youth conditional caution be an appropriate way of dealing with such a case. The decision to authorize a youth conditional caution in any indictable-only case must be approved by a Deputy Chief Crown Prosecutor.

Before a youth conditional caution is made, the following requirements must be satisfied:

(a) there is evidence that the offender committed the offence;
(b) there is sufficient evidence to charge the offender with the offence and it is determined that a youth conditional caution should be given in respect of that offence;
(c) the offender admits to the authorized person that they committed the offence;
(d) the authorized person explains the effect of the youth conditional caution to the offender and warns them that failure to comply with any of the conditions attached may result in their being prosecuted for the offence (if the offender is 16 or under, this must be done in the presence of an appropriate adult);
(e) the offender signs a document containing details of the offence, their admissions, their consent to being given a youth conditional caution, and details of the conditions attached to the caution.

The conditions that can be attached must be rehabilitative, reparative, and/or punitive. Rehabilitative conditions can include attendance at the local YOT or at a specific treatment course. Reparative conditions can include apologizing to the victim, paying compensation, and making good any damage. Punitive conditions can include unpaid work or a financial penalty. Conditions must always be appropriate, proportionate, and achievable.

The offender may be made subject to the sexual offences notification requirements if a conditional caution is administered for a relevant sexual offence. See **J21**. A youth conditional caution is spent three months from its imposition: Rehabilitation of Offenders Act 1974, s 8A and Sch 2.

Where a defendant who has been made subject of a youth conditional caution is prosecuted for an offence committed within two years of the date of the conditional caution, a sentencing court may not impose a conditional discharge unless it is satisfied that there are exceptional circumstances which justify it doing so.

If the offender fails, without reasonable excuse, to comply with any of the conditions of the caution, criminal proceedings may be initiated for the offence and the document signed by the offender confirming their admission of the offence is admissible in evidence.

G3.1 *Director's Guidance on Youth Conditional Cautions*

G3.1.1 *Sufficient evidence to charge*

The *Guidance* provides as follows:

> 9.1. Before a Youth Conditional Caution can be considered, there must be sufficient evidence available to provide a realistic prospect of conviction in accordance with the Full Code Test set out in the Code for Crown Prosecutors.
>
> 9.2. In making this assessment, an authorised person may offer a Conditional Caution where:

- the suspect has made a clear and reliable admission to the offence and has said nothing that could be used as a defence, or
- the suspect has made no admission but has not denied the offence or otherwise indicated it will be contested and the commission of the offence and the identification of the offender can be established by reliable evidence or the suspect can be seen clearly committing the offence on a good quality visual recording.

G3.1.2 *Post-charge review*

Once a case has reached court, it is not too late for a youth conditional caution to be offered. The *Guidance* sets out the procedure to be followed where a prosecutor's post-charge review concludes that a youth conditional cautions should have been offered.

> 8.1 Where an offender is charged with an offence, but it appears upon review by a Prosecutor that a Youth Conditional Caution is more appropriate, the reviewing Prosecutor should consult the Youth Offending Team and if it is still considered appropriate should direct an authorised person to offer a Youth Conditional Caution. This includes any case where authorised persons ordinarily make that decision. The current prosecution should be adjourned whilst this action is taken. The authorised person shall then offer a youth caution with conditions as specified by the Prosecutor. If it proves then not to be possible to administer the Youth Conditional Caution an alternative out of court disposal may not be offered and the prosecution must continue.

G3.1.3 *Financial penalty conditions*

Under the CDA 1998, s 66C, the Secretary of State prescribes the maximum amount which may be specified in a financial penalty condition. The *Guidance*, at Annex B, also suggests a mitigated amount to be imposed as appropriate:

Financial penalty conditions banding

Maximum amount that may be specified where the offender is aged 14 or over but under 18

- Any summary offence: £30
- Any offence triable either way: £50
- Any offence triable only on indictment: £75

Mitigated amount where the offender is aged 14 or over but under 18

- Any summary offence: Between £5 and £20
- Any offence triable either way: Between £5 and £30
- Any offence triable only on indictment: Between £30 and £50

Maximum amount that may be specified where the offender is aged 10 or over but under 14

- Any summary offence: £15
- Any offence triable either way: £25
- Any offence triable only on indictment: £35

Mitigated amount where the offender is aged 10 or over but under 14

- Any summary offence: Between £5 and £10
- Any offence triable either way: Between £5 and £15
- Any offence triable only on indictment: Between £15 and £20

NOTE: A financial penalty condition may not be imposed for loitering or soliciting for the purposes of prostitution, possession of any class of drug or an offence under the Road Traffic Act or Road Traffic Offenders Act 1998.

G3.1.4 *Compensation for personal injuries*

There is also assistance in Annex B as to the level of compensation for injury which can appropriately be made part of the conditions of the caution.

Compensation for personal injuries

Graze

- Description: Depending on size
- Award: Up to £75

Bruise

- Description: Depending on size
- Award: Up to £100

Black eye

- Award: Up to £125

Minor cut—no permanent scar

- Description: Depending on size and whether stitched
- Award: £100 to £200

Sprain

- Description: Depending on loss of mobility
- Award: £100 to £200

G4 Code for Crown Prosecutors

Special considerations apply to the prosecution of youths under the *Code for Crown Prosecutors*. Where the allegation arises in relation to someone who was under the age of 18 at the time and the prosecutor is considering whether a prosecution is in the public interest it states:

> 4.14 d) The criminal justice system treats children and young people differently from adults and significant weight must be attached to the age of the suspect if they are a child or young person under 18. The best interests and welfare of the child or young person must be considered including whether a prosecution is likely to have an adverse impact on his or her future prospects that is disproportionate to the seriousness of the offending. Prosecutors must have regard to the principal aim of the youth justice system which is to prevent offending by children and young people. Prosecutors must also have regard to the obligations arising under the United Nations 1989 Convention on the Rights of the Child . . .
>
> As a starting point, the younger the suspect, the less likely it is that a prosecution is required.

The *Directors' Guidance on Charging* states that the police may charge any summary only offence (including criminal damage where the value of the loss or damage is less than £5,000) irrespective of plea and any either way offence anticipated as a guilty plea and suitable for sentence in a magistrates' court, provided it is not:

- a case requiring the consent to prosecute of the DPP or law officer;
- a case involving a death;
- connected with terrorist activity or official secrets;
- classified as hate crime or domestic violence under CPS policies;
- an offence of violent disorder or affray;
- causing grievous bodily harm or wounding, or actual bodily harm;
- a Sexual Offences Act offence committed by or upon a person under 18; or
- an offence under the Licensing Act 2003.

Many cases are brought to court without prior CPS consideration. The decision to prosecute may still be reviewed once a charge or requisition has brought the matter to court.

Blackstone's Handbook of Youths in the Criminal Courts. Mark Ashford, Gareth Branston, and Naomi Redhouse, Oxford University Press.
 DOI: 10.1093/oso/9780198913146.003.0013

G4.1 **Representations**

There are two stages in the decision to prosecute: the evidential stage and the public interest stage. Representations can be made in relation to either or both.

As diversion from prosecution is only available if an admission is made, a defendant who made no comment at the investigations stage may now be allowed to make an admission. At the evidential stage, if no admission can be made, any representations must be addressed to the admissibility and reliability of the evidence.

Representations in relation to public interest matters will be assisted by the extensive guidance on '*Children as suspects and defendants*' in the *CPS Legal Guidance* available on the CPS website.

G4.2 **Continuing duty to review**

When a decision has been made to bring a youth before the court this can be reviewed, particularly if new information becomes available.

The CPS *Code for Crown Prosecutors* states:

> 2.4 The decision to prosecute or to recommend an out-of-court disposal is a serious step that affects suspects, victims, witnesses and the public at large and must be undertaken with the utmost care.
>
> 2.5 It is the duty of prosecutors to make sure that the right person is prosecuted for the right offence and to bring offenders to justice wherever possible. Casework decisions taken fairly, impartially and with integrity help to secure justice for victims, witnesses, defendants and the public. Prosecutors must ensure that the law is properly applied; that relevant evidence is put before the court and that obligations of disclosure are complied with.
>
> ...
>
> 3.6 Prosecutors review every case they receive from the police or other investigators. Review is a continuing process and prosecutors must take account of any change in circumstances that occurs as the case develops This includes what becomes known of the defence case, any further reasonable lines of inquiry that should be pursued, and receipt of any unused material that may undermine the prosecution case or assist the defence case, to the extent that charges should be altered or discontinued or the prosecution should not proceed ... Wherever possible, prosecutors should consult the investigator when considering changing the charges or stopping the case. Prosecutors and investigators work closely together, but the final responsibility for the decision whether or not a case should go ahead rests with the CPS.

G4.3 Legitimate expectation and abuse of process

The prosecution of a person who has received a promise, undertaking, or representation from the police that he will not be prosecuted is capable of being an abuse of process: *R v Croydon Justices (ex parte Dean)* [1993] QB 769.

The prosecution of a person denied a caution by the failure of the police to make appropriate disclosure to enable legal advice to be given may be an abuse: *DPP v Ara* [2001] EWHC 493 (Admin).

In *R v Guildford Youth Court* [2008] EWHC 506 (Admin), a police officer had indicated, prior to interview, that the case would be dealt with by way of diversion. Subsequent proceedings should have been stayed as an abuse of process.

The administration of a caution may make it an abuse for there to be a later prosecution: *Jones v Whalley* [2007] 1 AC 63.

The Crown may, where there is a proper basis such as fresh evidence, bring proceedings notwithstanding that a caution has been administered: *DPP v Alexander* [2010] EWHC 2266 (Admin).

G5 **CPS Legal Guidance**

The *CPS Legal Guidance on Children as suspects and defendants* is available on the CPS website. Within that guidance, the CPS has set out principles guiding the decision to prosecute:

> The CPS is committed to ensuring that the special considerations which apply to cases involving children are enshrined in its working practices and form part of the training of its prosecutors . . .
>
> A decision to prosecute a child is susceptible to judicial review if it can be shown that the prosecutor has not taken into account all the information about a child's background and the public interest factors set out in the Code. It is crucial that prosecutors therefore record the rationale for their review decisions and, in doing so, address all relevant considerations . . .
>
> **Senior Crown Prosecutors (SCP)**
>
> All [Senior Crown Prosecutors] can make the decision to prosecute cases involving children. However, in more serious or complex cases, oversight and mentoring should be sought from a Youth Justice Specialist. It is expected that all SCPs will have access to training that equips them to deal with standard cases involving children, including the decision to prosecute cases in Youth Courts and deal with cases involving children jointly charged with adults in the magistrates' court. All trained SCPs can carry out an initial review of files prior to the first hearing to enable a child to enter a guilty plea if offered . . .
>
> **Public Interest considerations**
>
> The starting point in asking whether a prosecution is required in the public interest is the Code for Crown Prosecutors, in particular paragraphs 4.9 to 4.14 and factors (a) to (g) in that latter paragraph. In addition to those principal considerations, the following may also be important to consider at the public interest stage. In particular, the circumstances of the individual child . . . may be highly relevant as part of the overall public interest assessment.
>
> It is essential in all cases involving children to ensure that all matters relevant to the public interest decision are clearly identified, considered, and balanced . . . The decision to prosecute must only be taken after a full review of the case and the background information, including information concerning the suspect provided by the Youth Justice Service, police, or local authority. Failure to show that the Code and the legal guidance has been followed and properly applied to all the information on the case may result in the decision to prosecute being quashed.

R (on the application of E, S and R) v DPP [2011] EWHC 1465 (Admin) concerned allegations of child sexual offences by E on her younger siblings. A multi-agency strategy group had formed the view that prosecution was not in the best interests of any of the children. Nonetheless, the

Blackstone's Handbook of Youths in the Criminal Courts. Mark Ashford, Gareth Branston, and Naomi Redhouse, Oxford University Press.
 DOI: 10.1093/oso/9780198913146.003.0014

decision was taken on full review of the papers to prosecute E. It was the court's view that the rationale for this decision was inadequately expressed.

Please also see *R v Chief Constable of Kent and Another ex parte L, R v DPP ex parte B* [1991] 93 Cr App R 416: whilst rare, decisions to prosecute can be overturned upon judicial review where they are made regardless of or contrary to a settled policy of the DPP . . .

Diversion from the court process - out of court disposals

Prosecutors, when making charge decisions or reviewing police charged cases, will consider the key principles of the youth justice system outlined earlier and consider whether the case is suitable for diversion.

If the case is suitable to be diverted, it is always preferable that this happens before the case enters the court system. However, prosecutors will advise the police at the point of charge and post-charge if suitable cases have been potentially missed, or if the child subsequently wishes to make admissions an adjournment may need to be requested to allow relevant enquiries to be made. Wherever possible that request will be made prior to the court hearing to prevent the child unnecessarily attending court . . .

Cautions and conditional cautions after charge

In some circumstances, after a child has been charged with an offence, a prosecutor can invite the court to adjourn a case so that the requisite enquiries can be made, and consideration given to a caution or conditional caution. This includes cases where an admission to an authorised person was not made in interview, pre-charge. If, after review, it is determined that a caution can be given, a clear and unambiguous admission is a statutory requirement prior to the administration of either the simple or conditional caution. If the conditional caution is found to be an inappropriate disposal, the prosecution must continue. All parties should be made aware that this is the position and best practice may be to announce this in open court at the same time as the application is made for an adjournment.

The guidance contains particular reference to the decision whether to prosecute in the following situations:

- First time entrants
- Physical and mental health of the child
- Children looked after
- Adverse childhood experiences
- Special educational needs and disabilities
- Offence-specific public interest guidance:
    - Weapons and knife crime
    - Modern slavery and county lines
    - Gang related offending
    - Joint enterprise
    - Sexual offences and child abuse by young offenders

- Driving offences
- Football related offences
- Firearms

G5.1 Young people in care

In response to concerns that young people in the care of local authorities are being unfairly criminalized in relation to their behaviour in children's homes, the CPS has issued specific guidance on looked after children. This is to be considered in conjunction with the Code when deciding whether to prosecute.

> Children in the care of the local authority for more than 24 hours are often referred to as Children Looked After (CLA), defined by the provisions of the Children Act 1989. They make up a disproportionate amount of those children who are prosecuted . . .
>
> The decision to prosecute children looked after for low level offences committed within a children's home is a major decision and should be taken under the supervision of a youth justice specialist with full consideration of the specific and unique circumstances of this group of children. The National Protocol to Reduce the Unnecessary Criminalisation of Looked After Children and Care Leavers (2018) may assist prosecutors with these public interest considerations. This protocol provides a framework to help practitioners reduce criminalisation of CLA and care leavers.
>
> They are vulnerable and at high risk of offending because they may be living in a completely different geographical area away from friends and family, with other children who have been remanded to local authority accommodation. They are often aged between 14-17, deemed to be the peak age range for offending, and may be susceptible to peer pressure to engage in group offending. They may display challenging behaviour and be living within a setting of others displaying challenging behaviour.
>
> Additionally, offences of violence or theft which might not have been reported to the police in a familial setting are more likely to be reported when the children are living away from home. Alternative disposals should be considered before prosecution, where appropriate. These may include restorative justice, reparation, Acceptable Behaviour Contracts and disciplinary measures by the home. Prosecution, caution or conditional caution should only follow if only these outcomes meet the public interest.
>
> To assist prosecutors in their decision-making it is expected that in cases involving CLA the police will provide relevant background information which they will have collated from social services and other agencies detailed within of the child looked after assessment form (CLAA). A prosecutor should also receive a copy of the children's home behaviour management policy to assist in the decision-making process. If the assessment or the relevant material is not provided prosecutors should escalate the matter through local escalation processes . . .

Behaviour Management policies

When making a review decision concerning an offence alleged to have been committed by a CLA in a placement or in the wider community, a prosecutor should receive a copy of the children's home behaviour management policy to assist in the decision-making process . . .

Each home should have a clear written policy, procedures and guidance for staff based on a code of conduct that sets out control, discipline and Restrictive Physical Interventions that are permitted and must reinforce positive messages to children for the achievement of acceptable behaviour.

A copy of this policy and a statement from the home setting out how the policy has been applied to this incident should accompany any request for advice on charging.

The consequences of unacceptable behaviour should be clear to staff and children and must be appropriate to the age, understanding and individual needs of the child. It must also be recognised that unacceptable or challenging behaviour may be the result of illness, bullying, disabilities such as Autism Spectrum Disorder (ASD), Attention Deficit Hyperactivity Disorder (ADHD) or communication difficulties . . .

Unless the registered person can show it is inappropriate, the home should also have procedures and guidance on police involvement in the home, which has been agreed with the local police. Staff should know about the agreement with the police and should be clear when the police should be involved (paragraph 22.15 National Minimum Standards for Children).

G6 Notification of Prosecution

The Children and Young Persons Act 1969 (CYPA 1969), ss 5(8) and 34(2) provide that, before any proceedings are commenced against a young person, notification of the prosecution should be given to the local authority and probation service for the area where the young person resides.

In *DPP v Cottier* [1996] 3 All ER 126, it was stated that the notice could be given orally. In practice, the notification is generally sent to the YOT. Failure to notify does not invalidate the proceedings: *R v Marsh* [1997] 1 WLR 649.

Blackstone's Handbook of Youths in the Criminal Courts. Mark Ashford, Gareth Branston, and Naomi Redhouse, Oxford University Press.
 DOI: 10.1093/oso/9780198913146.003.0015

Part H
Procedure

H1 Age

H1.1 Age of criminal responsibility

Children and Young Persons Act 1933, s 50

It shall be conclusively presumed that that no child under the age of ten years can be guilty of an offence.

H1.2 Presumption of *doli incapax*

At common law, there was a rebuttable presumption that a person aged under 14 was incapable of committing a crime. This presumption, often termed *doli incapax*, required the prosecution to establish not only that the accused had committed the offence but also that he knew what he had done was seriously wrong rather than merely naughty. The presumption of *doli incapax* was abolished by the CDA 1998, s 34 for all offences committed on or after 30 November 1998. In *R v JTB* [2009] 1 AC 1310, the House of Lords ruled that s 34 abolished both the presumption and the defence of *doli incapax*. It was therefore not open to the defence to argue that the accused had not understood that what had been done was seriously wrong.

H1.3 Determination of age

The Children and Young Persons Act 1933 (CYPA 1933), s 99(1) provides:

Children and Young Persons Act 1933

99 Presumption and determination of age

(1) Where a person, whether charged with an offence or not, is brought before any court otherwise than for the purpose of giving evidence, and it appears to the court that he is a child or young person, the court shall make due inquiry as to the age of that person, and for that purpose shall take such evidence as may be forthcoming at the hearing of the case, but an order or judgment of the court shall not be invalidated by any subsequent proof that the age of that person has not been correctly stated to the court, and the age presumed or declared by the court to be the age of the person so brought before it shall, for the purposes of this Act, be deemed to be the true age of that person, and, where it appears to the court that the person so

Blackstone's Handbook of Youths in the Criminal Courts. Mark Ashford, Gareth Branston, and Naomi Redhouse, Oxford University Press.
 DOI: 10.1093/oso/9780198913146.003.0016

> brought before it has attained the age of eighteen years, that person shall for the purposes of this Act be deemed not to be a child or young person.

The SC, s 405 and the CDA 1998, s 117 contain similar provisions providing that the age of a person shall be 'deemed' to be that which it appears to the court to be after considering 'any available evidence'.

H1.4 **Procedure**

Any dispute in relation to the age of a defendant should be raised at the first hearing, whether in the adult or youth court. An adjournment may be necessary to resolve the issue: *R v O* [2008] EWCA Crim 2835; *R (M) v Hammersmith Magistrates' Court* [2017] EWHC 1359 (Admin). The legislation does not expressly stipulate what inquiries are appropriate. Any assessment must be in accordance with the leading authority of *B v The Mayor and Burgesses of the London Borough of Merton* [2003] EWHC 1689 (Admin):

- It may be determined informally provided safeguards of minimum standards of inquiry and fairness are adhered to.
- It cannot be decided solely on the basis of appearance.
- The decision maker must seek to elicit the general background of the person, including their family circumstances and history, education, and activities during previous years.
- Ethnic and cultural information may be important.
- The defendant's credibility may have to be tested if there is any doubt as to their statement as to age.

The court shall take such evidence as may be forthcoming for the purposes of the 'deeming hearing' including:

- Input from the YOT, which will usually have been responsible for conducting the age inquiry during any adjournment.
- Oral evidence from the defendant, family, or friends concerning their stated age and details of their history.
- Domestic or foreign documentation, such as birth certificates, passports, PNC etc.
- Input from any other agency which has had involvement with the defendant or their family.
- The physical appearance of the defendant.

H1.5 **Determination of age is incorrect**

There is no difficulty if a defendant is deemed to be a youth but it subsequently transpires that they are an adult. Section 99(1) provides that no order or judgment is invalidated by later discovery of the true age. The CYPA 1933, s 48 also provides:

Children and Young Persons Act 1933

48 Miscellaneous provisions as to powers of juvenile courts

(1) A youth court sitting for the purpose of hearing a charge against a person who is believed to be a child or young person may, if it thinks fit to do so, proceed with the hearing and determination of the charge, notwithstanding that it is discovered that the person in question is not a child or young person.

H2 Allocation and Sending Proceedings

H2.1 Presumption of summary trial

The Magistrates' Courts Act 1980 (MCA 1980), s 24 establishes a presumption that youth defendants will be dealt with summarily for any indictable offence.

> **Magistrates' Courts Act 1980**
>
> **24 Summary trial of information against child or young persons for indictable offence**
>
> (1) Where a person under the age of 18 years appears or is brought before a magistrates' court on an information charging him with an indictable offence he shall, subject to sections 51 and 51A of the Crime and Disorder Act 1998 and to sections 24A and 24B below be tried summarily.

A youth defendant will only appear in the Crown Court for trial:

- when charged with homicide;
- when charged with a firearms offence subject to a mandatory minimum sentence;
- when charged with a 'grave crime' and a court has determined that it ought to be possible to impose a sentence under the SC, s 250;
- when charged with certain terrorism offences and a court has determined that it ought to be possible to impose a sentence of more than two years' detention for an offender of particular concern;
- when a notice has been given in a serious or complex fraud;
- when a notice has been given in a child case;
- when charged with a specified offence and it is considered that the criteria for imposing a sentence of extended detention are met (dangerous offender);
- when charged with an adult offender who has been sent to the Crown Court and it has been determined that it is in the interests of justice for the youth to be tried there too.

The CDA 1998, ss 51 and 51A set out the procedure for determining the allocation of a youth defendant. See flow chart following para 2.16 of the *Sentencing Children and Young People – Overarching Principles* definitive guideline in Appendix Y1.

Save where allocation to the Crown Court is mandatory (homicide and firearms cases), it is only rarely that a youth court should

Blackstone's Handbook of Youths in the Criminal Courts. Mark Ashford, Gareth Branston, and Naomi Redhouse, Oxford University Press.
 DOI: 10.1093/oso/9780198913146.003.0017

send a child or young person to the Crown Court for trial, because of the interrelationship between the allocation provisions and the general power to commit for sentence: *R (BB) v West Glamorgan Youth Court* [2020] EWHC 2888 (Admin). The youth court is best designed to meet the specific needs of children and young persons. It allows trials to be conducted in private, in a manner specifically adapted to the needs of young people; it allows the proceedings to be expedited and to avoid the delays that are frequently encountered in the Crown Court: *R (BH) v Norwich Youth Court* [2023] EWHC 25 (Admin); [2023] 1 Cr.App.R. 20.

H2.2 **Homicide**

A youth defendant charged with an offence of homicide must be sent to the Crown Court for trial forthwith: CDA 1998, s 51A(2), (3)(a), and (12)(a). In such cases, there will be no plea before venue or allocation procedure.

The term 'offence of homicide' has not been defined in general terms by either statute or case law. There is general agreement that the term will include charges of murder and manslaughter. It is likely also to include offences of infanticide, child destruction, and procuring an abortion. Attempted murder is subject to the same rules regarding venue of proceedings as the offence of murder, by virtue of the Criminal Attempts Act 1981, s 2(2)(c). It would therefore seem that a youth defendant charged with this offence should be sent for trial without a plea before venue or allocation procedure.

An offence of causing or allowing the death of a child or vulnerable adult is an offence of homicide for the purposes of the CDA 1998, s 51A: Domestic Violence, Crime and Victims Act 2004, s 6(5).

It is unlikely that the definition of 'offence of homicide' extends to driving offences where a fatality is caused and HMCTS records show that such offences have been tried in the youth court.

The following offences are punishable with 14 years' imprisonment in the case of an adult and may therefore be sent for trial as 'grave crimes':

- causing death by dangerous driving—Road Traffic Act 1988 (RTA 1988), s 1;
- causing death by careless driving whilst under the influence of drink or drugs or having failed to provide a specimen for analysis or to permit analysis of a blood sample—RTA 1988, s 3A;
- causing death by aggravated vehicle-taking—Theft Act 1968 (TA 1968), s 12A(2)(b) and (4).

If these offences are not offences of homicide, a plea before venue procedure must be conducted before an allocation determination is made.

The following offences are not 'grave crimes':

- causing death by careless or inconsiderate driving—RTA 1988, s 2B (maximum penalty five years' imprisonment);
- causing death by driving unlicensed or uninsured—RTA 1988, s 3ZB (maximum penalty two years' imprisonment);
- causing death by driving whilst disqualified—RTA 1988, s 3ZC (maximum penalty ten years' imprisonment).

H2.3 **Firearms offences**

By the CDA 1998, s 51A(2), (3)(a), (12)(b), and (12)(c), a youth defendant must be sent for trial if charged with a firearms offence where, on conviction, they would be subject to a mandatory minimum sentence of three years' detention under the SC, s 311 (see **MCH B5.1**).

In such cases, there will be no plea before venue or allocation procedure.

Defendants aged under 16 on the date of the offence are not subject to the mandatory minimum sentence. An allocation decision would still have to be made in relation to offences under the Firearms Act 1968, ss 16, 17, and 18 as they are 'grave crimes'.

H2.4 **'Grave crimes'**

By the CDA 1998, s 51A(2)(b), the court must send for trial a youth defendant charged with an offence for which long-term detention is available to the Crown Court under s 250 of the SC for so-called 'grave crimes' and the court considers that it ought to be possible to sentence them to detention for a period longer than a two year DTO. The term 'grave crimes' remains in general use but is no longer based in statute. The offences to which it relates are defined by the SC, s 249(1). The definition includes:

- **Offences punishable with 14 years or more**—the definition would include robbery, dwelling burglary, and handling stolen goods. It does not, however, include non-dwelling burglary where the maximum penalty is ten years' imprisonment: *R v Brown* (1995) 16 Cr App R (S) 932.
- **Sexual offences specifically defined as grave crimes**—the following sexual offences may be treated as grave crimes notwithstanding the fact that the maximum sentence is less than 14 years:

(a) sexual assault contrary to the Sexual Offences Act 2003 (SOA 2003), s 3;
(b) child sex offences committed by children and young persons contrary to the SOA 2003, s 13;
(c) sexual activity with a child family member contrary to the SOA 2003, s 25; and
(d) inciting a child family member to engage in sexual activity contrary to the SOA 2003, s 26.

The s 249(1) definition of offences for which detention under s 250 is available includes firearms offences to which the mandatory minimum sentence applies. This provides the Crown Court with the appropriate power to impose long-term detention for such offences. It is irrelevant to allocation decisions for 16- and 17-year-old defendants as these defendants liable to a mandatory minimum sentence must be sent for trial forthwith, pursuant to the CDA 1998, s 51A(3) and (12)(b) (see **H2.3** above and MCH **C17.1**).

H2.4.1 *Plea before venue*

Before making a decision on allocation of a grave crime, the court must deal with plea before venue: MCA 1980, s 24A(1) and (2).

The plea before venue procedure is set out in s 24A and Criminal Procedure Rules (Crim PR) rule 9.13:
(a) The procedure must be carried out in the presence of the accused (however, provision exists for the procedure to be carried out in the absence of the accused if their behaviour is disruptive and they are legally represented at the hearing—see the MCA 1980, s 24B).
(b) The court shall cause the charge to be written down (if this has not already been done) and to be read to the accused.
(c) The court shall explain to the accused in ordinary language that they may indicate whether (if the offence were to proceed to trial) they would plead guilty or not guilty, and if they indicate that they would plead guilty, the court will accept that indication as a guilty plea. In the case of a grave crime or a specified offence, the court must also warn the accused that committal for sentence could still be possible even after an indication of a guilty plea.
(d) If the accused indicates that they would plead guilty, the court shall proceed as if the indication were a guilty plea.
(e) If the accused indicates that they would plead not guilty, the court shall proceed to make a decision regarding allocation (the 'relevant determination').
(f) If the accused fails to indicate how they would plead, they shall be taken to indicate that they would plead not guilty.

A magistrates' court proceeding under the MCA 1980, s 24A (or s 24B) may adjourn the proceedings at any time, and on doing so on any occasion when the accused is present may remand the accused: MCA 1980, s 24C(1).

H2.4.2 *Committing a 'grave crime' for sentence*

Where a person under 18 charged with a grave crime has indicated a guilty plea at a plea before venue hearing, the court may commit them for sentence if the court is of the opinion that the offence, or the combination of the offence and one or more offences associated with it, was such that the Crown Court should have power to deal with the offender by imposing a sentence under the SC, s 250: SC, s 16(1). See **J4.1**.

This power to commit to the Crown Court for sentence can take place whether the defendant is convicted on their own plea or after summary trial.

H2.4.3 *Allocation*

If the accused gives a not guilty indication or no indication at all, the court must proceed to determine the allocation of the case.

The criterion for determining allocation: **Ought it be possible to sentence the accused in pursuance of the Sentencing Code, s 251(2) to long-term detention under s 250 for this alleged offence?** (MCA 1980, s 24A and CDA 1998, s 51A(3)(b).) Section 251(2) of the SC provides the Crown Court with the power to impose such a sentence if it is of the opinion that neither a YRO nor a DTO is suitable. The allocation decision for grave crimes has been the subject of extensive scrutiny by the Administrative Court. Reviewing those authorities, Leveson J in *R (H) v Southampton Youth Court* [2004] EWHC 2912 (Admin), [2005] 2 Cr App R (S) summarized the principles as follows:

1. The general policy of the legislature is that those who are under 18 years of age and in particular children of under 15 years of age should, wherever possible, be tried in the youth court. It is that court which is best designed to meet their specific needs. A trial in the Crown Court with the inevitably greater formality and greatly increased number of people involved (including a jury and the public) should be reserved for the most serious cases.
2. It is a further policy of the legislature that, generally speaking, first-time offenders aged 12 to 14 and all offenders under 12 should not be detained in custody and decisions as to jurisdiction should have regard to the fact that the exceptional power to detain for grave offences should not be used to water down the general

principle. Those under 15 will rarely attract a period of detention and, even more rarely, those who are under 12.

3. In each case the court should ask itself whether there is a real prospect, having regard to his or her age, that this defendant whose case they are considering might require a sentence of, or in excess of, two years or, alternatively, whether although the sentence might be less than two years, there is some unusual feature of the case which justifies declining jurisdiction, bearing in mind that the absence of a power to impose a detention and training order because the defendant is under 15 is not an unusual feature.

The *Sentencing Children and Young People – Overarching Principles* definitive guideline at para 2.10 states: 'Children and young people should only be sent for trial or committed for sentence to the Crown Court when charged with or found guilty of an offence of such gravity that a custodial sentence substantially exceeding two years is a realistic possibility. For children aged 10 or 11, and children/young people aged 12 to14 who are not persistent offenders, the court should take into account the normal prohibition on imposing custodial sentences.'

H2.4.4 ***Allocation procedure***

The allocation decision may be made by a single justice: MCA 1980, s 24D(1).

In relation to certain sexual offences there are special listing arrangements as set out in the CPD 2023, part 5.15: *Sexual Offences in the Youth Court*. See Appendix Y2. The allocation decision should be listed before an authorized district judge (who has received specific training in dealing with serious sexual offences), by live link if necessary. If jurisdiction is retained and the allegation involves actual, or attempted, penetrative activity, the case must be tried by an authorized district judge. If it is not practicable for an authorized district judge to determine allocation, any district judge or any youth court bench may consider that issue. If jurisdiction is then retained, the case papers must be referred to an authorized district judge as soon as possible for a decision to be made as to whether the case should be tried by an authorized district judge.

If the youth court is to make a satisfactory decision on allocation, it must have all the necessary information before it. The facts of the case as alleged should be accurately put before the court. The summary of facts must be scrupulously fair and balanced, and it is the duty of both advocates to ensure that is so: *R(W) v Brent Youth Court* [2006] EWHC 95 (Admin), (2006) 170 JP 198.

In recognition of the youth court as the appropriate place for trial in most cases and the court's power to commit for sentence after trial when more information about the allegation and the defendant would be available, the Divisional Court in *R (DPP) v South Tyneside Youth Court* [2015] EWHC 1455 (Admin) at para 31 stated:

> At the time of allocation and determination of venue, the court will doubtless take the views of the prosecution and defence into account; these views could include representations as the value of privacy of the proceedings or, alternatively, the desire for a jury trial. Subject to such submissions, however, in most cases whether there is such a 'real prospect' will generally be apparent only when the court has determined the full circumstances of the offence and has a far greater understanding of the position of the offender.

It is no longer necessary to take the prosecution case at its highest.

It is a useful discipline for a youth court declining jurisdiction to give reasons. By doing so, there is a better prospect that the court will consider and apply the appropriate legal test: *R (C) v Balham Youth Court* [2003] EWHC 1332 Admin, [2004] 1 Cr App R (S) 143.

The court is not obliged to consider the evidence but may decide the case is appropriate for trial on indictment after looking at the charges and hearing representations: *R v South Hackney Juvenile Court ex parte RB (a minor) and CB (a minor)* (1983) 77 Cr App R 294.

When considering allocation, a court may take into account previous convictions: *R (T) v Medway Magistrates' Court* [2003] EWHC 2279 (Admin), (2003) 167 JP 541.

In making its decision, the youth court should take into account undisputed mitigation (for example, good character) but contentious mitigation should be ignored: *R(C&D) v Sheffield Youth Court* [2003] EWHC 35 (Admin).

Where several defendants are charged together, the court must consider the position of each defendant separately, even if this results in one defendant being tried in the youth court and another in the Crown Court: *R (W) v Brent Youth Court* [2006] EWHC 95 (Admin), (2006) 170 JP 198.

H2.4.5 ***Related offences***

By the CDA 1998, s 51A(4), where a court sends a youth defendant for trial under s 51A(2), it may at the same time send them to the Crown Court for trial for any indictable or summary offence with which they are charged and which:

- (if it is an indictable offence) appears to the court to be related to the offence mentioned in s 51A(2); or

- (if it is a summary offence) appears to the court to be related to the offence mentioned in s 51A(2) or to the indictable offence (above), and which fulfils the 'requisite condition'.

A summary offence fulfils the requisite condition if it is punishable in the case of an adult with imprisonment or involves obligatory or discretionary disqualification from driving: s 51A(9).

The CDA 1998, s 51E provides:

- An either-way offence is related to an indictable offence if the charge for the either-way offence could be joined in the same indictment as the charge for the indictable offence.
- A summary offence is related to an indictable offence if it arises out of circumstances which are the same as or connected with those giving rise to the indictable offence.

H2.4.6 *Revisiting the allocation decision*

Section 25 of the CDA 1998 provides the magistrates' court with the power to change from summary trial to committal proceedings and vice versa. This power applies only in relation to adult defendants. There is no equivalent power for youth defendants. An allocation decision cannot be revisited by the youth court itself.

The Crown Court now has the power to remit a defendant back to the youth court whenever the lower court has sent the matter for trial as a grave crime: Senior Courts Act 1981, s 46ZA.

H2.4.7 *Challenging the decision to send to the Crown Court for trial*

On judicial review, the test is whether the court is satisfied that the original decision was wrong and not that it would have made a different decision: *R(C&D) v Sheffield Youth Court and R(N) v Sheffield Youth Court* [2003] EWHC 35 (Admin).

H2.4.8 *Prosecution challenge to a decision to try summarily*

The procedure to be used by the prosecution should be judicial review (and not the seeking of a voluntary bill of indictment): *R v (DPP) Camberwell Youth Court* [2004] EWHC 1805 (Admin).

H2.5 Terrorism offences

By the CDA 1998, s 51A(2) and (3)(ba), a youth defendant must be sent for trial if charged with an offence mentioned in s 252A(1)(a) of the SC and the court considers that if they are found guilty of the offence it ought to be possible to sentence them under that section to a term of detention of more than two years.

The offences mentioned in s 252A(1)(a) are those contained in part 1 of Schedule 13 to the SC and consist of a number of terrorism offences. Section 252A provides for a required special sentence of detention for terrorist offenders aged under 18 of particular concern. If convicted of a relevant offence, the court must impose a sentence consisting of the appropriate custodial term and a further period of one year for which the offender is to be subject to a licence.

A s 252A sentence can be imposed by a youth court or Crown Court. Any allocation decision will be dealt with by a district judge authorized to deal with terrorism offences. The test is similar to that for grave crimes, namely whether it ought to be possible to sentence the defendant to detention of more than two years. Those making the allocation decision should apply the same real prospect test and consider the same guidance as is provided for grave crimes. The court should follow the same procedure as for grave crimes, including taking a plea before venue.

H2.6 **Notices in serious or complex fraud cases**

A youth defendant must be sent for trial forthwith where notice is given under the CDA 1998, s 51B: CDA 1998 s 51A(2) and (3)(c). Where such a notice is served, there will be no plea before venue or allocation procedure.

A notice may be given by a designated authority under s 51B(1) in respect of an indictable offence if the authority is of the opinion that the evidence of the offence charged—

- is sufficient for the person charged to be put on trial for the offence; and
- reveals a case of fraud of such seriousness or complexity that it is appropriate that the management of the case should without delay be taken over by the Crown Court.

A notice under this section must be given to the magistrates' court at which the person charged appears or before which they are brought. Such a notice must be given to the magistrates' court before any summary trial begins: s 51B(4) and (5).

The definition of 'designated authority' includes the following:

- the DPP;
- the Director of the Serious Fraud Office; or
- the Secretary of State.

H2.7 Notices in certain cases involving children

A youth defendant must be sent for trial forthwith where notice is given under the CDA 1998, s 51C: CDA 1998 s 51A(2) and (3)(c). Where such a notice is served, there will be no plea before venue or allocation procedure.

A notice may be given by the DPP under the CDA 1998, s 51C(1) if they are of the opinion:

- that the evidence of the offence would be sufficient for the person charged to be put on trial for the offence;
- that a child would be called as a witness at the trial; and
- that, for the purpose of avoiding any prejudice to the welfare of the child, the case should be taken over and proceeded with without delay by the Crown Court.

By the CDA 1998, s 51C(3), this power applies to an offence:

(a) which involves an assault on, or injury or a threat of injury to, a person;
(b) under section 1 of the CYPA 1933 (cruelty to persons under 16);
(c) under the SOA 1956, the Protection of Children Act 1978 or the SOA 2003;
(d) of kidnapping or false imprisonment, or an offence under section 1 or 2 of the Child Abduction Act 1984;
(da) under section 1 or 2 of the Modern Slavery Act 2015;
(e) which consists of attempting or conspiring to commit, or of aiding, abetting, counselling, procuring, or inciting the commission of, an offence falling within paragraph (a), (b), (c), (d) or (da) above.

By the CDA 1998, s 51C(7) 'child' means—

- a person who is under the age of 17; or
- any person of whom a video recording (as defined in the Youth Justice and Criminal Evidence Act 1999 (YJCEA 1999), s 63(1)) was made when they were under the age of 17 with a view to its admission as his evidence in chief in the trial.

A notice under s 51C must be given to the magistrates' court before any summary trial begins: s 51B(4) and s 51C(4).

A decision to give notice under s 51C is not subject to appeal or liable to be questioned in any court: s 51C(6).

The CDA 1998, s 51C substantially re-enacts the CJA 1991, s 53. Case law relating to the use of s 53 of the 1991 Act suggest that, in the case of a 'grave crime':

- where the youth court has determined summary trial, the prosecution cannot reverse that decision by issue of a notice: *R v Fareham Youth Court and Morey ex parte CPS* (1999) 163 JP 812.

- it would be inappropriate for the DPP to use a notice unless satisfied that a magistrates' court would be likely to determine that trial on indictment was required under what is now the CDA 1998 s 51A(2) and (3)(b), i.e. a sentence substantially in excess of two years required: *R v T and K* [2001] 1 Cr App R 446, Kay LJ at [37].

H2.8 **Dangerousness**

By the CDA 1998, s 51A(2) and (3)(d), a youth defendant must be sent for trial forthwith if:

- the offence is a specified offence; and
- it appears to the court that, if they are found guilty of the offence, the criteria in the SC, s 255(1) for the imposition of a sentence of extended detention would be met.

There is no plea before venue procedure.

H2.8.1 ***Criteria for imposing extended detention***

The SC, ss 254 to 257 are considered in more detail at **K4.4** but, in summary, they provide that the Crown Court may impose an extended sentence of detention where:

- a person aged under 18 is convicted of a ***specified*** offence for which a sentence of detention is available under the SC, s 250 or s 252A;
- the court is of the opinion that there is a significant risk to members of the public of ***serious harm*** occasioned by the commission by the offender of further specified offences;
- the court is not required to impose a sentence of detention for life; and
- if the court were to impose an extended sentence of detention, the term that it would specify as the appropriate custodial term would be at least four years.

The SC, s 306 provides the following definitions:

- ***Specified offence***—a violent or sexual or terrorism offence listed in the SC, Schedule 18.
- ***Serious harm***—means death or serious person injury, whether physical or psychological.

H2.8.2 ***The assessment of dangerousness***

By the SC, s 308(2), the court:

- must take into account all such information as is available to it about the nature and circumstances of the offence;

- may take into account all the information that is available to it about the nature and circumstances of any other offences of which the offender has been convicted;
- may take into account any information which is before it about any pattern of behaviour of which the offence(s) forms part; and
- may take into account any information about the offender which is before it.

General advice about assessing dangerousness on sentence was given by Thomas LJ in *R v Lang* [2005] EWCA Crim 2864, [2006] 1 WLR 2509 (for which see K4.4.2). For the purposes of allocation, the most important points from the judgment are:

- 'significant risk' is more than the possibility of occurrence;
- 'significant risk' must be shown in relation to two matters: first, the commission of further specified, but not necessarily serious, offences; and secondly, the causing thereby of serious harm to a member of the public;
- assessment of risk should include the offending history—the kind of offences, their circumstances, and the sentence imposed.

In *CPS v South East Surrey Youth Court* [2005] EWHC 2929; [2006] 1 WLR 2543, the Administrative Court considered the approach that should be taken by a youth court at the allocation stage and provided the following guidance:

- The policy of the legislature is that those who are under 18 should, wherever possible, be tried in a youth court, which is best designed for their specific needs.
- The guidance given by the Court of Appeal in *R v Lang* is of relevance, particularly in relation to non-serious specified offences.
- The court must be particularly rigorous before concluding that there is a significant risk of serious harm by the commission of further offences; such a conclusion is unlikely to be appropriate in the absence of a pre-sentence report following assessment by a YOT.
- In most cases where a non-serious specified offence is charged, an assessment of dangerousness will not be appropriate until after conviction, when, if the dangerousness criteria are met, the defendant can be committed to the Crown Court for sentence.

The *Sentencing Children and Young People: Overarching Principles* definitive guideline, para 2.7 suggests that, in most cases, it would not be possible to form a view as to whether the criteria would be met until after plea or trial and that jurisdiction should be retained in the youth court until a decision can be made as to committal for sentence.

H2.8.3 *Co-defendants*

When dealing with youth co-defendants at an allocation hearing, the court must address the question of dangerousness for each defendant separately. Where one youth defendant is deemed to satisfy the criteria of s 51A(3)(d) and is sent for trial under s 51A(2), there is no provision to send a youth co-defendant who is not deemed to be dangerous. It would, however, be possible to send an adult co-defendant charged with an either-way offence which is a joint charge or related to the charge which the youth defendant faces: s 51A(6).

H2.8.4 *Related offences*

Where a court sends a youth defendant for trial under s 51A(2), s 51A(4) provides that it may at the same time send them to the Crown Court for trial for any indictable or summary offence with which they are charged and which:

- (if it is an indictable offence) appears to the court to be related to the offence mentioned in s 51A(2); or
- (if it is a summary offence) appears to the court to be related to the offence mentioned in s 51A(2) or to the indictable offence (above), and which fulfils the 'requisite condition'.

A summary offence fulfils the requisite condition if it is punishable with imprisonment in the case of an adult or involves obligatory or discretionary disqualification from driving: s 51A(9).

The CDA 1998, s 51E provides:

- An either-way offence is related to an indictable offence if the charge for the either-way offence could be joined in the same indictment as the charge for the indictable offence.
- A summary offence is related to an indictable offence if it arises out of circumstances which are the same as or connected with those giving rise to the indictable offence.

H2.8.5 *Post-conviction committal for sentence*

After the summary trial of a specified offence where a person under 18 is convicted of the offence, the court must commit the offender to the Crown Court for sentence if it appears to the court that the criteria for the imposition of a dangerous offender sentence would be met: SC, s 17. See **J4.3**.

H2.9 **Youth charged jointly with an adult**

By the CDA 1998, s 51(7), where:

- the court sends an adult defendant A for trial;

- a youth Y appears before the court on the same or a subsequent occasion charged jointly with A with that indictable offence or charged with a related indictable offence,

the court shall also send Y to the Crown Court for the indictable offence if it considers it necessary to do so in ***the interests of justice***.

Before allocation can be considered under s 51(7), the court must go through the plea before venue procedure (see **H.2.4.1**).

H2.9.1 *Jointly charged*

It is not necessary for the charge to specify that the offence was committed 'jointly' or 'together with' the adult concerned: *R v Rowlands* [1972] 1 All ER 306.

A defendant charged with driving a conveyance taken without consent and another defendant charged with allowing to be carried are properly considered to be 'jointly charged': *R v Peterborough Magistrates' Court ex parte Allgood* (1995) JP 627.

The power to send a youth for trial under s 51(7) is not confined to cases where the adult and youth defendant are before the same adult magistrates' court. A youth court can exercise the power under the MCA 1980, s 24(1)(b) in a case where a youth is to be jointly indicted with an adult who has already been sent for trial by an adult magistrates' court: *R v Coventry City Magistrates' Court ex parte M* (1992) JP 809.

H2.9.2 *Order of decision-making*

Where a youth is jointly charged with an adult and both appear before the court at the same time, the allocation procedure starts with the adult. The order of decision-making is set out in the CDA 1998, ss 50A, 51, and 51A. The complex provisions are summarized in two flow charts which can be found in Appendix Y1 at pages 377–9. The flow chart dealing with decision-making for a youth charged alone is followed by a flow chart dealing with the circumstances where the youth is jointly charged with an adult who is charged with an indictable-only offence. The next chart deals with the procedure where the adult is charged with an either-way offence.

H2.9.3 *Plea before venue*

Before the court determines whether to send the youth with the adult for trial in the Crown Court under s 51(7), it must deal with plea before venue and ask the youth to indicate a plea to the charge (MCA 1980 s 24A). For the prescribed procedure when dealing with plea before venue see **H2.4.1** above.

H2.9.4 *Interests of justice*

Every court making an allocation decision must follow any relevant sentencing guideline unless it is satisfied that it would be contrary to the interests of justice to do so (SC, s 59(1)). The *Sentencing Children and Young People – Overarching Principles* definitive guideline, when dealing with whether a youth defendant should be sent for trial with an adult, states:

> 2.11 The proper venue for the trial of any child or young person is normally the youth court. Subject to statutory restrictions, that remains the case where a child or young person is jointly charged with an adult. If the adult is sent for trial to the Crown Court, the court should conclude that the child or young person must be tried separately in the youth court unless it is in the interests of justice for the child or young person and the adult to be tried jointly.
>
> 2.12 Examples of factors that should be considered when deciding whether to send the child or young person to the Crown Court (rather than having a trial in the youth court) include:

- whether separate trials will cause injustice to witnesses or to the case as a whole (consideration should be given to the provisions of sections 27 and 28 of the Youth Justice and Criminal Evidence Act 1999);
- the age of the child or young person; the younger the child or young person, the greater the desirability that the child or young person be tried in the youth court;
- the age gap between the child or young person and the adult; a substantial gap in age militates in favour of the child or young person being tried in the youth court;
- the lack of maturity of the child or young person;
- the relative culpability of the child or young person compared with the adult and whether the alleged role played by the child or young person was minor; and/or
- the lack of previous findings of guilt on the part of the child or young person.

In July 2020, William Davis J, Judicial Lead for Youth Justice for England and Wales, issued a note to all magistrates' courts emphasizing a seventh factor in applying the interests of justice test, namely:

- the likely delay in trying the youth in the Crown Court, as compared to the youth court, because of the very large backlog of cases in the Crown Court.

H2.9.5 *Related offences*

The CDA 1998, s 51(8) provides that, where the court sends a youth for trial under subsection (7), it may at the same time send them to the Crown Court for trial for any indictable or summary offence with which they are charged and which—

- (if it is an indictable offence) appears to the court to be related to the offence for which they are sent for trial; and
- (if it is a summary offence) appears to the court to be related to the offence for which they are sent for trial or to the indictable offence (above), and which fulfils the 'requisite condition'.

A summary offence fulfils the requisite condition if it is punishable with imprisonment or involves obligatory or discretionary disqualification from driving: s 51(11).

The CDA 1998, s 51E provides:

- An either-way offence is related to an indictable offence if the charge for the either-way offence could be joined in the same indictment as the charge for the indictable offence.
- A summary offence is related to an indictable offence if it arises out of circumstances which are the same as or connected with those giving rise to the indictable offence.

H2.10 Allocation procedure—relevant legislation

Magistrates' Courts Act 1980

24A Child or young person to indicate intention as to plea in certain cases

(1) This section applies where—
 (a) a person under the age of 18 years appears or is brought before a magistrates' court on an information charging him with an offence other than one falling within section 51A(12) of the Crime and Disorder Act 1998 ('the 1998 Act'); and
 (b) but for the application of the following provisions of this section, the court would be required at that stage, by virtue of section 51(7) or (8) or 51A(3)(b), (4) or (5) of the 1998 Act to determine, in relation to the offence, whether to send the person to the Crown Court for trial (or to determine any matter, the effect of which would be to determine whether he is sent to the Crown Court for trial).

(2) Where this section applies, the court shall, before proceeding to make any such determination as is referred to in subsection (1)(b) above (the 'relevant determination'), follow the procedure set out in this section.

(3) Everything that the court is required to do under the following provisions of this section must be done with the accused person in court.

(4) The court shall cause the charge to be written down, if this has not already been done, and to be read to the accused.

(5) The court shall then explain to the accused in ordinary language that he may indicate whether (if the offence were to proceed to trial) he would plead guilty or not guilty, and that if he indicates that he would plead guilty—

(a) the court must proceed as mentioned in subsection (7) below; and

(b) (in cases where the offence is one mentioned in section 249(1)(a) or (b) of the Sentencing Code) he may be sent to the Crown Court for sentencing under section 16, 16A or 17 of that Act if the court is of such opinion as is mentioned in section 16(1)(c), 16A(1)(c) or (if applicable) section 17(1)(b).

(6) The court shall then ask the accused whether (if the offence were to proceed to trial) he would plead guilty or not guilty.

(7) If the accused indicates that he would plead guilty, the court shall proceed as if—

(a) the proceedings constituted from the beginning the summary trial of the information; and

(b) section 9(1) above was complied with and he pleaded guilty under it,

and, accordingly, the court shall not (and shall not be required to) proceed to make the relevant determination or to proceed further under section 51 or (as the case may be) section 51A of the 1998 Act in relation to the offence.

(8) If the accused indicates that he would plead not guilty, the court shall proceed to make the relevant determination and this section shall cease to apply.

(9) If the accused in fact fails to indicate how he would plead, for the purposes of this section he shall be taken to indicate that he would plead not guilty.

(10) Subject to subsection (7) above, the following shall not for any purpose be taken to constitute the taking of a plea—

(a) asking the accused under this section whether (if the offence were to proceed to trial) he would plead guilty or not guilty;

(b) an indication by the accused under this section of how he would plead.

Crime and Disorder Act 1998

50A Order of consideration for either-way offences

(1) Where an adult appears or is brought before a magistrates' court charged with an either-way offence (the 'relevant offence'), the court shall proceed in the manner described in this section.

(2) If notice is given in respect of the relevant offence under section 51B or 51C below, the court shall deal with the offence as provided in section 51 below.

(3) Otherwise—
  (a) if the adult (or another adult with whom the adult is charged jointly with the relevant offence) is or has been sent to the Crown Court for trial for an offence under section 51(2)(a) or 51(2)(c) below—
    (i) the court shall first consider the relevant offence under subsection (3), (4), (5) or, as the case may be, (6) of section 51 below and, where applicable, deal with it under that subsection;
    (ii) if the adult is not sent to the Crown Court for trial for the relevant offence by virtue of sub-paragraph (i) above, the court shall then proceed to deal with the relevant offence in accordance with sections 17A to 23 of the 1980 Act;
  (b) in all other cases—
    (i) the court shall first consider the relevant offence under sections 17A to 20 (excluding subsections (8) and (9) of section 20) of the 1980 Act;
    (ii) if, by virtue of sub-paragraph (i) above, the court would be required to proceed in relation to the offence as mentioned in section 17A(6), 17B(2)(c) or 20(7) of that Act (indication of guilty plea), it shall proceed as so required (and, accordingly, shall not consider the offence under section 51 or 51A below);
    (iii) if sub-paragraph (ii) above does not apply—
      (a) the court shall consider the relevant offence under sections 51 and 51A below and, where applicable, deal with it under the relevant section;
      (b) if the adult is not sent to the Crown Court for trial for the relevant offence by virtue of paragraph (a) of this sub-paragraph, the court shall then proceed to deal with the relevant offence as contemplated by section 20(9) or, as the case may be, section 21 of the 1980 Act.

(4) Subsection (3) above is subject to any requirement to proceed as mentioned in subsections (2) or (6)(a) of section 22 of the 1980 Act (certain offences where value involved is small).

(5) Nothing in this section shall prevent the court from committing the adult to the Crown Court for sentence pursuant to any enactment, if he is convicted of the relevant offence.

51 Sending cases to the Crown Court: adults

(1) Where an adult appears or is brought before a magistrates' court ('the court') charged with an offence and any of the conditions mentioned in subsection (2) below is satisfied, the court shall send him forthwith to the Crown Court for trial for the offence.

(2) Those conditions are—
  (a) that the offence is an offence triable only on indictment other than one in respect of which notice has been given under section 51B or 51C below;

(b) that the offence is an either-way offence and the court is required under section 20(9)(b), 21, 23(4)(b) or (5) or 25(2D) of the Magistrates' Courts Act 1980 to proceed in relation to the offence in accordance with subsection (1) above;

(c) that notice is given to the court under section 51B or 51C below in respect of the offence.

(3) Where the court sends an adult for trial under subsection (1) above, it shall at the same time send him to the Crown Court for trial for any either-way or summary offence with which he is charged and which—

(a) (if it is an either-way offence) appears to the court to be related to the offence mentioned in subsection (1) above; or

(b) (if it is a summary offence) appears to the court to be related to the offence mentioned in subsection (1) above or to the either-way offence, and which fulfils the requisite condition (as defined in subsection (11) below).

(4) Where an adult who has been sent for trial under subsection (1) above subsequently appears or is brought before a magistrates' court charged with an either-way or summary offence which—

(a) appears to the court to be related to the offence mentioned in subsection (1) above; and

(b) (in the case of a summary offence) fulfils the requisite condition, the court may send him forthwith to the Crown Court for trial for the either-way or summary offence.

(5) Where—

(a) the court sends an adult ('A') for trial under subsection (1) or (3) above;

(b) another adult appears or is brought before the court on the same or a subsequent occasion charged jointly with A with an either-way offence; and

(c) that offence appears to the court to be related to an offence for which A was sent for trial under subsection (1) or (3) above,

the court shall where it is the same occasion, and may where it is a subsequent occasion, send the other adult forthwith to the Crown Court for trial for the either-way offence.

(6) Where the court sends an adult for trial under subsection (5) above, it shall at the same time send him to the Crown Court for trial for any either-way or summary offence with which he is charged and which—

(a) (if it is an either-way offence) appears to the court to be related to the offence for which he is sent for trial; and

(b) (if it is a summary offence) appears to the court to be related to the offence for which he is sent for trial or to the either-way offence, and which fulfils the requisite condition.

(7) Where—

(a) the court sends an adult ('A') for trial under subsection (1), (3) or (5) above; and

(b) a child or young person appears or is brought before the court on the same or a subsequent occasion charged jointly with

A with an indictable offence for which A is sent for trial under subsection (1), (3) or (5) above, or an indictable offence which appears to the court to be related to that offence,

the court shall, if it considers it necessary in the interests of justice to do so, send the child or young person forthwith to the Crown Court for trial for the indictable offence.

(8) Where the court sends a child or young person for trial under subsection (7) above, it may at the same time send him to the Crown Court for trial for any indictable or summary offence with which he is charged and which—

(a) (if it is an indictable offence) appears to the court to be related to the offence for which he is sent for trial; and

(b) (if it is a summary offence) appears to the court to be related to the offence for which he is sent for trial or to the indictable offence, and which fulfils the requisite condition.

(9) Subsections (7) and (8) above are subject to sections 24A and 24B of the Magistrates' Courts Act 1980 (which provide for certain cases involving children and young persons to be tried summarily).

(10) The trial of the information charging any summary offence for which a person is sent for trial under this section shall be treated as if the court had adjourned it under section 10 of the 1980 Act and had not fixed the time and place for its resumption.

(11) A summary offence fulfils the requisite condition if it is punishable with imprisonment or involves obligatory or discretionary disqualification from driving.

(12) In the case of an adult charged with an offence—

(a) if the offence satisfies paragraph (c) of subsection (2) above, the offence shall be dealt with under subsection (1) above and not under any other provision of this section or section 51A below;

(b) subject to paragraph (a) above, if the offence is one in respect of which the court is required to, or would decide to, send the adult to the Crown Court under—

(i) subsection (5) above; or

(ii) subsection (6) of section 51A below,

the offence shall be dealt with under that subsection and not under any other provision of this section or section 51A below.

(13) The functions of a magistrates' court under this section, and its related functions under section 51D below, may be discharged by a single justice.

51A Sending cases to the Crown Court: children and young persons

(1) This section is subject to sections 24A and 24B of the Magistrates' Courts Act 1980 (which provide for certain offences involving children or young persons to be tried summarily).

(2) Where a child or young person appears or is brought before a magistrates' court ('the court') charged with an offence and any of the conditions mentioned in subsection (3) below is satisfied, the court shall send him forthwith to the Crown Court for trial for the offence.

(3) Those conditions are—
  (a) that the offence falls within subsection (12) below;
  (b) that the offence is such as is mentioned in section 249(1)(a) or (b) of the Sentencing Code (other than one mentioned in paragraph (d) below in relation to which it appears to the court as mentioned there) and the court considers that if he is found guilty of the offence it ought to be possible to sentence him in pursuance of section 251(s) of that Code;
  (ba) that the offence is such as is mentioned in section 252A(1)(a) of the Sentencing Code and the court considers that if he is found guilty of the offence it ought to be possible to sentence him under that section to a term of detention of more than two years;
  (c) that notice is given to the court under section 51B or 51C below in respect of the offence;
  (d) that the offence is a specified offence (within the meaning given by section 306 of the Sentencing Code) and it appears to the court that if he is found guilty of the offence the criteria in section 255(1) of that Code for the imposition of an extended sentence of detention would be met.

(4) Where the court sends a child or young person for trial under subsection (2) above, it may at the same time send him to the Crown Court for trial for any indictable or summary offence with which he is charged and which—
  (a) (if it is an indictable offence) appears to the court to be related to the offence mentioned in subsection (2) above; or
  (b) (if it is a summary offence) appears to the court to be related to the offence mentioned in subsection (2) above or to the indictable offence, and which fulfils the requisite condition (as defined in subsection (9) below).

(5) Where a child or young person who has been sent for trial under subsection (2) above subsequently appears or is brought before a magistrates' court charged with an indictable or summary offence which—
  (a) appears to the court to be related to the offence mentioned in subsection (2) above; and
  (b) (in the case of a summary offence) fulfils the requisite condition,

the court may send him forthwith to the Crown Court for trial for the indictable or summary offence.

(6) Where—
  (a) the court sends a child or young person ('C') for trial under subsection (2) or (4) above; and
  (b) an adult appears or is brought before the court on the same or a subsequent occasion charged jointly with C with an either-way offence for which C is sent for trial under subsection (2) or (4) above, or an either-way offence which appears to the court to be related to that offence,

the court shall where it is the same occasion, and may where it is a subsequent occasion, send the adult forthwith to the Crown Court for trial for the either-way offence.

(7) Where the court sends an adult for trial under subsection (6) above, it shall at the same time send him to the Crown Court for trial for any either-way or summary offence with which he is charged and which—
   (a) (if it is an either-way offence) appears to the court to be related to the offence for which he was sent for trial; and
   (b) (if it is a summary offence) appears to the court to be related to the offence for which he was sent for trial or to the either-way offence, and which fulfils the requisite condition.

(8) The trial of the information charging any summary offence for which a person is sent for trial under this section shall be treated as if the court had adjourned it under section 10 of the 1980 Act and had not fixed the time and place for its resumption.

(9) A summary offence fulfils the requisite condition if it is punishable with imprisonment or involves obligatory or discretionary disqualification from driving.

(10) In the case of a child or young person charged with an offence—
   (a) if the offence satisfies any of the conditions in subsection (3) above, the offence shall be dealt with under subsection (2) above and not under any other provision of this section or section 51 above;
   (b) subject to paragraph (a) above, if the offence is one in respect of which the requirements of subsection (7) of section 51 above for sending the child or young person to the Crown Court are satisfied, the offence shall be dealt with under that subsection and not under any other provision of this section or section 51 above.

(11) The functions of a magistrates' court under this section, and its related functions under section 51D below, may be discharged by a single justice.

(12) An offence falls within this subsection if—
   (a) it is an offence of homicide;
   (b) each of the requirements of section 311(1) of the Sentencing Code would be satisfied with respect to—
      (i) the offence; and
      (ii) the person charged with it,

      if he were convicted of the offence; or
   (c) section 29(3) of Violent Crime Reduction Act 2006 (minimum sentences in certain cases of using someone to mind a weapon) would apply if he were convicted of the offence.

H3 **Bail**

H3.1 **Introduction**

Under the UN Convention on the Rights of the Child, Article 37(1), depriving a child of their liberty during criminal proceedings should be a measure of last resort. To that end there are rules applicable only to defendants under the age of 18 and extra resources are devoted to supporting defendants on bail.

The Bail Act 1976 (BA 1976) applies to youth defendants but there are a number of differences which generally narrow the scope of the statutory grounds for refusing bail. In addition, if bail is refused, there is a presumption that the remand will be to local authority accommodation; further criteria must be satisfied before a remand in custody is made (see H4).

The main practical difference between applying for bail for a youth as opposed to an adult is the significant role played by the YOT. When a court is considering bail in relation to a young defendant, the YOT may be involved in the following ways:

- assessing the young defendant;
- providing bail information;
- implementing bail supervision and support; and
- providing a bail intensive supervision and surveillance programme (bail ISSP).

Assessment Prior to deciding whether to offer any services to the young defendant, the YOT will assess them. If the YOT is not already working with the youth defendant, an *Asset* Bail Profile will be completed.

Bail information The YOT may seek to verify information about the young person (eg regarding school attendance), obtain information from children's services databases, as well as checking out the suitability of a proposed bail address by carrying out child protection and police checks on the address and its occupants.

Bail supervision and support The YOT may offer a bail support package to the court. This could be in the form of an oral presentation or in a written report.

If the defendant is at a court outside their own local authority area, the YOT workers at the court will contact the 'home' YOT.

Blackstone's Handbook of Youths in the Criminal Courts. Mark Ashford, Gareth Branston, and Naomi Redhouse, Oxford University Press.
 DOI: 10.1093/oso/9780198913146.003.0018

There will always be a YOT worker present at court on a day when there is a scheduled youth court. When dealing with a young defendant who has been refused bail by the police, the advocate should make early contact with the worker to ensure that an early assessment of the young defendant is carried out. Where the defendant is in custody at an adult court, the advocate should ensure that the relevant YOT is aware of the defendant's presence at court.

H3.2 Right to bail

There is a general right to bail for any person accused of an offence when they appear or are brought before a youth court, adult magistrates' court, or the Crown Court in the course of or in connection with proceedings for the offence: BA 1976 s 4(1) and (2).

That presumption does not, however, apply in the following cases:

- following committal to the Crown Court for sentence or for breach of a Crown Court order;
- after conviction, unless the proceedings are adjourned for enquiries to be made or a report to be prepared for sentence;
- on appeal against conviction or sentence; or
- following a breach of bail.

The general right to bail is subject to the Coroners and Justice Act 2009, s 115(1) and the Criminal Justice and Public Order Act 1994, s 25.

Section 115 of the Coroners and Justice Act 2009 provides that bail decisions in murder cases may only be made by a Crown Court judge. No application for bail may be made in the magistrates' or youth court and that court must commit the defendant to custody to be brought before a judge of the Crown Court: s 115(4). A judge of the Crown Court must then make a decision about bail in respect of the person as soon as reasonably practicable and, in any event, within the period of 48 hours (excluding weekends and bank holidays) beginning with the day after the day on which the person appears or is brought before the magistrates' court: s 115 (3) and (7).

Section 25 of the Criminal Justice and Public Order Act 1994 provides that bail may only be granted in exceptional circumstances where a defendant is charged with or convicted of an offence of:

- murder, or
- manslaughter, or
- rape, or
- penetrative sexual offence under the SOA 2003, ss 2, 4, 5, 6, 8, 30 or 31, or

- an attempt to commit one of these offences,

and the defendant has been previously convicted in the United Kingdom or in an EU member state of any such offence or equivalent offence.

However, neither of these statutory restrictions on bail remove the requirement for a magistrates' or youth court to determine whether the remand will be to local authority accommodation or to youth detention (see H4).

H3.3 **Right to apply for bail**

An application for bail can be made at the first hearing of the case before a youth court or adult magistrates' court.

If bail is refused at the first hearing, the BA 1976 Sch 1 Part IIA provides:

Bail Act 1976, Sch 1, Part IIA

1. If the court decides not to grant the defendant bail, it is the court's duty to consider, at each subsequent hearing while the defendant is a person to whom section 4 above applies and remains in custody, whether he ought to be granted bail.
2. At the first hearing after that at which the court decided not to grant the defendant bail he may support an application for bail with any argument as to fact or law that he desires (whether or not he has advanced that argument previously).
3. At subsequent hearings the court need not hear arguments as to fact or law which it has heard previously.

A refusal of bail on the grounds of insufficient information should not be counted as a decision to refuse bail, thereby exhausting one of the two attempts: *R v Calderdale Justices, ex parte Kennedy* The Times, 18 February 1992. Similarly, a remand in absence should be discounted: *R v Dover and East Kent Justices, ex parte Dean* The Times, 22 August 1991. However, if a fully argued application is not made by the defendant at the first hearing, the effect is that one opportunity to argue for bail is lost, meaning that if bail is refused at the subsequent hearing, the two opportunities for bail are spent. Similarly, if an argument is made at the first hearing, but not at a second hearing, there is no right to a second application for bail at the third hearing.

Following two refusals to grant bail, further applications can be made if there has been a change in circumstances, for example:

1. Change in the case alleged against the defendant: *R v Reading Crown Court, ex parte Malik* [1981] QB 451 and *R v Slough Justices, ex parte Duncan* [1981] QB 451.

2. Increased surety: *R v Isleworth Crown Court, ex parte Commissioners of Customs and Excise* (1990) The Times, 27 July.
3. Passage of time: *Neumeister v Austria (No 1)* (1979–80) 1 EHRR 91.

In *R (B) v Brent Youth Court* [2010] EWHC 1893 (Admin), the court held that a different bail address amounted to a change of circumstances. It was not necessary that any new factor be exceptional in nature. The correct test is whether there is any new consideration which was not before the court when the accused was last remanded in custody. Similarly, an argument that the prosecution case against the defendant was significantly weaker than at first presented would qualify as a change in circumstance. The court ended by saying:

> [E]ven if the Bench had been entitled to form the view that each and every argument as to fact or law was an argument which it had heard previously, it manifestly failed to go on to consider whether, notwithstanding that, it should nonetheless consider substantively a bail application, given the provisions of [the CYPA 1933 s 44], having regard to the welfare of a child or young person.

H3.4 **Grounds to refuse bail**

The court may only refuse bail if it can identify one of the prescribed exceptions to the right to bail contained in the BA 1976, Sch 1.

Since the implementation of the Criminal Justice and Immigration Act 2008 (CJIA 2008), the BA 1976, Sch 1 is now split into three Parts:

- Part I—Indictable offences;
- Part IA—Imprisonable summary-only offences; and
- Part II—Non-imprisonable offences.

The grounds for refusing bail are different in each category and will be considered separately.

H3.4.1 ***Defendants accused of indictable offences***

The BA 1976, Sch 1, Part I provides that, in the case of indictable offences, bail may be refused if:

- the court is satisfied there are *substantial* grounds for believing that, if released on bail (whether subject to conditions or not) the defendant would:
  (a) fail to surrender to custody; or
  (b) commit an offence while on bail; or
  (c) interfere with witnesses or otherwise obstruct the course of justice, whether in relation to themselves or any other person (para 2);

- the court is satisfied that there are *substantial* grounds for believing that the defendant, if released on bail (whether subject to conditions or not), would commit an offence while on bail that would, or would be likely to, cause:
  (a) physical or mental injury to an 'associated person' (as defined in the Family Law Act 1996, s 62); or
  (b) an associated person to fear physical or mental injury (para 2ZA);
- it appears to the court that the defendant was on bail in criminal proceedings on the date of the offence (para 2A);
- the court is satisfied that the defendant should be kept in custody for their own protection or, if they are under 18, for their own welfare (para 3);
- the defendant is in custody in pursuance of a sentence of a court or a sentence imposed by an officer under the Armed Forces Act 2006 (para 4);
- the court is satisfied that it has not been practicable to obtain sufficient information for the purpose of taking the decisions required regarding bail for want of time since the institution of the proceedings against the defendant (para 5);
- having been released on bail in proceedings for the offence, the defendant has been arrested for breach of bail conditions under the BA 1976, s 7 (para 6);
- (where the case is adjourned for enquiries or a report) it appears to the court that it would be impracticable to complete the enquiries or make the report without keeping the defendant in custody (para 7).

For the purposes of para 2ZA above, 'associated person', as defined by the Family Law Act 1996, s 62, includes a parent, child, spouse, civil partner, intimate partner, relative, or any person who lives in the same household otherwise than merely by reason of one being the other's tenant, lodger, or boarder.

Unlike for an adult defendant, the BA 1976 does not require that there is a real prospect of a custodial sentence for a youth defendant for those exceptions in paras 2, 2A, and 6 to apply. There is, however, a requirement, in the Legal Aid Sentencing and Punishment of Offenders Act 2012 (LASPO 2012), ss 98 and 99, that the court must consider it very likely that the child or young person will be sentenced to a custodial sentence before it remands to youth detention (see **H4**).

Restrictions on the grant of bail which apply to certain drug users under the BA 1976, Sch 1, Part I, paras 6A and 6B do not apply to youth defendants.

If a defendant is charged with murder, the defendant may not be bailed unless the court is of the opinion that there is no significant risk of the defendant committing, while on bail, an offence that would, or would be likely to, cause physical or mental injury to any person other than the defendant (para 6ZA).

When considering if any of the grounds in para 2 or para 2ZA are made out, the BA 1976, Sch 1, Part 1, para 9 requires the court to take into account information available to it regarding the following:

- the nature and seriousness of the offence (and the probable means of dealing with the defendant for it);
- the character, antecedents (eg criminal record), associations, and community ties of the defendant;
- the defendant's previous record of complying with the obligation of bail;
- (except in the case of an adjournment for a pre-sentence report) the strength of the evidence against the defendant;
- if the court is satisfied that there are substantial grounds for believing that the defendant, if released on bail (whether subject to conditions or not), would commit an offence while on bail, the risk that the defendant may do so by engaging in conduct that would, or would be likely to, cause physical or mental injury to any person other than the defendant;
- any other consideration which the court considers relevant.

The seriousness of the offence (and the likely penalty) cannot of itself justify a refusal of bail on the inference that the person is likely to abscond (*Lettelier v France* (1992) 14 EHRR 83), although a judge is perfectly entitled to regard that as a significant factor: *R (Thompson) v Central Criminal Court* [2005] EWHC 2345. Before bail can be refused on the grounds of interfering with witnesses or obstructing justice, the prosecution must point to an identifiable risk and provide supporting evidence: *Clooth v Belgium* (1991) 14 EHRR 717.

The CJA 2003 inserted into the BA 1976 provisions which deal with how the court should approach the decision whether to grant bail when the defendant has committed an offence whilst on bail during the proceedings or has failed to surrender to custody during the proceedings. These provisions are more favourable than the comparable provisions for adult defendants.

Where the defendant has committed an offence on bail during the proceedings, the CJA 2003 s 14(2) inserts a new para 9AA. However, this provision is currently only in force in relation to offences punishable in the case of an adult with life imprisonment: Criminal Justice Act 2003 (Commencement No 14 and Transitional Provision) Order 2006 SI 2006/3217.

Bail Act 1976, Sch 1, para 9AA

(1) This paragraph applies if–
  (a) the defendant is a child or young person, and
  (b) it appears to the court that he was on bail in criminal proceedings on the date of the offence.

(2) In deciding for the purposes of paragraph 2(1) of this Part of this Schedule whether it is satisfied that there are substantial grounds for believing that the defendant, if released on bail (whether subject to conditions or not), would commit an offence while on bail, the court shall give particular weight to the fact that the defendant was on bail in criminal proceedings on the date of the offence.

Where the defendant has failed to surrender to custody during the proceedings, the CJA 2003 s 15(2) inserts a new para 9AB. However, this provision is currently only in force in relation to offences punishable in the case of an adult with life imprisonment: Criminal Justice Act 2003 (Commencement No 14 and Transitional Provision) Order 2006, SI 2006/3217.

Bail Act 1976, Sch 1, para 9AB

(1) Subject to sub-paragraph (2) below, this paragraph applies if–
  (a) the defendant is a child or young person, and
  (b) it appears to the court that, having been released on bail in or in connection with the proceedings for the offence, he failed to surrender to custody.

(2) Where it appears to the court that the defendant had reasonable cause for his failure to surrender to custody, this paragraph does not apply unless it also appears to the court that he failed to surrender to custody at the appointed place as soon as reasonably practicable after the appointed time.

(3) In deciding for the purposes of paragraph 2(1) of this Part of this Schedule whether it is satisfied that there are substantial grounds for believing that the defendant, if released on bail (whether subject to conditions or not), would fail to surrender to custody, the court shall give particular weight to–
  (a) where the defendant did not have reasonable cause for his failure to surrender to custody, the fact that he failed to surrender to custody, or
  (b) where he did have reasonable cause for his failure to surrender to custody, the fact that he failed to surrender to custody at the appointed place as soon as reasonably practicable after the appointed time.

(4) For the purposes of this paragraph, a failure to give to the defendant a copy of the record of the decision to grant him bail shall not constitute a reasonable cause for his failure to surrender to custody.

H3.4.2 *Defendants accused of summary-only imprisonable offences*

This category includes not only all imprisonable summary-only offences but also either-way offences specified in the MCA 1980, Sch 2 (criminal damage and aggravated vehicle-taking where the value is less than £5,000). Under the BA 1976, s 9A, where a child or young person is charged with such an offence and the court is considering whether to withhold or grant bail it must consider whether, having regard to any representations made by the prosecutor and the defence, the value involved does not exceed £5,000.

Under the BA 1976, Sch 1, Part IA, bail need not be granted if:

- it appears to the court that, having been previously granted bail in criminal proceedings, the defendant has failed to surrender to custody in accordance with their obligations under the grant of bail and the court believes, in view of that failure, that the defendant, if released on bail (whether subject to conditions or not) would fail to surrender to custody (para 2);
- it appears to the court that the defendant was on bail in criminal proceedings on the date of the offence and the court is satisfied that there are substantial grounds for believing that the defendant, if released on bail (whether subject to conditions or not), would commit an offence on bail (para 3);
- the court is satisfied that there are substantial grounds for believing that the defendant, if released on bail (whether subject to conditions or not), would commit an offence while on bail by engaging in conduct which would, or would be likely to, cause:
  (a) physical or mental injury to an 'associated person' (as defined in the Family Law Act 1996, s 62); or
  (b) an associated person to fear physical or mental injury (para 4);
- the court is satisfied that the defendant should be kept in custody for their own protection, or if they are a child or young person, for their own welfare (para 5);
- they are in custody serving a sentence of a court or a sentence imposed by an officer under the Armed Forces Act 1996 (para 6);
- having been released on bail in or in connection with the proceedings for the offence, the defendant has been arrested for breach of bail conditions under the BA 1976 s 7 and the court is satisfied that there are substantial grounds for believing that the defendant, if released on bail (whether subject to conditions or not) would fail to surrender to custody, commit an offence while on bail, or interfere with witnesses or otherwise obstruct

the course of justice (whether in relation to themselves or any other person) (para 7);
- the court is satisfied that it has not been practicable to obtain sufficient information for the purposes of making a decision regarding bail (para 8).

For the purposes of para 4 above, 'associated person', as defined by the Family Law Act 1996, s 62, includes a parent, child, spouse, civil partner, intimate partner, relative, or any person who lives in the same household otherwise than merely by reason of one being the other's tenant, lodger, or boarder.

Unlike for an adult defendant, the BA 1976 does not require that there is a real prospect of a custodial sentence for a youth defendant for those exceptions in paras 2, 3, and 7 to apply. There is, however, a requirement, in LASPO 2012, ss 98 and 99, that the court must consider it very likely that the child or young person will be sentenced to a custodial sentence before it remands to youth detention (see **H4**).

H3.4.3 *Defendants accused of non-imprisonable offences*

Under the BA 1976, Sch 1, Part II, bail need not be granted if:

- it appears to the court that, having been previously granted bail in criminal proceedings, a defendant under the age of 18 has failed to surrender to custody in accordance with their obligations under the grant of bail and the court believes, in view of that failure, that the defendant, if released on bail (whether subject to conditions or not), would fail to surrender to custody (para 2);
- the court is satisfied that the defendant should be kept in custody for their own protection or, if they are a child or young person, for their own welfare (para 3);
- if the defendant is in custody serving a sentence (para 4);
- having been released on bail in or in connection with the proceedings for the offence, a defendant under the age of 18 has been arrested for breach of bail conditions under the BA 1976 s 7 and the court is satisfied that there are substantial grounds for believing that the defendant, if released on bail (whether subject to conditions or not), would fail to surrender to custody, commit an offence on bail, or interfere with witnesses or otherwise obstruct the course of justice (whether in relation to themselves or any other person) (para 5);
- having been released on bail in or in connection with the proceedings for the offence, the defendant has been arrested for

breach of bail conditions under the BA 1976 s 7 and the court is satisfied that there are substantial grounds for believing that the defendant, if released on bail (whether subject to conditions or not), would commit an offence while on bail by engaging in conduct which would, or would be likely to, cause:

(a) physical or mental injury to an 'associated person' (as defined in the Family Law Act 1996, s 62); or
(b) an associated person to fear physical or mental injury (para 6).

For the purposes of para 6 above, 'associated person', as defined by the Family Law Act 1996, s 62, includes a parent, child, spouse, civil partner, intimate partner, relative, or any person who lives in the same household otherwise than merely by reason of one being the other's tenant, lodger, or boarder.

H3.5 **Conditional bail**

When granting bail, the court may order that:

- a surety or security be taken before the defendant is released on bail; or
- conditions be imposed with which the defendant must comply either before or after their release on bail.

The power to impose bail conditions is governed by the BA 1976, s 3.

Bail Act 1976

3 General provisions

(1) A person granted bail in criminal proceedings shall be under a duty to surrender to custody and that duty is enforceable in accordance with section 6 of this Act.
(2) No recognizance for his surrender to custody shall be taken from him.
(3) Except as provided by this section-
  (a) no security for his surrender to custody shall be taken from him,
  (b) he shall not be required to provide a surety or sureties for his surrender to custody, and
  (c) no other requirement shall be imposed on him as a condition of bail.
(4) He may be required, before release on bail, to provide a surety or sureties to secure his surrender to custody.
(5) He may be required, before release on bail, to give security for his surrender to custody. The security may be given by him or on his behalf.
(6) He may be required to comply, before release on bail or later, with such requirements as appear to the court to be necessary—

(a) to secure that he surrenders to custody,
(b) to secure that he does not commit an offence while on bail,
(c) to secure that he does not interfere with witnesses or otherwise obstruct the course of justice whether in relation to himself or any other person,
(ca) for his own protection, or if he is a child or young person, for his own welfare or in his own interests,
(d) to secure that he makes himself available for the purpose of enabling inquiries or a report to be made to assist the court in dealing with him for the offence.
(e) to secure that before the time appointed for him to surrender to custody, he attends an interview with a person who, for the purposes of the Legal Services Act 2007, is an authorised person in relation to an activity which constitutes the exercise of a right of audience or the conduct of litigation (within the meaning of that Act);

and, in any Act, 'the normal powers to impose conditions of bail' means the powers to impose conditions under paragraph (a), (b), (c) or (ca) above.

A person granted bail on a charge of murder must be required to undergo a psychiatric examination: BA 1976, s 3(6A).

H3.6 Electronic monitoring requirements

The BA 1976, s 3(6ZAA) provides that the power to impose bail conditions includes the power to impose electronic monitoring requirements. These are requirements imposed for the purpose of securing the electronic monitoring of a person's compliance with any other requirement imposed on him as a condition of bail: s 3(6ZAB). The most common electronic monitoring requirement is a tag to monitor compliance with a curfew.

In the case of a youth defendant, the use of electronic monitoring requirements is subject to s 3AA.

Bail Act 1976

3AA Conditions for the imposition of electronic monitoring requirements: children and young persons released on bail . . .

(1) A court may not impose electronic monitoring requirements on a child or young person released on bail in criminal proceedings . . . unless each of the following conditions is met.
(2) The first condition is that the child or young person has attained the age of twelve years.
(3) The second condition is that-
 (a) the child or young person is charged with or has been convicted of a violent, sexual or terrorism offence, or an offence

punishable in the case of an adult with imprisonment for a term of fourteen years of more; or

(b) he is charged with or has been convicted of one or more imprisonable offences which, together with any other imprisonable offences of which he has been convicted in any proceedings-
   (i) amount, or
   (ii) would, if he were convicted of the offences with which he is charged, amount

to a recent history of repeatedly committing imprisonable offences while remanded on bail or subject to a custodial remand.

(4) The third condition is that the court is satisfied that the necessary provision for dealing with the person concerned can be made under arrangements for the electronic monitoring of persons released on bail that are currently available in each local justice area which is a relevant area.

(5) The fourth condition is that a youth offending team has informed the court that in its opinion the imposition of electronic monitoring requirements will be suitable in the case of the child or young person.

The references in s 3AA(3)(b) to an imprisonable offence include a reference to a conviction for an equivalent offence outside England and Wales: s 3AA(11). Reference in that subsection to a custodial remand is to a remand to local authority accommodation or youth detention accommodation or equivalent custodial detention outside England and Wales: s 3AA(12).

At the time of introducing electronically monitored bail curfews, the Home Office issued a guidance document *Criminal Justice and Police Act 2001: Electronic Monitoring of 12- to 16-year-olds on Bail and on Remand to Local Authority Accommodation.* This guidance includes advice on what steps YOTs should take to assess the suitability of a proposed bail address for electronic monitoring.

At a minimum, contact must be made with a householder (i.e. the person holding the tenancy or the owner/occupier of the proposed bail address), and the parent or carer of the defendant (if different) to ascertain whether s/he consents to the monitoring.

Where the youth offending team has no information about the proposed address, information should be sought from social services departments and other partner agencies. A home visit may be needed before the suitability of an address can be determined. If it is not possible to arrange the home visit on the day of the court hearing then an electronic monitoring requirement may not be used.

For placements in local authority residential accommodation Social Services' consent should be sought for the use of electronic monitoring.

The youth offending team should contact the relevant local authority social services department to ascertain whether there are any current or previous child protection concerns that would indicate that tagging is not advisable in a particular case.

H3.7 **Bail supervision and support**

YOTs are under a statutory duty to provide support for children and young persons remanded or committed on bail while awaiting trial or sentence: CDA 1998, s 38(4)(c).

Most schemes aim to help defendants to comply with their conditions of bail and to provide constructive activities to occupy their time and lessen the risk of further offending.

The contents of bail support programmes vary across the country but may include:

- regular reporting to the YOT;
- monitored attendance at youth activities;
- monitoring of school attendance;
- programmes aimed at reintroducing the young defendant to school or to arrange specific educational provision;
- assistance with arranging training or finding employment;
- work with families to resolve conflicts and to ensure a continuing home base for the young defendant and to involve the parents in taking more responsibility for their children's behaviour;
- placements with volunteers during the evening and weekends; and
- intensive supervision and surveillance programmes (see **H3.7.1**).

H3.7.1 ***Intensive supervision and surveillance programme (ISSP)***

Bail ISSPs normally involve up to 25 hours of activities each week. The programme may include:

- electronic tagging and voice verification;
- tracking of the young offender by YOT staff;
- monitoring of young offenders by police;
- literacy and numeracy programmes;
- work with families; and
- offending behaviour workshops/cognitive behavioural therapy.

YOTs will only advise courts to consider the option of a bail ISSP where:

- the defendant fits the criteria for an ISSP;
- they are not considered to pose an unacceptable risk to the community if placed on an ISSP;
- the current offence before the court is of sufficient gravity for the court to be considering a custodial remand; and
- there is a place available.

H3.8 **Parental surety**

A surety taken under the BA 1976, s 3(4) is to secure that the defendant surrenders to custody. In the case of a defendant under the age of 17, the court may also take a surety from their parent or guardian to ensure the defendant's compliance with other bail conditions.

Bail Act 1976, s 3(7)

If a parent or guardian of a person under the age of seventeen consents to be surety for the person for the purposes of this subsection, the parent or guardian may be required to secure that the person complies with any requirement imposed on him by virtue of subsection (6), (6ZAA) or (6A) above, but—

(a) no requirement shall be imposed on the parent or guardian of a person by virtue of this subsection where it appears that the person will attain the age of seventeen before the time to be appointed for him to surrender to custody; and

(b) the parent or guardian shall not be required to secure compliance with any requirement to which his consent does not extend and shall not, in respect of those requirements to which his consent does extend, be bound in a sum greater than £50.

The words 'parent' and 'guardian' are not specifically defined in the BA 1976. For the definition in other statutory provisions see **M1**.

H3.9 **Prosecution appeal against grant of bail**

The Bail (Amendment) Act 1993 provides that a prosecutor may appeal to the Crown Court the grant of bail in any case where the defendant is charged with an offence punishable in the case of an adult with imprisonment: s 1(1).

An appeal may only be made if the prosecutor made representations against the grant of bail before the defendant was granted bail: s 1(3).

Where the prosecutor wishes to appeal the grant of bail, s 1(4) requires that oral notice be given to the court which granted bail at the conclusion of the proceedings in which such bail has been granted and before the defendant is released from custody. A delay of five minutes in giving an oral indication to the court (and after the defendant had been taken from the courtroom) was deemed to comply with the Act in *R v Isleworth Crown Court, ex parte Clarke* [1998] 1 Cr App R 257. Once an oral notice of appeal has been given, the court must remand the defendant until the appeal is determined or otherwise disposed of: s 1(6).

By s 1(5), a written notice of appeal must be served on the court which has granted bail and the defendant within two hours of the conclusion of the proceedings. Where the prosecution fails, within the period of two hours, to serve written notices upon both the court and the defendant, the appeal shall be deemed to be disposed of: s 1(7). In *R v Isleworth Crown Court ex parte Clarke*, above, it was held that there is no requirement to serve the written notice upon the magistrates or the defendant directly. Instead, it is valid service to give the notice to the court clerk and have the defendant's copy served via a court gaoler. In *R (Jeffrey) v Crown Court at Warwick* [2002] EWCA 2469 (Admin), a written notice was served three minutes late in circumstances where the court considered the prosecutor had acted with due diligence and there was no prejudice to the defendant. A challenge to the validity of that service failed and the court suggested that s 1(7) should have read into it the following words: 'unless such failure was caused by circumstances outside the control of the prosecution and not due to any fault on its part.'

This was confirmed in *R (Cardin) v Birmingham Crown Court* [2017] EWHC 2101 (Admin), where it was stated that the two hours allowed for the giving of written notice of appeal by the Crown against the grant of bail is to be liberally interpreted where the delay is no fault of the prosecution and the defendant is not prejudiced (having had oral notice).

Where the defendant is under the age of 18, any remand under s 1(6) is still subject to a determination of whether the remand is to local authority accommodation or youth detention: s 1(10)(b) (see H4). Having initially granted bail, it is difficult to see how a court could consider a remand to youth detention accommodation to be merited.

After written notice has been served, the Crown Court must hear the appeal within 48 hours, not counting weekends and public holidays: s 1(8). The YOT should be present at any hearing in the Crown Court to assist the court as to its views.

The prosecution may also appeal to the High Court against the grant of bail by a Crown Court: s 1(1B). This power does not apply if the grant of bail is made after a prosecution appeal against bail from the youth court or magistrates' court: s 1(1C).

H3.10 **Appeal against refusal of bail**

Following a refusal of bail in the youth court or adult magistrates' court, the defendant may appeal to the Crown Court: Senior Courts Act 1981, s 81(1).

The Crown Court may only grant bail on appeal if the youth court or adult magistrates' court has certified that it heard full argument on the application for bail before refusing the application: s 81(1J). It is the duty of the youth or adult magistrates' court to issue such certificates under the BA 1976, s 5(6A) and it is important that the advocate requests the certificate at the end of an unsuccessful bail application. The YOT should be present at any hearing in the Crown Court to assist the court as to its views.

H3.11 Appeal against imposition of a bail condition

The CJA 2003, s 16 provides that a defendant may appeal to the Crown Court against the imposition of any of the following bail conditions:

- that they reside away from a particular place or area;
- that they reside at a particular place other than a bail hostel;
- for the provision of a surety or sureties or the giving of a security;
- that they remain indoors between certain hours;
- any imposed under the BA 1976, s 3(6ZAA) (requirements with respect to electronic monitoring); or
- that they make no contact with another person.

The defendant may only appeal if:

- they previously made an application to the magistrates under the BA 1976, s 3(8)(a) to vary the bail conditions; or
- the conditions were imposed by the magistrates on the application of a constable or prosecutor: s 16(4) to (6).

H3.11.1 *Procedure for appealing to the Crown Court*

The procedure for appealing is set out in Crim PR, r 14.8:

- The defendant must apply to the Crown Court in writing as soon as practicable after the magistrates' court decision and serve a copy on the Crown Court officer, the magistrates' court officer, the prosecutor, and any affected/proposed surety.
- The application must specify:
    i. the decision that the defendant wants the Crown Court to make;
    ii. the charges;
    iii. why the Crown Court should not withhold bail or why it should vary the conditions under appeal; and
    iv. what further information or legal argument, if any, has become available since the magistrates' court decision;

- Unless the Crown Court otherwise directs, the court officer must arrange for the court to hear the application or appeal as soon as practicable and in any event no later than the business day after it was served.

H3.12 **Breach of bail conditions**

Breach of a bail condition does not constitute a separate criminal offence. There is, however, a power of arrest to allow the police to enforce bail conditions.

The BA 1976, s 7 provides:

Bail Act 1976

7 Liability to arrest for absconding or breaking conditions of bail

(3) A person who has been released on bail in criminal proceedings and is under a duty to surrender into the custody of a court may be arrested without warrant by a constable—
   (a) if the constable has reasonable grounds for believing that that person is not likely to surrender to custody;
   (b) if the constable has reasonable grounds for believing that that person is likely to break any of the conditions of his bail or has reasonable grounds for suspecting that that person has broken any of those conditions; or
   (c) in a case where that person was released on bail with one or more surety or sureties, if a surety notifies a constable in writing that that person is unlikely to surrender to custody and that for that reason the surety wishes to be relieved of his obligations as a surety.

(4) A person arrested in pursuance of subsection (3) above—
   (a) shall, except where he was arrested within 24 hours of the time appointed for him to surrender to custody, be brought as soon as practicable and in any event within 24 hours after his arrest before a justice of the peace; and
   (b) in the said excepted case shall be brought before the court at which he was to have surrendered to custody.

...

(5) A justice of the peace before whom a person is brought under subsection (4). . .above may, subject to subsections (5A) and (6) below, if of the opinion that that person—
   (a) is not likely to surrender to custody, or
   (b) has broken or is likely to break any condition of his bail,

   remand him in custody or commit him to custody, as the case may require, or alternatively, grant him bail subject to the same or to different conditions, but if not of that opinion shall grant him bail subject to the same conditions (if any) as were originally imposed.

(5A) *[applies only to those aged 18 or over]*

(6) Where the person brought before a justice under subsection (4) ... is a child or young person and the justice does not grant him

bail, subsection (5) above shall have effect subject to the provisions of section 91 of the Legal Aid, Sentencing and Punishment of Offenders Act 2012 (remands of children otherwise than on bail).

(7) In reckoning for the purposes of this section any period of 24 hours, no account shall be taken of Christmas Day, Good Friday or any Sunday.

If the defendant arrested under s 7(3) is charged with murder, then they must be brought before a Crown Court judge rather than a justice of the peace and, in such a case, when reckoning the period of 24 hours, no account shall be taken of any Saturday in addition to Christmas Day, Good Friday, and any Sunday: s 7(8).

The 24-hour requirement is absolute and requires that the detainee be brought, not merely to the court precincts or cells, but actually before a justice of the peace: *R v Governor of Glen Parva Young Offender Institution ex parte G (A Minor)* [1998] 2 Cr App R 349. The court's investigation and decision-making in relation to the alleged breach must be completed within the 24-hour period: *R (Culley) v Crown Court Sitting at Dorchester* [2007] EWHC 109 (Admin). A court can, however, bring a defendant into the dock and then adjourn the hearing until later in the court list or even before a differently constituted bench, subject to the proviso that the breach must be resolved within the 24-hour period: *R (Hussein) v Derby Magistrates' Court* [2001] 1 WLR 254. If a detainee cannot be brought before a justice of the peace within 24 hours then they have an absolute right to be released.

There is no defence of 'reasonable excuse' in relation to the breaching of bail conditions (*R (Vickers) v West London Magistrates' Court* [2004] Crim LR 63), although the reasons for breach would be relevant to the determination of whether or not subsequently to grant bail.

In *R v Liverpool Justices, ex parte Director of Public Prosecutions* (1992) 95 Cr App R 222, the court laid down the following guidance for a court to follow when considering bail breaches:

- strict rules of evidence do not apply and hearsay is admissible;
- the court must consider the type of evidence called and take account of the fact that there has been no cross-examination;
- the prosecution and defence can call witnesses if they so wish, and the other party has the right to cross-examine;
- the defendant has a right to give oral evidence.

If the breach is not proved, the defendant must be released on the same conditions as existed previously. If the breach is proved, that does not mean an automatic refusal of bail; it is simply a factor to be considered when the court decides on whether or not it should grant bail again.

H3.13 Failing to surrender to custody

A person granted bail in criminal proceedings is under a duty to surrender to custody: BA 1976, s 3(1). Having been granted bail, it is a criminal offence not to surrender to custody at the place and time appointed by the court.

The BA 1976, s 6 creates two separate criminal offences of absconding:

Bail Act 1976

6 Offence of absconding by person released on bail

(1) If a person who has been released on bail in criminal proceedings fails without reasonable cause to surrender to custody he shall be guilty of an offence.

(2) If a person who—
   (a) has been released on bail in criminal proceedings, and
   (b) having reasonable cause therefor, has failed to surrender to custody,

   fails to surrender to custody at the appointed place as soon after the appointed time as is reasonably practicable he shall be guilty of an offence.

(3) It shall be for the accused to prove that he had reasonable cause for his failure to surrender to custody.

(4) A failure to give to a person granted bail in criminal proceedings a copy of the record of the decision shall not constitute a reasonable cause for that person's failure to surrender to custody.

(5) An offence under subsection (1) or (2) shall be punishable either on summary conviction or as if it were a criminal contempt of court.

(6) Where a magistrates' court convicts a person of an offence under subsection (1) or (2) above the court may, if it thinks-
   (a) that the circumstances of the offence are such that greater punishment should be inflicted for that offence than the court has power to inflict, or
   (b) in a case where it sends that person for trial to the Crown Court for another offence, that it would be appropriate for him to be dealt with for the offence under subsection (1) or (2) above by the court before which he is tried for the other offence,

   commit him in custody or on bail to the Crown Court for sentence.

(7) A person who is convicted summarily of an offence under subsection (1) or (2) above and is not committed to the Crown Court for sentence shall be liable to imprisonment for a term not exceeding 3 months or to a fine not exceeding level 5 on the standard scale or to both and a person who is so committed for sentence or is dealt with as for such a contempt shall be liable to imprisonment for a term

> not exceeding the general limit in a magistrates' court or to a fine or to both.
>
> ...
>
> (8) In any proceedings for an offence under subsection (1) or (2) above a document purporting to be a copy of the part of the prescribed record which relates to the time and place appointed for the person specified in the record to surrender to custody and to be duly certified to be a true copy of that part of the record shall be evidence of the time and place appointed for that person to surrender to custody.
>
> (9) For the purposes of subsection (8) above—
>
> (a) 'the prescribed record' means the record of the decision of the court, officer or constable made in pursuance of section 5(1) of this Act;
>
> (b) the copy of the prescribed record is duly certified if it is certified by the appropriate officer of the court or, as the case may be, by the constable who took the decision or a constable designated for the purpose by the officer in charge of the police station from which the person to whom the record relates was released; ...

'Surrender to custody' means, in relation to a person released on bail, surrendering themselves into the custody of the court at the time and place for the time being appointed for them to do so (BA 1976, s 2(2)). What precisely constitutes surrendering may depend on the procedure followed by a particular court. Where a defendant reported to a particular court official in accordance with that court's normal procedure, they had surrendered to the court (sufficient to relieve a surety of their obligations), though they were thereafter under an implied obligation not to leave the building without permission: *DPP v Richards* [1989] QB 701.

A reasonable excuse need only be proved to the civil standard: *R v Carr-Bryant* (1944) 29 Cr App R 76. The mere fact that a defendant is only slightly late does not afford them a defence: *R v Scott* [2007] EWCA Crim 2757. A genuine, albeit mistaken, belief that bail was to another date would not in itself amount to a reasonable excuse: *Laidlaw v Atkinson* The Times, 2 August 1986. In *R v Liverpool Justices, ex parte Santos* The Times, 23 January 1997, the court held that reliance on mistaken information provided by a solicitor may constitute a reasonable excuse for failing to surrender. The court went on to say that all relevant factors would need to be considered and a mistake on the part of a solicitor in calculating the bail date did not automatically excuse the defendant's non-attendance.

The BA 1976, s 6(7) provides that a person who is convicted summarily of an offence under s 6(1) or s 6(2) shall be liable to imprisonment for a term not exceeding three months or to a fine not exceeding level 5 on the standard scale or to both. A magistrates' court may commit to the Crown Court for sentence but may not send an offence of absconding for trial at that court. The maximum sentence available to the Crown Court for an offence of absconding is 12 months' imprisonment (although a drafting error in secondary legislation temporarily reduced it to six months between 7 February 2023 and 17 October 2023 inclusive).

The Crown Court may impose a DTO (see, for example, *R v Mason Cooper* [2018] EWCA Crim 2628). A custodial sentence should not be imposed on a youth defendant by the youth court because:

- the minimum term of a DTO is four months and a person not committed to the Crown Court is not liable to custody exceeding three months; and
- a court may not impose detention as a punishment for contempt upon a youth defendant: *R v Byas* (1995) 16 Cr App R (S) 869.

H4 **Bail Refused**

H4.1 **General**

Where a youth defendant is refused bail, they are not automatically remanded into prison or a remand centre. Instead, the court must go on to consider the nature of the remand. The remand will ordinarily be to local authority accommodation unless the court orders that the remand is to youth detention accommodation. The child or young person becomes a 'looked after' child once bail is refused, whether the remand is to local authority accommodation or youth detention accommodation. The local authority's duties under the Children Act 1989 will apply.

The LASPO 2012, s 91 provides:

Legal Aid, Sentencing and Punishment of Offenders Act 2012

91 Remands of children otherwise than on bail

(1) This section applies where—
  (a) a court deals with a child charged with or convicted of one or more offences by remanding the child, and
  (b) the child is not released on bail.

. . .

(3) Subject to subsection (4), the court must remand the child to local authority accommodation in accordance with section 92.

(4) The court may instead remand the child to youth detention accommodation in accordance with section 102 where—
  (a) in the case of a child remanded under subsection (1), the first or second set of conditions for such a remand (see sections 98 and 99) is met in relation to the child . . .

(5) This section is subject to section 128(7) of the Magistrates' Courts Act 1980 (remands to police detention for periods of not more than 3 days); but that provision has effect in relation to a child as if for the reference to 3 clear days there were substituted a reference to 24 hours.

(6) In this Chapter, 'child' means a person under the age of 18.

(7) References in this Chapter . . . to the remand of a child include a reference to—
  (a) the sending of a child for trial, and
  (b) the committal of a child for sentence,

and related expressions are to be construed accordingly.

Blackstone's Handbook of Youths in the Criminal Courts. Mark Ashford, Gareth Branston, and Naomi Redhouse, Oxford University Press.
 DOI: 10.1093/oso/9780198913146.003.0019

The LASPO 2012, s 107 provides the following definitions:

- *Child*—a person under the age of 18.
- *Imprisonable offence* means—
  (a) an offence punishable in the case of an adult with imprisonment, or
  (b) in relation to an offence of which a child has been accused or convicted outside England and Wales, an offence equivalent to an offence that, in England and Wales, is punishable in the case of an adult with imprisonment;
  - *Sexual offence* means an offence specified in Part 2 of Schedule 18 to the SC;
  - *Terrorism offence* means an offence specified in Part 3 of Schedule 18 to the SC;
  - *Violent offence* means murder or an offence specified in Part 1 of Schedule 18 to the SC.

H4.2 **Remand to local authority accommodation**

A remand to local authority accommodation is a remand to accommodation provided by or on behalf of a local authority: LASPO 2012, s 92(1).

By s 92(2), a court that remands a child to local authority accommodation must designate the local authority that is to receive the child and, by s 92(3), that authority must be—

- in the case of a child who is being looked after by a local authority, that authority, and
- in any other case, the local authority in whose area it appears to the court that the child habitually resides or the offence or one of the offences was committed.

The LASPO 2012, s 92(4) provides that the designated authority must—

- receive the child, and
- provide or arrange for the provision of accommodation for the child whilst the child is remanded to local authority accommodation.

H4.3 **Conditions on remand to local authority accommodation**

Under the LASPO 2012, s 93(1), a court remanding a child to local authority accommodation may require the child to comply with any conditions that could be imposed under the BA 1976, s 3(6) if the child were then being granted bail.

The BA 1976, s 3(6) allows the court to impose conditions upon a defendant which appear to be necessary to secure that he:

- surrenders to custody;
- does not commit an offence on bail;
- does not interfere with witnesses or otherwise obstruct the course of justice;
- makes themselves available for the making of enquiries or a report to assist in sentencing; or
- attends an interview with a legal representative.

Tagging and other forms of electronic monitoring of the youth defendant's compliance with these requirements may be ordered (s 93(2)) but only if the conditions set out in s 94 are satisfied:

- The **first requirement** is that the child has reached the age of 12.
- The **second requirement** is that the youth defendant is charged with one or more imprisonable offences.
- **The third requirement is that—**
  (a) the youth defendant is charged with a violent, sexual, or terrorism offence or an offence punishable in the case of an adult with imprisonment for a term of 14 years or more, or
  (b) the current charges, together with any other imprisonable offences of which the child has been convicted in any proceedings, amount or would, if the youth were convicted of that offence or those offences, amount to a recent history of committing imprisonable offences while on bail or subject to a custodial remand.
- The **fourth requirement** is that the court is satisfied that the necessary provision for electronic monitoring can be made under arrangements currently available in each local justice area which is a relevant area.
- The **fifth requirement** is that a YOT team has informed the court that, in its opinion, the imposition of an electronic monitoring condition will be suitable in the youth defendant's case.

By the LASPO 2012, s 93(3), a court remanding a child to local authority accommodation may impose on the designated authority:

- requirements for securing compliance with any conditions imposed on the child under subsection (1) or (2), or
- requirements stipulating that the child must not be placed with a named person.

A court may only impose a condition upon a child or a requirement upon the local authority after consultation with the designated authority: s 93(4). References to consultation are to such consultation (if any) as is reasonably practical in all the circumstances of the case: s 93(9).

Where a youth defendant has been remanded to local authority accommodation, the local authority or the defendant may apply to a relevant court to vary or revoke any conditions or requirements made: s 93(6)). 'Relevant court' is defined as the court by which the defendant was remanded or any magistrates' court that has jurisdiction in the place where the defendant is for the time being: s 93(8).

H4.4 Breach of remand conditions

By the LASPO 2012, s 97(1), a youth defendant may be arrested without warrant by a police constable if:

- the defendant has been remanded to local authority accommodation;
  - conditions on the remand have been imposed upon them under s 93; and
  - the constable has reasonable grounds for suspecting that the defendant has broken any of those conditions.

It should be noted that, unlike the BA 1976, s 7, a constable may not arrest for breach of a remand condition if they only suspect that the condition is likely to be broken.

A youth defendant arrested under s 97(1) must be brought before a justice of the peace as soon as is practicable and in any event within the period of 24 hours beginning with the youth defendant's arrest: s 97(2). If the defendant is arrested within 24 hours of the next court hearing, then he should be taken to the court where the hearing is due to take place whether it is a youth court, other adult magistrates' court, or a Crown Court: s 97(3). In reckoning a period of 24 hours, no account is to be taken of Christmas Day, Good Friday, or any Sunday: s 97(4).

If a justice of the peace before whom the youth defendant is brought is of the opinion that the defendant has broken any remand condition imposed on them, the justice of the peace must remand the defendant: s 97(5). Such a remand is still subject to the requirements of s 91: s 97(6). This means that the remand will still be to local authority accommodation unless the court now considers that the criteria for a remand to youth detention accommodation are satisfied.

If a justice of the peace before whom the youth defendant is brought is not of the opinion that the defendant has broken any remand condition imposed on them, the justice of the peace must remand the defendant to the place to which they had been remanded at the time of their arrest subject to the same conditions as before: s 97(7).

H4.5 Remand to youth detention accommodation

A court may only remand to youth detention accommodation if *either* of the following set of remand conditions is satisfied:

A. First set of conditions (LASPO 2012, s 98):

- AGE: The child must have reached the age of 12.
- SENTENCING: It must appear very likely that the child will be sentenced to a custodial sentence.
- OFFENCE: The offence with which the child is charged—
  (a) is a violent, sexual, or terrorism offence, or
  (b) is an offence punishable in the case of an adult with imprisonment for a term of 14 years or more.
- NECESSITY: The court is of the opinion, after considering all the options for the remand of the child, that only remanding the child to youth detention accommodation would be adequate—
  (a) to protect the public from death or serious personal injury (whether physical or psychological) occasioned by further offences committed by the child, or
  (b) to prevent the commission by the child of imprisonable offences,

  and the risks posed by the child cannot be managed safely in the community.
- LEGAL REPRESENTATION: The child must be legally represented or have had legal representation withdrawn because of their conduct or refusal as to representation.

B. Second set of conditions (LASPO 2012, s 99):

- AGE: The child must have reached the age of 12.
- SENTENCING: It appears to the court that it is very likely that the child will be sentenced to a custodial sentence for the offence before the court or one or more of those offences.
- OFFENCE: The child is before the court charged with at least one imprisonable offence.
- HISTORY: Either:
  (a) the child has a recent and significant history of absconding while subject to a custodial remand and it appears to the court that the history is relevant in all the circumstances of the case, and the offence mentioned in section 91(1), or one or more of those offences, is alleged to be or has been found to have been committed while the child was remanded to local authority accommodation or youth detention accommodation; or
  (b) the offence or offences mentioned in section 91(1), together with any other imprisonable offences of which the child has been convicted in any proceedings, amount or would, if

the child were convicted of that offence or those offences, amount to a recent and significant history of committing imprisonable offences while on bail or subject to a custodial remand and this appears to the court relevant in all the circumstances of the case.

- NECESSITY: The court is of the opinion, after considering all the options for the remand of the child, that only remanding the child to youth detention accommodation would be adequate—
  - (a) to protect the public from death or serious personal injury (whether physical or psychological) occasioned by further offences committed by the child; or
  - (b) to prevent the commission by the child of imprisonable offences

  and that the risks posed by the child cannot be managed safely in the community.
- LEGAL REPRESENTATION: The child must be legally represented or have had legal representation withdrawn because of their conduct or refusal as to representation.

Sections 98(6) and 99(9) refer to legal representation being withdrawn because the child's financial resources make them ineligible for representation, but any defendant under the age of 18 is deemed to have financial resources such that they are eligible for legal representation: Criminal Legal Aid (Financial Resources) Regulations 2013, reg.22.

H4.6 **Placement in youth detention accommodation**

A remand to youth detention accommodation is a remand to such accommodation as the Secretary of State directs in the child's case: LASPO 2012, s 102(1).

By s 102(2), the accommodation may be any of the following:

- a secure children's home;
- a secure college;
- a secure training centre;
- a young offender institution; or
- accommodation, or accommodation of a description, for the time being specified by regulations under section 248(1)(f) of the SC (youth detention accommodation for purposes of DTO provisions).

The placement decision is the responsibility of the Youth Custody Service of HM Prison and Probation Service, based on the information provided by the YOT assessment.

H4.7 **Reports on 10- and 11-year-olds**

A remand to youth detention accommodation is not available to defendants aged 10 or 11.

By the CYPA 1969, s 23B, where a defendant aged 10 or 11 has been remanded on bail, the court may order a local authority to make an oral or written report specifying where the person is likely to be placed or maintained if they were to be refused bail and remanded to local authority accommodation.

This power to order such a report only exists if the 10- or 11-year-old defendant:

- is charged with or convicted of a serious offence (defined as an offence punishable in the case of an adult with imprisonment for a term of two years or more); or
- in the opinion of the court the person is a persistent offender.

The court must designate the local authority which will prepare the report. This must be the local authority the court would have designated under the LASPO 2012, s 92(2) if the person had been remanded to local authority accommodation. The report must be prepared within a maximum period of seven working days.

H5 Constitution of the Youth Court

Magistrates and District Judges sitting in the youth court will have received specialist training and must be authorized to sit. Magistrates will usually sit as a bench of three justices but hearings can be dealt with by two justices. A District Judge (Magistrates' Courts) can sit alone.

The CYPA 1933, s 45 provides for the constitution of the youth court.

Children and Young Persons Act 1933

Constitution of the youth court

45 Youth courts

(1) Magistrates' courts—
- (a) constituted in accordance with this section or section 66 of the Courts Act 2003 (judges having powers of District Judges (Magistrates' Courts)), and
- (b) sitting for the purpose of—
  - (i) hearing any charge against a child or young person, or
  - (ii) exercising any other jurisdiction conferred on youth courts by or under this or any other Act,

are to be known as youth courts.

(2) A justice of the peace is not qualified to sit as a member of a youth court for the purpose of dealing with any proceedings unless he has an authorisation extending to the proceedings.

(3) He has an authorisation extending to the proceedings only if he has been authorised by the Lord Chief Justice, with the concurrence of the Lord Chancellor, to sit as a member of a youth court to deal with—
- (a) proceedings of that description, or
- (b) all proceedings dealt with by youth courts.

(4) The Lord Chief Justice may, with the concurrence of the Lord Chancellor, by rules make provision about—
- (a) the grant and revocation of authorisations,
- (b) the appointment of chairmen of youth courts, and
- (c) the composition of youth courts.

(5) Rules under subsection (4) may confer powers on the Lord Chancellor or Lord Chief Justice with respect to any of the matters specified in the rules.

(6) Rules under subsection (4) may be made only after consultation with the Criminal Procedure Rule Committee.

(7) Rules under subsection (4) are to be made by statutory instrument.

(8) A statutory instrument containing rules under subsection (4) is subject to annulment in pursuance of a resolution of either House of Parliament.

Blackstone's Handbook of Youths in the Criminal Courts. Mark Ashford, Gareth Branston, and Naomi Redhouse, Oxford University Press.
 DOI: 10.1093/oso/9780198913146.003.0020

(9) The Lord Chief Justice may nominate a judicial office holder (as defined in section 109(4) of the Constitutional Reform Act 2005) to exercise his functions under subsection (3) or (4) or his powers under rules under subsection (4).

The latest rules made under s 45 are the Justice of the Peace Rules (SI 2016/709). Requirements for training and authorization to sit in the youth court are found in rules 19 and 30. The previous requirement that a youth court bench should include at least one man and at least one woman no longer applies.

H6 **Custody Time Limits**

The Prosecution of Offences (Custody Time Limits) Regulations 1987 set time limits during which the defendant can be in the custody of a court awaiting the start of his trial. Custody time limits apply to any youth defendant, whether remanded to local authority accommodation or youth detention accommodation (see definition of 'custody' in the Prosecution of Offences Act 1985, s 22(11)).

Category	Time limit
Summary-only offences Either-way offences	56 days to start of summary trial 56 days to start of summary trial
Indictable-only offences	56 days to start of summary trial Indictable-only cases that are tried summarily in the youth court are subject to the same time limits as either-way cases (*R v Stratford Youth Court, ex parte S (A Minor)* [1998] 1 WLR 1758)
Cases sent to the Crown Court	182 days from the date when the accused is sent for trial less any time spent in custody at the magistrates' court

H6.1 **Overview**

Custody time limits start at the end of the first day of remand and expire at midnight on the last day. A time limit expiring on a Saturday, Sunday, bank holiday, or on Christmas Day or Good Friday will be treated as having expired on the next preceding day which is not one of those days.

H6.2 **Exceptions**

Defendants who abscond from prison, or who have been released on bail following expiry of a custody time limit, but are then remanded following a breach of bail, do not enjoy the protections offered by custody time limits.

If a person spends time in custody, is granted bail, and is then later remanded into custody, the earlier period on remand will count towards the custody time limit.

Blackstone's Handbook of Youths in the Criminal Courts. Mark Ashford, Gareth Branston, and Naomi Redhouse, Oxford University Press.
 DOI: 10.1093/oso/9780198913146.003.0021

H6.3 **Extending custody time limits**

The case law on extending custody time limits is voluminous and, since applications will generally be made on notice, this topic is not covered in this book. In general the following considerations are relevant.

(1) The prosecution should give two days' notice of an intention to apply, but lack of notice is not fatal to the application and the court retains a discretion to extend the time limits: *R v Governor of Canterbury Prison, ex parte Craig* [1991] 2 QB 195.
(2) There is no power to extend once a time limit has lapsed: *R v Sheffield Justices, ex parte Turner* [1991] 2 WLR 987.
(3) The court must be satisfied, on a balance of probabilities, that the need for the extension is due to the illness or absence of the accused, a necessary witness, a judge, or magistrate; or a postponement which is occasioned by the ordering of separate trials, or some other good and sufficient cause; and that the prosecution has acted with all due diligence and expedition.
(4) The following have been held to amount to good and sufficient cause: lack of court time; listing difficulties due to the nature of the case; lack of a suitably experienced judge (or lack of any judge at all). Absent exceptional circumstances, resource difficulties do not amount to a good and sufficient case.

See *Blackstone's Criminal Practice 2024*.

H7 Jurisdiction of the Youth Court

The CYPA 1933, s 46(1) deals with the assignment of matters to the youth court.

> **Children and Young Persons Act 1933**
>
> **46 Assignment of certain matters to juvenile courts**
>
> (1) Subject as hereinafter provided, no charge against a child or young person, and no application whereof the hearing is by rules made under this section assigned to youth courts, shall be heard by a magistrates' court which is not a youth court: ...

H7.1 Criminal charges

All criminal charges against a child or young person are assigned to the youth court unless there is an adult co-defendant (see **H2**).

The youth court has power in certain cases to send a youth defendant to the Crown Court for trial (see **H2**) or to commit them for sentence (see **J4**).

H7.2 Applications

Applications involving youths can also be assigned to the youth court under s 46(1). Section 18 of the Crime and Courts Act 2013 assigns applications for gang injunctions to the youth court (see **N1**).

Applications for orders made under the civil jurisdiction of the summary courts are not specifically assigned to the youth court and therefore are made in the adult magistrates' court. This includes applications for:

- Bind overs under the MCA 1980, s 115;
- Orders relating to dangerous dogs under the Dogs Act 1871, s 2;
- Football banning orders (other than on conviction) under the Football Spectators Act 1989, s 14B.

Blackstone's Handbook of Youths in the Criminal Courts. Mark Ashford, Gareth Branston, and Naomi Redhouse, Oxford University Press.
 DOI: 10.1093/oso/9780198913146.003.0022

H8 Presence of Defendant in Court

H8.1 General principles

If a defendant has been remanded on bail to attend court, their presence is mandatory unless and until it is excused by the court. Where a defendant on bail fails to appear, a warrant can be issued for their arrest. If a defendant has been summonsed, they may be absent but represented by a legal representative: MCA 1980, s 122. This would be unusual in the youth court.

In *Westminster City Council v Owadally* [2017] EWHC 1092 (Admin), it was stated that the provisions of s 17A of the MCA 1980 require the plea to an either-way allegation faced by an adult to be entered personally by the defendant. The court observed that failure to do so nullified any proceedings as it went to jurisdiction. The wording of s 24A of the MCA 1980 in relation to plea for a youth defendant is very similar. The defendant, rather than a legal representative, should indicate the plea when an allocation decision is to be made.

H8.2 Defendant's presence at trial

The MCA 1980, s 11 details the court's powers when a defendant does not appear for trial:

Magistrates' Courts Act 1980

11 Non-appearance of accused: general provisions

(1) Subject to the provisions of this Act, where at the time and place appointed for the trial or adjourned trial of an information the prosecutor appears but the accused does not—

(a) if the accused is under 18 years of age, the court may proceed in his absence; and

(b) if the accused has attained the age of 18 years, the court shall proceed in his absence unless it appears to the court to be contrary to the interests of justice to do so.

This is subject to subsections (2), (2A), (3), and (4).

(2) Where a summons has been issued, the court shall not begin to try the information in the absence of the accused unless either it is proved to the satisfaction of the court, on oath or in such other manner as may be prescribed, that the summons was served on the accused within what appears to the court to be a reasonable time before the trial or adjourned trial or the accused has appeared on a previous occasion to answer to the information.

Blackstone's Handbook of Youths in the Criminal Courts. Mark Ashford, Gareth Branston, and Naomi Redhouse, Oxford University Press.
 DOI: 10.1093/oso/9780198913146.003.0023

(2A) The court shall not proceed in the absence of the accused if it considers that there is an acceptable reason for his failure to appear.

(3) In proceedings to which this subsection applies, the court shall not in a person's absence sentence him to imprisonment or detention in a young offender institution or make a detention and training order or an order under paragraph 13(1)(a) or (b) of Schedule 16 to the Sentencing Code that a suspended sentence passed on him shall take effect.

(3A) But where a sentence or order of a kind mentioned in subsection (3) is imposed or given in the absence of the offender, the offender must be brought before the court before being taken to a prison or other institution to begin serving his sentence (and the sentence or order is not to be regarded as taking effect until he is brought before the court).

(4) In proceedings to which this subsection applies, the court shall not in a person's absence impose any disqualification on him, except on resumption of the hearing after an adjournment under section 10(3) above; and where a trial is adjourned in pursuance of this subsection the notice required by section 10(2) above shall include notice of the reason for the adjournment.

(5) Subsections (3) and (4) apply to—
   - (a) proceedings instituted by an information, where a summons has been issued; and
   - (b) proceedings instituted by a written charge.

...

(6) Nothing in this section requires the court to enquire into the reasons for the accused's failure to appear before deciding whether to proceed in his absence.

(7) The court shall state in open court its reasons for not proceeding under this section in the absence of an accused who has attained the age of 18 years; and the court shall cause those reasons to be entered in its register of proceedings . . .

The distinction between adults and youths in s 11 is important and is emphasized in the Crim PR, r 24.12. In deciding whether or not to proceed in the defendant's absence, the Divisional Court in *Shirzadeh v Maidstone Magistrates' Court* [2003] EWHC 2216 (QB) stated that the trial bench should have regard to all the circumstances of the case including, in particular:

- the conduct of the defendant;
- the extent of the disadvantage to the defendant in not being able to give his account of events, having regard to the nature of the evidence against him;
- the seriousness of the offence, which affects defendant, victim, and public;
- the general public interest and the particular interest of victims and witnesses that a trial should take place within a reasonable time of the events to which it relates;

- the effect of delay on the memories of witnesses;
- the likelihood of obtaining the defendant's attendance on another occasion; and
- where there is more than one defendant and not all have absconded, the undesirability of separate trials, and the prospects of a fair trial for the defendants who are present.

The decision to try a person in their absence must be exercised with great care and only in exceptional circumstances such as cases where the absence was a deliberate absconding: *R (Drinkwater) v Solihull Magistrates' Court* [2012] EWHC 765 (Admin).

The involuntary absence of the defendant is not a reason to proceed in absence: *R v Thames Youth Court* (2002) 166 JP 613 (in this case detained in a police station). It is an important consideration that a youth may not have the same level of understanding as an adult. This is reflected in the different test applicable in the youth and adult courts.

See *Blackstone's Criminal Practice 2024*.

H9 Remand Periods

H9.1 Prior to conviction

- Remand to police cells for 24 hours.
- Remand to custody for maximum of eight clear days on first remand.
- Subsequent remand to custody for up to 28 clear days provided the next stage in the proceedings will be dealt with. If it is known that the next stage cannot be dealt with in that period, then eight-day remands will have to follow until such time as completion of the next stage within 28 days is achievable.
- Subsequent remand to custody for up to 28 clear days if the defendant is already in custody serving a sentence and will not be released before that date.
- Remand on bail for eight days, or longer if the defendant consents.
- Following a sending to the Crown Court, the magistrates have the power to adjourn for a period up to the date of trial (so the normal eight-day limit on first remand does not apply). It is important to note that the expression 'remand' has a particular meaning within the 1980 Act, and the court is not remanding a person when it sends someone for trial—therefore when a court sends a person for trial during their first appearance it can do so in custody for a period in excess of eight days.

The MCA 1980, s 129 allows for the remands of persons not produced before the court due to illness or accident. The court must have 'solid grounds' to justify an opinion that failure to be produced was due to illness or accident: *R v Liverpool Justices, ex parte Grogan* The Times, 8 October 1990).

H9.2 Post conviction

Maximum three weeks if in custody, four weeks if on bail.

See *Blackstone's Criminal Practice 2024.*

Blackstone's Handbook of Youths in the Criminal Courts. Mark Ashford, Gareth Branston, and Naomi Redhouse, Oxford University Press.
 DOI: 10.1093/oso/9780198913146.003.0024

H10 Reporting Restrictions in the Youth Court

Reporting restrictions apply automatically to defendants under the age of 18 appearing in the youth court.

The CYPA 1933, s 49 provides for reporting restrictions in the youth court and on appeal therefrom:

Children and Young Persons Act 1933

49 Restrictions on reports of proceedings in which children or young persons are concerned

(1) No matter relating to any child or young person concerned in proceedings to which this section applies shall while he is under the age of 18 be included in any publication if it is likely to lead members of the public to identify him as someone concerned in the proceedings.

(2) The proceedings to which this section applies are—
- (a) proceedings in a youth court;
- (b) proceedings on appeal from a youth court (including proceedings by way of case stated);
- (c) proceedings in a magistrates' court under Schedule 7 to the Sentencing Code (proceedings for breach, revocation or amendment of youth rehabilitation orders);
- (d) proceedings on appeal from a magistrates' court arising out of any proceedings mentioned in paragraph (c) (including proceedings by way of case stated).

(3) In this section 'publication' includes any speech, writing, relevant programme or other communication in whatever form, which is addressed to the public at large or any section of the public (and for this purpose every relevant programme shall be taken to be so addressed), but does not include an indictment or other document prepared for use in particular legal proceedings.

(3A) The matters relating to a person in relation to which the restrictions imposed by subsection (1) above apply (if their inclusion in any publication is likely to have the result mentioned in that subsection) include in particular—
- (a) his name,
- (b) his address,
- (c) the identity of any school or other educational establishment attended by him,
- (d) the identity of any place of work, and
- (e) any still or moving picture of him.

Blackstone's Handbook of Youths in the Criminal Courts. Mark Ashford, Gareth Branston, and Naomi Redhouse, Oxford University Press.
 DOI: 10.1093/oso/9780198913146.003.0025

(4) For the purposes of this section a child or young person is 'concerned' in any proceedings if he is—
 (a) a person against or in respect of whom the proceedings are taken, or
 (b) a person called, or proposed to be called, to give evidence in the proceedings.

...

(9) If a publication includes any matter in contravention of subsection (1) above, the following persons shall be guilty of an offence and liable on summary conviction to a fine not exceeding level 5 on the standard scale—
 (a) where the publication is a newspaper or periodical, any proprietor, any editor and any publisher of the newspaper or periodical;
 (b) where the publication is a relevant programme—
  (i) any body corporate or Scottish partnership engaged in providing the programme service in which the programme is included; and
  (ii) any person having functions in relation to the programme corresponding to those of an editor of a newspaper;
 (c) in the case of any other publication, any person publishing it.

(9A) Where a person is charged with an offence under subsection (9) above it shall be a defence to prove that at the time of the alleged offence he was not aware, and neither suspected nor had reason to suspect, that the publication included the matter in question.

(9B) If an offence under subsection (9) above committed by a body corporate is proved—
 (a) to have been committed with the consent or connivance of, or
 (b) to be attributable to any neglect on the part of,

an officer, the officer as well as the body corporate is guilty of the offence and liable to be proceeded against and punished accordingly.

(9C) In subsection (9B) above 'officer' means a director, manager, secretary or other similar officer of the body, or a person purporting to act in any such capacity.

(9D) If the affairs of a body corporate are managed by its members, 'director' in subsection (9C) above means a member of that body.

(9E) Where an offence under subsection (9) above is committed by a Scottish partnership and is proved to have been committed with the consent or connivance of a partner, he as well as the partnership shall be guilty of the offence and shall be liable to be proceeded against and punished accordingly.

(10) In any proceedings under Schedule 7 to the Sentencing Code (proceedings for breach, revocation or amendment of youth rehabilitation orders) before a magistrates' court other than a youth court or on appeal from such a court it shall be the duty of the magistrates' court or the appellate court to announce in the course of the proceedings that this section applies to the proceedings; and if the court fails to do so this section shall not apply to the proceedings.

(11) In this section—
'picture' includes a likeness however produced;
'relevant programme' means a programme included in a programme service, within the meaning of the Broadcasting Act 1990; . . .

The CYPA 1933, s 49 does not prevent representatives of the press attending the youth court but merely restricts what can be reported.

The reporting restrictions under s 49 cease to have effect once the defendant has attained 18: *T v DPP* [2003] EWHC 2408 (Admin).

H10.1 Lifting the restrictions during the proceedings

In rare circumstances, the court may lift reporting restrictions in the youth court before conviction. The court may do so during proceedings if it is appropriate for the purpose of avoiding injustice to the youth defendant (for example, where it is thought that publicizing the case might prompt witnesses to come forward) or if the defendant is unlawfully at large in order to apprehend them.

The CYPA 1933, s 49(5) to (8) provides for the dispensing of reporting restrictions in these circumstances:

Children and Young Persons Act 1933, s 49

(5) Subject to subsection (7) below, a court may, in relation to proceedings before it to which this section applies, by order dispense to any specified extent with the requirements of this section in relation to a child or young person who is concerned in the proceedings if it is satisfied—
- (a) that it is appropriate to do so for the purpose of avoiding injustice to the child or young person; or
- (b) that, as respects a child or young person to whom this paragraph applies who is unlawfully at large, it is necessary to dispense with those requirements for the purpose of apprehending him and bringing him before a court or returning him to the place in which he was in custody.

(6) Paragraph (b) of subsection (5) above applies to any child or young person who is charged with or has been convicted of—
- (a) a violent offence,
- (b) a sexual offence,
- (ba) a terrorism offence, or
- (c) an offence punishable in the case of a person aged 21 or over with imprisonment for fourteen years or more.

(7) The court shall not exercise its power under subsection (5)(b) above—
- (a) except in pursuance of an application by or on behalf of the Director of Public Prosecutions; and

(b) unless notice of the application has been given by the Director of Public Prosecutions to any legal representative of the child or young person.

(8) The court's power under subsection (4A) or (5) above may be exercised by a single justice.

. . .

(11) In this section—

. . .

'sexual offence' means an offence listed in Part 2 of Schedule 18 to the Sentencing Code;

'specified' means specified in an order under this section;

'terrorism offence' means an offence listed in Part 3 of Schedule 18 to the Sentencing Code;

'violent offence' means an offence listed in Part 1 of Schedule 18 to the Sentencing Code;

and a person who, having been granted bail, is liable to arrest (whether with or without a warrant) shall be treated as unlawfully at large.

H10.2 **Lifting the restrictions on conviction**

The youth court may also dispense with reporting restrictions once a youth defendant has been convicted if it is in the public interest to do so. In practice, this is unlikely to be considered until the sentencing hearing.

The CYPA 1933, s 49(4A), (4B) and (8) provides for the dispensing of reporting restrictions in these circumstances.

Children and Young Persons Act 1933, s 49

(4A) If a court is satisfied that it is in the public interest to do so, it may, in relation to a child or young person who has been convicted of an offence, by order dispense to any specified extent with the restrictions imposed by subsection (1) above in relation to any proceedings before it to which this section applies by virtue of subsection (2)(a) or (b) above, being proceedings relating to—

(a) the prosecution or conviction of the offender for the offence;

(b) the manner in which he, or his parent or guardian, should be dealt with in respect of the offence;

(c) the enforcement, amendment, variation, revocation or discharge of any order made in respect of the offence;

(d) where an attendance centre order is made in respect of the offence, the enforcement of any rules made under section 394(1)(d) or (e) of the Sentencing Code; or

(e) where a detention and training order is made, the enforcement of any requirements imposed under section 242(4)(b) of the Sentencing Code.

(4B) A court shall not exercise its power under subsection (4A) above without—
   (a) affording the parties to the proceedings an opportunity to make representations; and
   (b) taking into account any representations which are duly made.

...

(8) The court's power under subsection (4A) or (5) above may be exercised by a single justice.

H10.3 Judicial guidance

In *McKerry v Teesdale and Wear Valley* (2000) 164 JP 355, Lord Bingham CJ gave the following important guidance to justices on the exercise of the power under s 49(4A):

> It is a hallowed principle that justice is administered in public, open to full and fair reporting of the proceedings in court, so that the public may be informed about the justice administered in their name. That principle comes into collision with another important principle, also of great importance and reflected in international instruments ... that the privacy of a child or young person involved in legal proceedings must be carefully protected, and very great weight must be given to the welfare of such child or young person. It is in my judgment plain that power to dispense with anonymity, as permitted in certain cases by s 49(4A), must be exercised with very great care, caution and circumspection. It would be wholly wrong for any court to dispense with a juvenile's prima facie right to anonymity as an additional punishment. It is also very difficult to see any place for 'naming or shaming'. The court must be satisfied that the statutory criterion that it is in the public interest to dispense with the reporting restrictions is satisfied. This will be very rarely the case, and justices making an order under s 49(4A) must be clear in their minds why it is in the public interest to dispense with the restrictions.

H10.4 Application for post-conviction criminal behaviour order

By the SC, s 332(8), when a youth court makes a post-conviction criminal behaviour order (CBO) the automatic reporting restrictions imposed by the CYPA 1933, s 49 do not apply insofar as the proceedings relate to the making of the order. The court does have a discretionary power under the CYPA 1933, s 39 (which remains in force in civil applications despite the implementation of YJCEA 1999, s 45 in criminal matters (see **H11**)) to impose reporting restrictions in relation to the making of the CBO. The automatic reporting restrictions under the CYPA 1933, s 49 still apply to the substantive sentence.

H11 Reporting Restrictions in Other Criminal Courts

H11.1 Discretionary power

In the adult magistrates' court and Crown Court, the automatic reporting restrictions imposed by the CYPA 1933, s 49 do not apply. The court has a discretionary power to impose reporting restrictions in relation to those aged under 18 under the YJCEA 1999, s 45. This covers defendants and witnesses, including the alleged victim. There is also a power to restrict reporting of criminal proceedings for the lifetime of witnesses and victims under 18, if satisfied that the quality of their evidence or level of cooperation is likely to be diminished by fear or distress, but this power does not apply to defendants: YJCEA 1999, s 45A.

Youth Justice and Criminal Evidence Act 1999

45 Power to restrict reporting of criminal proceedings involving persons under 18

(1) This section applies (subject to subsection (2)) in relation to—
- (a) any criminal proceedings in any court (other than a service court) in England and Wales or Northern Ireland; and
- (b) any proceedings (whether in the United Kingdom or elsewhere) in any service court.

(2) This section does not apply in relation to any proceedings to which section 49 of the Children and Young Persons Act 1933 applies.

(3) The court may direct that no matter relating to any person concerned in the proceedings shall while he is under the age of 18 be included in any publication if it is likely to lead members of the public to identify him as a person concerned in the proceedings.

(4) The court or an appellate court may by direction ("an excepting direction") dispense, to any extent specified in the excepting direction, with the restrictions imposed by a direction under subsection (3) if it is satisfied that it is necessary in the interests of justice to do so.

(5) The court or an appellate court may also by direction ("an excepting direction") dispense, to any extent specified in the excepting direction, with the restrictions imposed by a direction under subsection (3) if it is satisfied—
- (a) that their effect is to impose a substantial and unreasonable restriction on the reporting of the proceedings, and
- (b) that it is in the public interest to remove or relax that restriction;

but no excepting direction shall be given under this subsection by reason only of the fact that the proceedings have been determined in any way or have been abandoned.

Blackstone's Handbook of Youths in the Criminal Courts. Mark Ashford, Gareth Branston, and Naomi Redhouse, Oxford University Press.
 DOI: 10.1093/oso/9780198913146.003.0026

(6) When deciding whether to make—
  (a) a direction under subsection (3) in relation to a person, or
  (b) an excepting direction under subsection (4) or (5) by virtue of which the restrictions imposed by a direction under subsection (3) would be dispensed with (to any extent) in relation to a person,

  the court or (as the case may be) the appellate court shall have regard to the welfare of that person.

(7) For the purposes of subsection (3) any reference to a person concerned in the proceedings is to a person—
  (a) against or in respect of whom the proceedings are taken, or
  (b) who is a witness in the proceedings.

(8) The matters relating to a person in relation to which the restrictions imposed by a direction under subsection (3) apply (if their inclusion in any publication is likely to have the result mentioned in that subsection) include in particular—
  (a) his name,
  (b) his address,
  (c) the identity of any school or other educational establishment attended by him,
  (d) the identity of any place of work, and
  (e) any still or moving picture of him.

(9) A direction under subsection (3) may be revoked by the court or an appellate court.

(10) An excepting direction—
  (a) may be given at the time the direction under subsection (3) is given or subsequently; and
  (b) may be varied or revoked by the court or an appellate court.

(11) In this section "appellate court", in relation to any proceedings in a court, means a court dealing with an appeal (including an appeal by way of case stated) arising out of the proceedings or with any further appeal.

The YJCEA 1999, s 45 applies only in criminal proceedings. The CYPA 1933, s 39 remains in force in relation to civil applications.

H11.2 **Judicial guidance**

Prior to the implementation of YJCEA 1999, s 45, the provisions were set out in the CYPA 1933, s 39 and case law relating to that section remains relevant. In *R v Winchester Crown Court* [2000] 1 Cr App R 11, Simon Brown LJ distilled the following propositions from earlier cases:

- In deciding whether to impose or thereafter to lift reporting restrictions, the court will consider whether there are good reasons for naming the defendant;
- In reaching that decision, the court will give considerable weight to the age of the offender and to the potential damage to any

young person of public identification as a criminal before the offender has the benefit or burden of adulthood;
- By virtue of section 44 of the 1933 Act, the court must 'have regard to the welfare of the child or young person';
- The prospect of being named in court with the accompanying disgrace is a powerful deterrent and the naming of a defendant in the context of his punishment serves as a deterrent to others. These deterrents are proper objectives for the court to seek;
- There is a strong public interest in open justice and the public knowing as much as possible about what has happened in court, including the identity of those who have committed crime;
- The weight to be attributed to the different factor may shift at different stages of the proceedings and, in particular, after the defendant has been found, or pleads guilty, and is sentenced. It may then be appropriate to place greater weight on the interest of the public in knowing the identity of those who have committed crimes, particularly serious and detestable crimes;
- The fact that an appeal has been made may be a material consideration.

There is authority for the proposition that there have to be exceptional circumstances justifying the refusal to make an order; this is an improper gloss on the language of s 39: *T v St Alban's Crown Court* [2002] EWHC 1129 (Admin).

In *R(Y) v Aylesbury Crown Court* [2012] EWHC 1140 (Admin), it was stated that, before making an order to restrict reporting under s 39, the court must be satisfied that there is a good reason to impose the restriction. The court must have regard to the welfare of the young person under the CYPA 1933, s 44, to the public interest, and to the right to freedom of expression under ECHR Article 10. Prior to any conviction, the defendant's welfare is likely to take precedence over other interests. After conviction, the age of the defendant and the seriousness of the crime will be particularly relevant. The court may permit the publication of some details but not all. Where the factors favouring restriction and those favouring publication are finely balanced, the court should make an order restricting publication.

See *Blackstone's Criminal Practice 2024*.

H12 Restricted Access to the Youth Court

The youth court is not a public court to which the public has free access. The CYPA 1933, s 47 provides:

Children and Young Persons Act 1933

47 Procedure in juvenile courts

(1) Youth courts shall sit as often as may be necessary for the purpose of exercising any jurisdiction conferred on them by or under this or any other Act.

(2) No person shall be present at any sitting of a youth court except—

(a) members and officers of the court;

(b) parties to the case before the court, their legal representatives, and witnesses and other persons directly concerned in that case;

(c) bona fide representatives of newspapers or news agencies;

(d) such other persons as the court may specially authorise to be present.

Blackstone's Handbook of Youths in the Criminal Courts. Mark Ashford, Gareth Branston, and Naomi Redhouse, Oxford University Press.
 DOI: 10.1093/oso/9780198913146.003.0027

H13 **Secure Accommodation Application (Children Act 1989, s 25)**

H13.1 **General power**

In addition to the court's power to remand a youth defendant to youth detention accommodation under the LASPO 2012, s 91(4), a local authority may apply to a court under the Children Act 1989, s 25 for permission to place a looked after child into secure accommodation for restricting their liberty.

Children Act 1989

25 Use of accommodation for restricting liberty

(1) Subject to the following provisions of this section, a child who is being looked after by a local authority in England or Wales may not be placed, and, if placed, may not be kept, in accommodation in England or Scotland provided for the purpose of restricting liberty ('secure accommodation') unless it appears—
 (a) that—
  (i) he has a history of absconding and is likely to abscond from any other description of accommodation; and
  (ii) if he absconds, he is likely to suffer significant harm; or
 (b) that if he is kept in any other description of accommodation he is likely to injure himself or other persons.

(2) The Secretary of State may by regulations—
 (a) specify a maximum period—
  (i) beyond which a child may not be kept in secure accommodation in England or Scotland without the authority of the court; and
  (ii) for which the court may authorise a child to be kept in secure accommodation in England or Scotland;
 (b) empower the court from time to time to authorise a child to be kept in secure accommodation in England or Scotland for such further period as the regulations may specify; and
 (c) provide that applications to the court under this section shall be made only by local authorities in England or Wales.

(3) It shall be the duty of a court hearing an application under this section to determine whether any relevant criteria for keeping a child in secure accommodation are satisfied in his case.

(4) If a court determines that any such criteria are satisfied, it shall make an order authorising the child to be kept in secure accommodation and specifying the maximum period for which he may be so kept.

Blackstone's Handbook of Youths in the Criminal Courts. Mark Ashford, Gareth Branston, and Naomi Redhouse, Oxford University Press.
 DOI: 10.1093/oso/9780198913146.003.0028

(5) On any adjournment of the hearing of an application under this section, a court may make an interim order permitting the child to be kept during the period of the adjournment in secure accommodation.

(5A) Where a local authority in England or Wales are authorised under this section to keep a child in secure accommodation in Scotland, the person in charge of the accommodation may restrict the child's liberty to the extent that the person considers appropriate, having regard to the terms of any order made by a court under this section.

(6) No court shall exercise the powers conferred by this section in respect of a child who is not legally represented in that court unless, having been informed of his right to apply for the provision of representation under Part 1 of the Legal Aid, Sentencing and Punishment of Offenders Act 2012 and having had the opportunity to do so, he refused or failed to apply.

(7) The Secretary of State may by regulations provide that—
- (a) this section shall or shall not apply to any description of children specified in the regulations;
- (b) this section shall have effect in relation to children of a description specified in the regulations subject to such modifications as may be so specified;
- (c) such other provisions as may be so specified shall have effect for the purpose of determining whether a child of a description specified in the regulations may be placed or kept in secure accommodation in England or Scotland;
- (d) a child may only be placed in secure accommodation that is of a description specified in the regulations (and the description may in particular be framed by reference to whether the accommodation, or the person providing it, has been approved by the Secretary of State or the Scottish Ministers).

(8) The giving of an authorisation under this section shall not prejudice any power of any court in England and Wales or Scotland to give directions relating to the child to whom the authorisation relates.

. . .

(9) This section is subject to section 20(8).

'A child who is being looked after' would include the following:

- a person for whom the local authority has an interim or full care order;
- a person accommodated by the local authority under the Children Act 1989, s 20 (except for a person aged 16 or 17 who is accommodated under s 20(5): Children (Secure Accommodation) Regulations 1991, reg 5(2)(a));
- a defendant remanded on bail with a condition that they reside as directed by a specified local authority: *Re C (a minor) (secure accommodation: bail)* [1994] 2 FCR 1153; and
- a defendant remanded to local authority accommodation under the LASPO 2012, s 91(3).

The Children Act 1989, s 25 does not apply to a defendant remanded to youth detention accommodation even though such a defendant is to be treated as a child who is looked after by a designated authority, in accordance with the LASPO 2012, s 104(1): Children (Secure Accommodation) Regulations 1991 reg 5A.

A child under the age of 13 shall not be placed in secure accommodation in a children's home without the prior approval of the Secretary of State to the placement of that child and such approval shall be subject to such terms and conditions as they see fit: Children (Secure Accommodation) Regulations 1991, reg 4.

H13.2 **Which court?**

Applications for secure accommodation orders are normally made to the family court and an application for civil legal aid should be made.

An application should, however, be made to the youth or adult magistrates' court where that court has remanded the defendant to local authority accommodation: CJA 1991, s 60(3).

> **Criminal Justice Act 1991**
>
> **60 Remands and committals to local authority accommodation**
>
> (3) In the case of a child or young person who has been remanded to local authority accommodation under section 91(3) of the Legal Aid, Sentencing and Punishment of Offenders Act 2012 by a youth court or a magistrates' court other than a youth court, any application under section 25 of the Children Act 1989 or section 119 of the Social Services and Well-being (Wales) Act 2014 (use of accommodation for restricting liberty) shall, notwithstanding anything in section 92(7) of the Children Act 1989, be made to that court.

The reference to 'that court' in s 60(3) is a generic term and allows an application to any court of that type: *Liverpool City Council v B* [1995] 1 WLR 505. Section 60(3) does not apply to the Crown Court; if the child or young person has been remanded to local authority accommodation by the Crown Court, any application for secure accommodation must be made to the family court. The same is the case if the defendant has been remanded on bail with a condition to reside as directed by the local authority: *Re W (Secure Accommodation Order: Jurisdiction)* [1995] 2 FCR 708.

H13.3 **Procedure**

An application for a secure accommodation order made to a youth court or adult magistrates' court is governed by Part III of the

Magistrates' Courts (Children and Young Persons) Rules 1992 (SI 1992/2071). Notice of the application must be served on the defendant and any parent or guardian whose whereabouts are known to the local authority or can be readily ascertained: r 14. There is no minimum notice period and no provision for the appointment of a litigation guardian in the proceedings.

The maximum period for which a court may make a secure accommodation order for a defendant remanded to local authority accommodation under the LASPO 2012, s 91(3) is the period of the remand: Children (Secure Accommodation) Regulations 1991, reg 13.

An application made to a youth court or adult magistrates' court would be incidental to the criminal proceedings and covered by the criminal legal aid certificate: LASPO 2012, Sch 3, para 5(3).

An application for a secure accommodation order made to the family court is governed by the Family Procedure Rules 2010, Part 12. Such applications are outside the scope of this Handbook.

H13.4 **Placement without court authority**

When the criteria of the Children Act 1989, s 25 are satisfied, a local authority looking after a child may place them in secure accommodation without the authority of a court for a maximum period of 72 hours (whether or not consecutive) in any period of 28 consecutive days: Children (Secure Accommodation) Regulations 1991, reg 10.

The Children (Secure Accommodation) Regulations 1991, reg 6 modifies the criteria for the use of secure accommodation in the case of a detained person aged 12 to 17 transferred after charge to local authority accommodation under the Police and Criminal Evidence Act 1984 (PACE 1984) s 38(6). In such cases, the local authority may not place them in secure accommodation unless it appears that any accommodation other than that provided for the purpose of restricting liberty is inappropriate because:

- they are likely to abscond from such other accommodation, or
- they are likely to injure themselves or other people if they are kept in any such other accommodation.

H14 Separation of Youth Defendants from Adult Defendants

Children and Young Persons Act 1933

31 Separation of children and young persons from adults in police stations, courts, &c.

Arrangements shall be made for preventing a child or young person while detained in a police station, or while being conveyed to or from any criminal court, or while awaiting before or after attendance in any criminal court, from associating with an adult (not being a relative) who is charged with any offence other than an offence with which the child or young person is jointly charged, and for ensuring that a girl (being a child or young person) shall while so detained, being conveyed, or waiting, be under the care of a woman.

The application of s 31 has been considered in *R(T) v Secretary of State* [2013] EWHC 111 (Admin). The court held that the object of s 31 is to prevent the moral risks of contact between young persons and adult defendants. The section does not oblige the use of separate court buildings or even entirely separate custody areas in one court building but arrangements must be in place to ensure that young persons at court are prevented from being able to speak, communicate, or interact with adult defendants. Ensuring that young persons and adults are not afforded the opportunity to speak or socialize by sharing a cell or by associating outside the cell are part of that duty, but arrangements may also be needed to address transitory contact or even physical proximity where these give rise to the risks to which the section is directed.

Blackstone's Handbook of Youths in the Criminal Courts. Mark Ashford, Gareth Branston, and Naomi Redhouse, Oxford University Press.
 DOI: 10.1093/oso/9780198913146.003.0029

Part I
Case Management

I1 Special Measures for Defendants

Special measures directions for vulnerable and intimidated witnesses, under ss 16 to 33 of the YJCEA 1999, are not available to defendants. The court, however, has wide and flexible powers to ensure that the accused receives a fair trial, which includes a fair opportunity to give the best evidence that they can: *R v SH* [2003] EWCA Crim 1208.

Some statutory provisions have been introduced to assist defendants, by way of amendment to the YJCEA 1999 and to the Crim PR. The special measures now available to a defendant are the use of live link and the use of an intermediary.

The court may also use its inherent common law powers in choosing how to regulate a criminal trial. It may choose, for example, to screen a defendant from their co-defendants whilst they are testifying: *R (S) v Waltham Forest Youth Court* [2004] EWHC 715 (Admin).

I1.1 Defendant's live link

Sections 33A and 33B of the YJCEA 1999 introduced live-link directions for defendants in a magistrates' court or the Crown Court. A live-link direction was a direction that any oral evidence to be given by the accused was to be given through a live link. Different conditions had to be satisfied depending on whether the accused was under 18 or over 18. For young defendants, the court had to be satisfied that the defendant's ability to participate effectively in the proceedings as a witness giving oral evidence was compromised by their level of intellectual ability or social functioning and the use of live link would enable them to participate more effectively. The Police Crime Sentencing and Courts Act 2022 (PCSCA 2022) has amended these provisions so that they only apply to service courts. Live-link directions for defendants are now subsumed by the much wider, general live-link powers in the CJA 2003, ss 51–52:

Criminal Justice Act 2003

51 Directions for live links in criminal proceedings

(1) The court may, by a direction, require or permit a person to take part in eligible criminal proceedings through—
   (a) a live audio link, or
   (b) a live video link.

(2) . . .

Blackstone's Handbook of Youths in the Criminal Courts. Mark Ashford, Gareth Branston, and Naomi Redhouse, Oxford University Press.
 DOI: 10.1093/oso/9780198913146.003.0030

(3) In this Part 'eligible criminal proceedings' mean—

. . .

(b) a summary trial,

(c) a criminal appeal to the Crown Court . . .

(d) a trial on indictment or any other trial in the Crown Court for an offence,

. . .

(4) The court may not give a direction under this section unless—

(a) the court is satisfied that it is in the interests of justice for the person to whom the direction relates to take part in the proceedings in accordance with the direction through the live audio link or live video link,

(b) the parties to the proceedings have been given the opportunity to make representations, and

(c) if so required by section 52(9), the relevant youth offending team has been given the opportunity to make representations.

(5) In deciding whether to give a direction under this section, the court must consider—

(a) any guidance given by the Lord Chief Justice, and

(b) all the circumstances of the case.

(6) Those circumstances include in particular—

(a) the availability of the person to whom the direction would relate,

(b) any need for that person to attend in person,

(c) the views of that person,

(d) the suitability of the facilities at the place where that person would take part in the proceedings in accordance with the direction,

(e) whether that person would be able to take part in the proceedings effectively if the person took part in accordance with the direction,

(f) in the case of a direction relating to a witness—

(i) the importance of the witness's evidence to the proceedings, and

(ii) whether the direction might tend to inhibit any party to the proceedings from effectively testing the witness's evidence, and

(g) the arrangements that would or could be put in place for members of the public to see or hear the proceedings as conducted in accordance with the direction.

52 Further provision about the giving, variation and rescission of live-link directions

(1) The power conferred by section 51 includes power to give—

(a) a direction that is applicable to several, or all, of the persons taking part in particular eligible criminal proceedings;

(b) a direction that is applicable to a particular person in respect of only some aspects of particular eligible criminal proceedings (such as giving evidence or attending the proceedings when not giving evidence); . . .

(2) The court may vary or rescind a direction under section 51 at any time before or during the eligible criminal proceedings to which it

relates (but this does not affect the court's power to give a further direction under that section in relation to the proceedings).

(3) A direction under section 51 may not be rescinded unless—
  (a) the court is satisfied that it is in the interests of justice for the direction to be rescinded,
  (b) the parties to the proceedings have been given the opportunity to make representations, and
  (c) if so required by subsection (9), the relevant youth offending team has been given the opportunity to make representations.

. . .

(6) A direction under section 51 may be given, varied or rescinded—
  (a) on an application by a party to the proceedings, or
  (b) of the court's own motion.

  But a party may not apply for a variation or rescission unless there has been a material change of circumstances since the direction was given or last varied.

(7) The court must state in open court its reasons for refusing an application for the giving, variation or rescission of a direction under section 51 and, if it is a magistrates' court, must cause them to be entered in the register of its proceedings.

. . .

(9) The requirements in section 51(4)(c) and subsection (3)(c) arises in a case where—
  (a) the defendant has not attained the age of 18 years, or
  (b) the defendant has attained the age of 18 years but the court is dealing with the case as if the defendant had not attained that age.

11.2 Defendant's intermediary

Amendments to the YJCEA 1999, introduced in 2009, to provide for examination of an accused through an intermediary have never been brought into force. Instead, the Divisional Court identified an inherent jurisdiction to direct that the accused be assisted by an intermediary in giving their evidence: see *R(C) v Sevenoaks Youth Court* [2009] EWHC 3088 (Admin) and *R v Head* [2009] EWCA Crim 140. The criminal courts have continued to appoint intermediaries on this basis, for the purposes of a defendant giving evidence and also to assist a defendant's participation in the whole trial process. In *R(OP) v Secretary of State for Justice* [2014] EWHC 1944 (Admin), the Divisional Court held that the withholding of access of vulnerable defendants to professionally regulated, registered intermediaries breached equality of arms with Crown witnesses under the ECHR Article 6. The welfare principle contained in the CYPA 1933, s 44 reinforces the need for a young defendant to be put on an equal footing to a young or vulnerable witness.

Special Measures for Defendants

As of April 2021, the Crim PR now include rules which deal expressly with the provision of intermediaries for defendants.

Criminal Procedure Rules

18.23 Appointment of intermediary to facilitate a defendant's participation

(1) The court must exercise its power to appoint an intermediary to facilitate a defendant's effective participation in the trial where—
  (a) the defendant's ability to participate is likely to be diminished by reason of
    (i) age, if the defendant is under 18, or
    (ii) mental disorder (as defined in section 1(2) of the Mental Health Act 1983), a significant impairment of intelligence and social functioning, or a physical disability or disorder; and
  (b) the appointment is necessary for that purpose.

(2) In determining whether such an appointment is necessary, who to appoint and the duration or purpose of the appointment, the court must have regard to—
  (a) the defendant's communication needs as reported to the court;
  (b) the recommendations in any intermediary's report received by the court;
  (c) any views that the defendant has expressed about—
    (i) receiving the assistance of an intermediary,
    (ii) other measures or arrangements to facilitate the defendant's effective participation in the trial;
  (d) the likely impact of the defendant's age, if under 18, level of intellectual ability or social functioning on the ability to—
    (i) give evidence, and
    (ii) understand what is said and done by the court and other participants;
  (e) the likely impact on such participation and on such understanding of any mental disorder or other significant impairment of intelligence or social functioning;
  (f) the adequacy of arrangements for questioning the defendant in the absence of an intermediary;
  (g) any assistance that the defendant has received in the past—
    (i) while giving evidence in legal proceedings,
    (ii) while being questioned during the investigation of an alleged offence, or
    (iii) as a defendant in a criminal case;
  (h) any assessment of the defendant's health by a mental health practitioner acting independently of the parties to assist the court;
  (i) any expert medical opinion that the court may have received; and
  (j) any other matter that the court thinks relevant.

(3) The court may exercise its power to appoint an intermediary—
  (a) for the duration of every hearing that the defendant is due to attend;

(b) for the duration of any specified such hearing or hearings, or for the duration of a specified part of such a hearing; or

(c) for a specified purpose during a hearing.

(4) Unless the court otherwise directs, the appointment of an intermediary extends to facilitating the defendant's communication with that defendant's legal representatives for the duration and for the purpose of the appointment.

(5) The court may decide whether to appoint an intermediary to facilitate a defendant's effective participation in the trial and whether to vary or discharge any such appointment—

(a) on application or on the court's own initiative;

(b) at a hearing, in public or in private, or without a hearing; and

(c) in a party's absence, if that party—

(i) applied for the appointment, variation or discharge, or

(ii) has had at least 10 business days in which to make representations.

(6) The court must not exercise its power to vary or discharge a direction for the appointment of an intermediary unless satisfied that—

(a) since the direction was made—

(i) the defendant's communication needs have changed materially, or

(ii) any other material circumstance has changed materially; and

(b) the defendant will be able to participate effectively in the trial despite the variation or discharge of the direction.

18.24.- Application to vary or discharge the appointment of an intermediary for a defendant

(1) A party who wants the court to vary or discharge the appointment of an intermediary to facilitate a defendant's effective participation in the trial must—

(a) apply in writing, as soon as reasonably practicable after becoming aware of the grounds for doing so; and

(b) serve the application on—

(i) the court officer, and

(ii) each other party.

(2) The applicant must—

(a) explain how the criteria listed in rule 18.23(6) are met (variation or discharge of appointment); and

(b) ask for a hearing, if the applicant wants one, and explain why it is needed.

18.25 Representations in response to application or proposal

(1) This rule applies where a party wants to make representations about—

(a) an application or proposal for the appointment of an intermediary to facilitate a defendant's effective participation in the trial; or

(b) an application or proposal for the variation or discharge of such an appointment.

> (2) Such a party must—
> (a) serve the representations on—
> (i) the court officer, and
> (ii) each other party;
> (b) do so not more than 10 business days after, as applicable—
> (i) service of the application, or
> (ii) notice of the appointment, variation or discharge that the court proposes; and
> (c) ask for a hearing, if that party wants one, and explain why it is needed.
>
> (3) Representations against such an appointment, variation or discharge must explain why the criteria that apply are not met.

Rules 18.26 to 18.28 provide for the duties, declaration, and contents of the report for an intermediary (whether for a witness or defendant). Part 6.2 of the CPDs gives guidance on the use of intermediaries. The CPDs emphasize that communication needs (such as short attention span, suggestibility, and reticence in relation to authority figures) are common to many witnesses and defendants under 18. The court must consider their communication needs, adapt the trial process to address those needs, and consider assessment by an intermediary. Where the court directs questioning through an intermediary, a ground rules hearing must be held at which the intermediary is required to be present.

A youth court acted irrationally in ruling that an accused with ADHD was not entitled to an intermediary: *R (AS) v Great Yarmouth Youth Court* [2011] EWHC 2059.

Where a direction is made that an intermediary should be appointed but no suitable person can be found, the trial judge must make an informed assessment as to whether it is possible nonetheless to have a fair trial by adapting procedures: *R v Cox* [2012] EWCA Crim 549. In cases where the defendant is vulnerable, the court should take an active role in ensuring their participation in the proceedings: *R v Dixon* [2013] EWCA 465.

The Divisional Court gave important guidance in *R (TI) v Bromley Youth Court* [2020] EWHC 1204 (Admin); [2020] 2 Cr.App.R. 22. Where a defendant cannot participate effectively in the proceedings, they will not have a fair trial. The court must be vigilant to consider how issues of concentration and understanding may affect a young defendant's ability to participate. Though the youth court is a specialist jurisdiction, this does not mean that a judge could not be assisted by another professional if the needs of the individual required such assistance. Whilst the appointment of an intermediary will be rare, it does not follow that there is a high hurdle to overcome for the appointment if one is necessary. The fact that a defendant participated in an earlier trial without an intermediary is of limited assistance. In a case where the evidence demonstrates that the defendant lacks the capacity to participate unaided in the trial process, it is incumbent on the judge to explain how the court will enable the defendant effectively to participate in the proceedings despite that evidence.

See **I2** Effective Participation.

12 Effective Participation

12.1 Introduction

The inability of a defendant to participate effectively in the criminal proceedings against them will be a breach of the right to a fair trial under the ECHR, Article 6(1). The right of the accused to participate effectively in their criminal trial includes the right to hear and follow the proceedings. In the case of a child, it is essential that they be dealt with in a manner which takes account of their age, level of maturity, and intellectual and emotional capacity. Steps must also be taken to promote their ability to understand and participate in the proceedings, including by conducting the hearing in such a way so as to reduce, as far as possible, any feelings of intimidation or inhibition. A child may be at risk of not being able to participate effectively because of their young age and/or limited intellectual capacity.

The question of fairness of trial in the Crown Court for young defendants was considered by the ECtHR in *V v UK* (2000) 30 EHRR 121. The importance of effective participation for a youth defendant, and the various measures employed to ensure that, have recently been re-emphasized by the Court of Appeal in *R v ZA* [2023] EWCA Crim 596.

The importance of the existence of a specialist tribunal, the youth court, was emphasized in *SC v UK* (2005) 40 EHRR 226.

12.2 Adapting the trial process

In order to prepare for trial, the court must take every reasonable step to facilitate the participation of any person, including the defendant: Crim PR, r3.8(3)(b).

Part 6 of the CPDs deals with the participation of vulnerable people, including vulnerable defendants. The CPDs apply in all criminal courts. They set out steps which should be taken to assist a young defendant to understand and participate in criminal proceedings, adapting the trial process where appropriate and necessary. Part 6 includes guidance on:

- Consulting the toolkits available through The Advocate's Gateway (para.6.1.2); The importance of following the guidance on the proper approach to asking questions of young persons and other vulnerable witnesses was emphasized in *R v Grant-Murray* [2017] EWCA Crim 1228 and *R v Rashid* [2017] EWCA Crim 2.

Blackstone's Handbook of Youths in the Criminal Courts. Mark Ashford, Gareth Branston, and Naomi Redhouse, Oxford University Press.
 DOI: 10.1093/oso/9780198913146.003.0031

- Conducting a ground-rules hearing (GRH) (paras.6.1.4 to 6.1.5 and 6.4.1);
- Restricting, limiting and adapting cross-examination (paras.6.1.6 to 6.1.10);
- Intermediaries (Part 6.2);
- Section 28 of the YJCEA 1999 (Part 6.3);
- Sitting in a court in which communication is more readily facilitated (para.6.4.2(a));
- Pre-trial familiarization visits to court (para.6.4.2(b));
- Live link (paras.6.4.2(c) and 6.4.4);
- Sitting with family or another supporting adult in a place which permits easy communication with their legal representative (para.6.4.2(d));
- Timetabling the case to accommodate the defendant's ability to concentrate (para.6.4.2(e));
- Whether to wear robes and wigs in the Crown Court (para.6.4.2(g));
- Limiting visible security uniforms or police officers in court (para.6.4.2(h));
- Avoiding exposure to intimidation, vilification, or abuse to a defendant in cases attracting widespread public or media interest (para.6.4.2(i));
- Limiting attendance by members of the public to a small number (paras.6.4.5 to 6.4.6).

The court must always have regard to the welfare of a young defendant (CYPA 1933, s 44) and must be provided with information concerning their welfare (para.6.4.2(j)).

In *R(TP) v West London Youth Court* [2005] EWHC 2583 (Admin), the minimum requirements for a fair trial were stated to be:

(i) the defendant had to understand what they were said to have done wrong;
(ii) the court had to be satisfied that the defendant, when they had done wrong by act or omission, had the means of knowing that was wrong;
(iii) they had to understand what, if any, defences were available to them;
(iv) they had to have a reasonable opportunity to make relevant representations if they wished; and
(v) they had to have the opportunity to consider what representations they wished to make once they had understood the issues involved.

They had, therefore, to be able to give proper instructions and to participate by way of providing answers to questions and suggesting questions to their lawyers in the circumstances of the trial as they arose. The case involved a defendant aged 15 with a mental age of 8. It was crucial that the tribunal hearing the case, in that case a youth court, was able to adapt its procedures so that the defendant could effectively participate in the proceedings. Emphasis was again placed on the specialist nature of the tribunal and legal representatives.

The trial judge must take an active role throughout the proceedings to ensure that the defendant is actively participating: *R v Dixon* [2013] EWCA 465.

12.3 Competence to give evidence

All persons, whatever their age, are competent to give evidence in criminal proceedings unless it appears to the court that they are not a person who is able to understand questions put to them as a witness and give answers to those questions which can be understood: YJCEA 1999, s 53.

Any question as to the competence of a young defendant to give evidence should be made before they are sworn and preferably at the beginning of the trial. It should not be an act of ratification after the evidence has been given. Expert evidence may be adduced but is not essential; the decision is for the court.

12.4 Child or young person's oath

No witness may be sworn unless they have attained the age of 14 and have a sufficient appreciation of the solemnity of the occasion and of the particular responsibility to tell the truth which is involved in taking an oath: YJCEA 1999, s 55(2). Any witness, including a defendant, aged 14 to 17 may take an oath but this will be in the form of 'I promise before Almighty God … ': Children and Young Persons Act 1963 (CYPA 1963), s 28. Alternatively, they may affirm, in which case the words used usually are: 'I promise that I shall tell the truth'.

Any witness, including an adult, before the youth court should also take the oath or affirmation as a promise.

Any defendant aged 10 to 13 will give unsworn evidence: YCJEA 1999, s 56(2).

12.5 Other sources of help for effective participation

Chapter 2 of the *Equal Treatment Bench Book* deals with 'Children, Young People and Vulnerable Adults', including young defendants.

It provides guidance on the rights of defendants to effective participation, the duty to safeguard young defendants, competence, expedited timescales and active case management, special measures, intermediaries, ground-rules hearings, and adjustments to cross-examination.

The *Advocate's Gateway* contains freely accessible and regularly updated 'toolkits' for advocates, judges, and other professionals who may have to communicate with, or question, vulnerable people. These have been endorsed by the Court of Appeal and the CPDs.

The *Crown Court Compendium* also includes guidance on special measures and the evidence of children. Appendix II to Part II includes guidance for writing and delivering sentencing remarks to child defendants.

12.6 Mental Health Act procedures

In *R (P) v Barking Youth Court* [2002] EWHC 734 (Admin), the question of fitness to plead was raised in the youth court in relation to a young person aged 12 years with a history of learning difficulties and mental health problems. The High Court stated that the procedure for dealing with matters of this kind in the magistrates' court is specifically provided for by a combination of s 37(3) of the Mental Health Act 1983 (MHA 1983) and s 11(1) of the Powers of Criminal Courts (Sentencing) Act 2000 (PCCSA 2000) (the latter remains in force notwithstanding the SC). An order can be made on a finding that the defendant 'did the act alleged' without conviction and disposals are then available under the MHA 1983. 'Fitness to plead' can be decided in the Crown Court but not in the youth or magistrates' court (where the court is concerned with fitness to participate in a trial).

The MHA 1983, s 37(3) provides:

Mental Health Act 1983

37 Powers of courts to order hospital admission or guardianship

(3) Where a person is charged before a magistrates' court with any act or omission as an offence and the court would have power, on convicting him of that offence, to make an order under subsection (1) above in his case, then, if the court is satisfied that the accused did the act or made the omission charged, the court may, if it thinks fit, make such an order without convicting him.

The PCCSA 2000, s 11 provides for remand by a magistrates' court for medical reports:

Powers of Criminal Courts (Sentencing) Act 2000

11 Remand by magistrates' court for medical examination

(1) If, on the trial by a magistrates' court of an offence punishable on summary conviction with imprisonment, the court—
  (a) is satisfied that the accused did the act or made the omission charged, but
  (b) is of the opinion that an inquiry ought to be made into his physical or mental condition before the method of dealing with him is determined,

the court shall adjourn the case to enable a medical examination and report to be made, and shall remand him.

(2) An adjournment under subsection (1) above shall not be for more than three weeks at a time where the court remands the accused in custody, nor for more than four weeks at a time where it remands him on bail.

(3) Where on an adjournment under subsection (1) above the accused is remanded on bail, the court shall impose conditions under paragraph (d) of section 3(6) of the Bail Act 1976 and the requirements imposed as conditions under that paragraph shall be or shall include requirements that the accused—
  (a) undergo medical examination by a registered medical practitioner or, where the inquiry is into his mental condition and the court so directs, two such practitioners; and
  (b) for that purpose attend such an institution or place, or on such practitioner, as the court directs and, where the inquiry is into his mental condition, comply with any other directions which may be given to him for that purpose by any person specified by the court or by a person of any class so specified.

12.7 A hybrid approach?

In *CPS v P* [2007] EWHC 946 (Admin), the court gave specific guidance as to how these issues should be approached by a youth court. The case involved a defendant against whom proceedings in the Crown Court had previously been stayed on the basis of a number of medical reports. Smith LJ at para [61] stated:

(i) The fact that a court of 'higher authority' has previously held that a person is unfit to plead does not make it an abuse of process to try that person for subsequent criminal acts. The issue of the child's ability to participate effectively must be decided afresh.

(ii) Where the court decides to proceed to decide whether the person did the acts alleged, the proceedings are not a criminal trial.

(iii) The court may consider whether to proceed to decide the facts at any stage. It may decide to do so before hearing any evidence or it may stop the criminal procedure and switch to the fact-finding procedure at any stage.

(iv) The DJ should not have stayed the proceedings at the outset as he did without considering the alternative of allowing the trial to proceed while keeping P's situation under constant review.

(v) If the court proceeds with fact-finding only, the fact that the defendant does not or cannot take any part in the proceedings does not render them unfair or in any way improper; the defendant's Article 6 rights are not engaged by that process.

The court stated that there would be a very small number of cases where it would be right to stay proceedings at the outset. This would only be where the child was clearly so severely impaired as to be unable to participate in the trial and where there is no useful purpose in finding the facts.

It is likely that some applications to adapt the trial process or to proceed under the PCCSA 2000, s 11(1) will need the support of specialist reports. It may be possible to obtain guidance from professionals who are already involved with the young person. Where proceedings take the form of a fact-finding hearing, rather than a trial, an order under the MHA 1983 does not necessarily have to be made.

Rule 3.10 of the Crim PR provides for directions for commissioning medical reports, other than for sentencing purposes. Rule 25.10 applies where a defendant in the Crown Court may not be fit to be tried. Rule 28.8 provides for directions for commissioning medical reports in any court for the purpose of sentencing or other disposal.

See **K** Youths in the Crown Court and **J10** Mentally Disordered Offenders.

13 Special Measures for Young and Vulnerable Witnesses

The YJCEA 1999, ss 16 and 17 provide:

Youth Justice and Criminal Evidence Act 1999

16 Witnesses eligible for assistance on grounds of age or incapacity

(1) For the purposes of this Chapter a witness in criminal proceedings (other than the accused) is eligible for assistance by virtue of this section—
   (a) if under the age of 18 at the time of the hearing; or
   (b) if the court considers that the quality of evidence given by the witness is likely to be diminished by reason of any circumstances falling within subsection (2).

(2) The circumstances falling within this subsection are—
   (a) that the witness—
      (i) suffers from mental disorder within the meaning of the Mental Health Act 1983, or
      (ii) otherwise has a significant impairment of intelligence and social functioning;
   (b) that the witness has a physical disability or is suffering from a physical disorder.

(3) In subsection (1)(a) 'the time of the hearing', in relation to a witness, means the time when it falls to the court to make a determination for the purposes of section 19(2) in relation to the witness.

(4) In determining whether a witness falls within subsection (1)(b) the court must consider any views expressed by the witness.

(5) In this Chapter references to the quality of a witness's evidence are to its quality in terms of completeness, coherence and accuracy; and for this purpose 'coherence' refers to a witness's ability in giving evidence to give answers which address the questions put to the witness and can be understood both individually and collectively.

17 Witnesses eligible for assistance on grounds of fear or distress about testifying

(1) For the purposes of this Chapter a witness in criminal proceedings (other than the accused) is eligible for assistance by virtue of this subsection if the court is satisfied that the quality of evidence given by the witness is likely to be diminished by reason of fear or distress on the part of the witness in connection with testifying in the proceedings.

(2) In determining whether a witness falls within subsection (1) the court must take into account, in particular—
   (a) the nature and alleged circumstances of the offence to which the proceedings relate;

Blackstone's Handbook of Youths in the Criminal Courts. Mark Ashford, Gareth Branston, and Naomi Redhouse, Oxford University Press.
 DOI: 10.1093/oso/9780198913146.003.0032

(b) the age of the witness;
(c) such of the following matters as appear to the court to be relevant, namely—
  (i) the social and cultural background and ethnic origins of the witness,
  (ii) the domestic and employment circumstances of the witness, and
  (iii) any religious beliefs or political opinions of the witness;
(d) any behaviour towards the witness on the part of—
  (i) the accused,
  (ii) members of the family or associates of the accused, or
  (iii) any other person who is likely to be an accused or a witness in the proceedings.

(3) In determining that question the court must in addition consider any views expressed by the witness.

(4) Where the complainant in respect of an offence listed in subsection (4A) is a witness in proceedings relating to that offence (or to that offence and any other offences), the witness is eligible for assistance in relation to those proceedings by virtue of this subsection unless the witness has informed the court of the witness' wish not to be so eligible by virtue of this subsection.

(4A) The offences are—
(a) a sexual offence;
(b) an offence under section 1 or 2 of the Modern Slavery Act 2015;
(c) any other offence where it is alleged that the behaviour of the accused amounted to domestic abuse within the meaning of the Domestic Abuse Act 2021 (see section 1 of that Act).

(5) A witness in proceedings relating to a relevant offence (or to a relevant offence and any other offences) is eligible for assistance in relation to those proceedings by virtue of this subsection unless the witness has informed the court of the witness's wish not to be so eligible by virtue of this subsection.

(6) For the purposes of subsection (5) an offence is a relevant offence if it is an offence described in Schedule 1A.

(7) The Secretary of State may by order amend Schedule 1A.

13.1 Special measures in force

The following special measures, applicable to prosecution and defence witness, are available in all youth and adult magistrates' courts:

- screening witness from accused, s 23
- evidence via live link, s 24
- evidence given in private, s 25
- video-recorded evidence in chief, s 27
- examination through an intermediary, s 29
- aids to communication, s 30.

Video-recorded cross-examination or re-examination (s 28) has been brought into force in all Crown Courts for witnesses eligible for assistance by virtue of s 16 or s 17(4) of the Act. On 26 September 2022, s 28 was also brought into force at Leeds Youth Court for witnesses eligible by virtue of s 16.

See 13.8 Special Measures.

13.2 Witnesses under the age of 18

Child witnesses are automatically eligible for special measures as provided in s 16(1)(a) without having to satisfy any other test. Furthermore, the YJCEA 1999, s 21 provides for the 'primary rule' for a child witness:

Youth Justice and Criminal Evidence Act 1999

21 Special provisions relating to child witnesses

(1) For the purposes of this section—
   (a) a witness in criminal proceedings is a 'child witness' if he is an eligible witness by reason of section 16(1)(a) (whether or not he is an eligible witness by reason of any other provision of section 16 or 17); and
   (b) . . .
   (c) a 'relevant recording', in relation to a child witness, is a video recording of an interview of the witness made with a view to its admission as evidence in chief of the witness.

(2) Where the court, in making a determination for the purposes of section 19(2), determines that a witness in criminal proceedings is a child witness, the court must—
   (a) first have regard to subsections (3) to (4C) below; and
   (b) then have regard to section 19(2);

   and for the purposes of section 19(2), as it then applies to the witness, any special measures required to be applied in relation to him by virtue of this section shall be treated as if they were measures determined by the court, pursuant to section 19(2)(a) and (b)(i), to be ones that (whether on their own or with any other special measures) would be likely to maximise, so far as practicable, the quality of his evidence.

(3) The primary rule in the case of a child witness is that the court must give a special measures direction in relation to the witness which complies with the following requirements—
   (a) it must provide for any relevant recording to be admitted under section 27 (video recorded evidence in chief); and
   (b) it must provide for any evidence given by the witness in the proceedings which is not given by means of a video recording (whether in chief or otherwise) to be given by means of a live link in accordance with section 24.

(4) The primary rule is subject to the following limitations—
- (a) the requirement contained in subsection (3)(a) or (b) has effect subject to the availability (within the meaning of section 18(2)) of the special measure in question in relation to the witness;
- (b) the requirement contained in subsection (3)(a) also has effect subject to section 27(2);
- (ba) if the witness informs the court of the witness's wish that the rule should not apply or should apply only in part, the rule does not apply to the extent that the court is satisfied that not complying with the rule would not diminish the quality of the witness's evidence; and
- (c) the rule does not apply to the extent that the court is satisfied that compliance with it would not be likely to maximise the quality of the witness's evidence so far as practicable (whether because the application to that evidence of one or more other special measures available in relation to the witness would have that result or for any other reason).

(4A) Where as a consequence of all or part of the primary rule being disapplied under subsection (4)(ba) a witness's evidence or any part of it would fall to be given as testimony in court, the court must give a special measures direction making such provision as is described in section 23 for the evidence or that part of it.

(4B) The requirement in subsection (4A) is subject to the following limitations—
- (a) if the witness informs the court of the witness's wish that the requirement in subsection (4A) should not apply, the requirement does not apply to the extent that the court is satisfied that not complying with it would not diminish the quality of the witness's evidence; and
- (b) the requirement does not apply to the extent that the court is satisfied that making such a provision would not be likely to maximise the quality of the witness's evidence so far as practicable (whether because the application to that evidence of one or more other special measures available in relation to the witness would have that result or for any other reason).

(4C) In making a decision under subsection (4)(ba) or (4B)(a), the court must take into account the following factors (and any others it considers relevant)—
- (a) the age and maturity of the witness;
- (b) the ability of the witness to understand the consequences of giving evidence otherwise than in accordance with the requirements in subsection (3) or (as the case may be) in accordance with the requirement in subsection (4A);
- (c) the relationship (if any) between the witness and the accused;
- (d) the witness's social and cultural background and ethnic origins;
- (e) the nature and alleged circumstances of the offence to which the proceedings relate.

. . .

Where a witness is eligible by reason of age, there may be agreement between the prosecution and defence as to the making of a special measures direction at an early stage in the proceedings, usually avoiding the need to make a formal written application. The court may raise the issue on completion of the case management form.

The provisions apply to prosecution and defence witnesses. They do not apply to the defendant.

13.3 Adult witness with physical or mental impairment

An adult witness suffering from a mental disorder, a significant impairment of intelligence and social functioning, a physical disability, or a physical disorder is entitled to special measures under s 16(2), if such impairment is likely to diminish the quality of their evidence. Any application is likely to need supporting evidence.

13.4 Witness in fear or distress

A witness whose evidence is likely to be diminished by reason of fear or distress is entitled to special measures under s 17(1). Section 17(2) sets out the factors which the court will take into account in considering an application.

13.5 Sexual, modern slavery, and domestic abuse complainants

Any adult complainant in proceedings for a sexual offence, an offence under s 1 or s 2 of the Modern Slavery Act 2015, or an offence which would amount to domestic abuse within the meaning of the Domestic Abuse Act 2021 (DAA 2021) is automatically entitled to special measures under s 17(4). In the Crown Court (but not a magistrates' or youth court), there is a presumption that the court will admit video-recorded evidence in chief for a complainant to a sexual offence: s 22A.

13.6 Witness to other relevant offences involving knives or guns

A witness in proceedings relating to any offence listed in Sch 1A of the YJCEA 1999 is eligible for special measures under s 17(5). Schedule 1A sets out various offences of violence involving weapons or firearms:

Youth Justice and Criminal Evidence Act 1999, Sch 1A

Relevant offences for the purposes of s 17

Murder and manslaughter

1 Murder in a case where it is alleged that a firearm or knife was used to cause the death in question.

2 Manslaughter in a case where it is alleged that a firearm or knife was used to cause the death in question.

3 Murder or manslaughter in a case (other than a case falling within paragraph 1 or 2) where it is alleged that—

(a) the accused was carrying a firearm or knife at any time during the commission of the offence, and

(b) a person other than the accused knew or believed at any time during the commission of the offence that the accused was carrying a firearm or knife.

Offences against the Person Act 1861 (c 100)

4 An offence under section 18 of the Offences against the Person Act 1861 (wounding with intent to cause grievous bodily harm etc) in a case where it is alleged that a firearm or knife was used to cause the wound or harm in question.

5 An offence under section 20 of that Act (malicious wounding) in a case where it is alleged that a firearm or knife was used to cause the wound or inflict the harm in question.

6 An offence under section 38 of that Act (assault with intent to resist arrest) in a case where it is alleged that a firearm or knife was used to carry out the assault in question.

7 An offence under section 47 of the Offences against the Person Act 1861 (assault occasioning actual bodily harm) in a case where it is alleged that a firearm or knife was used to inflict the harm in question.

8 An offence under section 18, 20, 38 or 47 of the Offences against the Person Act 1861 in a case (other than a case falling within any of paragraphs 4 to 7) where it is alleged that—

(a) the accused was carrying a firearm or knife at any time during the commission of the offence, and

(b) a person other than the accused knew or believed at any time during the commission of the offence that the accused was carrying a firearm or knife.

Prevention of Crime Act 1953 (c 14)

9 An offence under section 1 of the Prevention of Crime Act 1953 (having an offensive weapon in a public place).

9A An offence under section 1A of that Act (threatening with offensive weapon in public).

Firearms Act 1968 (c 27)

10 An offence under section 1 of the Firearms Act 1968 (requirement of firearm certificate).

11 An offence under section 2(1) of that Act (possession etc of a shot gun without a certificate).
12 An offence under section 3 of that Act (business and other transactions with firearms and ammunition).
13 An offence under section 4 of that Act (conversion of weapons).
14 An offence under section 5(1) of that Act (weapons subject to general prohibition).
15 An offence under section 5(1A) of that Act (ammunition subject to general prohibition).
16 An offence under section 16 of that Act (possession with intent to injure).
17 An offence under section 16A of that Act (possession with intent to cause fear of violence).
18 An offence under section 17 of that Act (use of firearm to resist arrest).
19 An offence under section 18 of that Act (carrying firearm with criminal intent).
20 An offence under section 19 of that Act (carrying firearm in a public place).
21 An offence under section 20 of that Act (trespassing with firearm).
22 An offence under section 21 of that Act (possession of firearms by person previously convicted of crime).
23 An offence under section 21A of that Act (firing an air weapon beyond premises).
24 An offence under section 24A of that Act (supplying imitation firearms to minors).

Criminal Justice Act 1988 (c 33)

25 An offence under section 139 of the Criminal Justice Act 1988 (having article with blade or point in public place).
26 An offence under section 139A of that Act (having article with blade or point (or offensive weapon) on school premises).
26A An offence under section 139AA of that Act (threatening with article with blade or point or offensive weapon).

Violent Crime Reduction Act 2006 (c 38)

27 An offence under section 28 of the Violent Crime Reduction Act 2006 (using someone to mind a weapon).
28 An offence under section 32 of that Act (sales of air weapons by way of trade or business to be face to face).
29 An offence under section 36 of that Act (manufacture, import and sale of realistic imitation firearms).

Serious Crime Act 2015

29A An offence under section 75A of the Serious Crime Act 2015 (strangulation or suffocation) in a case where it is alleged that—
(a) the accused was carrying a firearm or knife at any time during the commission of the offence, and

(b) a person other than the accused knew or believed at any time during the commission of the offence that the accused was carrying a firearm or knife.

General

30 A reference in any of paragraphs 1 to 8 or 29A to an offence ('offence A') includes—

(a) a reference to an attempt to commit offence A in a case where it is alleged that it was attempted to commit offence A in the manner or circumstances described in that paragraph,

(b) a reference to a conspiracy to commit offence A in a case where it is alleged that the conspiracy was to commit offence A in the manner or circumstances described in that paragraph,

(c) a reference to an offence under Part 2 of the Serious Crime Act 2007 in relation to which offence A is the offence (or one of the offences) which the person intended or believed would be committed in a case where it is alleged that the person intended or believed offence A would be committed in the manner or circumstances described in that paragraph, and

(d) a reference to aiding, abetting, counselling or procuring the commission of offence A in a case where it is alleged that offence A was committed, or the act or omission charged in respect of offence A was done or made, in the manner or circumstances described in that paragraph.

31 A reference in any of paragraphs 9 to 29 to an offence ('offence A') includes—

(a) a reference to an attempt to commit offence A,

(b) a reference to a conspiracy to commit offence A,

(c) a reference to an offence under Part 2 of the Serious Crime Act 2007 in relation to which offence A is the offence (or one of the offences) which the person intended or believed would be committed, and

(d) a reference to aiding, abetting, counselling or procuring the commission of offence A.

Interpretation

32 In this Schedule—

'firearm' has the meaning given by section 57 of the Firearms Act 1968;

'knife' has the meaning given by section 10 of the Knives Act.

13.7 Procedure and time limits

The issue of special measures may arise on application by the prosecution or the defence. It may also be raised of the court's own motion.

The YJCEA 1999, s 19 provides:

Youth Justice and Criminal Evidence Act 1999

19 Special measures direction relating to eligible witness

(1) This section applies where in any criminal proceedings—
 (a) a party to the proceedings makes an application for the court to give a direction under this section in relation to a witness in the proceedings other than the accused, or
 (b) the court of its own motion raises the issue whether such a direction should be given.

(2) Where the court determines that the witness is eligible for assistance by virtue of section 16 or 17, the court must then—
 (a) determine whether any of the special measures available in relation to the witness (or any combination of them) would, in its opinion, be likely to improve the quality of evidence given by the witness; and
 (b) if so—
  (i) determine which of those measures (or combination of them) would, in its opinion, be likely to maximise so far as practicable the quality of such evidence; and
  (ii) give a direction under this section providing for the measure or measures so determined to apply to evidence given by the witness.

(3) In determining for the purposes of this Chapter whether any special measure or measures would or would not be likely to improve, or to maximise so far as practicable, the quality of evidence given by the witness, the court must consider all the circumstances of the case, including in particular—
 (a) any views expressed by the witness; and
 (b) whether the measure or measures might tend to inhibit such evidence being effectively tested by a party to the proceedings.

(4) A special measures direction must specify particulars of the provision made by the direction in respect of each special measure which is to apply to the witness's evidence.

(5) In this Chapter 'special measures direction' means a direction under this section.

(6) Nothing in this Chapter is to be regarded as affecting any power of a court to make an order or give leave of any description (in the exercise of its inherent jurisdiction or otherwise)—
 (a) in relation to a witness who is not an eligible witness, or
 (b) in relation to an eligible witness where (as, for example, in a case where a foreign language interpreter is to be provided) the order is made or the leave is given otherwise than by reason of the fact that the witness is an eligible witness.

Part 18 of the Crim PR 2020 provides for special measures. Rules 18.8 to 18.13 provide for special measures directions. The court may decide to give, vary, or discharge a special measures direction at a hearing in public or private, or without a hearing. The court may also do so in a party's absence if that party has made the application or has had at least ten business days to respond (r 18.8). Rule 18.9 permits the court to exercise its power to give a special measures direction without requiring a formal application if notice as to the witness's eligibility is given and no other party opposes the giving of a special measures direction. Where an application is required, r 18.4 provides for time limits and r 18.10 provides for the contents of such an application:

Criminal Procedure Rules 2020

18.4 Making an application for a direction or order

A party who wants the court to exercise its power to give or make a direction or order must—

(a) apply in writing as soon as reasonably practicable, and in any event not more than—
  (i) 20 business days after the defendant pleads not guilty, in a magistrates' court, or
  (ii) 10 business days after the defendant pleads not guilty, in the Crown Court; and
(b) serve the application on—
  (i) the court officer, and
  (ii) each other party.

18.10 Content of application for a special measures direction

An applicant for a special measures direction must—

(a) explain how the witness is eligible for assistance;
(b) explain why special measures would be likely to improve the quality of the witness' evidence;
(c) propose the measure or measures that in the applicant's opinion would be likely to maximise, so far as practicable, the quality of that evidence;
(d) report any views that the witness has expressed about—
  (i) his or her eligibility for assistance,
  (ii) the likelihood that special measures would improve the quality of his or her evidence, and
  (iii) the measure or measures proposed by the applicant;
(e) in a case in which a child witness or a qualifying witness does not want the primary rule to apply, provide any information which the court may need to assess the witness' views;
(f) in a case in which the applicant proposes that the witness should give evidence by live link—
  (i) identify someone to accompany the witness while the witness gives evidence,
  (ii) name that person, if possible, and
  (iii) explain why that person would be an appropriate companion for the witness, including the witness' own views;

(g) in a case in which the applicant proposes the admission of video recorded evidence, identify—
  (i) the date and duration of the recording, and
  (ii) which part the applicant wants the court to admit as evidence, if the applicant does not want the court to admit all of it;

(h) attach any other material on which the applicant relies, and

(i) if the applicant wants a hearing, ask for one, and explain why it is needed.

Rule 18.11 provides for applications to vary or discharge a special measures direction. Rule 18.12 provides for applications which include information that an applicant wishes to withhold from another party. Rule 18.13 provides for representations in response.

13.7.1 *Disapplying a special measures direction*

The YJCEA 1999, s 21(4) allows the court to disapply all or part of a special measures direction if the witness informs the court that he does not wish to have the benefit of it. The court must also be satisfied that the quality of the evidence given by the witness will not be affected by the removal of the special measure. In considering the application the court must take account of the following factors and any others it considers relevant:

- the age and maturity of the witness;
- the ability of the witness to understand the consequences of giving evidence without the assistance of the special measure;
- the relationship (if any) between the witness and the accused;
- the witness's social and cultural background and ethnic origins; and
- the nature and alleged circumstances of the offence to which the proceedings relate.

13.8 Special measures

13.8.1 *Screens*

Section 23 of the YJCEA 1999 provides:

Youth Justice and Criminal Evidence Act 1999

23 Screening Evidence by live link

(1) A special measures direction may provide for the witness, while giving testimony or being sworn in court, to be prevented by means of a screen or other arrangement from seeing the accused.

(2) But the screen or other arrangement must not prevent the witness from being able to see, and to be seen by—
  (a) the judge or justices (or both) and the jury (if there is one);

(b) legal representatives acting in the proceedings; and
(c) any interpreter or other person appointed (in pursuance of the direction or otherwise) to assist the witness.

(3) Where two or more legal representatives are acting for a party to the proceedings, subsection (2)(b) is to be regarded as satisfied in relation to those representatives if the witness is able at all material times to see and be seen by at least one of them.

13.8.2 *Live links*

Section 24 of the YJCEA 1999 provides:

Youth Justice and Criminal Evidence Act 1999

24 Evidence by live link

(1) A special measures direction may provide for the witness to give evidence by means of a live link.

(1A) Such a direction may also provide for a specified person to accompany the witness while the witness is giving evidence by live link.

(1B) In determining who may accompany the witness, the court must have regard to the wishes of the witness.

(2) Where a direction provides for the witness to give evidence by means of a live link, the witness may not give evidence in any other way without the permission of the court.

(3) The court may give permission for the purposes of subsection (2) if it appears to the court to be in the interests of justice to do so, and may do so either—
(a) on an application by a party to the proceedings, if there has been a material change of circumstances since the relevant time, or
(b) of its own motion.

(4) In subsection (3) 'the relevant time' means—
(a) the time when the direction was given, or
(b) if a previous application has been made under that subsection, the time when the application (or last application) was made.

. . .

(8) In this Chapter 'live link' means a live television link or other arrangement whereby a witness, while absent from the courtroom or other place where the proceedings are being held, is able to see and hear a person there and to be seen and heard by the persons specified in section 23(2)(a) to (c).

13.8.3 *Recorded evidence in chief*

Where a witness has made a statement in the form of a recording, that evidence will be admitted as evidence in chief and their cross-examination will take place on the live link.

Section 27 of the YJCEA 1999 provides:

Youth Justice and Criminal Evidence Act 1999

27 Video recorded evidence in chief

(1) A special measures direction may provide for a video recording of an interview of the witness to be admitted as evidence in chief of the witness.

(2) A special measures direction may, however, not provide for a video recording, or a part of such a recording, to be admitted under this section if the court is of the opinion, having regard to all the circumstances of the case, that in the interests of justice the recording, or that part of it, should not be so admitted.

(3) In considering for the purposes of subsection (2) whether any part of a recording should not be admitted under this section, the court must consider whether any prejudice to the accused which might result from that part being so admitted is outweighed by the desirability of showing the whole, or substantially the whole, of the recorded interview.

(4) Where a special measures direction provides for a recording to be admitted under this section, the court may nevertheless subsequently direct that it is not to be so admitted if—

- (a) it appears to the court that—
  - (i) the witness will not be available for cross-examination (whether conducted in the ordinary way or in accordance with any such direction), and
  - (ii) the parties to the proceedings have not agreed that there is no need for the witness to be so available; or
- (b) any Criminal Procedure Rules requiring disclosure of the circumstances in which the recording was made have not been complied with to the satisfaction of the court.

(5) Where a recording is admitted under this section—

- (a) the witness must be called by the party tendering it in evidence, unless—
  - (i) a special measures direction provides for the witness's evidence on cross-examination to be given in any recording admissible under section 28, or
  - (ii) the parties to the proceedings have agreed as mentioned in subsection (4)(a)(ii); and
- (b) the witness may not without the permission of the court give evidence in chief otherwise than by means of the recording as to any matter which, in the opinion of the court, is dealt with in the witness's recorded testimony.

(6) Where in accordance with subsection (2) a special measures direction provides for part only of a recording to be admitted under this section, references in subsections (4) and (5) to the recording or to the witness's recorded testimony are references to the part of the recording or testimony which is to be so admitted.

(7) The court may give permission for the purposes of subsection (5)(b) if it appears to the court to be in the interests of justice to do so, and may do so either—
   (a) on an application by a party to the proceedings or
   (b) of its own motion.

(8) . . .

(9) The court may, in giving permission for the purposes of subsection (5)(b), direct that the evidence in question is to be given by the witness by means of a live link.

(9A) If the court directs under subsection (9) that evidence is to be given by live link, it may also make such provision in that direction as it could make under section 24(1A) in a special measures direction.

(10) . . .

(11) Nothing in this section affects the admissibility of any video recording which would be admissible apart from this section.

Important guidance is contained in *Achieving Best Evidence in Criminal Proceedings: Guidance on interviewing victims and witnesses, and guidance on using special measures* (4th edition, January 2022) which is available on the GOV.UK website. It is of particular use if there is to be a challenge to the admissibility of all, or part of, recorded evidence in chief.

13.8.4 *Video-recorded cross-examination or re-examination*

Section 28 of the YJCEA 1999 provides:

Youth Justice and Criminal Evidence Act 1999

28 Video recorded cross-examination or re-examination

(1) Where a special measures direction provides for a video recording to be admitted under section 27 as evidence in chief of the witness, the direction may also provide—
   (a) for any cross-examination of the witness, and any re-examination, to be recorded by means of a video recording; and
   (b) for such recording to be admitted, so far as it relates to any such cross-examination or re-examination, as evidence of the witness under cross-examination or on re-examination, as the case may be.

(2) Such a recording must be made in the presence of such persons as Criminal Procedure Rules or the direction may provide and in the absence of the accused, but in circumstances in which—
   (a) the judge or justices (or both) and legal representatives acting in the proceedings are able to see and hear the examination of the witness and to communicate with the persons in whose presence the recording is being made, and

(b) the accused is able to see and hear any such examination and to communicate with any legal representative acting for him.

(3) Where two of more legal representatives are acting for a party to the proceedings, subsection (2)(a) and (b) are to be regarded as satisfied in relation to those representatives if at all material times they are satisfied in relation to at least one of them.

(4) Where a special measures direction provides for a recording to be admitted under this section, the court may nevertheless subsequently direct that it is not to be so admitted if any requirement of subsection (2) or Criminal Procedure Rules or the direction has not been complied with to the satisfaction of the court.

(5) Where in pursuance of subsection (1) a recording has been made of any examination of the witness, the witness may not be subsequently cross-examined or re-examined in respect of any evidence given by the witness in the proceedings (whether in any recording admissible under section 27 of this section or otherwise than in such a recording) unless the court gives a further special measures direction making such provision as is mentioned in subsection (1)(a) and (b) in relation to any subsequent cross-examination, and re-examination, of the witness.

(6) The court may only give such a further direction if it appears to the court—

(a) that the proposed cross-examination is sought by a party to the proceedings as a result of that party having become aware, since the time when the original recording was made in pursuance of subsection (1), of a matter which the party could not with reasonable diligence have ascertained by then, or

(b) that for any other reason it is in the interests of justice to give the further direction.

(7) Nothing in this section shall be read as applying in relation to any cross-examination of the witness by the accused in person (in a case where the accused is to be able to conduct any such cross-examination).

13.8.5 *Intermediaries for witnesses*

Section 29 of the YJCEA 1999 provides:

Youth Justice and Criminal Evidence Act 1999

29 Examination of witness through intermediary

(1) A special measures direction may provide for any examination of the witness (however and wherever conducted) to be conducted through an interpreter or other person approved by the court for the purposes of this section ('an intermediary').

(2) The function of an intermediary is to communicate—

(a) to the witness, questions put to the witness, and

(b) to any person asking such questions, the answers given by the witness in reply to them,

and to explain such questions or answers so far as necessary to enable them to be understood by the witness or person in question.

(3) Any examination of the witness in pursuance of subsection (1) must take place in the presence of such persons as Criminal Procedure Rules or the direction may provide, but in circumstances in which—
   (a) the judge or justices (or both) and legal representatives acting in the proceedings are able to see and hear the examination of the witness and to communicate with the intermediary, and
   (b) (except in the case of a video recorded examination) the jury (if there is one) are able to see and hear the examination of the witness.

(4) Where two or more legal representatives are acting for a party to the proceedings, subsection (3)(a) is to be regarded as satisfied in relation to those representatives if at all material times it is satisfied in relation to at least one of them.

(5) A person may not act as an intermediary in a particular case except after making a declaration, in such form as may be prescribed by Criminal Procedure Rules, that he will faithfully perform his function as intermediary.

(6) Subsection (1) does not apply to an interview of the witness which is recorded by means of a video recording with a view to its admission as evidence in chief of the witness; but a special measures direction may provide for such a recording to be admitted under section 27 if the interview was conducted through an intermediary and—
   (a) that person complied with subsection (5) before the interview began, and
   (b) the court's approval for the purposes of this section is given before the direction is given . . .

Rule 18.26 of the Crim PR sets out an intermediary's duty to the court. Rule 18.27 provides the declaration that must be made by an intermediary before any video-recorded interview or oral evidence conducted through an intermediary. Rule 18.28 details the contents of any intermediary's report that must be present in every case.

Part J
Sentencing

J1 Age of Offender

J1.1 Relevant age

The powers of the court on sentence depend upon the age of the offender. The relevant age is the defendant's age on the date of conviction, that is the date on which they plead guilty or are found guilty (*R v Danga* [1992] 13 Cr App R (S) 408).

J1.2 Age at date of offence

Where an offender crosses a significant age threshold between the date of the commission of the offence and the date of conviction, the starting point for the court to consider is the sentence that the defendant would have been likely to receive if they had been sentenced at the date of the commission of the offence; where the date of conviction is only a few months after the date of the offence, it would rarely be appropriate to pass a longer sentence than that which could have been passed on the date of offence: *R v Ghafoor* [2002] EWCA Crim 1857, [2003] 1 Cr App R (S) 428. In *Ghafoor*, a 17-year-old was involved in a serious public disturbance. He was jointly charged with adults on a charge of riot. Riot is not a grave crime for which long-term detention (then under the PCCSA 2000, s 91(3)) is available but the appellant was sent to the Crown Court for trial as he was jointly charged with adults. He pleaded guilty in the Crown Court after he had turned 18. His sentence of four years' detention in a young offender institution (YOI) was quashed and 18 months' detention in a YOI substituted. The court held that, if he had been sentenced at the time of the offence, the maximum sentence would have been a 24-month DTO. With the discount for a guilty plea, the sentence passed would not have been more than 18 months and that should have been the sentence passed in the Crown Court, notwithstanding the fact that the appellant had attained 18 years of age. The fact that the sentence available to a 17-year-old may be deemed inadequate to reflect the gravity of the offence is not in itself a reason for departing from that starting point: *R v Britton* [2006] EWCA Crim 2875, [2007] 1 Cr App R (S) 121.

The *Sentencing Children and Young People – Overarching Principles* definitive guideline summarizes the principles:

Blackstone's Handbook of Youths in the Criminal Courts. Mark Ashford, Gareth Branston, and Naomi Redhouse, Oxford University Press.
 DOI: 10.1093/oso/9780198913146.003.0033

Crossing a significant age threshold between commission of offence and sentence

6.1 There will be occasions when an increase in the age of a child or young person will result in the maximum sentence on the date of the finding of guilt being greater than that available on the date on which the offence was committed (primarily turning 12, 15 or 18 years old).

6.2 In such situations the court should take as its starting point the sentence likely to have been imposed on the date at which the offence was committed. This includes young people who attain the age of 18 between the commission of the offence and the finding of guilt but when this occurs the purpose of sentencing adult offenders has to be taken into account, which is:

- the punishment of offenders;
- the reduction of crime (including its reduction by deterrence);
- the reform and rehabilitation of offenders;
- the protection of the public; and
- the making of reparation by offenders to persons affected by their offences.

6.3 When any significant age threshold is passed it will rarely be appropriate that a more severe sentence than the maximum that the court could have imposed at the time the offence was committed should be imposed. However, a sentence at or close to that maximum may be appropriate'

For the application of this principle to the age thresholds relevant to DTOs see **J5.2.1**.

J1.3 **Determining age**

If there is any doubt about the age of the offender, this will normally have been resolved at the start of the proceedings. If any doubt about the offender's real age is raised for the first time at the sentencing hearing, the court must make a determination before proceeding to sentence. See **H1.3** and **H.1.4**

The SC, s 405 provides:

Sentencing Code, s 405

(1) This section applies for the purposes of any provision of this Code which requires a person's age to be determined by the court of the Secretary of State.

(2) The person is to be deemed to be whatever age the person appears to the court, or, as the case may be, the Secretary of State, to be.

(3) For this purpose, the court or Secretary of State must consider any available evidence.

Where all the evidence before a sentencing court indicates a particular age, the sentence is not invalidated by the later discovery of the correct date of birth of the offender: *R v Brown* (1989) 11 Cr App R (S) 263. However, where a sentencing court does have evidence of the offender's correct date of birth but that is overlooked and the court proceeds to pass an invalid sentence on the basis of an incorrect age, the sentence will not be allowed to stand: *R v Harris* (1989) 12 Cr App R (S) 318.

J2 Criminal Behaviour Order

Sections 330 to 342 of the SC now provide for CBOs. A CBO is an order which, for the purpose of preventing an offender from engaging in behaviour likely to cause harassment, alarm, or distress to any person, prohibits the offender from doing anything described in the order or requires them to do anything described in the order: s 330. A CBO can be made by a youth court, magistrates' court, or Crown Court whenever an offender is convicted of any offence: s 331(1). The test applied is whether the court is satisfied that the offender has engaged in behaviour that caused or was likely to cause harassment, alarm, or distress and the court considers that a CBO will help prevent the offender from engaging in such behaviour: s 331(2). A CBO cannot be made alongside an absolute discharge: s 331(3).

J2.1 Notice

The Crim PR, r 31.3 requires the prosecutor to give notice, on the prescribed form, of the intention to apply for a CBO following conviction.

The notice must:

- summarize the relevant facts;
- identify the evidence in support on which the prosecutor relies;
- attach any written statement not previously served; and
- specify the terms of the proposed order.

The court may only make a CBO on the application of the prosecution, not of its own motion: s 331(1)(a). The prosecution must find out the views of the local YOT before applying for a CBO for an offender under the age of 18: s 331(5). There is power to adjourn the proceedings even after sentencing the offender: s 332(3). A warrant may be issued if the young person does not then attend: s 332(4).

J2.2 Interim order

If the court decides to adjourn the proceedings it may make an interim order if it considers that it is just to do so: s 335.

Blackstone's Handbook of Youths in the Criminal Courts. Mark Ashford, Gareth Branston, and Naomi Redhouse, Oxford University Press.
 DOI: 10.1093/oso/9780198913146.003.0034

J2.3 Criteria

The SC, s 331 provides:

Sentencing Code

331 Power to make criminal behaviour order

(1) This section applies where—
  (a) a person is convicted of an offence, and
  (b) the prosecution makes an application to the court for a criminal behaviour order to be made against the offender.

(2) The court may make a criminal behaviour order against the offender if it—
  (a) is satisfied that the offender has engaged in behaviour that caused or was likely to cause harassment, alarm or distress to any person, and
  (b) considers that making the order will help in preventing the offender from engaging in such behaviour.

(3) But the court may make a criminal behaviour order only if it—
  (a) does so in addition to dealing with the offender for the offence, and
  (b) does not make an order for an absolute discharge under section 79 in respect of the offence.

(4) Prohibitions and requirements in a criminal behaviour order must, so far as practicable, be such as to avoid—
  (a) any interference with the times, if any, at which the offender normally works or attends school or any other educational establishment, and
  (b) any conflict with the requirements of any other court order to which the offender may be subject.

(5) The prosecution must find out the views of the local youth offending team before applying for a criminal behaviour order to be made if the offender will be under the age of 18 when the application is made.

(6) In this section 'local youth offending team' means the youth offending team in whose area it appears to the prosecution that the offender resides.

J2.4 Length of the order

For an offender under the age of 18 years, the minimum length is one year and the maximum is three years.

The SC, s 334 provides:

Sentencing Code

s 334 Duration of order etc

(1) A criminal behaviour order takes effect on the day it is made, subject to subsection (2).

(2) If on the day a criminal behaviour order ('the new order') is made the offender is subject to another criminal behaviour order ('the previous order'), the new order may be made so as to take effect on the day on which the previous order ceases to have effect.
(3) A criminal behaviour order must specify the period ('the order period') for which it has effect.
(4) In the case of a criminal behaviour order made before the offender has reached the age of 18, the order period must be a fixed period of—
  (a) not less than 1 year, and
  (b) not more than 3 years.
(5) In the case of a criminal behaviour order made after the offender has reached the age of 18, the order period must be—
  (a) a fixed period of not less than 2 years, or
  (b) an indefinite period (so that the order has effect until further order).
(6) A criminal behaviour order may specify periods for which particular prohibitions or requirements have effect.

J2.5 **Procedure**

The court will already have heard evidence in relation to the offence but may also hear evidence which would not have been admissible in criminal proceedings: s 332(2). The court must be satisfied to the criminal standard that the offender has engaged in relevant behaviour: *R (McCann) v Crown Court at Manchester* [2002] UKHL 39; [2003] 1 AC 787.

Evidence of post-application behaviour is admissible both to show whether a person has acted in an anti-social manner and whether an order is necessary: *Birmingham City Council v Dixon* [2009] EWHC 761 (Admin).

That conduct was likely to cause harassment, alarm, or distress does not require evidence that the conduct was actually witnessed as long as there were people in the vicinity (street drug dealing) who were likely to see it, and thereby be caused harassment, alarm, or distress: *R v Hashi* [2014] EWCA Crim 2119.

The High Court in *DPP v Bulmer* [2015] EWHC 2323 (Admin) confirmed that the second requirement, under section 331(2)(b), that the order should help to prevent further harassment, alarm, or distress, is an easier test than that of 'necessity' which applied to applications for anti-social behaviour orders (ASBOs). There is no burden of proof as such; it is an evaluative exercise. However, such orders are not to be lightly imposed. The issue is not one of pure discretion. Whilst the availability of positive requirements is important, their absence does not mean that an order cannot be made. A failure to comply with past orders is a relevant consideration but not of itself a reason for refusing an order; variation of the existing order or imposition of a new one may assist. Any requirement must be proportionate and tailored to the specific circumstances. The ordinary power to arrest may not be sufficient, without an order, for the police to prevent anti-social behaviour in advance.

Many of the principles established in cases concerning ASBOs—*R v Boness* [2005] EWCA Crim 2395, *R v P (Shane Tony)* [2004] EWCA Crim 287, *R v McGrath* [2005] EWCA Crim 353, and *W v Director of Public Prosecutions* [2005] EWCA Civ 1333)—continue to apply to CBOs.

The sentence imposed by the court on conviction will be a relevant consideration.

The court should not make an order where the underlying objective was to give the court higher sentencing powers in the event of future similar offending: *R v Sunderland Youth Court* [2003] EWHC 2385. It is not necessary to make an order not to commit a specified criminal offence if the sentence which could be passed on conviction for the offence should be sufficient deterrence: *R v Boness and others* [2005] EWCA Crim 2395.

J2.6 **Terms of the order**

The terms must be:

- clear and easily understood;
- enforceable;
- commensurate with the seriousness of the offence;
- commensurate with the risk of future conduct; and
- tailor-made to the facts of the case and the circumstances of the offender.

In *R v McGrath* [2005] EWCA Crim 353, an order containing provisions preventing a prolific offender from entering any car park in three counties, from trespassing, and from having in their possession tools or implements capable of being used for breaking into cars was too wide and not justified.

In *R v H, Stevens and Lovegrove* [2006] EWCA Crim 255, an order excluding a young offender from entering an area which included their home was said to be likely to reduce their prospects of successful rehabilitation.

In *T v CPS* [2006] EWHC 728 (Admin), the terms of an order made on a 13-year-old which prevented them from 'acting in an anti-social manner in the City of Manchester' were said to be too vague and lacking in clarity. It was important that the offender would be able understand the terms of the order.

In *R (Cooke) v Director of Public Prosecutions* [2008] EWHC 2703 (Admin), the court held that an order was not appropriate in relation to an offender who, due to mental incapacity, was not able to understand its terms, as such an order would fail to protect the public.

A condition not to cause harassment, alarm, or distress was too imprecise; conditions should be clear as to what behaviour the order was seeking to discourage: *Heron v Plymouth City Council* [2009] EWHC 3562 (Admin).

J2.7 **Review**

An order made in respect of a youth under the age of 18 years must be reviewed by the police on an annual basis: s 337. The statutory guidance indicates that the YOT or other organizations working with the young person should be involved in any review. The review is likely to consider:

- the extent of compliance;
- the adequacy of support available to the offender; and
- any other matters relevant as to whether the order should be varied or discharged.

J2.8 **Reporting restrictions**

The reporting restrictions which automatically apply in the youth court do not apply to the making of a CBO: s 332(8)(a). The court has a discretionary power to impose an order under the CYPA 1933, s 39. The considerations outlined in **H11** will be relevant.

J2.9 **Appeal**

Appeal is to the Crown Court. The Crown Court will consider whether an order will help in preventing the offender from engaging in the behaviour and can also consider the terms of the order.

J2.10 **Breach of CBO**

Breach of a CBO, without a reasonable excuse, is an offence: s 339(1). The maximum sentence in the youth court is a 24-month DTO. On conviction for breach of a CBO, the court cannot impose a conditional discharge: s 339(3).

See *Blackstone's Criminal Practice 2024*.

J3 **Bind Over**

J3.1 **Criteria**

Any person before the court, as defendant or witness (provided that they have given evidence), can be bound over. The court has common law powers to do this of its own motion as a measure of preventive justice where the person's conduct amounts to a breach of the peace involving violence or an imminent threat of violence or that there is a real risk of violence in the future. The violence feared may be from the person being bound over or a third party as a result of their conduct.

The MCA 1980, s 115 provides a magistrates' court with the power to bind over to keep the peace or be of good behaviour following a complaint. This is not a matter assigned to the youth court under the CYPA 1933, s 46 and would therefore be heard in the adult magistrates' court.

A bind over can only be made by consent and the court should give the person who may be subject to the bind over the opportunity to make representations. Refusal to consent can result in committal to prison in the case of an adult but there is no such power for a youth. In *Veater v Glennan* [1981] 2 All ER 307, it was confirmed that there was no sanction to compel a binding over where youths aged 14 and 15 years refused to consent. The order must now be to keep the peace only. A bind over to be of good behaviour has been held to be too imprecise to be enforceable: *Hashman and Harrup v UK* [2000] Crim LR 185. Where a youth consents to enter into a recognizance, the court does have the power to bind them over, despite the court not having the power to imprison the youth, under the MCA 1980, s 115(3), for failure to comply; the remedy for breach is to estreat (forfeit) the recognizance, in whole or in part: *Conlan v Oxford* (1984) 79 Cr App R 157.

J3.2 **Procedure**

Bind overs are now subject to part 31 of the Crim PR. In particular, rr 31.10 and 31.11 apply.

J3.3 **Parental bind over**

See **M4**.

See *Blackstone's Criminal Practice 2024* **E9**.

Blackstone's Handbook of Youths in the Criminal Courts. Mark Ashford, Gareth Branston, and Naomi Redhouse, Oxford University Press.
 DOI: 10.1093/oso/9780198913146.003.0035

J4 Committal for Sentence

Cases involving defendants ged under 18 should ordinarily be sentenced in the youth court but there are a number of provisions which allow committal to the Crown Court for sentence following conviction (whether on a guilty plea or finding of guilt at trial). These are:

- Committal for sentence of a 'grave crime': SC, s 16;
- Committal for sentence of certain terrorist offenders of particular concern: SC, s 16A;
- Committal for sentence of specified offence (dangerous youth offender): SC, s 17;
- Committal because offender is subject to existing Crown Court order;
- Committal for sentence for confiscation procedure: Proceeds of Crime Act 2002 (POCA 2002), s 70.

If a defendant attains 18 before the date of conviction, then the committal powers applicable to adults may apply (see **L6.3**).

J4.1 Committal of grave crime for sentence

Where a person under 18 is convicted of an offence mentioned in the SC, s 249(1)(a) or (b), then, if the court is of the opinion that the offence (or that offence in combination with associated offences) is such that the Crown Court should have power to deal with the offender by imposing a sentence of long-term detention under s 250, the court may commit the defendant to the Crown Court for sentence: SC, s 16(1) and (2).

In *DPP v South Tyneside Youth Court* [2015] EWHC 1455 (Admin), the High Court stated that, when making its allocation decision, the court should ensure, by its clear pronouncement, that the decision to retain a case for trial in the youth court does not prevent it deciding that committal for sentence is necessary if a trial results in a finding of guilt.

Where an offender is committed for sentence under s 16, s 22(2) provides that the Crown Court shall inquire into the circumstances of the case and may deal with the offender in any way in which it could deal with them if they had just been convicted of the offence on indictment before the court.

Where the court sends a youth defendant to the Crown Court for trial, it may also commit them to be dealt with for any related

Blackstone's Handbook of Youths in the Criminal Courts. Mark Ashford, Gareth Branston, and Naomi Redhouse, Oxford University Press.
 DOI: 10.1093/oso/9780198913146.003.0036

offence to which they indicate a guilty plea if the related offence is a 'grave crime' or relevant terrorism offence: SC, s 19(1). If the court commits under s 19(1) but was of the opinion that it also had power to commit the offender under ss 16, 16A, or 17, it must make a statement of that opinion otherwise the Crown Court may be limited to the powers of the magistrates' court in dealing with the offender for that offence if the offender is not also convicted of the offence sent for trial: s 22(2), (4), and (5).

Where the court commits for sentence under s 16, it may also commit the offender to the Crown Court to be dealt with for any other offence with which the committing court has power to deal: s 20(2).

J4.2 Committal of terrorist offender of particular concern for sentence

Where a person under 18 is convicted of an offence mentioned in the SC, s 252A(1)(a), then, if the court is of the opinion that the offence (or that offence in combination with associated offences) is such that the Crown Court should have power to deal with the offender by imposing a sentence of detention under s 252A for a term of more than two years, the court may commit the defendant to the Crown Court for sentence: SC, s 16A(1) and (2).

The offences within s 252A(1)(a) are those contained in part 1 of Sch 13 to the SC.

Where an offender is committed for sentence under s 16A, s 22(2) provides that the Crown Court shall inquire into the circumstances of the case and may deal with the offender in any way in which it could deal with them if they had just been convicted of the offence on indictment before the court.

Where the court sends a youth defendant to the Crown Court for trial, it may also commit them to be dealt with for any related offence to which they indicate a guilty plea if the related offence is a 'grave crime' or relevant terrorism offence: SC, s 19(1). If the court commits under s 19(1) but was of the opinion that it also had power to commit the offender under ss 16, 16A, or 17, it must make a statement of that opinion otherwise the Crown Court may be limited to the powers of the magistrates' court in dealing with the offender for that offence if the offender is not also convicted of the offence sent for trial: s 22(2), (4), and (5).

Where the court commits for sentence under s 16A, it may also commit the offender to the Crown Court to be dealt with for any other offence with which the committing court has power to deal: s 20(2).

J4.3 Committal of dangerous offender for sentence

Where a person aged under 18 is convicted of a specified offence (within the meaning of the SC, s 306) and the court is of the opinion that an extended sentence of detention under s 254 would be available, then the court must commit the offender to the Crown Court for sentence: SC, s 17(1) and (2).

The specified offences are set out in the SC, Sch 18.

The criteria for a sentence under s 254 are met where:

- a person aged under 18 is convicted of a specified offence which is listed (a) in s 249(1) as an offence for which a sentence under s 250 is available, or (b) in s 252A(1)(a) and (b) as an offence for which a sentence under s 252A is available;
- the court considers that there is a significant risk to members of the public of serious harm (death or serious personal injury) occasioned by the commission by the offender of further specified offences;
- the court is not required to impose a sentence of detention for life;
- if the court were to impose an extended sentence of detention, the term that it would specify as the appropriate custodial term would be at least four years.

These criteria are considered in more detail at **K4**.

Where an offender is committed for sentence under s 17, s 22(2) provides that the Crown Court shall inquire into the circumstances of the case and may deal with the offender in any way in which it could deal with them if they had just been convicted of the offence on indictment before the court.

Where the court commits for sentence under s 17, it may also commit the offender to the Crown Court to be dealt with for any other offence with which the committing court has power to deal: s 20(2).

J4.4 Committal where offender already subject to certain Crown Court orders

The youth court or adult magistrates' court has the power to commit a youth defendant to the Crown Court for sentence where they:

- are subject to a conditional discharge imposed by the Crown Court and the new offence was committed during the period of the discharge: SC, Sch 2, para 5(4); or
- are convicted of the new offence whilst subject to YRO imposed by the Crown Court: SC, Sch 7, para 22(2) and (4) (see **K4**).

The Crown Court may have made provision for the youth court to deal with any breaches of the Crown Court order.

When the Crown Court deals with the new offence under either of these provisions, it is limited to the sentencing powers available to the youth court for the new offence.

J4.5 Committal for sentence under the Proceeds of Crime Act 2002, s 70

A youth court or adult magistrates' court has no power to make a confiscation order. Such a court may commit a youth offender to the Crown Court for the purposes of activating the confiscation regime under the POCA 2002. For youth defendants, this is most likely to arise in drug dealing cases. This power exists even where a discharge is considered the proper sentence: *R v Varma* [2012] UKSC 42.

In the event that the prosecution wishes to proceed with confiscation proceedings, the court *must* commit the offender to the Crown Court for sentence.

Proceeds of Crime Act 2002

70 Committal by magistrates' court

(1) This section applies if—
- (a) a defendant is convicted of an offence by a magistrates' court, and
- (b) the prosecutor asks the court to commit the defendant to the Crown Court with a view to a confiscation order being considered under section 6.

(2) In such a case the magistrates' court—
- (a) must commit the defendant to the Crown Court in respect of the offence, and
- (b) may commit him to the Crown Court in respect of any other offence falling within subsection (3).

(3) An offence falls within this subsection if—
- (a) the defendant has been convicted of it by the magistrates' court or any other court, and
- (b) the magistrates' court has power to deal with him in respect of it.

(4) If a committal is made under this section in respect of an offence or offences—
- (a) section 6 applies accordingly, and

(b) the committal operates as a committal of the defendant to be dealt with by the Crown Court in accordance with section 71.

(5) If a committal is made under this section in respect of an offence for which (apart from this section) the magistrates' court could have committed the defendant for sentence under section 14(2) of the Sentencing Code (offences triable either way) or under section 16(2) or 16A(2) of that Code (committal of child or young person) the court must state whether it would have done so.

(6) A committal under this section may be in custody or on bail.

When committal for sentence is under s 70, the Crown Court must enquire into the circumstances of the case and may deal with the youth defendant in any way in which the youth court could deal with them if it had just convicted them of the offence (s 71(3)), unless the offence is one which the lower court said it would have committed for sentence under the SC, ss 16(2) or 16A(2), in which case the Crown Court may deal with that offence as if the defendant had just been convicted of the offence on indictment before it: s 71(2).

J5 Detention and Training Order

J5.1 Introduction

The DTO is the primary custodial sentence that can be imposed in the youth court (the other being the special sentence of detention for terrorist offenders of particular concern). It is also available in the Crown Court.

The order may be imposed on a defendant who has attained the age of 12 by the date of conviction but, in the case of an offender under the age of 15, the court must determine that they are a persistent offender before an order can be imposed.

Pursuant to the SC, s 226, a DTO cannot be imposed by a youth court or a Crown Court if the offender is not legally represented unless the youth offender has refused to apply for legal aid or the legal aid has been withdrawn as a result of their conduct. An offender is only deemed to be legally represented for the purposes of s 226 if they have a solicitor or barrister to represent them in the court at some time after they are found guilty and before they are sentenced.

The SC, ss 233 to 235 provide:

Sentencing Code

233 Detention and training order

A detention and training order in respect of an offender is an order that the offender is subject, for the term specified in the order, to a period of detention and training followed by a period of supervision.

234 Detention and training order: availability

(1) A detention and training order is available where a court is dealing with an offender for an offence if—
 (a) the offender is aged under 18, but at least 12, when convicted,
 (b) the offence is an imprisonable offence, and
 (c) the court is not required to pass—
  (i) a sentence of detention under section 250 (see section 249(2)),
  (ia) a sentence of detention under section 252A, or
  (ii) a sentence of detention during Her Majesty's pleasure under section 259.

(2) For circumstances in which the court is required to impose a detention and training order, see—
 (a) section 312 (minimum sentence for offences of threatening with weapon or bladed article);

Blackstone's Handbook of Youths in the Criminal Courts. Mark Ashford, Gareth Branston, and Naomi Redhouse, Oxford University Press.
 DOI: 10.1093/oso/9780198913146.003.0037

(b) section 315 (minimum sentence for repeat offence involving weapon or corrosive substance or bladed article).

235 Exercise of power to make a detention and training order

(1) This section applies where a detention and training order is available.
(2) The court may not make a detention and training order if it imposes—
   (a) a sentence of detention under section 250, or
   (b) an extended sentence of detention under section 254, in respect of the offence.
(3) If the offender is aged under 15 when convicted the court may not make a detention and training order unless it is of the opinion that the offender is a persistent offender.
(4) The court's power to make a detention and training order is subject to (in particular) section 230 (threshold for imposing discretionary custodial sentence).

The relevant age is the offender's age when convicted. Where an offender attains 18 between the date of conviction and the date of sentence, the appropriate custodial sentence to impose remains a DTO rather than detention in a YOI. For the position where the offender attains 18 before conviction see **L6.5**.

J5.2 **Custody threshold**

Where a mandatory sentence is not applicable, the SC, s 230 provides:

Sentencing Code

230 Threshold for imposing discretionary custodial sentence

(1) Subsection (2) applies where a person is convicted of an offence which is punishable with a custodial sentence . . .
(2) The court must not pass a custodial sentence unless it is of the opinion that—
   (a) the offence, or
   (b) the combination of the offence and one or more offences associated with it,

   was so serious that neither a fine alone nor a community sentence can be justified for the offence . . .

A written pre-sentence report must be considered before a DTO can be imposed on an offender aged under 18: SC, ss 30 and 230(7). See **J16.2**.

The *Sentencing Children and Young People – Overarching Principles* definitive guideline considers the custody threshold when sentencing young offenders. In summary the guidance suggests the following general principles:

- a custodial sentence must be imposed only as a 'measure of last resort' (para 6.42);
- for a first-time offender who has pleaded guilty to an imprisonable offence, in most circumstances a referral order will be the most appropriate sentence (para 6.19);
- a custodial sentence is most likely to be unavoidable where it is necessary to protect the public from serious harm (para 6.44);
- even where the threshold is crossed, a court is not required to impose a custodial sentence (para 6.42).

The guideline also states:

> 6.42 If a custodial sentence is imposed, a court must state its reasons for being satisfied that the offence is so serious that no other sanction would be appropriate and, in particular, why a YRO with intensive supervision and surveillance or fostering could not be justified.

The court should also consider the effect of custody on children and young people:

> 6.49 The welfare of the child or young person must be considered when imposing any sentence but is especially important when a custodial sentence is being considered. A custodial sentence could have a significant effect on the prospects and opportunities of the child or young person and a child or young person is likely to be more susceptible than an adult to the contaminating influences that can be expected within a custodial setting. There is a high reconviction rate for children and young people that have had custodial sentences and there have been many studies profiling the effect on vulnerable children and young people, particularly the risk of self harm and suicide and so it is of utmost importance that custody is a last resort.

J5.2.1 *Persistent offender*

In the case of offenders aged 12 to 14 at the time of conviction, a DTO may only be imposed if the custody threshold is met and the court deems the offender to be a persistent offender (SC, s 235(3)). There is no statutory definition of a 'persistent offender'. A court may take into account not only convictions but also cautions: *R v B* [2001] Cr App R (S) 113. The *Sentencing Children and Young People – Overarching Principles* definitive guideline considers the meaning of 'persistent offender':

> 6.5 The term persistent offender is not defined in statute but has been considered by the Court of Appeal. In general it is expected that the child or young person would have had previous contact with authority as a result of criminal behaviour. This includes previous findings of guilt as well as admissions of guilt such as restorative justice disposals and conditional cautions.
>
> 6.6 A child or young person who has committed one previous offence cannot reasonably be classed as a persistent offender, and a child

or young person who has committed two or more previous offences should not necessarily be assumed to be one. To determine if the behaviour is persistent the nature of the previous offences and the lapse of time between the offences would need to be considered.

6.7 If there have been three findings of guilt in the past 12 months for imprisonable offences of a comparable nature (or the child or young person has been made the subject of orders as detailed above in relation to an imprisonable offence) then the court could certainly justify classing the child or young person as a persistent offender.

6.8 When a child or young person is being sentenced in a single appearance for a series of separate, comparable offences committed over a short space of time then the court could justifiably consider the child or young person to be a persistent offender, despite the fact that there may be no previous findings of guilt. In these cases the court should consider whether the child or young person has had prior opportunity to address their offending behaviour before imposing one of the optional sentences available for persistent offenders only; if the court determines that the child or young person has not had an opportunity to address their behaviour and believes that an alternative sentence has a reasonable prospect of preventing re-offending then this alternative sentence should be imposed.

6.9 The court may also wish to consider any evidence of a reduction in the level of offending when taking into account previous offending behaviour. Children and young people may be unlikely to desist from committing crime in a clear cut manner but there may be changes in patterns of criminal behaviour (e.g. committing fewer and/or less serious offences or there being longer lengths of time between offences) that indicate that the child or young person is attempting to desist from crime.

6.10 Even where a child or young person is found to be a persistent offender, a court is not obliged to impose one of the optional sentences. The approach should still be individualistic and all other considerations still apply. **Custodial sentences must be a last resort for all children and young people** and there is an expectation that they will be particularly rare for children and young people aged 14 or under.

In *R v Ghafoor* [2002] EWCA Crim 1857, [2003] 1 Cr App R (S) 428, it was held that, where an offender crosses a significant age threshold between the date of the commission of the offence and the date of conviction, the starting point for determining the sentence is the sentence that they would have been likely to receive if they had been sentenced at the date of the offence (see **J1.2**). The Court of Appeal has held that the *Ghafoor* principle means that a DTO should not be imposed on a youth offender who was 14 on the date of the offence but 15 on the date of conviction if they could not be deemed to be a persistent offender at the time of the offence: *R v LM* [2002] EWCA Crim 3047, [2003] 2 Cr App

R (S) 26, and *R v NH* [2004] EWCA 2674. The contrary view was taken by the Court of Appeal in *R v Jahmarl* [2004] EWCA Crim 2199, [2005] 1 Cr App R (S) 96. The appeal concerned an offence of robbery for which the court had decided that 12 months' long-term detention (then under the PCCSA 2000, s 91) could properly be imposed. Having received advice that the regime under a DTO would be more appropriate for the 15-year-old appellant, the court considered that a DTO should be imposed rather than a period of s 91 detention. It is arguable that this decision is based on its particular facts and in any event has no application to cases where long-term detention is not a sentencing option.

J5.2.2 *Length of order*

The SC, s 236 provides:

Sentencing Code

236 Term of detention and training order

(1) The term of a detention and training order made in respect of an offence (whether by a magistrates' court or otherwise) must be at least 4 months but must not exceed 24 months.
This is subject to subsection (2)

(2) The term of a detention and training order in respect of an offence may not exceed—
  (a) in the case of a summary offence, the maximum sentence of imprisonment that court be imposed (in the case of an offender aged 21 or over) for the offence;
  (b) in the case of any other offence, the maximum term of imprisonment that the Crown Court could impose (in the case of an offender aged 21 or over) for the offence.

(3) Section 231 (length of discretionary custodial sentences: general provision) in particular, applies in determining the term of a detention and training order.

(4) A detention and training order takes effect at the beginning of the day on which it is made, unless the court orders otherwise under section 237.

The minimum order applies to each offence not the aggregate sentence: *R v Ganley* [2001] 1 Cr App R (S) 60. The minimum term therefore creates a much higher custody threshold for young offenders than that applicable to adult offenders. As the maximum custodial sentence for an adult is a term of three months' imprisonment, a youth convicted of criminal damage to the value of less than £5,000 is not liable to a custodial sentence in the youth court: *Pye v Leeds Youth Court* [2006] EWHC 2527 (Admin).

The same principle also applies to (amongst others) the following offences:

- being found on enclosed premises (Vagrancy Act 1824, s 4—three months);
- motor vehicle interference (Criminal Attempts Act 1981, s 9—three months);
- obstructing a police officer (Police Act 1996, s 89(2)—one month);
- refusing to give COZART drugs sample (PACE 1984, s 63C—one month).

J5.2.3 *Consecutive orders*

A court may impose consecutive DTOs, though it may not make consecutive orders which would result in total DTOs exceeding 24 months. The SC, ss 237 and 238(1) provide:

Sentencing Code

237 Making of order where offender subject to other order or sentence of detention

(1) This section applies where a court make a detention and training order.

(2) The court may order that the term of the detention and training order is to take effect on the expiry of any other detention and training order which it imposes on the same occasion.
This is subject to section 238(1).

(3) If the offender—
(a) is subject to another relevant detention and training order ('the existing order'), and
(b) has not at any time been released for supervision under the existing order,
the court may order that the detention and training order is to take effect on the expiry of the existing order.
This is subject to section 238(1).

(4) If the offender—
(a) is subject to a relevant sentence of detention (see section 248), and
(b) has not at any time been released under Chapter 6 of Part 12 of the Criminal Justice Act 2003 (release on licence of fixed-term prisoners),
the court may order that the detention and training order is to take effect at the time when the offender would otherwise be released under that Chapter.

(5) . . .

(6) If the offender is subject to a further period of detention imposed—
(a) under paragraph 3(2)(a) of Schedule 12 (breach of supervision requirement of existing detention and training order), . . .

> the court may order that the detention and training order is to take effect at the end of the further period of detention.
>
> **238 Offender subject to more than one order: maximum overall term**
>
> (1) A court may not make a detention and training order as a result of which the offender would be subject to relevant detention and training orders for a term exceeding 24 months.

A court imposing DTOs for imprisonable summary offences is restricted by the MCA 1980, s 133 and cannot impose a series of consecutive DTOs amounting in aggregate to more than six months: *R(B) v Leeds Crown Court* [2016] EWHC 1230 (Admin).

J5.2.4 *Minimum sentences of detention*

The following offences require the court to impose, on a defendant aged 16 or 17 at the date of conviction, the relevant minimum sentence of a four-month DTO unless the court is of the opinion that there are exceptional circumstances which relate to the offence or the offender and which justify it not doing so. (If the court is dealing with a qualifying offence that took place before 28 June 2022, the test is whether there are particular circumstances which would make the minimum sentence unjust.)

- Threatening with an offensive weapon/bladed article: SC, s 312.
- Possessing an offensive weapon/bladed article/corrosive substance in a public place (second offence): SC, s 315.
- Possessing an offensive weapon/bladed article on school premises (second offence): SC, s 315.

The minimum sentence only applies where the offender is aged 16 or over at the date of the qualifying offence (age at the time of an earlier relevant offence does not matter). Such an offender is, however, entitled to full credit for a guilty plea, which means that they are entitled to a non-custodial sentence where appropriate: SC, s 73(5).

See E2.

J5.3 Remand to detention or to qualifying curfew

Time remanded to youth detention now automatically counts as time served on a DTO: CJA 2003, s 240ZA. Similarly, time spent on bail subject to a qualifying curfew counts towards time served (though the credit period has to be declared by the court): CJA 2003, s 240A, SC, s 325.

However, remand to local authority accommodation, even where an electronically monitored curfew of at least nine hours is imposed, does not automatically count towards time served on a DTO. It is open to the sentencing court to take such time into account, should it wish to, but there is no legal requirement to do so: *R v Secretary of State for the Home Office ex parte A (a juvenile)* [2000] UKHL 4, [2000] 2 AC 276.

J5.4 **Taking account of a guilty plea**

In determining the sentence to pass on an offender who has pleaded guilty, a court must take into account the stage in the proceedings at which the offender indicated their intention to plead guilty and the circumstances in which the indication was made: SC, s 73(1) and (2). Detailed guidance on the amount of the discount and the limited grounds for refusing to give a discount is contained in section five of the *Sentencing Children and Young People – Overarching Principles* definitive guideline.

Previous appeal decisions have established the following principles:

- where an offender has pleaded guilty to an offence and long-term detention (now under the SC, s 250) is not a sentencing option, the court should not impose the maximum 24-month DTO unless there are proper grounds for withholding a discount for an offender's plea: *R v Kelly* [2001] EWCA 1030, *R v March* [2002] EWCA Crim 551;
- where the offence is a grave crime and the option of long-term detention exists, a maximum 24-month DTO may be imposed after a guilty plea if the sentencing judge decides, in light of the guilty plea, not to impose a sentence of long-term detention: *R v Fieldhouse and Watts* [2001] 1 Cr App R (S) 104.

These principles will now apply in the youth court in the case of a grave crime where the offender indicated a guilty plea prior to allocation being determined. The discount for pleading guilty could lead to the court choosing not to exercise the power to commit for sentence under the SC, s 16 (for which see **J4.1**). Where a committal for sentence is not an option, credit for a guilty plea should normally result in a discount from the 24-month maximum.

Where the court is dealing with two or more offences in circumstances where consecutive sentences are justified, the guilty plea discount should result in a reduction of the aggregate sentence from the 24-month maximum: *R v Dunkley* [2012] EWCA Crim 619).

J5.5 Interaction with other custodial sentences

Sentencing Code

244 Offender subject concurrently to detention and training order and sentence of detention in a young offender institution

(1) This section applies where an offender is subject concurrently—
(a) to a relevant detention and training order (see section 248), and
(b) to a sentence of detention in a young offender institution,
at least one of which is imposed in respect of an offence of which the offender was convicted on or after 1 December 2020.

(2) The offender is to be treated for the purposes of the following provisions as if subject only to the sentence of detention in a young offender institution—
(a) sections 241 to 243 and Schedule 12 (periods of detention and training and supervision, breach of supervision requirements and further offences);
(b) section 271 (detention in a young offender institution: place of detention);
(c) with the exception of sections 240ZA and 240A, Chapter 6 of Part 12 of the Criminal Justice Act 2003 (release, licences, supervision and recall).
This is subject to subsection (3).

(3) Nothing in subsection (2) requires the offender to be released in respect of either the order or the sentence unless and until the offender is required to be released in respect of each of them.

(4) In subsection (1), 'sentence of detention in a young offender institution' includes any sentence of detention in a young offender institution, whether imposed under this Code or otherwise.

(5) Subsection (2) has effect in relation to an order or sentence imposed in respect of an offence of which the offender was convicted before 1 December 2020 as if the provisions referred to in paragraphs (a) to (c) included the provisions referred to in section 106(4) of the Powers of Criminal Courts (Sentencing) Act 2000 (interaction of detention and training orders with sentences of detention in a young offender institution).

245 Offender subject concurrently to detention and training order and other sentence of detention

(1) This section applies where an offender is subject concurrently to—
(a) a relevant detention and training order, and
(b) a relevant sentence of detention,
at least one of which is imposed in respect of an offence of which the offender was convicted on or after 1 December 2020.
(See section 248 for the meaning of 'relevant detention and training order' and 'relevant sentence of detention'.)

(2) The offender is to be treated as if subject only to the relevant sentence of detention for the purposes of the following provisions—
(a) sections 241 to 243 and Schedule 12 (periods of detention and training and supervision, breach of supervision requirements and further offences);

(b) section 260 and section 261 (place of detention);
(c) Chapter 6 of Part 12 of the Criminal Justice Act 2003 (release and supervision following release);
(d) section 210 of the Armed Forces Act 2006 (place of detention etc);
(e) section 214 of the Armed Forces Act 2006 (offences committed during a detention and training order under that Act).

This is subject to subsection (3).

(3) Nothing in subsection (2) requires the offender to be released in respect of either the order or the sentence unless and until the offender is required to be released in respect of each of them.

(4) Subsection (2) has effect in relation to a relevant detention and training order or relevant sentence of detention that is imposed in respect of an offence of which the offender was convicted before 1 December 2020 as if the provisions referred to in paragraphs (a) to (e) included the provisions referred to in section 106A(8) of the Powers of Criminal Courts (Sentencing) Act 2000.

J5.6 Placement and release from detention

The SC, s 241 provides:

Sentencing Code

241 The period of detention and training

(1) An offender must serve the period of detention and training under a detention and training order in such youth detention accommodation as may be determined by the Secretary of State.

Release at half-way point

(2) Subject to subsections (3) to (5), the period of detention and training under a detention and training order is half of the term of the order.

Early release on compassionate grounds

(3) The Secretary of State may release the offender at any time if satisfied that exceptional circumstances exist which justify the offender's release on compassionate grounds.

Release before half-way point

(4) The Secretary of State may release the offender—
(a) in the case of an order for a term of—
(i) 8 months or more, but
(ii) less than 18 months,

at any time during the period of 1 month ending with the half-way point of the term of the order, and
(b) in the case of an order for a term of 18 months or more, at any time during the period of 2 months ending with that point.

Release after half-way point

(5) If a youth court so orders on an application made by the Secretary of State for the purpose, the Secretary of State must release the offender—
   (a) in the case of an order for a term of—
      (i) 8 months or more, but
      (ii) less than 18 months,
   1 month after the half-way point of the term of the order, and
   (b) in the case of an order for a term of 18 months or more, 1 month or 2 months after that point.

Consecutive detention and training order and sentence of detention

(5A) Where the offender is also subject to a sentence of any of the following kinds that is to take effect, by virtue of an order to which subsection (7) applies, when the offender would otherwise be released for supervision—
   (a) a sentence of detention under section 250 or 252A,
   (b) a sentence of detention under section 209 or 224A of the Armed Forces Act 2006, or
   (c) an extended sentence of detention under section 254 (including one passed as a result of section 221A of the Armed Forces Act 2006), subsection (4) is to be read as if, instead of conferring a power to release the offender, it conferred a power to determine that the Secretary of State would, but for the sentence concerned, have released the offender.

(6) Where—
   (a) the court makes an order under subsection (5), and
   (b) the offender is also subject to a sentence of any of the following kinds that is to take effect, by virtue of an order to which subsection (7) applies, when the offender would otherwise be released for supervision—
      (i) a sentence of detention under section 250,
      (ia) a sentence of detention under section 252A,
      (ii) a sentence of detention under section 209 of the Armed Forces Act 2006, or
      (iii) an extended sentence of detention under section 254 (including one passed as a result of section 221A of the Armed Forces Act 2006),
   the order under subsection (5) must be expressed as an order that the period of detention and training attributable to the detention and training order is to end at the time determined under that subsection.

(7) This subsection applies to orders under the following provisions (which provide for sentences of detention to take effect when an offender is released for supervision under a detention and training order)—
   (a) section 253(2) (offender under 18: sentence of detention to take effect on release for supervision under detention and training order),
   (b) section 257(2) (offender under 18: extended sentence of detention), or
   (c) any corresponding provision relating to an order under section 209 of, or made as a result of section 221A of, the Armed Forces Act 2006.

Detention to be legal custody

(8) An offender detained under a detention and training order is deemed to be in legal custody.

The choice of placement is not made by the court but by the Youth Custody Service Placement team. The YOT is required to forward details of the young offender, highlighting any disability or other reason to consider them exceptionally vulnerable. Details of how to contact the Youth Custody Service Placement team and the placement procedure are available at: *https://www.gov.uk/guidance/youth-custody-service-placement-team#sending-documents*

There is a presumption in favour of detainees being granted early release under s 241(4). All trainees released early under that provision will be subject to an electronically monitored curfew from the date of early release until the halfway point of the order: The Ministry of Justice policy framework for early and late release for DTOs (2022) is available at: *https://assets.publishing.service.gov.uk/government/uploads/system/uploads/attachment_data/file/1100450/early-and-late-release-for-DTOs-PF.pdf*

J5.7 Supervision after release

No matter the length of the order, the young offender will be subject to supervision upon release for the remainder of the order.

The SC, s 242 provides:

Sentencing Code

242 The period of supervision

(1) The period of supervision of an offender who is subject to a detention and training order—
 (a) begins when the offender is released for supervision (whether at the half-way point of the term of the order or otherwise), and
 (b) ends when the term of the order ends.

(2) During the period of supervision, the offender—
 (a) is to be under the supervision of—
  (i) an officer of a provider of probation services, or
  (ii) a member of a youth offending team, and
 (b) may be required to comply with particular requirements.

(3) Any such requirements, and the category of person to supervise the offender, are to be determined from time to time by the Secretary of State.

(4) The offender must be notified by the Secretary of State of—
 (a) the category of person responsible for the offender's supervision, and
 (b) any requirements with which the offender must comply.

(5) A notice under subsection (4) must be given to the offender—
  (a) before the period of supervision begins, and
  (b) before any change in the matters mentioned in that subsection.
(6) Where the supervision is to be provided by an officer of a provider of probation services, the officer must be an officer acting in the local justice area within which the offender resides for the time being.
(7) Where the supervision is to be provided by a member of a youth offending team, the member must be a member of a youth offending team established by the local authority in whose area the offender resides for the time being.

J5.8 Breach of supervision requirements

Unlike for adult offenders, enforcement action is not carried out administratively by notifying the Ministry of Justice of any breach of the requirements; instead the young offender must be taken back to court. Enforcement is by a youth court whatever court passed the original sentence or whatever the age of the offender at the time of the breach proceedings.

The SC, s 243(a) and Sch 12 provide:

Sentencing Code

243 Breach of supervision requirement and further offences during order

Schedule 12 makes provision about—
(a) breach of supervision requirements imposed under a detention and training order etc . . .

Schedule 12 – DETENTION AND TRAINING ORDER: BREACH OF SUPERVISION REQUIREMENTS AND FURTHER OFFENCES

1 Interpretation

In this Schedule—
'breach', in relation to a supervision requirement, means a failure to comply with it, and related expressions are to be read accordingly;
'supervision requirement' means a requirement with which an offender must comply under—
  (a) section 242(4)(b), or
  (b) paragraph 4(4)(b);
'further detention order' means an order under paragraph 3(2)(a);
'further supervision order' means an order under paragraph 3(2)(b).

2 Breach of supervision requirement: issue of summons or warrant by justice of the peace

(1) Sub-paragraph (2) applies where—
  (a) a detention and training order, or a further supervision order, is in force in respect of an offender, and

(b) it appears on information to a justice of the peace that the offender has breached any of the supervision requirements imposed under the order.

(2) The justice—

(a) may issue a summons requiring the offender to appear at the place and time specified in the summons, or

(b) if the information is in writing and on oath, may issue a warrant for the offender's arrest.

(3) Any summons or warrant issued under this paragraph must direct the offender to appear or be brought—

(a) before a youth court acting for the local justice area in which the offender resides, or

(b) if it is not known where the offender resides, before a youth court acting for same local justice area as the justice who issued the summons or warrant.

3 Power of youth court to deal with offender for breach of supervision requirement

(1) Sub-paragraph (2) applies if it is proved to the satisfaction of the youth court before which an offender appears or is brought under paragraph 2 that the offender has breached a supervision requirement imposed under a relevant order.

(2) The court may—

(a) order the offender to be detained for such period, not exceeding the maximum period found under sub-paragraph (3), as the court may specify,

(b) order the offender to be subject to such period of supervision, not exceeding the maximum period found under sub-paragraph (3), as the court may specify, or

(c) impose on the offender a fine not exceeding level 3 on the standard scale.

(3) The maximum period referred to in sub-paragraph (2)(a) and (b) is the shorter of—

(a) 3 months, and

(b) the period between—

(i) the date of the offender's breach, and

(ii) the last day of the term of the relevant order.

(4) For the purposes of sub-paragraph (3), a breach that is found to have occurred—

(a) over 2 or more days, or

(b) at some time during a period of 2 or more days, is to be taken to have occurred on the first of those days.

(5) A court may make an order under sub-paragraph (2) before or after the end of the term of the relevant order.

(6) A period of detention or supervision ordered under sub-paragraph (2)—

(a) begins with the day on which the order is made, and

(b) may overlap to any extent with the period of supervision under the relevant order.

This is subject to paragraph 5(1) (further detention order made where offender detained under other detention and training order).

(7) An offender detained under a further detention order is deemed to be in legal custody.

(8) Detention under a further detention order is—

(a) if the offender has reached the age of 21, to be in prison,

(b) otherwise, to be in such youth detention accommodation as the Secretary of State may determine.

(9) Where—

(a) the offender is aged under 18, and

(b) but for this sub-paragraph, the court would impose a fine on the offender under sub-paragraph (2)(c),

section 380 (order for payment by parent or guardian) applies to the fine.

(10) A fine imposed under sub-paragraph (2)(c) is to be treated, for the purposes of any enactment, as being a sum adjudged to be paid by a conviction.

(11) An offender may appeal to the Crown Court against any order made under sub-paragraph (2).

(12) In this paragraph—

(a) 'relevant order' means—

(i) a detention and training order, or

(ii) a further supervision order;

(b) any reference to the term of a relevant order is—

(i) in the case of a detention and training order, to the term of the order, and

(ii) In the case of a further supervision order, to the period of supervision imposed by the order.

4 Supervision where order made under paragraph 3(2)(b)

(1) This paragraph applies where an offender is subject to a period of supervision by virtue of a further supervision order.

(2) During that period of supervision, the offender—

(a) is to be under the supervision of—

(i) an officer of a provider of probation services, or

(ii) a member of a youth offending team, and

(b) may be required to comply with particular requirements.

(3) Any such requirements, and the category of person to supervise the offender, are to be determined from time to time by the Secretary of State.

(4) The offender must be notified by the Secretary of State of—

(a) the category of person responsible for the offender's supervision, and

(b) any requirements with which the offender must comply.

(5) A notice under sub-paragraph (4) must be given to the offender—

(a) as soon as reasonably practicable after the further supervision order is made, and

(b) before any change in the matters mentioned in that sub-paragraph.

(6) Where the supervision is to be provided by an officer of a provider of probation services, that officer must be an officer acting in the local justice area within which the offender resides for the time being.

> (7) Where the supervision is to be provided by a member of a youth offending team, the member must be a member of a youth offending team established by the local authority in whose area the offender resides for the time being.

The law and procedure of proceedings for breach of the supervision requirements was considered in *S v Doncaster Youth Offending Team* [2003] EWHC 1128 (Admin), (2003) 167 JP 381. In his judgment, Scott Baker LJ gave the following guidance:

- Where several DTOs are made on the same occasion, they are to be treated as a single term and therefore the information laid to institute breach proceedings should only allege breach of one order.
- Failing to attend four separate supervision appointments is a manifestation of the offender's failure to keep in touch with their supervising officer and it would be entirely artificial to split this up into four quite separate offences.
- Breach of quite separate licence conditions (e.g. failing to keep in touch with the supervisor and failure to live at the address approved by the supervisor) should not be the subject of the same information.
- Proof of service upon the young offender of the supervision requirements is required. Proof by inference is sufficient but, for the future, it seems desirable that, when an offender is given notice, they should be asked to sign a copy so that there can be no dispute that they have been given it.
- Where a failure is alleged of a requirement to comply with a specific order, such as to live at a specified address or attend on a specified occasion, the person who gave the order should, if it is disputed, be at court to give evidence about it.

Paragraphs 5 and 6 of Sch 12 make detailed provision for the interaction between a period of further detention with other DTOs and other custodial sentences.

J5.9 **Offence during currency of the order**

When a young offender commits an offence whilst still subject to a DTO supervision, the court dealing with the new offence has a power to recall the young offender.

The SC, s 243(b) and Sch 12 provide:

Sentencing Code

243 Breach of supervision requirement and further offences during order

Schedule 12 makes provision about—

...

(b) offences committed during the term of a detention and training order.

Schedule 12 – DETENTION AND TRAINING ORDER: BREACH OF SUPERVISION REQUIREMENTS AND FURTHER OFFENCES

7 Offence after release for supervision or during further supervision period

(1) This paragraph applies where an offender commits an imprisonable offence ('the new offence')—
   (a) after having been released for supervision under a detention and training order but before the date on which the term of the order ends, or
   (b) during a period of supervision under a further supervision order.

(2) The court which deals with the offender for the new offence may order the offender to be detained for all or part of the period mentioned in sub-paragraph (3).

(3) That period is the period which—
   (a) begins with the date of the order under sub-paragraph (2), and (b) is equal in length to the period between—
      (i) the date on which the new offence was committed, and
      (ii) the date on which the term of the detention and training order, or the period of supervision, mentioned in sub-paragraph (1) ends.

(4) A court may make an order under sub-paragraph (2) whether or not it passes any other sentence on the offender.

(5) Detention under sub-paragraph (2) is to be in such youth detention accommodation as the Secretary of State may determine.

(6) The period for which an offender is ordered under sub-paragraph (2) to be detained—
   (a) must, as the court may direct—
      (i) be served before and be followed by, or
      (ii) be served concurrently with,
   any sentence imposed for the new offence, and
   (b) in either case, is to be disregarded in determining the appropriate length of that sentence.

(7) Where the new offence is found to have been committed—
   (a) over a period of 2 or more days, or
   (b) at some time during a period of 2 or more days,
   it is be taken for the purposes of this paragraph to have been committed on the last of those days.

(8) A person detained under an order under sub-paragraph (2) is deemed to be in legal custody.

J6 Discharges (Absolute and Conditional)

J6.1 Criteria

By ss 79 and 80 of the SC, where an offender is convicted of an offence (not being an offence where the sentence is fixed by law or subject to a mandatory minimum sentence) and the court is of the opinion, having regard to the circumstances including the nature of the offence and the character of the offender, that it is inexpedient to inflict punishment, the court may make an order either:

- discharging them absolutely; or
- discharging them subject to the condition that they commit no offence during such period, not exceeding three years from the date of the order, as may be specified in the order.

J6.2 Combining discharge with other sentences or orders

A discharge may be combined with the following orders:

- Order to pay prosecution costs;
- Compensation order;
- Deprivation order;
- Restitution order;
- Unlawful profit order; and
- Any disqualification: SC, ss 79(7) and 80(7).

J6.3 Restrictions on use of conditional discharge

An order for a conditional discharge is not available in the following circumstances:

- Where a person who has received two or more youth cautions is convicted of an offence committed within two years beginning with the date of the last of those cautions (unless there are exceptional circumstances): CDA 1998, s 66ZB(5)(a) and (6);
- Where a person who has received a youth conditional caution followed by a youth caution is convicted of an offence committed within two years beginning with the date of the youth caution (unless there are exceptional circumstances): CDA 1998, s 66ZB(5)(b) and (6);

Blackstone's Handbook of Youths in the Criminal Courts. Mark Ashford, Gareth Branston, and Naomi Redhouse, Oxford University Press.
 DOI: 10.1093/oso/9780198913146.003.0038

- For breach of a sexual harm prevention order (SHPO) (or interim SHPO), whether on conviction or complaint: SOA 2003, s 103I(4); SC, s 354(5);
- For breach of a CBO: SC, s 339(3).

J6.4 Effect of a discharge

By the SC, s 82, a conviction for an offence for which the offender is discharged either absolutely or conditionally shall be deemed not to be a conviction for any purpose other than the purpose of the proceedings in which the order is made and for any subsequent proceedings for breach of a conditional discharge.

J6.5 Breach of a conditional discharge

The SC, s 81 and Sch 2 provide that, if a person commits an offence during the life of a conditional discharge, they may be re-sentenced for that original offence, even if the period of discharge has expired at the date of sentence. The offender will be sentenced with reference to their age at the date of sentence, not the date of the previous offence, and can be sentenced in any way as if they had just been convicted of the offence: s 402. If the conditional discharge was imposed by the Crown Court, the offender can be committed to that court for re-sentence.

There is no requirement to re-sentence and a court can sentence for a new offence and leave the conditional discharge in place if it sees fit to do so.

See *Blackstone's Criminal Practice 2024.*

J7 **Financial Order Enforcement**

J7.1 **Payment**

Where a court has ordered financial penalties against the offender, it will enforce the order against them. The court will, depending on the age of the offender, consider making the financial penalties the responsibility of the parent or guardian (for which see **M3**).

J7.2 **Enforcement**

- The CYPA 1933, s 46 assigns charges against children and young persons to the youth court. It does not deal with enforcement of financial penalties. As the orders were made as part of the proceedings in the youth court, there is an argument that it is that court which should deal with subsequent enforcement.
- Welfare issues are relevant.
- Where payment is not made as ordered at the sentencing hearing, a warrant with or without bail may be issued.

J7.3 **Powers of the court**

The court may deal with a fine defaulter in the following ways:

- Conduct a means enquiry: MCA 1980, s 86(1);
- Allow further time to pay: MCA 1980, s 85A;
- Remit of all or part of the fine: MCA 1980, s 85; SC, s 127;
- Make an attachment of earnings order: Courts Act 2003, Sch 5;
- Make a money payment supervision order: MCA 1980, s 88;
- Make an attendance centre order: PCCSA 2000, s 60;
- Make a youth default order: CJIA 2008, s 39 (not yet in force);
- Order parents to pay or to enter into a recognizance to ensure that the youth pays: MCA 1980, s 81.

There is no power to make a fines collection order, a deduction from benefit order, or to order time in custody in default of payment for an offender under the age of 18.

J7.4 **Attendance centre order**

An attendance centre order may be made where the court would have power to impose imprisonment in default of payment but for the restriction in the SC, s 227 on imposing imprisonment for those aged under 21.

Blackstone's Handbook of Youths in the Criminal Courts. Mark Ashford, Gareth Branston, and Naomi Redhouse, Oxford University Press.
 DOI: 10.1093/oso/9780198913146.003.0039

- Where the offender is aged under 14 years, the maximum length of the order is 12 hours.
- Where the offender is aged 14 or 15 years, the order may be for 12 to 24 hours.
- Where the offender is aged 16 years or over, the order may be for 12 to 36 hours.

The financial penalty will be reduced or considered paid in proportion to the number of hours completed.

The court must conduct a full investigation into the financial circumstances of the defaulter in their presence before making an attendance centre order: MCA 1980, s 81(3).

J8 Fines

J8.1 Criteria

The explanatory materials to the *Magistrates' Courts Sentencing Guidelines* set out the approach to fines in relation to **adult** offenders. There is no specific guidance in relation to youths.

J8.2 Power to fine

The SC, s 123 provides that the maximum fine in the magistrates' court for a youth depends on age:

Aged 10–13 years inclusive	£250
Aged 14–17 years inclusive	£1,000

There is no limit where a youth defendant is convicted on indictment in the Crown Court.

A fine must not exceed the statutory limit. Where this is expressed in terms of a 'level', the maximum fines for adults are:

Level 1	£200
Level 2	£500
Level 3	£1,000
Level 4	£2,500
Level 5	Unlimited

Where the maximum fine for an adult is less than the limit for a youth, the adult maximum will apply.

There is no statutory limit on the amount of fine which may be imposed in the Crown Court.

If the court orders costs to be paid by a youth defendant alongside a fine, the amount of the costs must not exceed the amount of the fine: Prosecution of Offences Act 1985, s 18(5).

J8.3 Assessment of fines

- The amount of a fine must reflect the seriousness of the offence.
- Account should be taken of any guilty plea.
- The court must take into account the financial circumstances of the offender.

Blackstone's Handbook of Youths in the Criminal Courts. Mark Ashford, Gareth Branston, and Naomi Redhouse, Oxford University Press.
 DOI: 10.1093/oso/9780198913146.003.0040

- Normally a fine should be of an amount that is capable of being paid within 12 months.
- Priority should be given to payment of compensation and surcharge.

J8.4 Assessment of financial circumstances

The court may require a defendant to provide details of their financial circumstances. Most youth defendants are unlikely to have income aside from money provided by their parents or guardians. It is important to establish whether any weekly allowance includes travel to school or college and any lunch money whilst there. In the case of young defendants who live independently, their benefits will be taken into account.

J8.5 Surcharge

See **J23**.

J8.6 Payment

The payment in full of any financial order is due on the day it is made. The court will ordinarily consider allowing time to pay. It will set payment terms allowing payment in full within a specified period or payment by instalments. The court will determine whether parents or guardians should be ordered to make payment (for which see **M3**).

See *Blackstone's Criminal Practice 2024* **E5**.

J9 Hospital and Guardianship Orders

A youth court or a Crown Court may impose a hospital order or guardianship order upon a youth defendant when the requirements of the MHA 1983, s 37 are satisfied.

Mental Health Act 1983

37 Powers of courts to order hospital admission or guardianship

(1) Where a person is convicted before the Crown Court of an offence punishable with imprisonment other than an offence the sentence for which is fixed by law, or is convicted by a magistrates' court of an offence punishable on summary conviction with imprisonment, and the conditions mentioned in subsection (2) below are satisfied, the court may by order authorise his admission to and detention in such hospital as may be specified in the order or, as the case may be, place him under the guardianship of a local social services authority or of such other person approved by a local social services authority as may be so specified.

(1A) In the case of an offence the sentence for which would otherwise fall to be imposed under section 258, 258A, 268A, 273, 274, 274A, 282A, 283, 285 or 285A of the Sentencing Code or under Chapter 7 of Part 10 of that Code, nothing in those provisions shall prevent a court from making an order under subsection (1) above for the admission of the offender to a hospital.

(1B) For the purposes of subsection (1A) above—

- (a) a sentence falls to be imposed under section 258 or 258A of the Sentencing Code if the court is obliged by that section to pass a sentence of detention for life under section 250 of that Code;
- (aa) a sentence falls to be imposed under section 268A or 282A of that Code if it is required by section 268B(2) or 282B(2) of that Code and the court is not of the opinion there mentioned;
- (b) a sentence falls to be imposed under section 273, 274 or 274A of that Code if the court is obliged by that section to pass a sentence of custody for life;
- (c) a sentence falls to be imposed under section 283, 285 or 285A of that Code if the court is obliged by that section to pass a sentence of imprisonment for life;
- (d) a sentence falls to be imposed under Chapter 7 of Part 10 of that Code if it is required by section 311(2), 312(2A), 313(2A), 314(2A) or 315(2A) of that Code and the court is not of the opinion there mentioned.

(2) The conditions referred to in subsection (1) above are that—

- (a) the court is satisfied, on the written or oral evidence of two registered medical practitioners, that the offender is suffering from mental disorder and that either—

Blackstone's Handbook of Youths in the Criminal Courts. Mark Ashford, Gareth Branston, and Naomi Redhouse, Oxford University Press.
 DOI: 10.1093/oso/9780198913146.003.0041

(i) the mental disorder from which the offender is suffering is of a nature or degree which makes it appropriate for him to be detained in a hospital for medical treatment and appropriate medical treatment is available for him; or
(ii) in the case of an offender who has attained the age of 16 years, the mental disorder is of a nature or degree which warrants his reception into guardianship under this Act; and
(b) the court is of the opinion, having regard to all the circumstances including the nature of the offence and the character and antecedents of the offender, and to the other available methods of dealing with him, that the most suitable method of disposing of the case is by means of an order under this section.

(3) Where a person is charged before a magistrates' court with any act or omission as an offence and the court would have power, on convicting him of that offence, to make an order under subsection (1) above in his case, then, if the court is satisfied that the accused did the act or made the omission charged, the court may, if it thinks fit, make such an order without convicting him.

(4) An order for the admission of an offender to a hospital (in this Act referred to as 'a hospital order') shall not be made under this section unless the court is satisfied on the written or oral evidence of the approved clinician who would have overall responsibility for his case or of some other person representing the managers of the hospital that arrangements have been made for his admission to that hospital, and for his admission to it within the period of 28 days beginning with the date of the making of such an order; and the court may, pending his admission within that period, given such directions as it thinks fit for his conveyance to and detention in a place of safety.

(5) If within the said period of 28 days it appears to the Secretary of State that by reason of an emergency or other special circumstances it is not practicable for the patient to be received into the hospital specified in the order, he may give directions for the admission of the patient to such other hospital as appears to be appropriate instead of the hospital so specified; and where such directions are given—
(a) the Secretary of State shall cause the person having the custody of the patient to be informed, and
(b) the hospital order shall have effect as if the hospital specified in the directions were substituted for the hospital specified in the order.

(6) An order placing an offender under the guardianship of a local social services authority or of any other person (in this Act referred to as 'a guardianship order') shall not be made under this section unless the court is satisfied that that authority or person is willing to receive the offender into guardianship.

(7) . . .

(8) Where an order is made under this section, the court shall not—
(a) pass sentence of imprisonment or impose a fine or make a community order (within the meaning given by section 200 of the Sentencing Code) or a youth rehabilitation order (within the

meaning given by section 173 of that Code) in respect of the offence,

(b) if the order under this section is a hospital order, make a referral order (within the meaning given by section 83 of that Code) in respect of the offence, or

(c) make in respect of the offender an order under section 376 of that Code (binding over of parent or guardian),

but the court may make any other order which it has power to make apart from this section; and for the purposes of this subsection 'sentence of imprisonment' includes any sentence or order for detention.

For the definition of mentally disordered see **J10.1**.

While a hospital order may be made upon conviction, under s 37(3) a hospital order may also be imposed without a formal conviction. A youth court is a magistrates' court for the purposes of s 37(3): *R (P) v Barking Youth Court* [2002] EWHC 734 (Admin), [2002] 2 Cr App R 294. For the use of this provision where the court considers that the youth defendant is unable to participate effectively in the proceedings see **I2.3**.

J9.1 Restriction order

A restriction order is a hospital order where the court orders that the offender's release shall be subject to special restrictions. It may only be made if it appears to the court, having regard to the nature of the offence, the antecedents of the offender, and the risk of their committing further offences if set at large, that it is necessary for the protection of the public from serious harm from them: MHA 1983, s 41.

A restriction order may only be made by the Crown Court. An offender who has attained the age of 14 may be committed to the Crown Court for such an order to be considered. This power to commit is exercisable by a youth court.

Mental Health Act 1983

43 Power of magistrates' courts to commit for restriction order

(1) If in the case of a person of or over the age of 14 years who is convicted by a magistrates' court of an offence punishable on summary conviction with imprisonment—

(a) the conditions which under section 37(1) above are required to be satisfied for the making of a hospital order are satisfied in respect of the offender; but

(b) it appears to the court, having regard to the nature of the offence, the antecedents of the offender and the risk of his committing further offences if set at large, that if a hospital order is made a restriction order should also be made,

the court may, instead of making a hospital order or dealing with him in any other manner, commit him in custody to the Crown Court to be dealt with in respect of the offence.

(2) Where an offender is committed to the Crown Court under this section, the Crown Court shall inquire into the circumstances of the case and may—

(a) if that court would have power so to do under the foregoing provisions of this Part of this Act upon the conviction of the offender before that court of such an offence as is described in section 37(1) above, make a hospital order in his case, with or without a restriction order;

(b) if the court does not make such an order, deal with the offender in any other manner in which the magistrates' court might have dealt with him . . .

J9.2 **Obtaining reports**

Rule 3.10 of the Crim PR provides for directions for commissioning medical reports, other than for sentencing purposes. Rule 25.10 applies where a defendant in the Crown Court may not be fit to be tried. Rule 28.8 provides for directions for commissioning medical reports in any court for the purpose of sentencing or other disposal.

See **J10** (Mentally Disordered Offenders).

J10 Mentally Disordered Offenders

J10.1 Definition of mentally disordered

The MHA 1983, s 1 provides:

Mental Health Act 1983

1 Application of Act: 'mental disorder'

(1) The provisions of this Act shall have effect with respect to the reception, care and treatment of mentally disordered patients, the management of their property and other related matters.

(2) In this Act—
'mental disorder' means any disorder or disability of the mind; and 'mentally disordered' shall be construed accordingly;
. . .

(2A) But a person with learning disability shall not be considered by reason of that disability to be—
(a) suffering from mental disorder for the purposes of the provisions mentioned in subsection (2B) below; or
(b) requiring treatment in hospital for mental disorder for the purposes of sections 17E and 50 to 53 below,
unless that disability is associated with abnormally aggressive or seriously irresponsible conduct on his part.

(2B) The provisions are—
(a) sections 3, 7, 17A, 20 and 20A below;
(b) sections 35 to 38, 45A, 47, 48 and 51 below; and
(c) section 72(1)(b) and (c) and (4) below.

(3) Dependence on alcohol or drugs is not considered to be a disorder or disability of the mind for the purposes of subsection (2) above.

(4) In subsection (2A) above, 'learning disability' means a state of arrested or incomplete development of the mind which includes significant impairment of intelligence and social functioning.

J10.2 Restrictions on imposing a custodial sentence

The SC, s 232 provides:

Sentencing Code

232 Additional requirements in case of offender suffering from mental disorder

(1) This section applies where—
(a) the offender is or appears to be suffering from a mental disorder, and

Blackstone's Handbook of Youths in the Criminal Courts. Mark Ashford, Gareth Branston, and Naomi Redhouse, Oxford University Press.
 DOI: 10.1093/oso/9780198913146.003.0042

(b) the court passes a custodial sentence other than one fixed by law ('the sentence').

(2) Before passing the sentence, the court must obtain and consider a medical report unless, in the circumstances of the case, it considers that it is unnecessary to obtain a medical report.

(3) Before passing the sentence, the court must consider—
(a) any information before it which relates to the offender's mental condition (whether given in a medical report, a pre-sentence report or otherwise), and
(b) the likely effect of such a sentence on that condition and on any treatment which may be available for it.

(4) If the court did not obtain a medical report where required to do so by this section, the sentence is not invalidated by the fact that it did not do so.

(5) Any court, on an appeal against the sentence, must—
(a) obtain a medical report if none was obtained by the court below, and
(b) consider any such report obtained by it or by that court.

(6) In this section—
'medical report' means a report as to an offender's mental condition made or submitted orally or in writing by a registered medical practitioner who is approved for the purposes of section 12 of the Mental Health Act 1983—
(a) by the Secretary of State, or
(b) by another person by virtue of section 12ZA or 12ZB of that Act, as having special experience in the diagnosis or treatment of mental disorder;
'mental disorder' has the same meaning as in the Mental Health Act 1983.

(7) Nothing in this section is to be taken to limit—
(a) the pre-sentence report requirements (see section 30), or
(b) any requirement for a court to take into account all information that is available to it about the circumstances of any offence, including any aggravating or mitigating factors.

J10.3 **Guidance for sentence**

The Sentencing Council's definitive guideline, *Sentencing Offenders with Mental Disorders, Developmental Disorders or Neurological Impairments,* applies only to offenders aged 18 or older. Guidance on these issues for youth defendants can be found in *R v PS* [2019] EWCA Crim 2286; [2020] 2 Cr App R (S) 9.

Mental health conditions and disorders might be relevant to sentencing in a number of ways:

- A consideration of the impact of a mental health condition or disorder at the time of the offence might be relevant to the assessment of the defendant's culpability in committing the crime, whether by impairing their ability to exercise appropriate judgment, to make rational choices, to understand the consequences of their actions, or causing them to behave in a disinhibited way.

- The defendant's mental health at the time of sentence might be relevant to the decision about the type of sentence imposed and, where a custodial sentence is necessary, the length of that sentence. The court should also have regard to any additional impact of a custodial sentence on the offender because of their mental health and to any personal mitigation to which their mental health is relevant.
- Mental health conditions and disorders might be relevant to an assessment of whether the defendant is dangerous.
- They might need to be taken into account in ensuring that the effect of the sentence is understood by the defendant and in ensuring that the requirements of a community order or ancillary order are capable of being fulfilled by them.

There must be a close focus on the offender's mental health (both at time of offence and at time of sentence). The impact of mental health on culpability may vary from little impact to significantly reduced. The ability to cope with a particular type of sentence will also vary amongst offenders with mental health difficulties. The impact on sentencing outcome will depend on all the circumstances.

Where a serious offence has been committed by a child or young person, both the court and those representing them must be alert to the possibility that mental health may be a relevant feature of the case. The younger the offender, and the more serious the offence, the more likely the need for expert reports.

The *Sentencing Children and Young People – Overarching Principles* definitive guideline reminds the court (at para 1.12) that, as part of its duty to have regard to the welfare of the young offender, the court should ensure that it is alert to any mental health problems or learning difficulties/disabilities.

J10.4 **Possible disposals**

If there are concerns regarding the mental health of a youth offender, the following disposals may be available:

- YRO with mental health treatment requirement (see **J24.5.12**);
- guardianship order (see **J9**); or
- hospital order (see **J9**).

J11 Previous Convictions

J11.1 Criteria

The SC, s 65 provides:

Sentencing Code

65 Previous convictions

(1) This section applies where a court is considering the seriousness of an offence ('the current offence') committed by an offender who has one or more relevant previous convictions.

(2) The court must treat as an aggravating factor each relevant previous conviction that it considers can reasonably be so treated, having regard in particular to—

(a) the nature of the offence to which the relevant previous conviction relates and its relevance to the current offence, and

(b) the time that has elapsed since the relevant previous conviction.

(3) Where the court treats a relevant previous conviction as an aggravating factor under subsection (2) it must state in open court that the offence is so aggravated.

(4) In subsections (1) to (3) 'relevant previous conviction' means—

(a) a previous conviction by a court in the United Kingdom, or

(b) . . .

(c) a previous conviction of a service offence (see subsection (5)) . . .

. . .

Whilst a court is required to find the seriousness of an offence aggravated by one or more previous convictions, a sentence that follows re-offending does not need to be more severe than the previous sentence solely because there has been a previous conviction.

The absence of previous convictions may affect the sentencing powers of the court. (See **J12**.)

See *Blackstone's Criminal Practice 2024*.

Blackstone's Handbook of Youths in the Criminal Courts. Mark Ashford, Gareth Branston, and Naomi Redhouse, Oxford University Press.
 DOI: 10.1093/oso/9780198913146.003.0043

J12 Referral Order

J12.1 *Referral order*

A referral order is an order which requires an offender to attend each of the meetings of a youth offender panel established for the offender by a YOT and by virtue of which the offender is required to comply, for a particular period, with a programme of behaviour to be agreed between the offender and the panel: SC, s 83(1). A referral order is the primary sentence for first-time offenders under the age of 18 who plead guilty. The order is unique in the criminal justice system in that the sentencing court determines the length of the referral but the requirements of the order are subsequently determined by a youth offender panel convened by the YOT.

There is no requirement to consider a pre-sentence report before imposing a referral order.

J12.1.1 *Availability of a referral order*

The SC, s 84(1) provides that a referral order is available where:

- the court is a youth court or other magistrates' court,
- the offender is aged under 18 when convicted,
- the offence does not attract a sentence fixed by law,
- the court is not proposing to impose a custodial sentence or make a hospital order,
- the court is not proposing to order an absolute or conditional discharge, and
- the offender pleaded guilty.

Though a referral order may only be made by a youth court or other magistrates' court, it is available to a Crown Court judge if that judge remits the defendant back to the youth court for sentence (pursuant to the SC, s 25(2)) and then exercises the power to sit as a District Judge (Magistrates' Courts) (pursuant to the Courts Act 2003, s 66) and sits as a youth court: *R v S* [2021] EWCA Crim 960; [2023] 1 Cr App R (S) 33.

The referral order conditions set out below apply where a court is dealing with a person aged under 18 at the date of conviction. The conditions still apply where the court adjourns the case and the offender attains 18 before the sentence date.

Blackstone's Handbook of Youths in the Criminal Courts. Mark Ashford, Gareth Branston, and Naomi Redhouse, Oxford University Press.
 DOI: 10.1093/oso/9780198913146.003.0044

Compulsory referral order conditions—By the SC, s 85(1)(a) and (2), a court **must** make a referral order if:

- the offence is an imprisonable offence,
- the offender pleaded guilty to the offence and to any connected offence, and
- the youth defendant has not previously been convicted of any offence.

The compulsory referral order conditions can lead to a difficult sentencing exercise as the court has a limited choice of sentence, often having to make a stark choice between custody and a referral order.

A Crown Court judge is not bound to remit a youth defendant to the youth court even where the compulsory referral order conditions would be satisfied: *R v Y* [2023] EWCA Crim 977.

Discretionary referral order conditions—By the SC, s 85(1)(b), where the compulsory referral order conditions are not met, the court maintains a power to make a referral order, as long as the conditions in s 84(1) are met. A referral order is not available unless there has been a guilty plea.

An offence is connected with another offence if the offender is to be dealt with for both offences at the same time (whether or not they are convicted of the offences at the same time or by or before the same court): s 108(1).

Sentencing Code

84 Referral order: availability

(1) A referral order is available to a court dealing with an offender for an offence where—
   (a) the court is a youth court or other magistrates' court,
   (b) the offender is aged under 18 when convicted,
   (c) neither the offence nor any connected offence is an offence the sentence for which is fixed by law,
   (d) the court is not proposing to—
      (i) impose a custodial sentence, or
      (ii) make a hospital order (within the meaning of the Mental Health Act 1983),
   in respect of the offence or any connected offence,
   (e) the court is not proposing to make—
      (i) an order for absolute discharge, or
      (ii) an order for conditional discharge, in respect of the offence, and
   (f) the offender pleaded guilty to the offence or to any connected offence.

(2) But a referral order is not available unless the court has been notified by the Secretary of State that arrangements for the implementation of referral orders are available in the area in which it appears to the

court that the offender resides or will reside (and the notice has not been withdrawn).

85 Duty and power to make referral order

(1) Where a referral order is available—
  (a) the court must make a referral order if the compulsory referral conditions are met;
  (b) otherwise, the court may make a referral order.

(2) The compulsory referral conditions are met where—
  (a) the offence is an imprisonable offence,
  (b) the offender pleaded guilty to the offence and to any connected offence, and
  (c) the offender has never been—
    (i) convicted by or before a court in the United Kingdom of any offence other than the offence and any connected offence.
    (ii) . . .

(3) For the effect of making a referral order on the court's other sentencing powers, see section 89.

J12.2 Length of referral order

The court must specify the length of the referral order: s 86(1)(b). A referral order may be for a period not less than three nor more than12 months: s 86(2). The *Sentencing Children and Young People – Overarching Principles* definitive guideline, at para 6.22, suggests the following bands:

Offence seriousness	Length of referral
Low	3–5 months
Medium	5–7 months
High	7–9 months
Very High	10–12 months

Because a referral order is only available on a guilty plea, there should be no discount given for such a plea.

The order does not start on the day of sentence but instead on the date when the youth offender contract is signed: s 97(2). The order ends when that contract is successfully completed: s 97(5).

J12.3 Custody threshold cases and intensive referral orders

Before a custodial sentence can be considered, the court will have to order a pre-sentence report: SC, ss 30(3) and 230(7).

The sentencing guideline states at paras 6.19–6.21:

6.19 A referral order is the mandatory sentence in a youth court or magistrates' court for most children and young people who have committed an offence for the first time and have pleaded guilty to an imprisonable offence. Exceptions are for offences where a sentence is fixed by law or if the court deems a custodial sentence, an absolute or conditional discharge or a hospital order to be more appropriate.

6.20 A discretionary referral order can also be imposed for any offence where there has been a plea of guilty regardless of previous offending history. It should be remembered that they are not community orders and in general terms may be regarded as orders which fall between community disposals and fines. However, bearing in mind that the principal aim of the youth justice system is to prevent children and young people offending, second or subsequent referral orders should be considered in those cases where

1. the offence is not serious enough for a YRO but the child or young person does appear to require some intervention OR
2. the offence is serious enough for a YRO but it is felt that a referral order would be the best way to prevent further offending (as an example, this may be because the child or young person has responded well in the past to such an order and the offence now before the court is dissimilar to that for which a referral order was previously imposed).

Referral orders are the main sentence for delivering restorative justice and all panel members are trained Restorative Conference Facilitators; as such they can be an effective sentence in encouraging children and young people to take responsibility for their actions and understand the effect their offence may have had on their victim.

6.21 In cases where children or young people have offended for the first time and have pleaded guilty to committing an offence which is on the cusp of the custody threshold, YOTs should be encouraged to convene a Youth Offender Panel prior to sentence (sometimes referred to as a 'pseudo-panel' or 'pre-panel') where the child or young person is asked to attend before a panel and agree an intensive contract. If that contract is placed before the sentencing youth court, the court can then decide whether it is sufficient to move below custody on this occasion. The proposed contract is not something the court can alter in any way; the court will still have to make a decision between referral order and custody but can do so on the basis that if it makes a referral order it can have confidence in what that will entail in the particular case.

J12.4 Mixing referral orders with other referral orders and other sentences (SC, ss 87–89)

A court may impose a later referral order on an offender who is subject to an earlier referral order and may direct that the later order is not to take effect until the earlier order is revoked or discharged: s 87(1).

Where a court makes referral orders in respect of two or more connected offences, the referral orders have the effect of referring the offender to a single youth offender panel: s 88(1) and (2). The court can make these referral orders consecutive or concurrent but the total period must not exceed 12 months: s 88(4) and (5).

When making a referral order, the court may make an order for an absolute discharge for a connected offence: s 88(2).

When imposing a referral order, the court may not, for that offence or a connected offence:

- order the offender to pay a fine;
- make a YRO;
- make an order for conditional discharge: s 89(3);
- bind over the offender to keep the peace or to be of good behaviour, or
- bind over a parent or guardian: s 89(4).

When making a referral order, a court may still be able to make the following:

- a compensation order;
- a restitution order;
- a deprivation order; and
- a parenting order.

J12.5 Procedural requirements (Sentencing Code, s 86)

A referral order must:

- specify the YOT which is to establish a youth offending panel for the offender;
- specify the period for which the youth offender contract is to have effect: s 86(1).

The YOT specified must be the team having the function of implementing referral orders in the area in which it appears to the court that the offender resides or will reside: s 86(3).

On making a referral order, the court must explain to the offender in ordinary language the effect of the order and the consequences of failure to agree a contract or breach of the requirements of such a contract: s 86(4).

J12.6 Ordering attendance of parent/guardian at panel meetings

The SC, s 90 provides:

Sentencing Code

90 Order requiring parents etc to attend meetings

(1) This section applies where a court makes a referral order.

(2) The court—

(a) may make an order requiring—

(i) the appropriate person, or

(ii) if there are two or more appropriate persons, one or more of them, to attend the meetings of the youth offender panel, and

(b) must do so if the offender is aged under 16 when the referral order is made.

(3) If the offender is—

(a) a looked-after child, and

(b) aged under 16 when the referral order is made,

the person or persons required under subsection (2) to attend those meetings must include at least one representative of the responsible authority.

(4) But an order under subsection (2) must not require a person to attend those meetings—

(a) if the court is satisfied that it would be unreasonable to do so, or

(b) to an extent which the court is satisfied would be unreasonable.

(5) For the purposes of this section, each of the following is an appropriate person in relation to an offender—

(a) if the offender is a looked-after child—

(i) a representative of the responsible authority, and

(ii) each person who is a parent or guardian of the offender with whom the offender is allowed to live;

(b) otherwise, each person who is a parent or guardian of the offender.

(6) In this section—

'looked-after child' means a child who is (within the meaning of the Children Act 1989 or the Social Services and Well-being (Wales) Act 2014 (anaw 4)) looked after by a local authority, and

'responsible authority', in relation to a looked-after child, means the authority by which the child is looked after.

(7) The court must forthwith send a copy of an order under subsection (2)—

(a) to each person required by the order to attend meetings of the panel, and

(b) to any responsible authority whose representative is required by the order to attend meetings of the panel,

unless the person was present, or the authority was represented, in court when the order was made.

J12.7 Establishing a youth offender panel (SC, s 91)

It is the duty of the specified YOT to establish a youth offender panel for the offender, which will be constituted and will discharge its functions in accordance with guidance issued by the Secretary of State. At each of its meetings, the panel shall consist of at least one representative of the YOT and two other panel members who are not members of the team.

The specified YOT must notify the offender and any appropriate parent/guardian required to attend of the time and place at which they are required to attend the meeting: s 92(2).

The panel may also allow the following to attend:

- a person over 18 chosen by the offender;
- a person who is capable of having a good influence on the offender; and
- a victim of the offence (accompanied to the meeting by one person chosen by the victim with the agreement of the panel): s 94.

If the offender fails to attend any part of a meeting the panel may:

- adjourn the meeting to such place and time as it may specify; or
- end the meeting and refer the offender back to court: s 92(3).

J12.8 Youth offender contract (Sentencing Code, ss 96, 97, Sch 3)

At the first meeting of the panel, the members of the panel shall seek to reach agreement with the offender on a programme of behaviour. The aim of this programme is the prevention of re-offending by the offender: s 96(1) and (2).

The programme may, in particular, include requiring the offender to:

- make financial or other reparation to any victim;
- attend mediation sessions with any victim;
- carry out unpaid work or service in or for the community;
- be at home at times specified in or determined under the programme;

- attend at a school or other educational establishment or a place of work;
- participate in specified activities designed to address the offending behaviour, offering education/training or assisting with drug/alcohol rehabilitation;
- meet specified persons at times and places specified in or determined under the programme;
- stay away from specified places;
- stay away from specified persons: Sch 3, paras 2 and 4.

The programme may include provision for the offender's compliance with the programme to be supervised and recorded: para 3.

The programme may not, however, provide for:

- electronic monitoring of the offender's whereabouts; or
- any physical restriction on the offender's movements: para 5.

No term which provides for anything to be done to or with any victim may be included in the programme without the consent of the victim: para 6.

When a programme has been agreed, it should be confirmed in writing and signed by a representative of the panel and the young offender. This written record becomes the youth offender contract: s 96(4) and (5). The contract starts on the day it is signed and lasts for the length of the compliance period specified by the court (unless revoked earlier): s 97.

J12.9 Progress meetings (Sentencing Code, ss 99–100)

At any time after a youth offender contract has taken effect and before the expiry of the period for which the contract has effect, the specified YOT must arrange a further meeting of the youth offender panel if the panel requests it: s 99(2).

A progress meeting may be requested if it appears to the panel to be expedient to review:

- the offender's progress in implementing the programme of behaviour contained in the contract; or
- any other matter arising in connection with the contract: s 99(3).

The panel must request the YOT to arrange a progress meeting if:

- the offender has notified the panel that they wish the contract to be varied;
- the offender has notified the panel that they wish to be referred back to court for the order to be revoked because of a significant change in circumstances which makes compliance impractical;

- it appears to the panel that the offender is in breach of the contract: s 99(4)–(6).

At the progress meeting, the panel will review progress, discuss any apparent breach, consider any proposed variation, and consider any request to be referred back to court, as appropriate: s 100(2).

J12.10 Final meeting (Sentencing Code, s 101)

Where the compliance period of a youth offender contract is due to expire, the specified YOT must arrange a final meeting of the panel: s 101(1) and (2).

At the final meeting the panel must:

- review the extent of the offender's compliance with the contract;
- decide whether or not the offender's compliance with the contract justifies the conclusion that the offender will have satisfactorily completed the contract by the end of the compliance period; and
- give the offender written confirmation of its decision: s 101(3).

A decision that the offender will have satisfactorily completed the contract has the effect of discharging the referral order (or orders) as from the end of the compliance period. That decision can be made in the offender's absence: s 101(4).

J12.11 Further conviction while referral order in force

When a young offender under the age of 18 is convicted of an offence whilst subject to a referral order:

(i) A youth court or other magistrates' court may sentence for the new offence by extending the compliance period of the referral order (up to a maximum order of 12 months);
(ii) Any court may:
  - make an order for absolute or conditional discharge for the new offence;
  - sentence for the new offence and revoke the referral order without re-sentencing;
  - sentence for the new offence, revoke the referral order, and re-sentence for the offence in respect of which the revoked order was made (but assuming that a referral order is not available).

There is no statutory requirement that the offender has pleaded guilty to the new offence before the court can consider extending the compliance period.

The detailed statutory provisions relating to the powers of the court on a further conviction are set out in the SC, Sch 4, Part 2.

Sentencing Code

104 Offender referred back to court or convicted while subject to referral order

In Schedule 4 –

...

(b) Part 2 makes provision for what is to happen when an offender is convicted of further offences while subject to a referral order.

SCHEDULE 4 – PART 2

FURTHER CONVICTIONS DURING REFERRAL

14 Introductory

This Part of this Schedule applies where—

(a) a referral order has been made in respect of an offender and has not been discharged or revoked,
(b) the offender is aged under 18, and
(c) a court is dealing with the offender for an offence ('the new offence').

15 Power of magistrates' court to deal with further offence by extending compliance period

(1) This paragraph applies if the court dealing with the offender for the new offence is a youth court or other magistrates' court.
(2) An order under this paragraph is available in respect of the new offence if neither the new offence nor any offence connected with it is one the sentence for which is fixed by law.
(3) The court may sentence the offender for the new offence by making an order extending the length of the compliance period, but not to more than 12 months.

16 Supplementary

(1) This paragraph applies where a court makes an order under paragraph 15 in respect of the new offence.
(2) The court must not deal with the offender for the new offence, or any offence connected with it, by making an order of the kind mentioned in section 89(3) (orders not available where court makes referral order).
(3) In respect of any offence connected with the new offence, the court must make—
    (a) an order under paragraph 15, or
    (b) an order for absolute discharge.

17 Further convictions: power of any court to revoke referral orders

(1) This paragraph applies where, in dealing with the offender for the new offence, the court makes an order other than—
    (a) an order under paragraph 15, or
    (b) an order for absolute discharge or an order for conditional discharge.
(2) If it appears to the court to be in the interests of justice to do so, the court—
    (a) may revoke the referral order (or any one or more of the referral orders), and

(b) if it revokes a referral order, may re-sentence the offender for the offence in respect of which the revoked order was made (but assuming that a referral order is not available).

(3) Revocation of a referral order under sub-paragraph (2) has the effect of revoking any related order under paragraph 9(2), 12 or 15 (extension of compliance period).

(4) When re-sentencing the offender under sub-paragraph (2)(b), if a youth offender contract has taken effect between the offender and the panel, the court must take into account the extent of the offender's compliance with the contract.

(5) For the purposes of this paragraph it does not matter whether the new offence was committed before or after the offender was referred to the panel.

J12.12 **Referral back to court**

The youth offender panel may refer the young offender back to the appropriate court for one of four main reasons: These are:

- for breach of the requirements of the order;
- for early revocation;
- to extend the contract period; and
- for revocation for change in circumstances (at offender's request).

The panel will send a report to the appropriate court explaining why the offender is being referred back to court: Sch 4, para 2. The appropriate court may then issue a summons or warrant to bring the offender before it: para 3.

The appropriate court is a youth court, if the offender is still under 18 at the time of referral back, or a magistrates' court if they are 18 or over: s 108.

J12.12.1 ***Referral back for breach of order***

A youth offending panel may refer an offender back to the appropriate court if:

- the offender fails to attend any part of a panel meeting: s 92(3);
- it appears that there is no prospect of reaching an agreement with the offender on an appropriate programme of behaviour within a reasonable period after the making of the referral order: s 98(3);
- the offender unreasonably refuses to sign a contract which has been agreed at a meeting: s 98(4);
- the panel considers that the offender is in breach of the youth offender contract: s 100(3);
- the offender unreasonably refuses to sign an amended contract: s 100(6); or

- the panel considers that the offender's compliance does not justify the conclusion that they have successfully completed the contract: s 101(5).

Where the court is satisfied that the panel have appropriately referred the matter back to court the court has power to:

- take no action, allowing the order to continue;
- revoke the referral order(s); or
- revoke the referral order(s) and re-sentence for the original offence(s): Sch 4, para 7(1)–(4).

In re-sentencing the offender, the court must take into account the circumstances of the referral and the extent of the offender's compliance with the contract (if one has taken effect): para 7(5).

If a referral order is to be revoked, the offender must be before the appropriate court. The power to revoke (and re-sentence) is not affected by the expiry of the compliance period: para 7(6).

If the referral back is for failure to attend any part of a panel meeting (s 92(3)), for breach of contract (s 100(3)), or for not completing the contract (s 101(5)), then as long as the offender is before it, the appropriate court may instead of revoking the referral order:

- extend the compliance period up to 12 months (but not if it has already expired), or
- fine the offender up to £2,500: para 9.

J12.12.2 *Referral back for early revocation for good progress etc.*

A youth offending panel may refer the offender back to court where it appears to be in the interests of justice for the referral order(s) to be revoked: s 102(1) and (2). In making this decision, the panel must have regard to circumstances which have arisen since the contract took effect, which may include the offender's making good progress under the contract: s 102(3).

In referring back to court, the panel will request the appropriate court:

- to revoke the referral order (or each of the referral orders); or
- to revoke the referral order(s) and re-sentence the offender for the offence in respect of which the revoked order was made: s 102(2).

If the court is satisfied of the youth offender panel's decision as to referral back to court, the court may:

- revoke the referral order(s);
- revoke the referral order(s) and re-sentence the offender for the offence (assuming that a referral order is not available): Sch 4, para 7(2) and (4).

If re-sentencing, the court shall have regard to the circumstances of the offender's referral back to the court and the extent of their compliance with the contract: para 7(5).

Where the panel refers back to court under s 102 and the appropriate court decides not to revoke the order, the panel may not make a further referral for early revocation within three months of the court's decision: s 102(4).

J12.12.3 *Referral back to extend period of order*

A youth offending panel may refer the offender back to court where a referral order with a compliance period less than 12 months has not yet been completed but, having regard to the circumstances since the contract took effect, the panel considers that it is in the interests of justice for the length of the compliance period to be extended: s 103(1). The panel may request the court to extend the length of the compliance period for up to three months: s 103(2), (3).

If it appears to the appropriate court that it would be in the interests of justice to do so, the court may extend the length of the compliance period but not by more than three months and not to more than 12 months in total. The court must take into account the extent of the offender's compliance with the contract: Sch 4, para 12.

J12.12.4 *Revocation of the referral order at request of young offender*

The offender may notify the panel that they wish to be referred back to court with a view to the referral order(s) being revoked on account of a significant change in the offender's circumstances (such as being taken to live abroad) which makes compliance with the contract impractical. If the panel receives such notification, it must request the specified YOT to arrange a progress meeting: s 99(4) and (5).

Having discussed the request with the offender at a progress meeting, if the panel is satisfied that there is (or is soon to be) a significant change in circumstances which make compliance with the contract impractical, the panel may refer the offender back to court: s 100(8).

If the court is satisfied of the youth offender panel's decision as to referral back to court, the court may:

- revoke the referral order(s);
- revoke the referral order(s) and re-sentence the offender for the offence (assuming that a referral order is not available): Sch 4, para 7(2) and (4).

There is no provision for the young offender to apply directly to the court for the order to be revoked.

Sentencing Code

104 Offender referred back to court or convicted while subject to referral order

In Schedule 4—

(a) Part 1 makes provision for what is to happen when a youth offender panel refers an offender back to court . . .

SCHEDULE 4 – PART 1

REFERRAL BACK TO COURT FOR FURTHER PROCEEDINGS

Introductory

1

This Part of this Schedule applies where a youth offender panel refers an offender back to court under Chapter 1 of Part 6 (referral orders).

Mode of referral back to court

2

To make the referral, the panel must send a report to the appropriate court explaining why the offender is being referred back to court.

Bringing the offender before the court

3

(1) Where the appropriate court receives a report under paragraph 2, the court must cause the offender to appear before it.

(2) For that purpose, a justice acting in the same local justice area as the appropriate court may—
   (a) issue a summons requiring the offender to appear before the appropriate court at the place and time specified in the summons, or
   (b) if the report is substantiated on oath, issue a warrant for the offender's arrest which requires the offender to be brought before the appropriate court.

Detention and remand of arrested offender

4

(1) This paragraph applies where an offender—
   (a) is arrested under a warrant issued under paragraph 3(2), and
   (b) cannot immediately be brought before the appropriate court.

(2) The person in whose custody the offender is—
   (a) may arrange for the offender to be detained in a place of safety for a period of not more than 72 hours from the time of the arrest, and
   (b) must, within that period, bring the offender before a youth court (or, if the offender is aged 18 or over, a magistrates' court other than a youth court).

(3) A person detained in accordance with arrangements under sub-paragraph (2)(a) is deemed to be lawfully detained.

5

(1) This paragraph applies where the court before which the offender is brought under paragraph 4(2) ('the alternative court') is not the appropriate court.

(2) The alternative court may—
 (a) direct that the offender is to be released immediately, or
 (b) remand the offender.

(3) Section 128 of the Magistrates' Courts Act 1980 (remand in custody or on bail) applies as if the court referred to in subsections (1)(a), (3), (4)(a) and (5) were the appropriate court.

(4) If the offender is aged under 18, any power conferred by that section to remand the offender in custody includes a power to remand the offender to accommodation provided by or on behalf of a local authority.

(5) If a court remands the offender to accommodation provided by or on behalf of a local authority, it must designate, as the authority which is to receive the offender, the local authority for the area in which it appears to the court that the offender resides or will reside.

Powers of court on referral back

6

Paragraphs 7 to 10 apply where the offender was referred back to court under—
(a) section 92(3) (offender's failure to attend panel meeting);
(b) section 98(3) (no prospect of agreement on youth offender contract);
(c) section 98(4) (unreasonable failure to sign record of agreement);
(d) section 100(3) (breach of contract);
(e) section 100(6) (unreasonable failure to sign record of variation);
(f) section 100(8) (change of circumstances);
(g) section 101(5) (final meeting: order not discharged);
(h) section 102(2) (panel requesting revocation of order).

Power of court where it upholds panel's decision

7

(1) Sub-paragraph (2) applies where the appropriate court is satisfied, for any decision of the youth offender panel which resulted in the referral back to court, that—
 (a) so far as the decision relied on any finding of fact by the youth offender panel, the panel was entitled to make that finding in the circumstances, and
 (b) so far as the decision involved any exercise of discretion by the youth offender panel, the panel reasonably exercised that discretion in the circumstances.

(2) The court may revoke the referral order (or each of the referral orders).

(3) Revocation of an order under sub-paragraph (2) has the effect of revoking any related order under paragraph 9(2), 12 or 15 (extension of compliance period).

(4) Where an order is revoked under sub-paragraph (2) or by virtue of sub-paragraph (3), the appropriate court may re-sentence the offender for the offence in respect of which the revoked order was made (but assuming that a referral order is not available).

(5) In re-sentencing the offender under sub-paragraph (4), the appropriate court must take into account—
  (a) the circumstances of the offender's referral back to the court, and
  (b) where a youth offender contract has taken effect between the offender and the panel, the extent of the offender's compliance with the contract.

(6) A power under sub-paragraph (2) or (4)—
  (a) may not be exercised unless the offender is before the appropriate court, and
  (b) is not affected by the expiry of the compliance period (whether before or after the offender was referred back to court), in a case where a youth offender contract has taken effect.

Appeal

8

An offender re-sentenced under paragraph 7(4) for an offence may appeal to the Crown Court against the sentence.

Power of court to impose fine or extend period for which contract has effect

9

(1) This paragraph applies where—
  (a) the reference back to court was made under—
    (i) section 92(3) (offender's failure to attend panel meeting),
    (ii) section 100(3) (breach of contract), or
    (iii) section 101(5) (final meeting: order not discharged),
  (b) the offender is before the appropriate court,
  (c) the appropriate court is satisfied that the offender has failed without reasonable excuse to comply with a youth offender contract which has taken effect between the offender and a youth offender panel, and
  (d) the appropriate court does not revoke the order under paragraph 7.

(2) The appropriate court may make an order extending the length of the compliance period, but—
  (a) not to more than 12 months, and
  (b) not if the compliance period has already expired.

(3) The court may order the offender to pay a fine of an amount not exceeding £2,500.

(4) Expiry of the compliance period (whether before or after the offender was referred back to court) does not affect the power to impose a fine under sub-paragraph (3).

(5) A fine imposed under sub-paragraph (3) is to be treated, for the purposes of any enactment, as being a sum adjudged to be paid by a conviction.

Consequences of court not revoking referral order or orders

10

(1) This paragraph applies where, having considered the matters in sub-paragraph (1) of paragraph 7, the appropriate court does not revoke the referral order (or orders) to which the offender is subject.

(2) The offender remains subject to the referral order (or orders) in all respects as if the referral back to court had not occurred (subject to any order under paragraph 9(2) (extension of compliance period)).

(3) But if—

(a) a youth offender contract has taken effect in pursuance of the referral order (or orders),

(b) the compliance period has expired, and

(c) the referral order (or each of the referral orders) has not been revoked,

the court must make an order declaring that the referral order (or each of the referral orders) is discharged.

(4) An order under sub-paragraph (3) has the effect of discharging any related order under paragraph 9(2), 12 or 15 (extension of compliance period).

Exception where court satisfied as to completion of contract

11

(1) This paragraph applies where—

(a) the reference back to court was made under section 101(5) (final meeting: order not discharged), and

(b) the court decides (contrary to the decision of the panel) that the offender's compliance with the youth offender contract has, or will by the end of the compliance period have, been such as to justify the conclusion that the offender has, or will have, satisfactorily completed the youth offender contract.

(2) The court must make an order declaring that the referral order (or each of the referral orders) is discharged.

(3) An order under sub-paragraph (2) has the effect of discharging any related order under paragraph 9(2), 12 or 15 (extension of compliance period).

12

(1) This paragraph applies where—

(a) the reference back to court was made under section 103(2) (request for extension of compliance period),

(b) the youth offender contract has taken effect and the compliance period has not expired, and

(c) the offender is before the appropriate court.

(2) If it appears to the appropriate court that it would be in the interests of justice to do so, having regard to circumstances which have arisen since the contract took effect, it may make an order extending the length of the compliance period but—

(a) not by more than 3 months, and

(b) not to more than 12 months.

(3) When deciding whether to make an order under sub-paragraph (2), the court must take into account the extent of the offender's compliance with the contract.

Power to adjourn hearing and remand offender

13

(1) This paragraph applies where a youth court or other magistrates' court holds a hearing in proceedings under this Part of this Schedule.

(2) The court may adjourn the hearing.

(3) Where the court adjourns the hearing under sub-paragraph (2), it may—
   (a) direct that the offender be released immediately, or
   (b) remand the offender.

(4) Where the court remands the offender under sub-paragraph (3)—
   (a) it must fix the time and place at which the hearing is to be resumed, and
   (b) the remand must require the offender to be brought before the court at that time and place.

(5) Where the court adjourns the hearing under sub-paragraph (2), but does not remand the offender—
   (a) it may fix the time and place at which the hearing is to be resumed, but
   (b) if it does not do so, it must not resume the hearing unless it is satisfied that the following persons have had adequate notice of the time and place for the resumed hearing—
      (i) the offender,
      (ii) if the offender is aged under 14, a parent or guardian of the offender, and
      (iii) a member of the specified youth offending team.

(6) The powers of a magistrates' court under this paragraph may be exercised by a single justice of the peace, notwithstanding anything in the Magistrates' Courts Act 1980.

(7) This paragraph—
   (a) applies to any hearing in proceedings under this Part of this Schedule in place of section 10 of the Magistrates' Courts Act 1980 (adjournment of trial) where that section would otherwise apply, but
   (b) is not to be taken to affect the application of that section to hearings of any other description.

J12.12.5 *Amendment of referral order because of offender's change of address*

The court which made the referral order may vary the order to specify a different YOT if it appears that the young offender has moved or is about to move to an address outside the area covered by the current YOT: s 105.

J12.12.6 ***Referral to court of parent or guardian***

The youth offender panel may refer a parent or guardian to the youth court if they fail to comply with an order requiring their attendance at youth offender panel meetings: s 93.

See M6.

J13 Rehabilitation of Offenders Act 1974

The Rehabilitation of Offenders 1974 Act establishes a scheme whereby a person convicted of a criminal offence can be rehabilitated for most purposes. This is achieved by deeming that offences are 'spent' after a certain period of time. Once a conviction is spent, the Act deems that the person concerned shall be treated as if they were never convicted of the offence. This means that, unless exceptions apply, spent convictions do not need to be declared when applying for employment or for financial services. Convictions are never spent for the purposes of criminal proceedings.

The length of time before a conviction is spent depends on the sentence passed not the offence.

J13.1 Sentences excluded from rehabilitation

Certain sentences are excluded from rehabilitation under the Act. These include:

- detention under the SC, s 250 for a term exceeding 48 months;
- detention under the SC, s 252A for a term exceeding 48 months;
- extended detention under the SC, s 254;
- detention during His Majesty's pleasure.

J13.2 Excluded occupations

The Rehabilitation of Offenders Act 1974 (Exceptions) Order 1975 lists professions and occupations which are excluded from the operation of the Act. These include

- all health professionals;
- veterinary surgeons;
- pharmacists;
- solicitors and barristers;
- accountants;
- probation officers;
- prison staff;
- police officers;
- traffic wardens;
- teachers;

Blackstone's Handbook of Youths in the Criminal Courts. Mark Ashford, Gareth Branston, and Naomi Redhouse, Oxford University Press.
 DOI: 10.1093/oso/9780198913146.003.0045

- employees of social services departments (or voluntary organizations) who in the course of ordinary duties would have access to various vulnerable groups (eg elderly, mentally ill, disabled, etc); and
- any employment concerned with the provision of services to persons under the age of 18.

However, unless an enhanced criminal record certificate is issued, many cautions and convictions become "protected" from disclosure after defined periods of time.

Full details on all aspects of rehabilitation appear in MCH Appendix 3.

J13.3 Rehabilitation periods

Below are the rehabilitation periods for an offender aged under 18 on the date of conviction.

Sentence/disposal	Rehabilitation period
Youth caution	Spent as soon as issued
Youth conditional caution	3 months from imposition
Absolute discharge	Spent on day of sentence
Conditional discharge	The last day of the period of discharge
Fine	6 months after the date of conviction
Compensation order	The day on which the payment is made in full
Referral order	The last day on which the order is to have effect (i.e. the day the youth offending contract is successfully completed)
YRO	The end of the period of 6 months beginning with the day specified on sentence as the last day on which the order is to have effect
DTO of 6 months or less	The end of the period of 18 months beginning with the day on which the sentence (including any supervision period) is completed
DTO of more than 6 months	The end of the period of 24 months beginning with the day on which the sentence (including any supervision period) is completed

Detention under the SC, s 250 or s 252A of more than 6 months and up to 30 months	The end of the period of 24 months beginning with the day on which the sentence (including any licence period) is completed
Detention under the SC, s 250 or s 252A of more than 30 months and up to 48 months	The end of the period of 42 months beginning with the day on which the sentence (including any licence period) is completed

J13.4 **Effect of further convictions**

If a person is convicted of a further offence whilst a conviction is unspent, the rehabilitation period is extended until the end of the rehabilitation period for the new offence(s).

J14 Remittal to Youth Court for Sentence

The SC, s 25 provides for the power to remit to the offender's local youth court for sentence, which in certain circumstances is a duty so to remit. It applies whenever a person aged under 18 is convicted by or before a court of an offence other than homicide:

- If the convicting court is the Crown Court, it must remit the offender to an appropriate youth court: s 25(2);
- If the convicting court is a magistrates' court which commits the offender to the Crown Court for sentence, the Crown Court may remit the offender back to an appropriate youth court: s 25(2A);
- If the convicting court is a youth court, it may remit the offender to another youth court: s 25(3);
- If the convicting court is an adult magistrate's court, it must remit the offender to the youth court unless:
  - the compulsory referral order conditions apply and it will therefore make a referral order, or
  - it is of the opinion that the case can properly be dealt with by an absolute/conditional discharge, a fine, or a parental bind over

  in which case it may remit but is not required to do so: s 25(4) and (5).

Remittal for sentence by the Crown Court is considered in more detail at **K3**.

The power of a youth court to remit to the youth offender's local youth court is of considerable practical benefit. Not only will it usually be more convenient and less expensive for the youth defendant to attend their local youth court, but it also means that the YOT which will be preparing any pre-sentence report will be present at court when the matter comes up for sentence.

It should be noted that the power to remit to a local youth court is not subject to the same preconditions as the power under s 28 to remit an adult offender to a different magistrates' court. The power under s 25 can be exercised without the need for another matter to be listed for sentence at the local court. There is also no requirement to seek the consent of the local court before remitting the case for sentence.

The youth court receiving the case under s 25 may hear an application to vacate a guilty plea and, if it considers it appropriate,

Blackstone's Handbook of Youths in the Criminal Courts. Mark Ashford, Gareth Branston, and Naomi Redhouse, Oxford University Press.
 DOI: 10.1093/oso/9780198913146.003.0046

proceed to try the defendant: *R v Stratford Youth Court ex parte Conde* [1997] 1 WLR 113.

Sentencing Code

25 Power and duty to remit offenders aged under 18 to youth courts for sentence

(1) This section applies where a person aged under 18 is convicted by or before a court ('the convicting court') of an offence other than homicide.

(2) If the convicting court is the Crown Court, it must remit the offender to a youth court acting for the place where the sending court sat, unless satisfied that it would be undesirable to do so. The 'sending court' is the magistrates' court which sent the offender to the Crown Court for trial.

(2A) If—

(a) the convicting court is a magistrates' court, and

(b) that court commits the offender to the Crown Court for sentence,

the Crown Court may remit the offender to a youth court acting for the place where the convicting court sat.

(3) If the convicting court is a youth court, it may remit the offender to another youth court.

(4) If the convicting court is a magistrates' court other than a youth court—

(a) it may remit the offender to a youth court, and

(b) must do so unless subsection (5) applies.

(5) This subsection applies where the convicting court—

(a) would be required by section 85(1)(a) to make a referral order if it did not remit the offender to a youth court, or

(b) is of the opinion that the case is one which can properly be dealt with by means of—

(i) an order for absolute discharge or an order for conditional discharge,

(ii) a fine, or

(iii) an order (under section 376) requiring the offender's parent or guardian to enter into a recognizance to take proper care of, and exercise proper control over, the offender,

with or without any other order that the court has power to make when making an order for absolute discharge or an order for conditional discharge.

(6) For the purposes of subsection (5)(b)(iii)—

(a) 'care' and 'control' are to be read in accordance with section 376(3) (binding over of parent or guardian), and

(b) section 404 (certain references to parent or guardian to be read as references to local authority) does not apply.

(7) Any remission of an offender under subsection (3) or (4) must be to a youth court acting for—

(a) the same place as the remitting court, or

(b) the place where the offender habitually resides.

(8) Where an offender is remitted to a youth court under this section, that court may deal with the offender in any way in which it could deal with the offender if it had convicted the offender of the offence.

(9) A court which remits an offender to a youth court under this section must provide the designated officer for the youth court with a certificate which—

(a) sets out the nature of the offence, and

(b) states—

(i) that the offender has been convicted of the offence, and

(ii) that the offender has been remitted for the purpose of being dealt with under subsection (8).

(10) A document which purports—

(a) to be a copy of an order made by a court under this section, and

(b) to be certified as a true copy by the designated officer for the court,

is to be evidence of the order.

J15 **Reparation Order**

Reparation orders have been abolished by the PCSCA 2022, s 162, as of 28 June 2022.

Blackstone's Handbook of Youths in the Criminal Courts. Mark Ashford, Gareth Branston, and Naomi Redhouse, Oxford University Press.
 DOI: 10.1093/oso/9780198913146.003.0047

J16 Reports

J16.1 Duty to provide information about the youth defendant

Local authorities are under a statutory duty to provide information about a youth charged with a criminal offence. Although the duty extends to children's services departments and education departments, the information is generally provided by the YOT. Information is most commonly provided through sentencing reports.

The CYPA 1969, s 9 provides:

Children and Young Persons Act 1969

9 Investigations by local authorities

(1) Where a local authority bring proceedings for an offence alleged to have been committed by a young person or are notified that any such proceedings are being brought, it shall be the duty of the authority, unless they are of opinion that it is unnecessary to do so, to make such investigations and provide the court before which the proceedings are heard with such information relating to the home surroundings, school record, health and character of the person in respect of whom the proceedings are brought as appear to the authority likely to assist the court.

(2) If the court mentioned in subsection (1) of this section requests the authority aforesaid to make investigations and provide information or to make further investigations and provide further information relating to the matters aforesaid, it shall be the duty of the authority to comply with the request.

J16.2 Pre-sentence report

A pre-sentence report is a report made or submitted by an appropriate officer with a view to assisting the court in determining the most suitable method of dealing with an offender: SC, s 31(1). For an offender aged under 18, the appropriate officer is usually a member of the YOT, but may be a probation officer or social worker: s 31(2).

The statutory requirement to obtain and consider a pre-sentence report before deciding on sentence is much tighter in the case of a youth defendant. In particular, a court may not impose a custodial sentence without considering a pre-sentence report.

Blackstone's Handbook of Youths in the Criminal Courts. Mark Ashford, Gareth Branston, and Naomi Redhouse, Oxford University Press.
 DOI: 10.1093/oso/9780198913146.003.0048

The SC, s 30 provides:

Sentencing Code

30 Pre-sentence report requirements

(1) This section applies where, by virtue of any provision in this Code, the pre-sentence report requirements apply to a court in relation to forming an opinion.

(2) If the offender is aged 18 or over, the court must obtain and consider a pre-sentence report before forming the opinion unless, in the circumstances of the case, it considers that it is unnecessary to obtain a pre-sentence report.

(3) If the offender is aged under 18, the court must obtain and consider a pre-sentence report before forming the opinion unless—

(a) there exists a previous pre-sentence report obtained in respect of the offender, and

(b) the court considers—

(i) in the circumstances of the case, and

(ii) having had regard to the information contained in that report or, if there is more than one, the most recent report,

that it is unnecessary to obtain a pre-sentence report.

Where a court does not obtain and consider a pre-sentence report before forming an opinion in relation to which the pre-sentence report requirements apply, no custodial sentence or community sentence is invalidated by the fact that it did not do so.(4) Where a court does not obtain and consider a pre-sentence report before forming an opinion in relation to which the pre-sentence report requirements apply, no custodial sentence or community sentence is invalidated by the fact that it did not do so.

The pre-sentence report requirement is scattered throughout the SC. In relation to offenders aged under 18, the requirement applies to the following determinations:

- whether an offence is serious enough to warrant a YRO: s 179(4);
- whether an offence is serious enough to cross the custodial threshold such that a YRO with ISS or with fostering is warranted: s 180(4);
- what particular requirement(s) are suitable as part of a YRO: s 186(4);
- whether restrictions imposed by a YRO are commensurate with the seriousness of the offence: s 186(8);
- whether an offence is serious enough to cross the custodial threshold: s 230(7);
- the length of a discretionary custodial sentence: s 231(8);
- whether the offender is dangerous for the purposes of imposing an extended sentence: s 255(2);

- whether the offender is dangerous for the purpose of imposing a sentence of detention for life: s 258(3).

A pre-sentence report may be presented orally in open court (often called a stand-down report) but, in the case of an offender aged under 18, a written report must be obtained and considered before a court may make any determination that relates to a custodial sentence: s 31(4) and (5).

The MoJ/YJB *Standards for Children in the Youth Justice System 2019* require that individual reports prepared by the YOT:

- focus on children's best interests
- constructively promote their potential and desistance from crime
- are balanced and impartial
- take account of the impact on victims
- promote fairness by making sure that diverse needs are met.

The *Standards* require magistrates and the judiciary to have reports which provide them with the required range of recommendations to make informed decisions regarding sentencing. To that end, they require the YOT to produce reports requested by the court within the stipulated timeframe and to base all reports on an up-to-date and relevant YJB approved assessment, and demonstrate engagement with the child and parents/carers.

Case management guidance from the YJB (October 2022, available on the GOV.UK website), states that stand-down reports are used where the child is well known to the youth justice service, the matters before the court are straightforward, and it would speed up the outcome. The guidance stipulates that a verbal stand-down report must not be used if there is any prospect of a custodial sentence. If community supervision is likely to be under consideration, a five-day adjournment should be requested.

The guidance states that pre-sentence reports should include information from:

- one (or more) conversation(s) and any other work with the child
- at least one discussion with the parents or carers
- CPS documents about the case
- the nature of any victim contacts regarding the offence
- AssetPlus and any additional specialist assessments
- other professionals involved, including the child's school, social worker etc.

The SC, s 32 requires the court to provide a copy of any written pre-sentence report to:

- the offender or their legal representative;

- if the offender is aged under 18, any parent or guardian of theirs who is present in court; and
- the prosecutor.

In the case of an offender aged under 18, a complete copy of the report need not be given to the offender or their parent or guardian if it appears to the court that the disclosure of information contained in the report would be likely to create a risk of significant harm to the offender: s 32(3).

J16.3 Medical report

Rule 3.10 of the Crim PR provides for directions for commissioning medical reports, other than for sentencing purposes. Rule 25.10 applies where a defendant in the Crown Court may not be fit to be tried. Rule 28.8 provides for directions for commissioning medical reports in any court for the purpose of sentencing or other disposal.

See **J10** Mentally Disordered Offenders.

J17 **The Scaled Approach**

In 2009, the YJB introduced a tiered approach to interventions by YOTs in order to reduce the likelihood of re-offending and risk of serious harm. This is called the Scaled Approach.

Under the Scaled Approach, the YOT will assess the young person using the standardized assessment tool *AssetPlus*. An initial assessment will calculate the risk of re-offending; where necessary an additional assessment will consider the risk of serious harm likely to be involved in further offending.

On the basis of this assessment, the YOT will identify a level of intervention:

- **Standard level**—for those who show a low likelihood of re-offending and a low risk of serious harm; in those circumstances, the order primarily will seek to repair the harm caused by the offence—typically, this will involve interventions to meet the requirements of the order and the engagement of parents in those interventions to meet the requirements of the order and the engagement of parents in those interventions and/ or in supporting the young person.
- **Enhanced level**—for those who show a medium likelihood of re-offending or a medium risk of serious harm; in those circumstances, the order will, in addition, seek to enable help or change as appropriate—typically this will involve greater activity in motivating the young person and in addressing the reasons for non-compliance with the law and may involve external interventions.
- **Intensive level**—for those with a high likelihood of re-offending or a high or very high risk of serious harm; in these circumstances, the order will, in addition, seek to ensure control of the young person as necessary to minimize the risk of further offending or of serious harm—typically this will involve additional control, restrictions, and monitoring.

The *Sentencing Children and Young People – Overarching Principles* definitive guideline gives the following guidance on the Scaled Approach:

> 6.28 When determining the nature and extent of the requirements [of a YRO] the court should primarily consider the likelihood of the child or young person re-offending and the risk of the child or young person causing serious harm. A higher risk of re-offending does not in itself justify a greater restriction on liberty than is warranted

Blackstone's Handbook of Youths in the Criminal Courts. Mark Ashford, Gareth Branston, and Naomi Redhouse, Oxford University Press.
 DOI: 10.1093/oso/9780198913146.003.0049

by the seriousness of the offence; any requirements should still be commensurate with the seriousness of the offence and regard must still be had for the welfare of the child or young person.

6.29 The YOT will assess this as part of their report and recommend an intervention level to the court for consideration. It is possible for the court to ask the YOT to consider a particular requirement.

	Child or young person profile	**Requirements of order**[1]
Standard	Low likelihood of re-offending **and** a low risk of serious harm	Primarily seek to repair harm caused through, for example: • reparation; • unpaid work; • supervision; and/or • attendance centre.
Enhanced	Medium likelihood of re-offending **or** a medium risk of serious harm	Seek to repair harm caused and to enable help or change through, for example: • supervision; • reparation; • requirement to address behaviour e.g. drug treatment, offending behaviour programme, education programme; and/or • a combination of the above.
Intensive	High likelihood of re-offending **or** a very high risk of serious harm	Seek to ensure the control of and enable help or change for the child or young person through, for example: • supervision; • reparation; • requirement to address behaviour; • requirement to monitor or restrict movement, e.g. prohibited activity, curfew, exclusion or electronic monitoring; and/or • a combination of the above.

[1] The examples provided here are not exclusive; the YOT will make recommendations based upon their assessment of the young offender which may vary from some of the examples given.

6.30 If a child or young person is assessed as presenting a high risk of re-offending or of causing serious harm but the offence that was committed is of relatively low seriousness then the appropriate requirements are likely to be primarily rehabilitative or for the protection of the public.

6.31 Likewise if a child or young person is assessed as presenting a low risk of re-offending or of causing serious harm but the offence was of relatively high seriousness then the appropriate requirements are likely to be primarily punitive.

A YOT is required to supervise the following orders in line with Scaled Approach model contacts as set out in the table below:

- YRO with a supervision requirement and other requirements where appropriate;
- Referral orders; and
- Community element of DTO.

Scaled Approach model

Intervention level	Minimum contact for first 12 weeks (per month)	Minimum contact after 12 weeks (per month)
Intensive	8	4
Enhanced	4	2
Standard	2	1

J18 Sentence: Procedure in the Youth Court

Pursuant to the CYPA 1933, s 59, the words 'conviction' and 'sentence' should not be used in relation to a youth defendant dealt with in the youth court or adult magistrates' court. Instead, the terms 'finding of guilt' and 'order made upon a finding of guilt' should be used. In practice, this provision is rarely observed. It does not apply, in any event, to youth defendants tried on indictment in the Crown Court.

The procedure for the sentencing hearing in the youth court is governed by the Crim PR, r 24.11.

The prosecutor must:

- summarize the prosecution case, if the sentencing court has not heard evidence;
- identify any offence to be taken into consideration (TIC) in sentencing;
- provide information relevant to sentence, including any statement to the effect of the offence on the victim, the victim's family, or others; and
- where it is likely to assist the court, identify any other matter relevant to sentence, including:
  - (i) the legislation applicable,
  - (ii) any sentencing guidelines or guideline cases,
  - (iii) aggravating and mitigating features, affecting the defendant's culpability, and the harm which the offence caused, was intended to cause, or might foreseeably have caused, and
  - (iv) the effect of any information in a defendant's means statement and/or pre-sentence report as the court may need to take into account: r 24.11(3).

The defendant must provide information relevant to sentence, including details of financial circumstances: r 24.11(4).

Before the court passes sentence, it must give the defendant an opportunity to make representations and introduce evidence relevant to sentence. Where the defendant is under 18, the court must give the defendant's parents, guardian, or other supporting adult, if present, such an opportunity as well: r 24.11(7).

Blackstone's Handbook of Youths in the Criminal Courts. Mark Ashford, Gareth Branston, and Naomi Redhouse, Oxford University Press.
 DOI: 10.1093/oso/9780198913146.003.0050

When the court has taken into account all the evidence, information, and any report available, the general rule is that the court will:

- pass sentence there and then;
- explain the reasons for deciding on that sentence;
- explain to the defendant the effect of the sentence, the consequences of failing to comply, and any power that the court has to vary or review the sentence;
- give any such explanation in terms the defendant can understand (with help, if necessary); and
- consider exercising any power it has to make a costs or other order: r 24.11(9).

J19 Sentences Available in the Youth Court

For offenders aged under 18 on the date of conviction, the youth court may impose the following:

- Absolute discharge
- Conditional discharge (for restrictions see **J6**)
- Fine
- Compensation order
- Referral order (where referral conditions apply—see **J12.11**)
- Youth rehabilitation order
  - YRO with intensive supervision and surveillance
  - YRO with fostering
- Detention and training order
- Special sentence of detention for terrorist offenders of particular concern (SC, s 252A). See **K4.3**.

A court may not suspend any custodial sentence imposed on an offender who was under the age of 18 on the date of conviction.

For sentences available to the youth court when the offender has attained 18 by the date of conviction, see **L3**.

For offenders aged under 18 on the date of conviction, the following sentences are only available in the Crown Court and are not available in the youth court:

- Long-term detention under the SC, s 250
- Special sentence of detention, longer than two years, for terrorist offenders of particular concern (SC, s 252A)
- Extended sentence of detention
- Detention for life
- Detention during His Majesty's pleasure

See **K4** for further details about Crown Court powers.

See **H2** and **J4** for further details about sending and committing for sentence to the Crown Court.

Blackstone's Handbook of Youths in the Criminal Courts. Mark Ashford, Gareth Branston, and Naomi Redhouse, Oxford University Press.
 DOI: 10.1093/oso/9780198913146.003.0051

J20 Sentencing Youth Offenders: General Approach

J20.1 General principles

An entirely different approach is required to sentencing children and young people; it is categorically wrong to set about it as if they are 'mini-adults': *R v ZA* [2023] EWCA Crim 596.

The *Sentencing Children and Young People – Overarching Principles* definitive guideline sets out at the outset the fundamental principles when sentencing children and young people.

The court must have regard to:

- the principal aim of the youth justice system; i.e. to prevent offending by children and young people (see **F1**); and
- the welfare of the child or young person (see **F4**).

The guideline then states:

> 1.2 While the seriousness of the offence will be the starting point, the approach to sentencing should be individualistic and focused on the child or young person, as opposed to offence focused. For a child or young person the sentence should focus on rehabilitation where possible. A court should also consider the effect the sentence is likely to have on the child or young person (both positive and negative) as well as any underlying factors contributing to the offending behaviour.
>
> 1.3 Domestic and international laws dictate that a custodial sentence should always be a measure of last resort for children and young people and statute provides that a custodial sentence may only be imposed when the offence is so serious that no other sanction is appropriate . . .
>
> 1.4 It is important to avoid 'criminalising' children and young people unnecessarily; the primary purpose of the youth justice system is to encourage children and young people to take responsibility for their own actions and promote re-integration into society rather than to punish. Restorative justice disposals may be of particular value for children and young people as they can encourage them to take responsibility for their actions and understand the impact their offence may have had on others.
>
> 1.5 It is important to bear in mind any factors that may diminish the culpability of a child or young person. Children and young people are not fully developed and they have not attained full maturity. As such, this can impact on their decision making and risk taking behaviour. It is important to consider the extent to which the child or young person has been acting impulsively and whether their conduct has been affected by inexperience, emotional volatility or negative

Blackstone's Handbook of Youths in the Criminal Courts. Mark Ashford, Gareth Branston, and Naomi Redhouse, Oxford University Press.
 DOI: 10.1093/oso/9780198913146.003.0052

influences. They may not fully appreciate the effect their actions can have on other people and may not be capable of fully understanding the distress and pain they cause to the victims of their crimes. Children and young people are also likely to be susceptible to peer pressure and other external influences and changes taking place during adolescence can lead to experimentation, resulting in criminal behaviour. When considering a child or young person's age their emotional and developmental age is of at least equal importance to their chronological age (if not greater).

1.6 For these reasons, children and young people are likely to benefit from being given an opportunity to address their behaviour and may be receptive to changing their conduct. They should, if possible, be given the opportunity to learn from their mistakes without undue penalisation or stigma, especially as a court sanction might have a significant effect on the prospects and opportunities of the child or young person and hinder their re-integration into society.

1.7 Offending by a child or young person is often a phase which passes fairly rapidly and so the sentence should not result in the alienation of the child or young person from society if that can be avoided.

1.8 The impact of punishment is likely to be felt more heavily by a child or young person in comparison to an adult as any sentence will seem longer due to their young age. In addition penal interventions may interfere with a child or young person's education and this should be considered by a court at sentencing.

The guideline goes on:

The sentence should focus on rehabilitation where possible and the court should consider the effect of the sentence on the child or young person.

The guideline sets out how the court should determine sentence:

4.1 In determining the sentence, the key elements to consider are:

- the principal aim of the youth justice system (to prevent re-offending by children and young people);
- the welfare of the child or young person;
- the age of the child or young person (chronological, developmental and emotional);
- the seriousness of the offence;
- the likelihood of further offences being committed; and
- the extent of harm likely to result from those further offences.

J20.2 **Seriousness**

Sentencing Code

63 Assessing seriousness

Where a court is considering the seriousness of any offence, it must consider—

(a) the offender's culpability in committing the offence, and

(b) any harm which the offence–
 (i) caused,
 (ii) was intended to cause, or
 (iii) might foreseeably have caused.

The *Sentencing Children and Young People – Overarching Principles* definitive guideline states that the approach of the court should be:

The seriousness of the offence

(This applies to all offences; when offence specific guidance for children and young people is available this should be referred to.)

4.2 The seriousness of the offence is the starting point for determining the appropriate sentence; the sentence imposed and any restriction on liberty must be commensurate with the seriousness of the offence.

4.3 The approach to sentencing children and young people should always be individualistic and the court should always have in mind the principal aims of the youth justice system.

4.4 In order to determine the seriousness of the offence the court should assess the culpability of the child or young person and the harm that was caused, intended to be caused or could foreseeably have been caused.

4.5 In assessing **culpability** the court will wish to consider the extent to which the offence was planned, the role of the child or young person (if the offence was committed as part of a group), the level of force that was used in the commission of the offence and the awareness that the child or young person had of their actions and its possible consequences. There is an expectation that in general a child or young person will be dealt with less severely than an adult offender. In part, this is because children and young people are unlikely to have the same experience and capacity as an adult to understand the effect of their actions on other people or to appreciate the pain and distress caused and because a child or young person may be less able to resist temptation, especially where peer pressure is exerted. Children and young people are inherently more vulnerable than adults due to their age and the court will need to consider any mental health problems and/or learning disabilities they may have, as well as their emotional and developmental age. Any external factors that may have affected the child or young person's behaviour should be taken into account.

4.6 In assessing **harm** the court should consider the level of physical and psychological harm caused to the victim, the degree of any loss caused to the victim and the extent of any damage caused to property. (This assessment should also include a consideration of any harm that was intended to be caused or could foreseeably have been caused in the committal of the offence.)

4.7 The court should also consider any aggravating or mitigating factors that may increase or reduce the overall seriousness of the offence. **If any of these factors are included in the definition of the committed offence they should not be taken into account when considering the relative seriousness of the offence before the court.**

J20.2.2 *Aggravating and mitigating factors of the offence*

The guideline sets out the aggravating and mitigating factors which may be considered:

Aggravating factors	**Factors reducing seriousness or reflecting personal mitigation (non-exhaustive)**
Statutory aggravating factors: Previous findings of guilt, having regard to a) the **nature** of the offence to which the finding of guilt relates and its relevance to the current offence; and b) the **time** that has elapsed since the finding of guilt; Offence committed whilst on bail; Offence motivated by, or demonstrating hostility based on any of the following characteristics or presumed; characteristics of the victim: religion, race, disability, sexual orientation, or transgender identity. *Other aggravating factors (non-exhaustive):* Steps taken to prevent the victim reporting or obtaining assistance; Steps taken to prevent the victim from assisting or supporting the prosecution; Victim is particularly vulnerable due to factors including but not limited to age, mental or physical disability; Restraint, detention or additional degradation of the victim; Prolonged nature of offence; Attempts to conceal/dispose of evidence; Established evidence of community/ wider impact; Failure to comply with current court orders; Attempt to conceal identity; Involvement of others through peer pressure, bullying, coercion or manipulation; Commission of offence whilst under the influence of alcohol or drugs; History of antagonising or bullying the victim; Deliberate humiliation of victim, including but not limited to filming of the offence, deliberately committing the offence before a group of peers with the intention of causing additional distress, or circulating details/photos/videos etc. of the offence on social media or within peer groups.	No previous findings of guilt or no relevant/recent findings of guilt; Remorse, particularly where evidenced by voluntary reparation to the victim; Good character and/or exemplary conduct; Unstable upbringing including but not limited to: • time spent looked after • lack of familial presence or support • disrupted experiences in accommodation or education • exposure to drug/ alcohol abuse, familial criminal behaviour or domestic abuse • victim of neglect or abuse, or exposure to neglect or abuse of others, • experiences of trauma or loss; Participated in offence due to bullying, peer pressure, coercion or manipulation; Limited understanding of effect on victim; Serious medical condition requiring urgent, intensive, or long-term treatment; Communication or learning disabilities or mental health concerns; In education, work, or training; Particularly young or immature child or young person (where it affects their responsibility); Determination and/or demonstration of steps taken to address addiction or offending behaviour.

J20.3 Personal mitigation

The SC, s 77(1) provides that a sentencing court may take into account any matters that, in the opinion of the court, are relevant in mitigation of sentence. Section 177(2) expressly confirms that personal mitigation can result in a court imposing a community order where the seriousness of the offence crosses the custody threshold.

J21 Sexual Offences Notification Requirements

J21.1 Criteria

The law relating to notification as a sex offender is contained in the SOA 2003, Part II (ss 80–92). The regime applicable to offenders who were under the age of 18 at the time of the offence is substantially different to that applicable to adult offenders. The most significant differences are:

- the notification requirements are triggered in a narrower set of circumstances; and
- the notification period is half that applicable to adult offenders.

An offender becomes subject to the notification requirements if they are convicted of or cautioned for an offence listed in the SOA 2003, s 80. The date when the offender is convicted or receives a caution is referred to as the 'relevant date': s 82(6).

Where the offender was under 18 years at the time of the offence, there are automatic notification requirements if they are convicted of, or cautioned for, the following offences in the SOA 2003:

- Rape (s 1);
- Assault by penetration (s 2);
- Causing sexual activity without consent (s 4);
- Rape of child under 13 (s 5);
- Assault of child under 13 by penetration (s 6);
- Causing or inciting a child under 13 to engage in sexual activity (s 8);
- Offences against persons with a mental disorder (ss 30–37);
- Offences by care workers (ss 38–41);
- Administering a substance with intent (s 61).

For these offences, notification requirements arise as soon as the defendant is convicted or cautioned. They must therefore provide relevant details to the police within three days of that date. If a conditional discharge is subsequently imposed on the defendant, the matter will still be treated as a conviction notwithstanding the SC, s 82(2): SOA 2003, s 134(1).

For other offences under the SOA 2003 committed by youth offenders, as well as offences relating to taking/making/distributing/possessing indecent photographs, notification requirements only arise if the sentencing threshold criteria contained in Sch 3 to the

Blackstone's Handbook of Youths in the Criminal Courts. Mark Ashford, Gareth Branston, and Naomi Redhouse, Oxford University Press.
 DOI: 10.1093/oso/9780198913146.003.0053

SOA 2003 are satisfied. Notification requirements only apply if the offender (aged under 18 at the date of the offence) is sentenced to a term of 'imprisonment' of 12 months or more. They will not therefore apply if a lesser sentence is imposed or if the offender is cautioned.

Under the SOA 2003, s 131, 'sentence of imprisonment' is to be construed to include reference to:

- a period of detention which a person is liable to serve under a DTO;
- a sentence of detention under the SC, s 250 or s 252A;
- a sentence of extended detention under the SC, s 254.

In the case of a DTO, 'term of imprisonment' has been held to mean the length of the period served in custody and not the full length of the order: *R v Slocombe* [2005] EWCA Crim 2997. This means that no DTO for less than the 24-month maximum satisfies the sentencing threshold condition of 'sentenced to a term of imprisonment of 12 months or more'.

Where the offence has a sentencing threshold condition, the notification requirements only arise once the sentence is passed: SOA 2003, s 132.

It should be noted that some sexual offences do not attract notification requirements for offenders aged under 18 at the time of the offence:

- possession of extreme pornography (CJIA 2008, s 63);
- possession of prohibited images of children (Coroners and Justice Act 2009, s 62(1));
- Possession of paedophile manual (Serious Crime Act 2015, s 69).

J21.2 **Notification period**

The length of the notification period depends on the sentence or other disposal. The relevant periods are set out in the SOA 2003, s 82. When the offender is under the age of 18 on the date of conviction the applicable period is half that of an adult offender (s 82(2)). These reduced periods are set out in the table below:

Disposal	Applicable period for offender under 18
Sentence of imprisonment for a term of 30 months or more	An indefinite period
A person admitted to hospital under a restriction order	An indefinite period

Sentence of imprisonment for a term of more than 6 months but less than 30 months	5 years
Sentence of imprisonment for a term of 6 months or less	3 ½ years
A person made subject to a hospital order without a restriction requirement	3 ½ years
A person who has received a youth caution or youth conditional caution for the offence	1 year
A person in whose case an order for conditional discharge is made in respect of the offence	The period of conditional discharge
A person of any other description (i.e. referral order, YRO, fine)	2 ½ years

If a DTO is imposed, the length of the applicable period is determined by the length of the custodial part of the order; i.e. half the length of the DTO: *R v Slocombe*, see above.

J21.3 **Notification obligations**

Pursuant to the SOA 2003, s 83, within three days of the relevant date, the offender must provide to the police the following information:

- their name;
- any other names used;
- date of birth;
- national insurance number (where the offender has attained 16);
- home address; and
- any other premises in the United Kingdom at which they regularly reside or stay.

The last requirement would mean that, where an offender spends part of the week with one parent and part of the week with the other, then both addresses would have to be provided.

Whilst subject to notification requirements the offender must also:

- notify the police of any change of circumstances including, a stay of seven days or more at a temporary address (s 84);
- renew registration annually (s 85); and
- notify the police of any proposed travel outside the United Kingdom for a period of three days or longer (s 86).

Failure without reasonable excuse to comply with the notification requirements is a criminal offence punishable in the case of an adult with five years' imprisonment: s 91.

J21.4 Parental directions

Pursuant to the SOA 2003, s 89, a court sentencing a defendant under the age of 18 for an offence where the notification requirements apply may make a parental direction against an individual who has parental responsibility for the defendant. The direction takes immediate effect and applies until the offender attains the age of 18 or for such shorter period as the court may, at the time the direction is given, direct.

The effect of a parental direction is that the notification obligations normally imposed on the offender are to be treated instead as obligations of the parent. The parent must still ensure that the young offender attends at the police station with him, when a notification is being given. Failure by the parent without a reasonable excuse to ensure that the notification requirements are satisfied is a criminal offence punishable with five years' imprisonment: s 91.

See *Blackstone's Criminal Practice 2024.*

J22 Sexual Orientation, Disability, Transgender Identity, Race, or Religion

The SC, s 66 provides:

Sentencing Code

66 Hostility

(1) This section applies where the court is considering the seriousness of an offence which is aggravated by—
 (a) racial hostility,
 (b) religious hostility,
 (c) hostility related to disability,
 (d) hostility related to sexual orientation, or
 (e) hostility related to transgender identity.
 This is subject to subsection (3).

(2) The court—
 (a) must treat the fact that the offence is aggravated by hostility of any of those types as an aggravating factor, and
 (b) must state in open court that the offence is so aggravated.

(3) So far as it relates to racial and religious hostility, this section does not apply in relation to an offence under sections 29 to 32 of the Crime and Disorder Act 1998 (racially or religiously aggravated offences).

(4) For the purposes of this section, an offence is aggravated by hostility of one of the kinds mentioned in subsection (1) if—
 (a) at the time of committing the offence, or immediately before or after doing so, the offender demonstrated towards the victim of the offence hostility based on—
  (i) the victim's membership (or presumed membership) of a racial group,
  (ii) the victim's membership (or presumed membership) of a religious group,
  (iii) a disability (or presumed disability) of the victim,
  (iv) the sexual orientation (or presumed sexual orientation) of the victim, or (as the case may be)
  (v) the victim being (or being presumed to be) transgender, or
 (b) the offence was motivated (wholly or partly) by—
  (i) hostility towards members of a racial group based on their membership of that group,
  (ii) hostility towards members of a religious group based on their membership of that group,
  (iii) hostility towards persons who have a disability or a particular disability,

Blackstone's Handbook of Youths in the Criminal Courts. Mark Ashford, Gareth Branston, and Naomi Redhouse, Oxford University Press.
 DOI: 10.1093/oso/9780198913146.003.0054

(iv) hostility towards persons who are of a particular sexual orientation, or (as the case may be)

(v) hostility towards persons who are transgender.

(5) For the purposes of paragraphs (a) and (b) of subsection (4), it is immaterial whether or not the offender's hostility is also based, to any extent, on any other factor not mentioned in that paragraph.

(6) In this section—

(a) references to a racial group are to a group of persons defined by reference to race, colour, nationality (including citizenship) or ethnic or national origins;

(b) references to a religious group are to a group of persons defined by reference to religious belief or lack of religious belief;

(c) 'membership' in relation to a racial or religious group, includes association with members of that group;

(d) 'disability' means any physical or mental impairment;

(e) references to being transgender include references to being transsexual, or undergoing, proposing to undergo or having undergone a process or part of a process of gender reassignment;

(f) 'presumed' means presumed by the offender.

See *Blackstone's Criminal Practice 2024*.

J23 Surcharge

There are different rates of surcharge applicable depending on the age of the offender on the date of the commission of the offence.

J23.1 Criteria

In any case relating to any offence committed on or after 1 April 2007, the court must impose a surcharge order. The surcharge may be reduced if the offender is not able to pay both the surcharge and compensation.

The SC, s 42 provides:

Sentencing Code

42 Court's duty to order payment of surcharge

(1) A court when dealing with an offender for one or more offences committed on or after 1 April 2007 must also order the offender to pay a surcharge.
This is subject to subsections (2) to (4).

(2) Subsection (1)—
   (a) does not apply in such cases as may be prescribed by regulations made by the Secretary of State, and
   (b) is subject to section 15 of the Proceeds of Crime Act 2002 (effect on duty in subsection (1) when proceedings on confiscation order are postponed).

(3) Where a court dealing with an offender considers—
   (a) that it would be appropriate to make one or more of—
      (i) a compensation order,
      (ii) an unlawful profit order, and
      (iii) a slavery and trafficking reparation order, but
   (b) that the offender has insufficient means to pay both the surcharge and appropriate amounts under such of those orders as it would be appropriate to make,

the court must reduce the surcharge accordingly (if necessary to nil).
But see section 13(4) of the Proceeds of Crime Act 2002 (court not to take confiscation order into account).

(4) Where an offender aged under 18 is convicted of an offence and, but for this subsection, a court would order the offender to pay a surcharge—
   (a) section 380 (orders for payment by parent or guardian) applies to the surcharge, and
   (b) for the purposes of any order under that section in respect of the surcharge, subsection (3)(b) of this section is to be read as if the reference to the offender's means were to the means of the offender's parent or guardian.

Blackstone's Handbook of Youths in the Criminal Courts. Mark Ashford, Gareth Branston, and Naomi Redhouse, Oxford University Press.
 DOI: 10.1093/oso/9780198913146.003.0055

(5) For the purposes of this section a court does not 'deal with' a person if it—
   (a) discharges the person absolutely, or
   (b) makes an order under the Mental Health Act 1983 in respect of the person.

(6) In this section—
   'slavery and trafficking reparation order' means an order under section 8 of the Modern Slavery Act 2015;
   'unlawful profit order' means an unlawful profit order under section 4 of the Prevention of Social Housing Fraud Act 2013.

(7) Regulations under subsection (2) are subject to the negative resolution procedure.

Surcharge rates where the offender was under 18 when the offence was committed:

	Pre 28.06.19	28.06.19 to 13.04.20	14.04.20 to 15.06.22	16.06.22 to present
Conditional discharge	£15	£16	£17	£20
Fine, youth rehabilitation or community order	£20	£21	£22	£26
Custodial sentence	£30	£32	£34	£41

J23.2 **Payment by parent or guardian**

The SC, s 380(1)(a) and (2) provides that, where the offender is under the age of 16 on the date of conviction, the court must order the parent or guardian to pay the surcharge in place of the youth offender unless the court is satisfied that:

- the parent or guardian cannot be found; or
- it would be unreasonable to make an order for payment having regard to the circumstances of the case.

In the case of an offender aged 16 or 17, the court may order the parent or guardian to pay the surcharge: s 380(1)(b).

It would, for example, normally be unreasonable to order a parent or guardian to pay the surcharge where they were the victim of the offence.

See M3.

J24 Youth Rehabilitation Order

Where a person under 18 is convicted of an offence, they may be sentenced to a YRO: SC, s 177(1).

As part of the order, the court may impose any of the following requirements specified in s 174:

- an activity requirement;
- an extended activity requirement;
- a supervision requirement;
- an unpaid work requirement (only available for offenders aged 16 or 17 on the date of conviction);
- a programme requirement;
- an attendance centre requirement;
- a prohibited activity requirement;
- a curfew requirement;
- an exclusion requirement;
- a residence requirement (only available for offenders aged 16 or 17 on the date of conviction);
- a local authority residence requirement;
- a fostering requirement;
- a mental health treatment requirement;
- a drug treatment requirement;
- a drug testing requirement;
- an intoxicating substance treatment requirement;
- an education requirement; and
- an electronic monitoring requirement (not yet fully in force).

A court must not make a YRO unless it is of the opinion that the offence, or the combination of the offence and one or more offences associated with it, was serious enough to warrant the making of such an order: s 179(2).

J24.1 Date of taking effect

Normally a YRO takes effect on the day on which the order is made: s 198(1).

But a court making a YRO may order that it is to take effect instead on a later date: s 198(2). If a DTO is in force in respect of an offender, a court making a YRO in respect of the offender may order that it is to take effect instead either when the period of supervision begins in relation to the DTO or on the expiry of the term of the DTO: s 181(2).

Blackstone's Handbook of Youths in the Criminal Courts. Mark Ashford, Gareth Branston, and Naomi Redhouse, Oxford University Press.
 DOI: 10.1093/oso/9780198913146.003.0056

J24.2 Existing orders

A court must not make a YRO in respect of an offender at a time when another YRO or a reparation order is in force, unless when it makes the new order it revokes the earlier order: s 181(4).

When a YRO is already in force when an offender is convicted of an offence, the sentencing court may revoke and re-sentence for the original offence: Sch 7, para 21 (see **J24.9**). Where the existing YRO was made by the Crown Court and that court did not include a direction that the YRO was to be subject to magistrates' court supervision (s 189), the youth court has no power to revoke the existing order. Instead, if the court considers that a new YRO is appropriate for the new offence, it must commit the case to the Crown Court for sentence: Sch 7, para 23 (see **J24.9** and **K4.1.1**).

J24.3 Concurrent and consecutive orders

Where the court is dealing with an offender for two or more associated offences on the same occasion, it may impose YROs for each offence but the court cannot combine any of the three kinds of YRO: (a) a YRO with ISS, (b) a YRO with fostering, or (c) a simple YRO: s 183(2).

Where the court includes requirements of the same kind in two or more YROs, the court must direct, for each kind of requirement, whether the requirements are to be concurrent or consecutive: s 183(5). Where the court directs that two or more requirements of the same kind are to be consecutive, the number of hours, days, or months specified are to be aggregated but must not, in aggregate, exceed the maximum number which may be specified in relation to any one of them: s 183(7). For example, if two unpaid work requirements are to run consecutively, the aggregate length of the requirement must not exceed 240 hours.

J24.4 Procedural requirements

The court must not make a YRO unless it is of the opinion that the offence(s) was/were serious enough to warrant the making of such an order: s 179(2). In forming that opinion, the court must take into account all the information that is available about the circumstances of the offence(s): s 179(3). The pre-sentence report (PSR) requirement under the SC, s 30 applies: s 179(4). Before making a YRO, the court must obtain and consider information about the offender's family circumstances and the likely effect of such an order on those circumstances: s 179(6).

The sentencing court must specify the end date (not more than three years after the date the order takes effect) for compliance with the requirements of the order. Different deadlines may be specified for different requirements and the last of those dates must be the same as the end date: s 187.

A YRO must specify the local justice area in which the offender resides or will reside: s 188.

Where the YRO is made by the Crown Court, the judge may include a direction that the order is to be subject to magistrates' court supervision (to deal with breach proceedings and any applications to amend or revoke the order): s 189. Without such a direction, the Crown Court will be the only court able to deal with such proceedings.

J24.5 **Requirements of the order**

Where a court passes a YRO, the particular requirements or combination of requirements imposed by the order must, in the opinion of the court, be the most suitable for the offender: s 186(3). The restrictions on liberty imposed by the order must be such as are in the opinion of the court commensurate with the seriousness of the offence(s): s 186(6).

If a YRO imposes two or more requirements, the court must, before making the order, consider whether, in the circumstances of the case, the requirements are compatible with each other: s 186(10).

The court must ensure, as far as practicable, that any requirement imposed by a YRO is such as to avoid:

- any conflict with the offender's religious beliefs,
- any interference with the times, if any, at which the offender normally works or attends school or any other educational establishment, and
- any conflict with the requirements of any other court order to which the offender may be subject: s 186(11).

The available requirements under a YRO are listed in the SC, s 174. The detailed provisions relating to the requirements which may be imposed are contained in the SC, Sch 6.

J24.5.1 ***Activity requirement (SC, Sch 6, paras 1 to 8)***

This requires the young offender to comply with one or more of the following:

- a specified place obligation (requiring the offender, in accordance with instructions of the responsible officer, to present themselves at a specified place to a person of the specified description and participate in activities),

- a specified activities obligation (requiring the offender, in accordance with instructions of the responsible officer, to participate in a specified activity, one of whose purpose may be reparation),
- a specified residential exercise obligation (requiring an offender, in accordance with the instructions of the responsible officer, to present themselves to a specified place and reside there for a specified number of days or to participate in an activity at a specified place for a specified number of days),
- an obligation to engage in activities as instructed by the responsible officer (requiring the offender to engage in activities in accordance with instructions of the responsible officer).

The number of days contained in the activity requirement must not exceed in aggregate 90 days (unless imposed as part of an ISS requirement, for which see **J24.5.18**).

A court may not impose an activity requirement unless:

- it has consulted with the YOT or local probation services;
- it is satisfied that it is feasible to secure compliance with the requirement; and
- it is satisfied that there are adequate provisions for the offender to participate in the activities proposed to be specified in the order in the local justice area in which the offender resides or is to reside.

A court may not include an activity requirement in a YRO if compliance with that requirement would involve the cooperation of a person other than the offender and the responsible officer, unless that other person consents to its inclusion.

J24.5.2 ***Supervision requirement (SC, Sch 6, para 9)***

This requires an offender to attend appointments with the responsible officer or another person determined by the responsible officer, at such times and places as may be determined by the responsible officer.

The requirement lasts for the length of the YRO. The frequency of the appointments will be determined by the responsible officer.

J24.5.3 ***Unpaid work requirement (SC, Sch 6, paras 10 to 11)***

This requirement may only be imposed where the offender is aged 16 or 17 at the time of the conviction for the offence: s 185(2).

The number of hours which a person may be required to work under an unpaid work requirement must be specified in the order and must be, in aggregate:

- not less than 40; and
- not more than 240.

A court may not impose an unpaid work requirement unless it is satisfied that:

- the offender is a suitable person to perform work under such a requirement as notified by the YOT or probation service; and
- provision for the offender to work under such a requirement is available in the local justice area in which the offender resides or is to reside.

The offender must perform for the number of hours specified in the order such work at such times as the responsible officer may specify in instructions.

The unpaid work must normally be performed during the period of 12 months beginning with the day on which the order takes effect. However, this period may be extended, on application to the court by either the responsible officer or the offender, where it appears to the court that it would be in the interests of justice to do so having regard to the circumstances which have arisen since the order was made: Sch 7, para 19.

Unless revoked, a YRO imposing an unpaid work requirement remains in force until the offender has completed the hours specified in the order.

Youth offenders sentenced to an unpaid work requirement will often carry out any work placement in the company of adult offenders. Previous guidance advised YOTs to consider carefully the circumstances of the young person concerned before proposing an unpaid work requirement and it suggested that, in general, an unpaid work requirement will only be suitable for young people with reasonable levels of maturity.

J24.5.4 *Programme requirement (SC, Sch 6, paras 12 to 13)*

This requires the offender to participate in a particular systematic set of activities ('a programme') specified in the order at a place or places so specified on such number of days as may be so specified.

The offender may be required to reside at any place specified in the YRO for any period so specified if it is necessary for the offender to reside there for that period in order to participate in the programme.

A court may not include a programme requirement in a YRO unless:

- the programme which the court proposes to specify in the order has been recommended to the court by the YOT or the probation service as being suitable for the offender; and
- the court is satisfied that the programme is available at the place or places proposed to be specified.

A court may not include a programme requirement in a YRO if compliance with that requirement would involve the cooperation of a person other than the offender and the offender's responsible officer, unless that other person consents to its inclusion.

A requirement to participate in a programme operates to require the offender:

- in accordance with instructions given by the responsible officer to participate in the programme at the place or places specified in the order on the number of days so specified, and
- while at any of those places, to comply with instructions given by, or under the authority of, the person in charge of the programme.

J24.5.5 *Attendance centre requirement (SC Sch 6, paras 14 to 15)*

This requires the offender to attend at a particular attendance centre specified in the order for a particular number of hours.

For an offender aged 16 or 17 at the date of conviction, the aggregate number of hours for which the offender may be required to attend must be:

- not less than 12, and
- not more than 36.

For an offender aged 14 or 15 at the date of conviction, the aggregate number of hours for which the offender may be required to attend must be:

- not less than 12, and
- not more than 24.

For an offender aged under 14 at the time of conviction, the aggregate number of hours for which the offender may be required to attend must not be more than 12.

A court may not include an attendance centre requirement in a YRO unless it—

- has been notified by the Secretary of State that an attendance centre is available for persons of the offender's description and provision can be made at the centre for the offender; and

- is satisfied that the attendance centre proposed to be specified is reasonably accessible to the offender, having regard to the means of access available to the offender and any other circumstances.

The responsible officer will notify the offender of the first time that they are required to attend at the attendance centre. The subsequent hours are to be fixed by the officer in charge of the centre:

- in accordance with arrangements made by the responsible officer, and
- having regard to the offender's circumstances.

An offender may not be required to attend at an attendance centre:

- more than once on any day, or
- for more than three hours at a time.

A requirement to attend at an attendance centre for any period on any occasion operates as a requirement, during that period, to engage in occupation, or receive instruction, under the supervision of and in accordance with instructions given by, or under the authority of, the officer in charge of the centre, whether at the centre or elsewhere.

J24.5.6 *Prohibited activity requirement (SC, Sch 6, paras 16 to 17)*

This requires the offender to refrain from participating in particular activities specified in the order:

- on one or more particular days, or
- for a particular period.

A court may not include a prohibited activity requirement in a YRO unless it has consulted the YOT or the probation service.

A prohibited activity requirement may, in particular, include a requirement that the offender does not possess, use, or carry a firearm within the meaning of the Firearms Act 1968.

J24.5.7 *Curfew requirement (SC, Sch 6, paras 18 to 19)*

This requires the offender to remain at a particular place for particular periods specified in the order. The order may specify different places or different periods for different days.

The curfew period cannot be for less than two hours a day nor for more than 20 hours a day. The curfew period must be not more than 112 hours in any period of seven days. The order may not specify periods which fall outside the period of 12 months beginning with the day on which the requirement first takes effect.

Before making a YRO imposing a curfew requirement, the court must obtain and consider information about each place proposed to be specified in the order (including information as to the attitude of persons likely to be affected by the enforced presence there of the offender).

The curfew must be electronically monitored unless:

- in the particular circumstances of the case, the court considers it inappropriate; or
- the court does not have the consent of any person (other than the offender) without whose cooperation it will not be practicable to secure that the monitoring takes place (para 44).

J24.5.8 *Exclusion requirement (SC, Sch 6, paras 20 to 21)*

This means that the youth offender is prohibited from entering a particular place or area specified in the order for a particular period. The specified period must not be more than three months.

The requirement may specify:

- more than one prohibited place;
- more than one exclusion period; and
- different prohibited places for different exclusion periods or different days.

The exclusion requirement must be electronically monitored unless:

- in the particular circumstances of the case, the court considers it inappropriate; or
- the court does not have the consent of any person (other than the offender) without whose cooperation it will not be practicable to secure that the monitoring takes place (para 44).

J24.5.9 *Residence requirement (SC, Sch 6, paras 22 to 23)*

This requires the youth offender, for a particular period, to:

- reside with a particular person (that person's consent must be obtained); or
- reside at a particular place (known as a 'place of residence requirement').

A place of residence requirement may not be imposed unless the offender was 16 or over at the time of conviction. Before making such a requirement, the court must consider the home surroundings of the offender. The court may not specify a hostel or other institution except on the recommendation of a YOT worker, probation officer, or local authority social worker. On making the place of residence requirement, the court may provide that the offender may reside in a place not specified in the order with the prior approval of the responsible officer. If this provision is not made, then any change of address will require an application to the court to vary the requirements of the YRO.

J24.5.10 *Local authority residence requirement (SC, Sch 6, paras 24 to 25)*

This requires the offender, during the particular period specified in the order, to reside in accommodation provided by or on behalf of a local authority specified in the order.

The court may also stipulate that the offender is not to reside with a person specified in the order.

A court may not include a local authority residence requirement in a YRO made in respect of an offence unless it is satisfied that:

- the behaviour which constituted the offence was due to a significant extent to the circumstances in which the offender was living; and
- the imposition of that requirement will assist in the offender's rehabilitation.

A court may not include a local authority residence requirement in a YRO unless it has consulted:

- a parent or guardian of the offender (unless it is impracticable to do so); and
- the local authority which is to receive the offender (i.e. the authority in whose area the offender resides or is to reside).

A court may not include a local authority residence requirement in a YRO in respect of an offender unless the offender was legally represented at the relevant time in court. This requirement does not apply if a representation order was originally granted for the proceedings but it was withdrawn because of the offender's conduct or if the offender failed to apply for a representation order at all.

The period for which the offender must reside in local authority accommodation must:

- not be longer than six months, and
- end before the offender reaches the age of 18.

J24.5.11 *Fostering requirement (SC, Sch 6, paras 26 to 27)*

A fostering requirement means a requirement that, for a particular period, the offender must reside with a local authority foster parent. A YRO with fostering is intended to be a community alternative to custody. A court may only impose the requirement if:

- the court is dealing with the offender for an offence which is punishable in the case of an adult with imprisonment: s 178;
- the court is of the opinion that the offence, or the combination of the offence and one or more offences associated with it, was so serious that, but for the availability of a YRO with fostering, a custodial sentence would be appropriate (or, if the offender was aged under 12, it would have been appropriate for an offender aged 12): s 180(2)(a); and
- if the offender was aged under 15 at the time of conviction, the court is of the opinion that the offender is a persistent offender (for definition of persistent offender see **J5.2.1**): s 180(2)(b).

Under a YRO with fostering, the offender must reside with a local authority foster parent for a period specified in the order, which must be no longer than 12 months and must not extend beyond the offender's 18th birthday. There is no minimum fostering period.

The court must specify the local authority which is to place the offender with a local authority foster parent under the Children Act 1989, s 22C or the Social Services and Well-being (Wales) Act 2014, s 81. The authority so specified must be the local authority in whose area the offender resides or is to reside.

A fostering requirement may be imposed if the court is satisfied—

- that the behaviour which constituted the offence was due to a significant extent to the circumstances in which the offender was living, and
- that the imposition of a fostering requirement would assist in the offender's rehabilitation.

A court may not impose a fostering requirement unless—

- it has consulted the offender's parents or guardians (unless it is impracticable to do so), and
- it has consulted the local authority which is to place the offender with a local authority foster parent.

A YRO which imposes a fostering requirement must also impose a supervision requirement. A YRO may not include an ISS requirement at the same time as a fostering requirement.

The court may not include a fostering requirement in a YRO in respect of an offender unless the offender was legally represented at the relevant time in court. This requirement does not apply if a representation order was originally granted for the proceedings but it was withdrawn because of the offender's conduct or if the offender failed to apply for a representation order at all.

A court may not include a fostering requirement in a YRO unless the court has been notified by the Secretary of State that arrangements for implementing such a requirement are available in the area of the local authority which is to place the offender with a local authority foster parent.

J24.5.12 *Mental health treatment requirement (SC, Sch 6, paras 28 to 30)*

This requires the offender to submit, during a particular period or periods specified in the order, to treatment by or under the direction of a registered medical practitioner or a registered psychologist (or both, for different periods) with a view to the improvement of the offender's mental condition.

The mental health treatment may be:

- in-patient treatment (treatment as a resident patient in a care home, independent hospital, or hospital within the meaning of the MHA 1983, but not where high security psychiatric services are provided);
- institution-based out-patient treatment (treatment as a non-resident patient at a particular institution or place); or
- practitioner-based treatment (treatment by or under the direction of a particular registered medical practitioner or registered psychologist, or both).

The YRO must specify the period(s) during which the offender is required to submit to mental health treatment and

- the care home or hospital where it is to be provided; or
- the institution or places where it is to be provided; or
- the registered medical practitioner and/or registered psychologist by whom or under whose direction it is to be provided;

but the order must not otherwise specify the nature of the treatment.

A court may not include a mental health treatment requirement in a YRO unless:

- the court is satisfied that the mental condition of the offender requires treatment, may be susceptible to treatment, but is not such as to warrant the making of a hospital order or guardianship order within the meaning of the MHA 1983;

- the court is satisfied that arrangements have been or can be made for the treatment intended to be specified in the order; and
- the offender has expressed willingness to comply with the requirement.

While the offender is under treatment as a resident patient in pursuance of a mental health treatment requirement, the responsible officer is to carry out the supervision of the offender to such extent only as may be necessary for the purpose of the revocation or amendment of the order.

J24.5.13 *Drug treatment requirement (SC, Sch 6, paras 31 to 33)*

This requires the offender to submit, during a period or periods specified in the order, to treatment, by or under the direction of a person so specified having the necessary qualifications or experience, with a view to the reduction or elimination of the offender's dependency on, or propensity to misuse, drugs.

A court may not include a drug treatment requirement in a YRO unless—

- the court is satisfied that the offender is dependent on, or has a propensity to misuse, drugs, and that the offender's dependency or propensity requires treatment and may be susceptible to treatment;
- the court has been notified by the Secretary of State that arrangements for implementing drug treatment requirements are in order in the local justice area in which the offender resides or is to reside;
- the court is satisfied that arrangements have been, or can be, made for the specified treatment;
- the requirement has been recommended to the court as suitable for the offender by a member of a YOT or a probation officer; and
- the offender has expressed willingness to comply with the requirement.

'Drug' means a controlled drug as defined by the Misuse of Drugs Act 1971 (MDA 1971), s 2.

J24.5.14 *Drug testing requirement (SC, Sch 6, paras 34 to 35)*

This requires the offender, for the purpose of ascertaining whether there is any drug in their body during any treatment period, to provide samples during the treatment period in accordance with instructions given by the responsible officer or the treatment director.

A court may not include a drug testing requirement in a YRO unless:

- the court has been notified by the Secretary of State that arrangements for implementing drug testing requirements are in force in the local justice area in which the offender resides or is to reside; and
- the offender has expressed willingness to comply with the requirement.

A YRO which imposes a drug testing requirement:

- must specify for each month the minimum number of occasions on which samples are to be provided, and
- may specify times at which, and circumstances in which, the responsible officer or treatment director may require samples to be provided, and descriptions of the samples which may be so required.

A YRO may impose a drug testing requirement only if it also imposes a drug treatment requirement.

J24.5.15 *Intoxicating substance treatment requirement (SC, Sch 6, paras 36 to 38)*

This requires the offender to submit, during a period or periods specified in the order, to treatment, by or under the direction of a person so specified having the necessary qualifications or experience, with a view to the reduction or elimination of the offender's dependency on, or propensity to misuse, intoxicating substances.

'Intoxicating substance' means:

- alcohol, or
- any other substance or product (other than a controlled drug within the meaning of the MDA 1971) which can be used for the purpose of causing intoxication, whether through inhaling it or its fumes or otherwise.

A court may not include an intoxicating substance treatment requirement in a YRO unless—

- the court is satisfied that the offender is dependent on, or has a propensity to misuse, intoxicating substances, and that the offender's dependency or propensity requires treatment and may be susceptible to treatment;
- the court is satisfied that arrangements have been, or can be, made for the specified treatment;

- the requirement has been recommended to the court as suitable for the offender by a member of a YOT or a probation officer; and
- the offender has expressed willingness to comply with the requirement.

Such treatment may be resident treatment (at a particular institution or place) or non-resident treatment (at a particular institution or place).

J24.5.16 *Education requirement (SC, Sch 6, paras 39 to 40)*

This requires the offender to comply, during a period or periods specified in the order, with arrangements for the offender's education:

- made for the time being by the offender's parent or guardian, and
- approved by the local education authority specified in the order.

The specified local education authority must be the authority for the area in which the offender resides or is to reside.

A court may not include an education requirement in a YRO unless:

- it has consulted the local education authority proposed to be specified in the order with regard to the proposal to include the requirement: and
- it is satisfied—
  - (i) that, in the view of that local education authority, arrangements exist for the offender to receive efficient full-time education suitable to the offender's age, ability, aptitude, and special educational needs (if any), and
  - (ii) that, having regard to the circumstances of the case, the inclusion of the education requirement is necessary for securing the good conduct of the offender or for preventing the commission of further offences.

Any period specified in a YRO as a period during which an offender must comply with approved education arrangements must not include any period after the offender has ceased to be of compulsory school age.

J24.5.17 *Electronic monitoring requirement (SC, Sch 6, paras 41 to 48)*

An electronic monitoring requirement means a requirement for securing the electronic monitoring of the offender's compliance with other requirements imposed by a YRO during a particular period ('the monitoring period'). It monitors compliance with:

- a curfew requirement;
- an exclusion requirement; or
- an attendance centre requirement.

A YRO imposing such a requirement must include provision for making a person responsible for the monitoring. The YRO must specify the monitoring period or provide for the responsible officer to determine the monitoring period. The offender must submit to being fitted with, or the installation of, any necessary apparatus and inspection or repair of that apparatus. The offender must not interfere with the working of any apparatus.

The court may not include an electronic monitoring requirement unless:

- any person (other than the offender) without whose cooperation it will not be practicable to secure the monitoring has provided their consent;
- the court has been notified by the Secretary of State that arrangements for electronic monitoring of offenders are available in the offender's home local justice area and for the requirement with which electronic monitoring will secure compliance; and
- the court is satisfied that the necessary provision can be made under the arrangements currently available.

In due course, the PCSCA 2022 will amend this requirement so that it becomes an 'electronic compliance monitoring requirement'. The amendments include provision for an 'electronic whereabouts monitoring requirement' which can stand alone from other requirements. These amendments are being piloted, between 3 July 2023 and 3 January 2025, in London, the North East, the West Midlands, and Wales.

J24.5.18 *Intensive supervision and surveillance (ISS) requirements (SC, Sch 6, para 2)*

A YRO may be a YRO with ISS: s 175.

A YRO with ISS is intended to be a community alternative to custody. A court may only impose the requirement if:

- the court is dealing with the offender for an offence which is punishable in the case of an adult with imprisonment: s 178;
- the court is of the opinion that the offence, or the combination of the offence and one or more offences associated with it, was so serious that, but for the availability of a YRO with ISS, a custodial sentence would be appropriate (or, if the offender was aged under 12, it would have been appropriate for an offender aged 12): s 180(2)(a); and

- if the offender was aged under 15 at the time of conviction, the court is of the opinion that the offender is a persistent offender (for definition of persistent offender see **J5.2.1**): s 180(2)(b).

A YRO with ISS must include the following requirements:

- an extended activity requirement (specified number of days more than 90 but not more than 180);
- a supervision requirement; and
- a curfew requirement.

In due course, the PCSCA 2022 will amend the maximum number of extended activity requirement days available to 365. This amendment is being piloted, between 3 July 2023 and 3 January 2025, in London, the North East, the West Midlands, and Wales.

The curfew must be electronically monitored unless:

- in the particular circumstances of the case, the court considers it inappropriate; or
- the court does not have the consent of any person (other than the offender) without whose cooperation it will not be practicable to secure that the monitoring takes place (para 44).

A YRO with ISS may also include other requirements but may not impose a fostering requirement: s 175(2).

The pre-sentence report will propose a level of ISS in accordance with the Scaled Approach. National standards have required the following number of contacts:

ISS type	Contacts per week		
Extended ISS (180 days)	1–4 months	5–6 months	7–12 months
	25 hours	15 hours	5 hours
Band 1 ISS (91 days)	1–3 months	4–6 months	
	25 hours	5 hours	
Band 2 ISS (91 days)	1–2 months	3 months	4–6 months
	20 hours	10 hours	5 hours

Where a high intensity ISS is considered appropriate, those national standards have allowed the requirement to be adjusted in the following cases:

- *ISS Junior version*—offender aged 13 years or younger—12.5 hours programmed contact time each week (of which seven and a half hours can be education) for three months followed by a minimum of five hours a week for the next three months.
- *ISS Education, training, and employment version*—minimum of one programmed contact each day totalling seven hours of

contact per week for three months, followed by a minimum of three hours a week for the next three months.

J24.6 Management of the order

There will be a responsible officer to manage each YRO. The SC, s 191 defines this as:

- if the only YRO requirement imposed is an attendance centre requirement, the officer in charge of the specified attendance centre;
- in any other case, the qualifying officer who is for the time being responsible for discharging the functions conferred on the responsible officer.

'Qualifying officer' means—

- a member of a YOT established by a local authority for the time being specified in the order for the purposes of this section, or
- an officer of a provider of probation services acting in the offender's home local justice area.

J24.7 Obligations of responsible officer

By the SC, s 192, where a YRO is in force, the responsible officer must—

- make any arrangements that are necessary in connection with the requirements imposed by the order,
- promote the offender's compliance with those requirements, and
- where appropriate, take steps to enforce those requirements.

By s 192(4), when giving instructions in pursuance of a YRO, the responsible officer must ensure, as far as practicable, that any instruction is such as to avoid:

- any conflict with the offender's religious beliefs,
- any interference with the times, if any, at which the offender normally works or attends school or any other educational establishment, and
- any conflict with the requirements of any other court order to which the offender may be subject.

J24.8 Duties of offender

By the SC, s 193, an offender in respect of whom a YRO is in force:

- must keep in touch with the responsible officer in accordance with such instructions as the offender may from time to time be given by that officer; and
- must notify the responsible officer of any change of address.

These obligations are enforceable as if they were a requirement imposed by the YRO.

J24.9 Further convictions while youth rehabilitation order in force

If an offender is convicted of an offence while a YRO is in force, the requirement that a new order cannot be made while another YRO is in force means that that provision has to be made for the convicting court to deal with the existing order. That power is set out in the SC, Sch 7, paras 20–23:

Sentencing Code, Sch 7

20

Paragraphs 21 and 22 apply where—
(a) a youth rehabilitation order ('the existing youth rehabilitation order') is in force in respect of an offender, and
(b) the offender is convicted of an offence (the 'further offence') by a youth court or other magistrates' court ('the convicting court').

21

(1) This paragraph applies if—
  (a) the existing youth rehabilitation order is subject to magistrates' court supervision, and
  (b) the convicting court is dealing with the offender for the further offence.
(2) If it appears to the convicting court to be in the interests of justice to do so, having regard to circumstances which have arisen since the youth rehabilitation order was made, the convicting court may—
  (a) revoke the youth rehabilitation order, or
  (b) both—
    (i) revoke the youth rehabilitation order, and
    (ii) re-sentence the offender for the offence in respect of which the order was made.
(3) Unless the offender is before it, the convicting court may not deal with the offender under sub-paragraph (2)(b) unless it has summoned the offender to appear before it.
(4) If the offender fails to appear in answer to a summons under sub-paragraph (3) the court may issue a warrant for the offender's arrest.
(5) If the convicting court deals with the offender under sub-paragraph (2)(b), it must take into account the extent to which the offender has complied with the requirements of the order.
(6) A person sentenced under sub-paragraph (2)(b) for an offence may appeal to the Crown Court against the sentence.

22

(1) Sub-paragraph (2) applies if—
  (a) the existing youth rehabilitation order was made by the Crown Court but is subject to magistrates' court supervision, and
  (b) the convicting court would, but for this paragraph, deal with the offender for the further offence.

(2) The convicting court may, instead of proceeding under paragraph 21—
(a) commit the offender to custody, or
(b) release the offender on bail,
until the offender can be brought before the Crown Court.
(3) Sub-paragraph (4) applies if the youth rehabilitation order is a Crown Court youth rehabilitation order.
(4) The convicting court may—
(a) commit the offender to custody, or
(b) release the offender on bail,
until the offender can be brought or appear before the Crown Court.
(5) Where the convicting court deals with an offender's case under sub-paragraph (2) or (4), it must send the Crown Court such particulars of the case as may be desirable.
(6) Unless the offender is before it, the convicting court may not deal with the offender under this paragraph unless it has summoned the offender to appear before it.
(7) If the offender fails to appear in answer to a summons under sub-paragraph (6) the court may issue a warrant for the offender's arrest.

23 Powers of Crown Court following subsequent conviction

(1) This paragraph applies where a youth rehabilitation order is in force in respect of an offender, and the offender—
(a) is convicted by the Crown Court of an offence, or
(b) is brought or appears before the Crown Court—
(i) by virtue of paragraph 22(2) or (4), or
(ii) having been committed by a magistrates' court to the Crown Court for sentence.
(2) If it appears to the Crown Court that it would be in the interests of justice to do so, having regard to circumstances which have arisen since the youth rehabilitation order was made, the Crown Court may—
(a) revoke the order, or
(b) both—
(i) revoke the order, and
(ii) re-sentence the offender for the offence in respect of which the order was made.
(3) Unless the offender is before it, the Crown Court may not deal with the offender under sub-paragraph (2)(b) unless it has summoned the offender to appear before it.
(4) If the offender fails to appear in answer to a summons under sub-paragraph (3) the Crown Court may issue a warrant for the offender's arrest.
(5) If the Crown Court deals with the offender under sub-paragraph (2)(b), it must take into account the extent to which the offender has complied with the requirements of the order.
(6) If the offender is brought or appears before the Crown Court by virtue of paragraph 22(2) or (4), the Crown Court may deal with the offender for the further offence in any way which the convicting court could have dealt with the offender for that offence.
(7) In sub-paragraph (6), 'further offence' and 'the convicting court' have the meanings given by paragraph 20.

J24.10 **Breach of a youth rehabilitation order**

Proceedings for breach of the requirements of the YRO normally start in the youth court (or adult magistrates' court if the offender has attained 18) unless the order was made in the Crown Court.

On breach of the requirements of a YRO, a court has the following options:

- take no action and allow the order to continue;
- fine the offender up to £2,500 for the breach and allow the order to continue;
- amend the requirements of the order; or
- revoke the order and re-sentence the offender for the original offence.

If the YRO was made by a Crown Court and no direction under the SC, s 189 was made for the order to be subject to magistrates' court supervision, then the youth court must commit the offender to the Crown Court (see **J24.4**).

Where the offender has 'wilfully and persistently' failed to comply with the order, and the court proposes to sentence again for the offence(s) in respect of which the order was made, additional powers are available. These additional powers are:

- If the offender has failed to comply with a YRO, the court may impose a YRO with ISS even if the original offence is not imprisonable or does not cross the custody threshold;
- If the offender has failed to comply with a YRO with ISS, the court may impose a custodial sentence (for an imprisonable offence) even if the original offence did not cross the custody threshold;
- If the offender has previously been re-sentenced to a YRO with ISS because of wilful and persistent failure to comply, and the court is having to deal with continuing wilful and persistent failure to comply, the court may impose a four-month DTO, even if the offence was not punishable with imprisonment.

The *Sentencing Children and Young People – Overarching Principles* definitive guideline summarizes the approach to dealing with young offenders for breach of the requirements of a YRO at paras 7.12 to 7.19:

> 7.13 If the terms of the order are amended the new requirements must be capable of being complied with before the expiry of the overall period. The court may impose any requirement that is currently available (provided the requirement is available to a child or young person who is the age that the offender was at the time in fact convicted) and this may be in addition to, or in substitution for, any requirements contained in the order. If the YRO did not contain an unpaid work requirement and the court includes such a requirement using this power, the minimum period of unpaid work is 20 hours; this will give greater flexibility when responding to less

serious breaches or where there are significant other requirements to be complied with.

7.14 A court may not amend the terms of a YRO that did not include an extended activity requirement or a fostering requirement by inserting them at this stage; should these requirements be considered appropriate following breach, the child or young person must be re-sentenced and the original YRO revoked.

7.15 A court must ensure that it has sufficient information to enable it to understand why the order has been breached and should be satisfied that the YOT and other local authority services have taken all steps necessary to ensure that the child or young person has been given appropriate opportunity and the support necessary for compliance. This is particularly important if the court is considering imposing a custodial sentence as a result of the breach.

7.16 Where the failure arises primarily from non-compliance with reporting or other similar obligations and a sanction is necessary, the most appropriate response is likely to be the inclusion of (or increase in) a primarily punitive requirement such as the curfew requirement, unpaid work, the exclusion requirement and the prohibited activity requirement or the imposition of a fine. However, continuing failure to comply with the order is likely to lead to revocation of the order and re-sentencing for the original offence.

7.17 Where the child or young person has 'wilfully and persistently' failed to comply with the order, and the court proposes to sentence again for the offence(s) in respect of which the order was made, additional powers are available.

A child or young person will almost certainly be considered to have 'wilfully and persistently' breached a YRO where there have been three breaches that have demonstrated a lack of willingness to comply with the order that have resulted in an appearance before court.

7.18 . . .

The primary objective when sentencing for breach of a YRO is to ensure that the child or young person completes the requirements imposed by the court.

7.19 If an offender has attained the age of 18 by the first court hearing then breach proceedings must be dealt with by the adult magistrates' court. If the court chooses to revoke the order then its powers are limited to those available to the court at the time of the original sentence.

The detailed provisions are contained in the SC, Sch 7, paras 4 to 11:

Sentencing Code, Sch 7

4 Duty to give warning or lay information relating to breach of order

(1) This paragraph applies where the responsible officer is of the opinion that the offender has without reasonable excuse breached a requirement of a youth rehabilitation order.

(2) Sub-paragraph (3) applies if—
  (a) the breach occurred during a warned period relating to an earlier breach of the order, and
  (b) during that warned period the offender had been given a further warning in relation to the order.

(3) The responsible officer must cause an information to be laid before a justice of the peace in respect of that breach unless of the opinion that there are exceptional circumstances which justify not doing so.

(4) If sub-paragraph (3) does not apply, the responsible officer must either—
  (a) give the offender a warning under this paragraph, or
  (b) cause an information to be laid before a justice of the peace in respect of that breach.

(5) A warning under this paragraph must—
  (a) describe the circumstances of the breach,
  (b) state that the breach is unacceptable, and
  (c) inform the offender that the offender will be liable to be brought before a court if the offender breaches a requirement of the order again—
    (i) more than once during the warned period, or
    (ii) if the warning is given during the warned period relating to an earlier breach of the order, during that warned period.

(6) For the purposes of this paragraph, 'warned period', in relation to a breach of a requirement of the youth rehabilitation order, means the period of 12 months beginning with the date on which a warning is given under this paragraph in relation to the breach.

(7) As soon as practicable after giving a warning under this paragraph, the responsible officer must record that fact.

5 Issue of summons or warrant by justice of the peace

(1) This paragraph applies where—
  (a) a youth rehabilitation order is in force, and
  (b) it appears on information to a justice of the peace that the offender has breached a requirement of the order.

(2) The justice may—
  (a) issue a summons requiring the offender to appear at the place and time specified in it, or
  (b) if the information is in writing and on oath, issue a warrant for the offender's arrest.

(3) A summons or warrant issued under this paragraph must direct the offender to appear or be brought—
  (a) in the case of a Crown Court youth rehabilitation order, before the Crown Court, and
  (b) in any other case, before the appropriate court.

(4) In sub-paragraph (3), 'appropriate court' means—
  (a) if the offender is aged under 18, a youth court acting in the relevant local justice area, and
  (b) if the offender is aged 18 or over, a magistrates' court (other than a youth court) acting in that local justice area.

(5) In sub-paragraph (4), 'relevant local justice area' means—
  (a) the local justice area in which the offender resides, or

(b) if it is not known where the offender resides, the offender's home local justice area.

(6) Sub-paragraphs (7) and (8) apply where—

(a) a summons is issued under this paragraph, and

(b) the offender does not appear in answer to it.

(7) If the summons required the offender to appear before the Crown Court, the Crown Court may—

(a) if the summons was issued by a justice of the peace, issue a further summons requiring the offender to appear at the place and time specified in it, or

(b) in any case, issue a warrant for the arrest of the offender.

(8) If the summons required the offender to appear before a magistrates' court, the magistrates' court may issue a warrant for the arrest of the offender.

6 Powers of magistrates' court

(1) This paragraph applies where—

(a) an offender appears or is brought before a youth court or other magistrates' court under paragraph 5, and

(b) it is proved to the satisfaction of the court that the offender has breached a requirement of the youth rehabilitation order without reasonable excuse,

and must be read with paragraphs 8 to 11.

(2) The court may deal with the case under sub-paragraph (5).

(3) If the youth rehabilitation order was made by the Crown Court, the court may instead—

(a) commit the offender to custody, or

(b) release the offender on bail,

until the offender can be brought or appear before the Crown Court.

(4) Where a court deals with the offender's case under sub-paragraph (3) it must send the Crown Court—

(a) a certificate signed by a justice of the peace certifying that the offender has breached the youth rehabilitation order in the respect specified in the certificate, and

(b) such other particulars of the case as may be desirable;

and a certificate purporting to be so signed is admissible as evidence of the failure before the Crown Court.

(5) Where the court deals with the case under this sub-paragraph, it may deal with the offender in respect of the breach in any one of the following ways—

(a) by ordering the offender to pay a fine of an amount not exceeding £2,500;

(b) by amending the terms of the youth rehabilitation order to add or substitute any requirement which it could include in a youth rehabilitation order if, applying the relevant assumptions, it were now making such an order in respect of the relevant offence;

(c) by re-sentencing the offender for the relevant offence.

(6) In this paragraph—

'relevant offence' means the offence in respect of which the youth rehabilitation order was made, and

the 'relevant assumptions' are that—
(a) the court has just convicted the offender of the relevant offence, and
(b) the offender is the same age as when in fact convicted of that offence.
(7) Sub-paragraph (5)(b) is subject to paragraph 10.
(8) In dealing with the offender under sub-paragraph (5), the court must take into account the extent to which the offender has complied with the requirements of the youth rehabilitation order.
(9) Where the court—
(a) deals with the offender under sub-paragraph (5)(b), and
(b) does not act in the offender's home local justice area,
it may exercise the power in paragraph 15 (amendment by reason of change of residence) as if it were the appropriate court for the purposes of that paragraph.
(10) Where the court deals with the offender under sub-paragraph (5)(c), it must revoke the youth rehabilitation order if it is still in force.
(11) An offender may appeal to the Crown Court against a sentence imposed under sub-paragraph (5)(c).

7 Powers of Crown Court

(1) This paragraph applies where—
(a) an offender appears or is brought before the Crown Court under paragraph 5 or by virtue of paragraph 6(3), and
(b) it is proved to the satisfaction of that court that the offender has breached a requirement of the youth rehabilitation order without reasonable excuse,
and must be read with paragraphs 8 to 11.
(2) The Crown Court may deal with the offender in respect of that breach in any one of the following ways—
(a) by ordering the offender to pay a fine of an amount not exceeding £2,500;
(b) by amending the terms of the youth rehabilitation order to add or substitute any requirement which it could include in a youth rehabilitation order if, applying the relevant assumptions, it were now making such an order in respect of the relevant offence;
(c) by re-sentencing the offender for the relevant offence.
(3) In this paragraph—
'relevant offence' means the offence in respect of which the youth rehabilitation order was made, and
the 'relevant assumptions' are that—
(a) the offender has just been convicted of the relevant offence by or before the court dealing with the offender, and
(b) the offender is the same age as when in fact convicted of that offence.
(4) Sub-paragraph (2)(b) is subject to paragraph 10.
(5) In dealing with the offender under sub-paragraph (2), the Crown Court must take into account the extent to which the offender has complied with the requirements of the youth rehabilitation order.

(6) Where the Crown Court deals with an offender under sub-paragraph (2)(c), it must revoke the youth rehabilitation order if it is still in force.
(7) In proceedings before the Crown Court under this paragraph any question whether the offender has breached a requirement of the youth rehabilitation order is to be determined by the court and not by the verdict of a jury.

8 Restriction of powers in paragraphs 6 and 7 where treatment required

(1) Sub-paragraph (2) applies where the offender—
 (a) is required by a treatment requirement of the youth rehabilitation order to submit to treatment, and
 (b) has refused to undergo any surgical, electrical or other treatment.
(2) The offender is not to be treated for the purposes of paragraph 6 or 7 as having breached the requirement on the ground only of that refusal if, in the opinion of the court, the refusal was reasonable having regard to all the circumstances.
(3) In this paragraph, 'treatment requirement' means—
 (a) a mental health treatment requirement,
 (b) a drug treatment requirement, or
 (c) an intoxicating substance treatment requirement.

9 Fines imposed under paragraphs 6 and 7

(1) A fine imposed under paragraph 6(5)(a) or 7(2)(a) is to be treated, for the purposes of any enactment, as being a sum adjudged to be paid by a conviction.
(2) Where—
 (a) a court is dealing with an offender for breach of a requirement of a youth rehabilitation order,
 (b) the offender is aged under 18, and
 (c) but for this sub-paragraph, the court would impose a fine under paragraph 6(5)(a) or 7(2)(a),
 section 380 (order for payment by parent or guardian) applies to the fine.

10 Powers in paragraphs 6 and 7 to impose other requirements: further provisions

(1) This paragraph applies where—
 (a) the magistrates' court deals with the offender under paragraph 6(5)(b), or
 (b) the Crown Court deals with the offender under paragraph 7(2)(b).
(2) Paragraphs 6(5)(b) and 7(2)(b) have effect subject to any provision that applies to the court in making a youth rehabilitation order as if the court were imposing the requirements on making the order.
 That is subject to the following provisions of this paragraph and to paragraph 11.
(3) Subject to sub-paragraph (4), any requirement imposed under paragraph 6(5)(b) or 7(2)(b) must be capable of being complied with before the end date.
(4) In dealing with an offender under paragraph 6(5)(b) or 7(2)(b) the court may substitute a later date for the end date.

(5) A date substituted under sub-paragraph (4)—
  (a) must not be more than 6 months after the existing end date;
  (b) subject to that, may be more than 3 years after the date on which the order took effect.
(6) Once the power in sub-paragraph (4) has been exercised in relation to the order, it may not be exercised again in relation to it by any court.
(7) Where—
  (a) in dealing with the offender under paragraph 6(5)(b) or 7(2)(b), the court imposes an unpaid work requirement, and
  (b) the youth rehabilitation order does not already contain an unpaid work requirement,
 the number of hours for which the offender may be required to work under the requirement (see paragraph 10(3) of Schedule 6) must not, in aggregate, be less than 20.
(8) The court may not under paragraph 6(5)(b) or 7(2)(b) impose—
  (a) an extended activity requirement, or
  (b) a fostering requirement,
 if the order does not already impose such a requirement.
(9) Sub-paragraph (10) applies where—
  (a) the order includes a fostering requirement (the 'original requirement'), and
  (b) under paragraph 6(5)(b) or 7(2)(b) the court proposes to substitute a new fostering requirement ('the substitute requirement') for the original requirement.
(10) The fostering period (see paragraph 26(3) of Schedule 6) for the substitute requirement must end—
  (a) within 18 months beginning with the day on which the original requirement first took effect, and
  (b) before the offender reaches the age of 18.

11 Powers in paragraphs 6 and 7 to re-sentence: further provisions relating to intensive supervision and surveillance

(1) This paragraph applies where—
  (a) the court is dealing with the offender under paragraph 6(5)(c) or 7(2)(c) for an offence, and
  (b) the offender has wilfully and persistently failed to comply with the youth rehabilitation order.
(2) The court may impose a youth rehabilitation order with intensive supervision and surveillance even if—
  (a) the offence is not an imprisonable offence, or
  (b) the court is not of the opinion mentioned in section 180(2)(a) (custodial sentence otherwise appropriate).
(3) If—
  (a) the order is a youth rehabilitation order with intensive supervision and surveillance, and
  (b) the offence is an imprisonable offence,
 the court may impose a custodial sentence even if it is not of the opinion mentioned in section 230(2) (threshold for imposing discretionary custodial sentence).

(4) If—
  (a) the order is a youth rehabilitation order with intensive supervision and surveillance which was imposed by virtue of sub-paragraph (2), and
  (b) the offence is not an offence punishable with imprisonment,

  the court's powers under paragraph 6(5)(c) or 7(2)(c) to deal with the offender for the offence include power to make a detention and training order for a term not exceeding 4 months.

J24.11 **Revocation of a youth rehabilitation order**

Sentencing Code, Sch 7

12 Youth rehabilitation order subject to magistrates' court supervision

(1) This paragraph applies where—
  (a) a youth rehabilitation order subject to magistrates' court supervision is in force in respect of an offender,
  (b) the offender or the responsible officer makes an application to the appropriate court under this sub-paragraph.

(2) In this paragraph, 'the appropriate court' means—
  (a) if the offender is aged under 18 when the application under sub-paragraph (1) is made, a youth court acting in the offender's home local justice area, and
  (b) if the offender is aged 18 or over at that time, a magistrates' court (other than a youth court) acting in that local justice area.

(3) No application may be made under sub-paragraph (1) while an appeal against the youth rehabilitation order is pending.

(4) Unless the application was made by the offender, the appropriate court—
  (a) must, before exercising its powers under sub-paragraph (5)(b), summon the offender to appear before it, and
  (b) if the offender does not appear in answer to the summons, may issue a warrant for the offender's arrest.

(5) If it appears to the appropriate court to be in the interests of justice to do so, having regard to circumstances which have arisen since the youth rehabilitation order was made, the appropriate court may—
  (a) revoke the order, or
  (b) both—
    (i) revoke the order, and
    (ii) re-sentence the offender for the offence in respect of which the order was made.

(6) The circumstances in which a youth rehabilitation order may be revoked under sub-paragraph (5) include the offender's—
  (a) making good progress, or

(b) responding satisfactorily to supervision or treatment (as the case requires).

(7) If the court deals with the offender under sub-paragraph (5)(b), it must take into account the extent to which the offender has complied with the requirements of the youth rehabilitation order.

(8) A person sentenced under sub-paragraph (5)(b) for an offence may appeal to the Crown Court against the sentence.

(9) If the application is dismissed, no-one may make a further application under sub-paragraph (1) during the 3 month period beginning with the date of the dismissal, except with the consent of the appropriate court.

13 Crown Court youth rehabilitation order

(1) This paragraph applies where a Crown Court youth rehabilitation order is in force and—
   (a) the offender, or
   (b) the responsible officer,
   makes an application to the Crown Court under this sub-paragraph.

(2) No application may be made under sub-paragraph (1) while an appeal against the youth rehabilitation order is pending.

(3) Unless the application was made by the offender, the Crown Court—
   (a) must, before exercising its powers under sub-paragraph (4)(b), summon the offender to appear before the court, and
   (b) if the offender does not appear in answer to the summons, may issue a warrant for the offender's arrest.

(4) If it appears to the Crown Court to be in the interests of justice to do so, having regard to circumstances which have arisen since the youth rehabilitation order was made, the Crown Court may—
   (a) revoke the order, or
   (b) both—
      (i) revoke the order, and
      (ii) re-sentence the offender for the offence in respect of which the order was made.

(5) The circumstances in which a youth rehabilitation order may be revoked under sub-paragraph (4) include the offender's—
   (a) making good progress, or
   (b) responding satisfactorily to supervision or treatment (as the case requires).

(6) If the Crown Court deals with the offender under sub-paragraph (4)(b), it must take into account the extent to which the offender has complied with the requirements of the youth rehabilitation order.

(7) If the application is dismissed, no-one may make a further application under sub-paragraph (1) during the 3 month period beginning with the date of the dismissal, except with the consent of the Crown Court.

J24.12 Amendment of a youth rehabilitation order

Sentencing Code, Sch 7

14 Appropriate court

In this Part of this Schedule, 'the appropriate court', in relation to an application relating to a youth rehabilitation order, means—

(a) if the order is subject to magistrates' court supervision—
  - (i) if the offender is aged under 18 when the application is made, a youth court acting in the offender's home local justice area, and
  - (ii) if the offender is aged 18 or over at that time, a magistrates' court (other than a youth court) acting in that local justice area;

(b) if the order is a Crown Court youth rehabilitation order, the Crown Court.

15 Amendment by appropriate court

(1) This paragraph applies where—
  - (a) a youth rehabilitation order is in force, and
  - (b) an application for the amendment of the order is made to the appropriate court by—
    - (i) the offender, or
    - (ii) the responsible officer.

(2) If the appropriate court is satisfied that the offender proposes to reside, or is residing, in a local justice area (a 'new local justice area') other than the offender's home local justice area for the time being specified in the order, the court—
  - (a) must, if the responsible officer made the application under sub-paragraph (1)(b), or
  - (b) may, in any other case,

  amend the youth rehabilitation order to specify the new local justice area as the offender's home local justice area.

  This is subject to paragraph 16.

(3) The appropriate court may by order amend the youth rehabilitation order—
  - (a) by cancelling any of the youth rehabilitation requirements of the order, or
  - (b) by replacing any of those requirements with a youth rehabilitation requirement of the same kind which it could include in a youth rehabilitation order if, applying the relevant assumptions, it were now making such an order in respect of the relevant offence.

  This is subject to paragraph 17.

(4) In this paragraph—

  'relevant offence' means the offence in respect of which the youth rehabilitation order was made, and

  the 'relevant assumptions' are that—
  - (a) the offender has just been convicted by or before the appropriate court of the relevant offence, and

(b) the offender is the same age as when in fact convicted of that offence.

16 Exercise of powers under paragraph 15(2): further provision

(1) This paragraph applies where—

(a) an application has been made under paragraph 15(1)(b) in respect of a youth rehabilitation order, and

(b) the court proposes to exercise its powers under paragraph 15(2) to specify a new local justice area in the order.

(2) Sub-paragraphs (3) and (4) apply if the youth rehabilitation order contains one or more requirements which, in the opinion of the court, cannot be complied with unless the offender continues to reside in the area then specified as the offender's home local justice area (each, a 'specific area requirement').

(3) The court may not amend the order under paragraph 15(2) to specify a new local justice area unless it also exercises the power in paragraph 15(3) (by cancelling or substituting each specific area requirement) so that the order can be complied with if the offender resides in the new local justice area.

(4) If the application was made by the responsible officer, the court must exercise the power in paragraph 15(3) in that way unless it considers it inappropriate to do so.

(5) Sub-paragraph (6) applies if the youth rehabilitation order imposes a programme requirement.

(6) The court may not amend the order under paragraph 15(2) unless it is satisfied that a programme which—

(a) corresponds as nearly as practicable to the programme specified in the order for the purposes of the programme requirement, and

(b) is suitable for the offender,

is available in the new local justice area.

17 Exercise of powers under paragraph 15(3)(b): further provision

(1) Before exercising its powers under paragraph 15(3)(b) (replacing requirements of a youth rehabilitation order), the court must summon the offender to appear before it, unless—

(a) the application under paragraph 15(1)(b) was made by the offender, or

(b) the court would exercise the powers only to—

(i) replace any requirement of the youth rehabilitation order with one of a shorter duration, or

(ii) substitute a new local justice area or place for one specified in the order.

(2) If the offender fails to appear in answer to a summons under sub-paragraph (1) the court may issue a warrant for the offender's arrest.

(3) Any requirement imposed under paragraph 15(3)(b) must be capable of being complied with before the end date.
This is subject to paragraph 18.

(4) Any provision that applies to a court where it imposes a requirement on making a youth rehabilitation order applies also to the court where it imposes such a requirement under paragraph 15(3)(b).
That is subject to the following provisions of this paragraph and paragraphs 18 and 19.

(5) Sub-paragraph (6) applies where—
  (a) the order includes a fostering requirement (the 'original requirement'), and
  (b) under paragraph 15(3)(b) the court proposes to substitute a new fostering requirement ('the substitute requirement') for the original requirement.

(6) The fostering period (see paragraph 26(3) of Schedule 6) for the substitute requirement must end—
  (a) within 18 months beginning with the day on which the original requirement first took effect, and
  (b) before the offender reaches the age of 18.

(7) The court may not under paragraph 15(3)(b) impose—
  (a) a mental health treatment requirement,
  (b) a drug treatment requirement, or
  (c) a drug testing requirement,
unless the offender has expressed willingness to comply with the requirement.

(8) If the offender fails to express willingness to comply with a mental health treatment requirement, a drug treatment requirement or a drug testing requirement which the court proposes to impose under paragraph 15(3)(b), the court may—
  (a) revoke the youth rehabilitation order, and
  (b) re-sentence the offender for the offence in respect of which the order was made.

(9) If the court deals with the offender under sub-paragraph (8)(b), it must take into account the extent to which the offender has complied with the requirements of the order.

J24.13 **Extension of a youth rehabilitation order**

On application by the responsible officer or the offender, a court may extend the length of a YRO by up to six months if the requirements of the order have not been completed. This power may only be exercised once.

In the case of an unpaid work requirement, the court may extend the period in which the work must be completed. In this case only, the extension is not limited to six months.

Sentencing Code, Sch 7

18 Extension of order

(1) The appropriate court may, on the application of–
  (a) the offender, or
  (b) the responsible officer,
  amend a youth rehabilitation order by substituting a later date for the end date.
(2) Unless the application was made by the offender, the court–
  (a) must, before exercising its powers under this paragraph, summon the offender to appear before the court, and
  (b) if the offender fails to appear in answer to the summons, may issue a warrant for the offender's arrest.
(3) A date substituted under sub-paragraph (1)–
  (a) must not be more than 6 months after the existing end date;
  (b) subject to that, may be more than 3 years after the date on which the order took effect.
(4) Once the power in sub-paragraph (1) has been exercised in relation to the order, it may not be exercised again in relation to it by any court.

19 Extension of unpaid work requirement

(1) This paragraph applies where a youth rehabilitation order imposing an unpaid work requirement is in force in respect of an offender.
(2) The appropriate court may, on the application of–
  (a) the offender, or
  (b) the responsible officer,
  extend the period of 12 months specified in paragraph 10(1)(b) of Schedule 6, if it appears to the appropriate court to be in the interests of justice to do so having regard to circumstances which have arisen since the order was made.
(3) Unless the application was made by the offender, the court–
  (a) must, before exercising its powers under this paragraph, summon the offender to appear before the court, and
  (b) if the offender fails to appear in answer to the summons, may issue a warrant for the offender's arrest.

J24.14 Warrants and adjournments

Sentencing Code, Sch 7

24

(1) Sub-paragraph (2) applies where an offender–
  (a) is arrested under a warrant issued by virtue of this Schedule, and

(b) cannot immediately be brought before the court before which the warrant directs the offender to be brought ('the relevant court').

(2) The person in whose custody the offender is—

(a) may arrange for the offender to be detained in a place of safety for a period of not more than 72 hours from the time of the arrest, and

(b) must, within that period, bring the offender before a youth court or, if the offender is aged 18 or over, a magistrates' court other than a youth court.

(3) In the case of a warrant issued by the Crown Court, section 81(5) of the Senior Courts Act 1981 (duty to bring person before magistrates' court) does not apply.

(4) A person detained in accordance with arrangements under sub-paragraph (2)(a) is deemed to be lawfully detained.

25

(1) This paragraph applies where the court before which the offender is brought under paragraph 24(2) ('the alternative court') is not the relevant court.

(2) If the relevant court is a magistrates' court—

(a) the alternative court may—

(i) direct that the offender be released forthwith, or

(ii) remand the offender, and

(b) section 128 of the Magistrates' Courts Act 1980 (remand in custody or on bail) applies as if the court referred to in subsections (1)(a), (3), (4)(a) and (5) were the relevant court.

(3) If the relevant court is the Crown Court, section 43A of the Magistrates' Courts Act 1980 (functions of magistrates' court where a person in custody is brought before it with a view to appearance before the Crown Court) applies as if, in subsection (1)—

(a) the words 'issued by the Crown Court' were omitted, and

(b) the reference to section 81(5) of the Senior Courts Act 1981 were a reference to paragraph 24(2)(b).

(4) If the offender is aged under 18, any power conferred by section 43A or 128 of the Magistrates' Courts Act 1980 to remand the offender in custody is to be taken to be a power to remand the offender to accommodation provided by or on behalf of a local authority.

(5) If the court remands the offender to accommodation provided by or on behalf of a local authority, it must designate, as the authority which is to receive the offender, the local authority for the area in which it appears to the court that the offender resides.

(6) In this paragraph 'relevant court' has the same meaning as in paragraph 24.

26

(1) This paragraph applies to any hearing relating to an offender held by a youth court or other magistrates' court in any proceedings under this Schedule.

(2) The court may adjourn the hearing.

(3) Where the court adjourns the hearing under sub-paragraph (2), it may—

(a) direct that the offender be released forthwith, or

(b) remand the offender.

(4) Where the court remands the offender under sub-paragraph (3)—

(a) it must fix the time and place at which the hearing is to be resumed, and

(b) the remand must require the offender to be brought before the court at that time and place.

(5) Where the court adjourns the hearing under sub-paragraph (2) but does not remand the offender—

(a) it may fix the time and place at which the hearing is to be resumed, but

(b) if it does not do so, must not resume the hearing unless it is satisfied that the following persons have had adequate notice of the time and place of the resumed hearing—

(i) the offender,

(ii) if the offender is aged under 14, a parent or guardian of the offender, and

(iii) the responsible officer.

(6) The powers of a magistrates' court under this paragraph may be exercised by a single justice of the peace, notwithstanding anything in the Magistrates' Courts Act 1980.

(7) This paragraph—

(a) applies to any hearing in any proceedings under this Schedule in place of section 10 of the Magistrates' Courts Act 1980 (adjournment of trial) where that section would otherwise apply, but

(b) is not to be taken to affect the application of that section to hearings of any other description.

J24.15 **Youth rehabilitation order requirements**

Requirement	Age on conviction	Possible range	Defence consent required	Preconditions	Other comments
Activity **J24.5.1**	10–17	Up to 90 days	No	Court must consult with YOT or probation service. It must be feasible to secure compliance with the requirement.	
Supervision **J24.5.2**	10–17	Up to 3 years	No	–	
Unpaid work **J24.5.3**	16–17	40 to 240 hours	No	The court must be satisfied that the offender is suitable to perform the work and provision for such work is available.	
Programme **J24.5.4**	10–17		No	The programme must have been recommended by the YOT or probation service. Consent of third party required if their cooperation is needed.	

Requirement	Age on conviction	Possible range	Defence consent required	Preconditions	Other comments
Attendance centre **J24.5.5**	10–17	16–17 years: 12–36 hours; 14–15 years: 12–24 hours;10–14 years: 0–12 hours	No	The court must be satisfied that the centre is reasonably accessible for the offender.	
Prohibited activity **J24.5.6**	10–17		No	Court must consult with YOT or probation service.	
Curfew **J24.5.7**		Max 12 months; 2–16 hours a day; Max 112 hours a week	No	Court must obtain and consider information about the proposed curfew address. Consent of third party required if their cooperation is needed	Electronic monitoring requirement should normally be imposed as well
Exclusion **J24.5.8**	10–17	Max 3 months	No		Electronic monitoring requirement should normally be imposed as well
Residence with specified person **FJ24.5.9**	10–17		No	The specified person must consent.	

Requirement	Age on conviction	Possible range	Defence consent required	Preconditions	Other comments
Place of residence **J24.5.9**	16–17		No	Court must consider the offender's home surroundings. Residence specified must be recommended by YOT or probation service.	
Residence in local authority accommodation **J24.5.10**		Max 6 months (must not include any period after offender has reached age of 18)	No	The behaviour which led to the offence was, to a significant extent, due to the living conditions of the young person. The addition of the requirement will assist the rehabilitation of the young person. The court must consult with parent/guardian and local authority. Offender must be legally represented	
Fostering **J24.5.11**	10–17	Max 12 months (must not include any period after offender has reached age of 18)	No	Statutory threshold—see **J24.5.11** The behaviour which led to the offence was, to a significant extent, due to the living conditions of the young person. The imposition of the requirement would assist in the offender's rehabilitation. The court must consult with parent/guardian and local authority. Offender must be legally represented.	

Requirement	Age on conviction	Possible range	Defence consent required	Preconditions	Other comments
Mental health treatment **J24.5.12**	10–17		Yes	The mental condition of the young person is such that it requires and may be susceptible to treatment, but is not such as to warrant the making of a hospital order or guardianship order under the MHA 1983.	
Drug treatment **J24.5.13**	10–17		Yes	Offender is dependent on, or has the propensity to misuse, drugs and their dependency or propensity is such that it requires and may be susceptible to treatment. Requirement recommended by YOT or probation service has recommended treatment.	Drug testing requirement may also be imposed—See **J24.5.14**
Drug testing **J24.5.14**	10–17		Yes	Only if court also imposes a drug treatment requirement.	
Intoxicating substance treatment **J24.15**	10–17		Yes	The young person is dependent on, or has the propensity to misuse, intoxicating substances and their dependency or propensity is such that it requires treatment and may be susceptible to treatment.	

Requirement	Age on conviction	Possible range	Defence consent required	Preconditions	Other comments
Education **J24.5.16**	Compulsory school age	Length of YRO	No	In the view of the local authority, arrangements exist for the young person to receive efficient full-time education suitable to the young person's age, ability, aptitude, and special educational need (if any). Requirement is necessary for securing the good conduct of the young person or for preventing re-offending.	
Electronic monitoring **J24.5.17**	10–17		No	**Dependent on other requirements**	Monitors compliance with curfew, exclusion or attendance centre requirement
Intensive supervision and surveillance (ISS) **J24.5.18**	10–17	Extended activity: 90–180 days; Supervsn.: up to 3 years; Curfew: Max 12 months; 2–16 hours a day; Max 112 hours a week	No	Statutory threshold – see **J24.5.18**	Electronic monitoring requirement should normally be imposed as well.

Part K
Youths in the Crown Court

K1 Routes to Trial on Indictment

The circumstances when a youth may be sent to the Crown Court for trial on indictment are set out in the CDA 1998, ss 51 and 51A. A youth will only appear in the Crown Court for trial:

- when charged with homicide: s 51A(2), (3)(a) and (12)(a);
- when charged with a firearms offence subject to a mandatory minimum sentence: s 51A(2), (3)(a), (12)(a) and 12(b);
- when charged with a grave crime and a court has determined that it ought to be possible to impose a sentence of more than two years' detention: s 51A(2) and (3)(b);
- when charged with a terrorism offence mentioned in the SC, s 252A(1)(a) and the court has determined that it ought to be possible to impose a sentence of more than two years' detention: s 51A(2) and (3)(ba);
- when notice is served in a serious or complex fraud case: ss 51A(2), (3)(c) and 51B;
- when notice is served in a child case: ss 51A(2), (3)(c) and 51C;
- when charged with a specified offence and it is considered that the criteria for imposing a sentence of extended detention are met: s 51A(2) and (3)(d);
- when charged with an adult offender who has been sent to the Crown Court and it has been determined that the cases should be kept together in the interests of justice: s 51(7).

Crime and Disorder Act 1998

51 Sending cases to the Crown Court: adults

(7) Where—

(a) the court sends an adult ('A') for trial under subsection (1), (3) or (5) above; and

(b) a child or young person appears or is brought before the court on the same or a subsequent occasion charged jointly with A with an indictable offence for which A is sent for trial under subsection (1), (3) or (5) above, or an indictable offence which appears to the court to be related to that offence,

the court shall, if it considers it necessary in the interests of justice to do so, send the child or young person forthwith to the Crown Court for trial for the indictable offence.

51A Sending cases to the Crown Court: children and young persons

(1) This section is subject to sections 24A and 24B of the Magistrates' Courts Act 1980 (which provide for certain offences involving children or young persons to be tried summarily).

Blackstone's Handbook of Youths in the Criminal Courts. Mark Ashford, Gareth Branston, and Naomi Redhouse, Oxford University Press.
 DOI: 10.1093/oso/9780198913146.003.0057

(2) Where a child or young person appears or is brought before a magistrates' court ('the court') charged with an offence and any of the conditions mentioned in subsection (3) below is satisfied, the court shall send him forthwith to the Crown Court for trial for the offence.

(3) Those conditions are—

(a) that the offence falls within subsection (12) below;

(b) that the offence is such as is mentioned in section 249(1)(a) or (b) of the Sentencing Code (other than one mentioned in paragraph (d) below in relation to which it appears to the court as mentioned there) and the court considers that if he is found guilty of the offence it ought to be possible to sentence him in pursuance of section 251(2) of that Code;

(ba) that the offence is such as is mentioned in section 252A(1)(a) of the Sentencing Code and the court considers that if he is found guilty of the offence it ought to be possible to sentence him under that section to a term of detention of more than two years;

(c) that notice is given to the court under section 51B or 51C below in respect of the offence;

(d) that the offence is a specified offence (within the meaning given by section 306 of the Sentencing Code) and it appears to the court that if he is found guilty of the offence the criteria in section 255(1) of that Code for the imposition of an extended sentence of detention would be met.

(4) Where the court sends a child or young person for trial under subsection (2) above, it may at the same time send him to the Crown Court for trial for any indictable or summary offence with which he is charged and which—

(a) (if it is an indictable offence) appears to the court to be related to the offence mentioned in subsection (2) above; or

(b) (if it is a summary offence) appears to the court to be related to the offence mentioned in subsection (2) above or to the indictable offence, and which fulfils the requisite condition (as defined in subsection (9) below).

(5) Where a child or young person who has been sent for trial under subsection (2) above subsequently appears or is brought before a magistrates' court charged with an indictable or summary offence which—

(a) appears to the court to be related to the offence mentioned in subsection (2) above; and

(b) (in the case of a summary offence) fulfils the requisite condition, the court may send him forthwith to the Crown Court for trial for the indictable or summary offence.

(6) Where—

(a) the court sends a child or young person ('C') for trial under subsection (2) or (4) above; and

(b) an adult appears or is brought before the court on the same or a subsequent occasion charged jointly with C with an either-way offence for which C is sent for trial under subsection (2) or

(4) above, or an either-way offence which appears to the court to be related to that offence,

the court shall where it is the same occasion, and may where it is a subsequent occasion, send the adult forthwith to the Crown Court for trial for the either-way offence.

(7) Where the court sends an adult for trial under subsection (6) above, it shall at the same time send him to the Crown Court for trial for any either-way or summary offence with which he is charged and which—

(a) (if it is an either-way offence) appears to the court to be related to the offence for which he was sent for trial; and

(b) (if it is a summary offence) appears to the court to be related to the offence for which he was sent for trial or to the either-way offence, and which fulfils the requisite condition.

(8) The trial of the information charging any summary offence for which a person is sent for trial under this section shall be treated as if the court had adjourned it under section 10 of the 1980 Act and had not fixed the time and place for its resumption.

(9) A summary offence fulfils the requisite condition if it is punishable with imprisonment or involves obligatory or discretionary disqualification from driving.

(10) In the case of a child or young person charged with an offence—

(a) if the offence satisfies any of the conditions in subsection (3) above, the offence shall be dealt with under subsection (2) above and not under any other provision of this section or section 51 above;

(b) subject to paragraph (a) above, if the offence is one in respect of which the requirements of subsection (7) of section 51 above for sending the child or young person to the Crown Court are satisfied, the offence shall be dealt with under that subsection and not under any other provision of this section or section 51 above.

(11) The functions of a magistrates' court under this section, and its related functions under section 51D below, may be discharged by a single justice.

(12) An offence falls within this subsection if—

(a) it is an offence of homicide;

(b) each of the requirements of section 311(1) of the Sentencing Code would be satisfied with respect to—

(i) the offence; and

(ii) the person charged with it,

if he were convicted of the offence; or

(c) section 29(3) of Violent Crime Reduction Act 2006 (minimum sentences in certain cases of using someone to mind a weapon) would apply if he were convicted of the offence.

K1.1 **Remittal for trial**

The Crown Court now has a general power to remit proceedings to the magistrates' court and, in relation to youth defendants, it has a duty to consider whether to send them back for trial and must give reasons if it does not remit. The Crown Court cannot remit a youth facing a homicide offence or a firearms offence carrying a mandatory minimum sentence.

Section 46ZA of the Senior Courts Act 1981 was introduced by the JRCA 2022:

Senior Courts Act 1981

46ZA Remitting proceedings to magistrates' courts for trial

(1) In a case where a person has been sent by a magistrates' court to the Crown Court for trial for an offence, the Crown Court may send the person back to a magistrates' court for trial.

(2) The Crown Court may not exercise the power in subsection (1)—
  (a) in respect of a person who has attained the age of 18, or is not an individual, if the offence in question is triable only on indictment;
  (b) in respect of a person who has not attained the age of 18, if the offence in question falls within section 51A(12) of the Crime and Disorder Act 1998.

(3) In the case of an offence that is triable either way, the Crown Court may not exercise the power in subsection (1)—
  (a) unless the person appears in court or consents to the power being exercised in the person's absence, and
  (b) in the case of a person who has attained the age of 18, or is not an individual, unless the person consents to the power being exercised.

(4) If a person under the age of 18 appears before the Crown Court having been sent to it as mentioned in subsection (1), the Crown Court—
  (a) must consider whether to send the person back to a magistrates' court under subsection (1), and
  (b) if it decides not to send the person back, must give reasons for not doing so.

(5) In deciding whether to exercise the power in subsection (1), the Crown Court must—
  (a) take into account any other offence before the Crown Court that appears to the court to be related to that offence (whether the same, or a different, person is accused or has been convicted of the other offence), and
  (b) have regard to any allocation guidelines (or revised allocation guidelines) issued as definitive guidelines under section 122 of the Coroners and Justice Act 2009.

(6) Where the Crown Court exercises the power in subsection (1) it may, subject to section 25 of the Criminal Justice and Public Order Act 1994 (restrictions on granting bail), give such directions as appear to be necessary—

(a) with respect to the custody of the accused, or
(b) for the accused's release on bail,
until the accused can appear or be brought before the magistrates' court.
(7) There is no right of appeal against an order under subsection (1).

K1.2 Committal for sentence

Changes to the powers of the youth court to commit for sentence and guidance from the Sentencing Council, Court of Appeal, and High Court have resulted in a reduction in the number of cases being sent from the youth court to the Crown Court for trial. The youth court can retain jurisdiction for trial and, if appropriate, commit for sentence in the event of a conviction. Cases may now be sent for sentence following a guilty plea or a finding of guilt after trial.

Section 16 of the SC provides:

Sentencing Code

16 Committal for sentence of young offenders on summary trial of certain serious offences

(1) This section applies where—
(a) on the summary trial of an offence within paragraph (a) or (b) of the table in section 249(1) (offences punishable with imprisonment for 14 years or more and certain sexual offences), a person is convicted of the offence,
(b) the person is aged under 18 at the time of conviction, and
(c) the court is of the opinion that—
(i) the offence, or
(ii) the combination of the offence and one or more offences associated with it, was such that the Crown Court should have power to deal with the offender by imposing a sentence of detention under section 250.
(2) The court may commit the offender in custody or on bail to the Crown Court for sentence in accordance with section 22(2).
(3) For powers of the court, where it commits a person under subsection (2), also to commit in respect of other offences, see section 20.

This power, restored in relation to findings of guilt at trial by the Criminal Justice and Courts Act 2015, s 53, means that a youth court dealing with a 'grave crime' can commit the case to the Crown Court for sentence either on indication of plea (see **H2**) or after conviction. Guidance on use of the power can be found in *DPP v South Tyneside Youth Court* [2015] EWHC 1455 (Admin), where it was suggested that, in most cases, a decision as to whether there was a 'real prospect' of a sentence of long-term detention will generally only be apparent when the court has determined the full circumstances of the offence and has a greater understanding of the offender. The greater suitability, in most cases, of the youth court as a venue for a trial hearing was emphasized.

On committal for sentence under s 16, the Crown Court has all the powers set out in **K4** and may still impose a sentence which the youth court would have had the power to impose. Where related offences have also been committed for sentence under the SC, s 19, unless the youth or magistrates' court stated that they were of the opinion that they could also have been committed under s 16, then the Crown Court is restricted to the power of the committing court in sentencing them.

K2 Case Management and Effective Participation

K2.1 Fair trial

The fair trial guarantee of ECHR Article 6 includes the ability of the youth defendant to participate effectively in the trial process (*V v United Kingdom* (2000) EHRR 121—see **I2**).

The demands of a trial on indictment are considerably greater than those of a summary trial. It is therefore in the Crown Court that concerns regarding effective participation arise in a higher proportion of cases. It is good practice for a defence lawyer to collect background information about a youth defendant's educational history as well as any information about any mental disorder. If significant doubts exist about their ability to participate effectively, consideration should be given to instructing a chartered psychologist to carry out psychometric testing and to advice on the defendant's ability to participate effectively in the proceedings.

Careful consideration should be given to the guidance contained in the CPDs, part 6.4 *Vulnerable Defendants*. The guidance applies to all defendants under the age of 18. It advises that all possible steps should be taken to assist a youth defendant to understand and participate in criminal proceedings and the ordinary trial process should, so far as necessary, be adapted to meet those needs. The appropriate time to address these issues is at the plea and trial preparation hearing and the appropriate trial modifications should be raised in the case management form.

K2.2 Fitness to plead

In *R v Pritchard* (1836) 7 C& P 303, it was held that the test was:

> Whether he is of sufficient intellect to comprehend the course of proceedings on the trial, so as to make a proper defence—to know that he might challenge [any jurors] to whom he may object—and to comprehend the details of the evidence . . . if you think that there is no certain mode of communicating the details of the trial to the prisoner, so that he can clearly understand them, and be able properly to make his defence to the charge; you ought to find that he is not of sane mind. It is not enough, that he may have a general capacity of communicating on ordinary matters.

Blackstone's Handbook of Youths in the Criminal Courts. Mark Ashford, Gareth Branston, and Naomi Redhouse, Oxford University Press.
 DOI: 10.1093/oso/9780198913146.003.0058

The test has been further considered in *R v Podola* [1960] 1 QB 325, where the court held that the test was whether:

> he is of sufficient intellect to comprehend the course of proceedings on the trial, so as to make a proper defence—to know that he might challenge (the jurors) to whom he may object—and to comprehend the details of the evidence, which in a case of this nature must constitute a minute investigation, upon this issue, therefore, if you think that there is no certain mode of communicating details of the trial to the prisoner, so that he can clearly understand them, and be able properly to make his defence to the charge; you ought to find that he is not of sane mind.

Although not stated in either of the formulations of the test, it is generally accepted that the defendant must also be able to give coherent and reliable evidence in their own defence (if they so wish).

In the case of youth defendants, the reason for being unfit to plead could be because of any one or more of:

- mental illness;
- learning disability or other mental disorder; or
- developmental immaturity.

K2.2.1 *Procedure*

The procedure is covered by the Criminal Procedure (Insanity) Act 1964:

- The question of fitness to plead may be raised by any party to the proceedings, but is normally raised by the defence.
- If raised by the defence, the burden of proof rests upon the defendant on the balance of probabilities.
- If the question of fitness to plead is raised before the defendant is asked to plead, a judge sitting without a jury will determine whether the defendant is unfit to stand trial. The court shall not make a finding of unfitness except on the written or oral evidence of two or more registered medical practitioners, at least one of whom is approved under the MHA 1983, s 12.
- If the judge finds the defendant fit to plead, a jury shall be empanelled to try them.
- If the judge finds the defendant unfit to plead, a jury shall be empanelled to determine whether the defendant did the act or made the omission alleged as the offence.

This statutory procedure is compatible with the ECHR as it strikes a proper balance between the rights of those accused of crime and the victims of the crime, as well as the general public: *R v H* [2003] UKHL 1, [2003] 1 WLR 411.

K2.2.2 *Possible disposals in the Crown Court*

Where an accused has been found both unfit to plead and to have done the act or made the omission alleged, the court may make one of the following orders:

- a hospital order (with or without a restriction order); or
- a supervision order; or
- an order for their absolute discharge.

Hospital orders and restriction orders may only be made if the criteria of the MHA 1983, ss 37 and 41 are satisfied (for which see **J9**). There will need to be medical evidence that justifies detention on the grounds of the accused's mental state.

K2.2.3 *Fitness to plead as measure of last resort*

In *R v Walls* [2011] EWCA Crim 443, Thomas LJ stressed that the adequacy of measures such as intermediaries to assist the defendant in the trial process should be carefully considered before embarking on the statutory fitness to plead procedure. He pointed out the disadvantages of the statutory procedure both for the defendant (who is not able to testify in their own defence) and for the protection of the general public (limited range of disposals). Therefore, where the procedure is invoked, courts must rigorously examine the evidence of psychiatrists adduced before them and then subject that evidence to careful analysis against the *Pritchard* criteria as interpreted in *Podola*. Save in cases where the unfitness is clear, the fact that psychiatrists agree is not enough; a court would be failing in its duty to both the public and a defendant if it did not rigorously examine the evidence and reach its own conclusion.

K2.3 Reporting restrictions

In proceedings involving youth defendants in the Crown Court, the automatic reporting restrictions applicable in the youth court under the CYPA 1933, s 49 do not apply.

Instead, the court may make an order under the YJCEA 1999, s 45 imposing reporting restrictions (see **H11**).

At the plea and trial preparation hearing, the Crown Court should be ready, if it has not already done so, to make an order under s 45. Though the magistrates' court has the power to give a direction under s 45 that will apply in the Crown Court (see Crim PR, r 3.5(3)), the Crown Court will need to ascertain whether such a direction has been given.

K3 **Remittal for Sentence**

The power to remit to the youth court for sentence is contained in the SC, s 25 (see **J14**). It should be noted that, when exercised by the Crown Court, remittal must be to a youth court acting for the place where the youth was sent to the Crown Court for trial, unless the court is satisfied that it would be undesirable to do so.

The wording of s 25 creates a presumption in favour of remittal for sentence but this is not necessarily how the power has been exercised in practice. When considering the similar provision in the CYPA 1933, s 56 in *R v Lewis* (1984) 79 Cr App R 94, Lord Lane identified the following reasons for not remitting:

- that, in a case where the youth pleaded not guilty and was convicted, the Crown Court judge who presided at the trial will be better informed about the facts of the offence and general nature of the case than the youth court could hope to be;
- that, in a case where an adult and juvenile have been jointly tried on indictment and both convicted, sentencing the youth in the Crown Court will avoid the risk of unacceptable disparity in sentencing that would arise if he were to be remitted to the youth court;
- that remitting would cause delay, unnecessary duplication of proceedings, and extra expense.

It was suggested by the Court of Appeal, in the case of *R v Allen* (1999) 163 JP 841, that in the case of a grave crime it will generally be undesirable for the Crown Court to remit the case to the youth court for sentence, since the youth court has already determined that the case is too serious for its powers. It is submitted that this principle would not necessarily apply if the youth defendant has been convicted of the offence on a less serious basis or where not all of the original charges have resulted in convictions.

The *Sentencing Children and Young People – Overarching Principles* definitive guideline suggests, at paras 2.15 and 2.16, that, when considering whether to remit to the youth court for sentence, the Crown Court judge should balance the need for expertise in the sentencing of young offenders with the benefits of sentence being imposed by the court which had determined guilt. Particular attention should be given where a young person appears before the Crown Court only because they are jointly charged with an adult offender.

Blackstone's Handbook of Youths in the Criminal Courts. Mark Ashford, Gareth Branston, and Naomi Redhouse, Oxford University Press.
 DOI: 10.1093/oso/9780198913146.003.0059

K4 Sentences Available to Crown Court

The following sentences are available:

- Absolute and conditional discharge (see **J6**)
- Fine (see **J8**)
- Youth rehabilitation order (see **J24** for the general principles and **K4.1** below for its application in the Crown Court)
- Detention and training order (see **J5**)
- Long-term detention under the SC, s 250 (see **K4.2** below)
- Special sentence of detention for terrorist offenders of particular concern (see **K4.3** below)
- Extended sentence of detention (see **K4.4** below)
- Detention for life (see **K4.5** below)
- Detention during His Majesty's pleasure (see **K4.6** below).

Referral orders may only be made by a youth court or other magistrates' court: SC, s 84(1). The Divisional Court has confirmed that a Crown Court judge can make such an order if they remit the case back to the youth court and then exercise their power under the Courts Act 2003, s 66 to sit as a district judge: *R v S* [2021] EWCA Crim 960; [2023] 1 Cr App R (S) 33.

It has been the practice of some youth courts to adjourn sentence on summary-only matters where the youth is due to appear at the Crown Court on other matters and to invite the Crown Court to deal with the summary offence at the same time (by sitting as a district judge). In the case of *R v Iles* [2012] EWCA Crim 1610, it was said that before this is done the youth court must carefully consider whether this is in the interests of justice and ensure there is a power to do so. Moreover, before sitting as a district judge, the Crown Court judge must consider whether it is appropriate in the light of submissions from both prosecution and defence. If this route is followed, the judge's powers for the summary-only offences would be limited to those of the magistrates' court and the sentence imposed by a judge sitting as a district judge would have a different route of appeal.

K4.1 Youth rehabilitation order

When a Crown Court judge is imposing a YRO, it is important to draw the court's attention to the SC, s 189:

Blackstone's Handbook of Youths in the Criminal Courts. Mark Ashford, Gareth Branston, and Naomi Redhouse, Oxford University Press.
 DOI: 10.1093/oso/9780198913146.003.0060

Sentencing Code

189 Power for Crown Court to direct magistrates' court supervision

(1) This section applies where the Crown Court makes a youth rehabilitation order otherwise than on appeal from a magistrates' court.

(2) The Crown Court may include a direction that the order is to be subject to magistrates' court supervision.

For the effect of such a direction, see Schedule 7 (breach, revocation or amendment of youth rehabilitation order).

Without such a direction, the youth court dealing with any new offence while the youth defendant is subject to the Crown Court order will have to commit the young offender to the Crown Court if it considers that the new matter can properly be dealt with by a new YRO (for which see **K4.1.1** below). If the direction for magistrates' court supervision is made, a youth court can deal with any subsequent breach.

K4.1.1 *Subsequent conviction*

Where a defendant is convicted of an offence whilst they are subject to a YRO made in the Crown Court, the SC, Sch 7, para 22(3) and (4) provides that the convicting court may commit the offender in custody or release them on bail until they can be brought before the Crown Court. When such a committal takes place, the SC, Sch 7, para 23 provides:

Sentencing Code, Sch 7

23 Powers of Crown Court following subsequent conviction

(1) This paragraph applies where a youth rehabilitation order is in force in respect of an offender, and the offender—
  (a) is convicted by the Crown Court of an offence, or
  (b) is brought or appears before the Crown Court—
    (i) by virtue of paragraph 22(2) or (4), or
    (ii) having been committed by a magistrates' court to the Crown Court for sentence.

(2) If it appears to the Crown Court that it would be in the interests of justice to do so, having regard to circumstances which have arisen since the youth rehabilitation order was made, the Crown Court may—
  (a) revoke the order, or
  (b) both—
    (i) revoke the order, and
    (ii) re-sentence the offender for the offence in respect of which the order was made.

(3) Unless the offender is before it, the Crown Court may not deal with the offender under sub-paragraph (2)(b) unless it has summoned the offender to appear before it.
(4) If the offender fails to appear in answer to a summons under sub-paragraph (3) the Crown Court may issue a warrant for the offender's arrest.
(5) If the Crown Court deals with the offender under sub-paragraph (2)(b), it must take into account the extent to which the offender has complied with the requirements of the order.
(6) If the offender is brought or appears before the Crown Court by virtue of paragraph 22(2) or (4), the Crown Court may deal with the offender for the further offence in any way which the convicting court could have dealt with the offender for that offence.
(7) In sub-paragraph (6), 'further offence' and 'the convicting court' have the meanings given by paragraph 20.

K4.1.2 *Breach of Crown Court order*

Where an offender is to be brought before a court for failing to comply with a YRO made by the Crown Court, the proceedings are initiated by the responsible officer applying to the relevant youth court (or magistrates' court if the offender has attained 18) for the issue of a summons directing attendance at the Crown Court: SC, Sch 7, para 5 (see **J24.10**). Once the offender is before the Crown Court, the SC, Sch 7, paras 7, 10, and 11 provide:

Sentencing Code, Sch 7

7 Powers of Crown Court

(1) This paragraph applies where—
  (a) an offender appears or is brought before the Crown Court under paragraph 5 or by virtue of paragraph 6(3), and
  (b) it is proved to the satisfaction of that court that the offender has breached a requirement of the youth rehabilitation order without reasonable excuse,

  and must be read with paragraphs 8 to 11.
(2) The Crown Court may deal with the offender in respect of that breach in any one of the following ways—
  (a) by ordering the offender to pay a fine of an amount not exceeding £2,500;
  (b) by amending the terms of the youth rehabilitation order to add or substitute any requirement which it could include in a youth rehabilitation order if, applying the relevant assumptions, it were now making such an order in respect of the relevant offence;
  (c) by re-sentencing the offender for the relevant offence.

(3) In this paragraph—
'relevant offence' means the offence in respect of which the youth rehabilitation order was made, and
the 'relevant assumptions' are that—
(a) the offender has just been convicted of the relevant offence by or before the court dealing with the offender, and
(b) the offender is the same age as when in fact convicted of that offence.
(4) Sub-paragraph (2)(b) is subject to paragraph 10.
(5) In dealing with the offender under sub-paragraph (2), the Crown Court must take into account the extent to which the offender has complied with the requirements of the youth rehabilitation order.
(6) Where the Crown Court deals with an offender under sub-paragraph (2)(c), it must revoke the youth rehabilitation order if it is still in force.
(7) In proceedings before the Crown Court under this paragraph any question whether the offender has breached a requirement of the youth rehabilitation order is to be determined by the court and not by the verdict of a jury.

...

10 Powers in paragraphs 6 and 7 to impose other requirements: further provisions

(1) This paragraph applies where—
(a) the magistrates' court deals with the offender under paragraph 6(5)(b), or
(b) the Crown Court deals with the offender under paragraph 7(2)(b).
(2) Paragraphs 6(5)(b) and 7(2)(b) have effect subject to any provision that applies to the court in making a youth rehabilitation order as if the court were imposing the requirements on making the order.
That is subject to the following provisions of this paragraph and to paragraph 11.
(3) Subject to sub-paragraph (4), any requirement imposed under paragraph 6(5)(b) or 7(2)(b) must be capable of being complied with before the end date.
(4) In dealing with an offender under paragraph 6(5)(b) or 7(2)(b) the court may substitute a later date for the end date.
(5) A date substituted under sub-paragraph (4)—
(a) must not be more than 6 months after the existing end date;
(b) subject to that, may be more than 3 years after the date on which the order took effect.
(6) Once the power in sub-paragraph (4) has been exercised in relation to the order, it may not be exercised again in relation to it by any court.
(7) Where—
(a) in dealing with the offender under paragraph 6(5)(b) or 7(2)(b), the court imposes an unpaid work requirement, and
(b) the youth rehabilitation order does not already contain an unpaid work requirement,

the number of hours for which the offender may be required to work under the requirement (see paragraph 10(3) of Schedule 6) must not, in aggregate, be less than 20.

(8) The court may not under paragraph 6(5)(b) or 7(2)(b) impose—
(a) an extended activity requirement, or
(b) a fostering requirement,
if the order does not already impose such a requirement.

(9) Sub-paragraph (10) applies where—
(a) the order includes a fostering requirement (the 'original requirement'), and
(b) under paragraph 6(5)(b) or 7(2)(b) the court proposes to substitute a new fostering requirement ('the substitute requirement') for the original requirement.

(10) The fostering period (see paragraph 26(3) of Schedule 6) for the substitute requirement must end—
(a) within 18 months beginning with the day on which the original requirement first took effect, and
(b) before the offender reaches the age of 18.

11 Powers in paragraphs 6 and 7 to re-sentence: further provisions relating to intensive supervision and surveillance

(1) This paragraph applies where—
(a) the court is dealing with the offender under paragraph 6(5)(c) or 7(2)(c) for an offence, and
(b) the offender has wilfully and persistently failed to comply with the youth rehabilitation order.

(2) The court may impose a youth rehabilitation order with intensive supervision and surveillance even if—
(a) the offence is not an imprisonable offence, or
(b) the court is not of the opinion mentioned in section 180(2)(a) (custodial sentence otherwise appropriate).

(3) If—
(a) the order is a youth rehabilitation order with intensive supervision and surveillance, and
(b) the offence is an imprisonable offence,
the court may impose a custodial sentence even if it is not of the opinion mentioned in section 230(2) (threshold for imposing discretionary custodial sentence).

(4) If—
(a) the order is a youth rehabilitation order with intensive supervision and surveillance which was imposed by virtue of sub-paragraph (2), and
(b) the offence is not an offence punishable with imprisonment,
the court's powers under paragraph 6(5)(c) or 7(2)(c) to deal with the offender for the offence include power to make a detention and training order for a term not exceeding 4 months.

K4.2 Long-term detention under section 250

Detention under the SC, s 250 permits a Crown Court judge to impose a sentence of detention beyond the two-year maximum of a DTO (though there is, in fact, no minimum period for a s 250 sentence). It is only available if:

- the offender was aged under 18 on the date of conviction;
- the offender was convicted on indictment; and
- the offence is one specified in section 249(1) ('grave crimes').

Where a youth defendant has been convicted at a trial in the youth court but committed for sentence, the SC, s 22(2) provides that the Crown Court may deal with the offender in any way in which it could deal with the offender if they had been convicted of the offence on indictment.

Sentencing Code

249 Sentence of detention under section 250: availability

(1) A sentence of detention under section 250 is available where a person aged under 18 is convicted on indictment of an offence listed in the following table (but the court is not required to pass a sentence of detention under section 252A)—

Offences punishable with imprisonment for at least 14 years

(a) an offence which—
  (i) is not an offence for which the sentence is fixed by law, and
  (ii) is punishable in the case of a person aged 21 or over with imprisonment for 14 years or more;

Sexual offences

(b) an offence under any of the following provisions of the Sexual Offences Act 2003—
  (i) section 3 (sexual assault);
  (ii) section 13 (child sex offences committed by children or young persons);
  (iii) section 25 (sexual activity with a child family member);
  (iv) section 26 (inciting a child family member to engage in sexual activity);

Offences related to firearms

(c) an offence (other than one within paragraph (a)) which—
  (i) is listed in Schedule 20 (firearms offences to which minimum sentence applies), and
  (ii) was committed when the offender was aged 16 or over.

(2) For circumstances in which a court is required to impose a sentence of detention under section 250, see—
  (a) sections 258 and 258A (required sentence of detention for life);
  (b) section 311 (minimum sentence for certain offences involving firearms that are prohibited weapons).

(3) Where an offence is found to have been committed—
  (a) over a period of 2 or more days, or
  (b) at some time during a period of 2 or more days,

it is to be taken for the purposes of paragraph (c)(ii) of the table in subsection (1) to have been committed on the last of those days.

250 Sentence of detention: offender convicted of certain serious offences

A sentence of detention under this section is a sentence requiring the offender to be detained for the period specified in the sentence.

251 Exercise of power to impose sentence of detention under section 250

(1) Subsection (2) applies where a sentence of detention under section 250 is available by virtue of section 249(1).

(2) The court may impose such a sentence if it is of the opinion that neither a youth rehabilitation order nor a detention and training order is suitable.

(3) This is subject to (in particular) section 230 (threshold for imposing discretionary custodial sentence) and section 231 (length of discretionary custodial sentences: general provision).

252 Maximum sentence

(1) This section applies where the court imposes a sentence of detention under section 250 by virtue of—

(a) section 251, or

(b) section 311 (minimum sentence for certain offences involving firearms that are prohibited weapons).

(2) The period of detention specified in the sentence must not exceed—

(a) the maximum term of imprisonment with which the offence is punishable in the case of a person aged 21 or over, or

(b) life, if the offence is punishable with imprisonment for life in the case of a person aged 21 or over.

253 Sentence of detention passed on offender subject to detention and training order

(1) This section applies where a court imposes a sentence of detention under section 250 or 252A in the case of an offender who is subject to a relevant detention and training order.

(2) If the offender has not at any time been released for supervision under the relevant detention and training order, the court may order that the sentence of detention is to take effect at the time when the offender would otherwise be released for supervision under the relevant detention and training order (see section 248(5)).

(3) Otherwise, the sentence of detention takes effect at the beginning of the day on which it is passed.

(4) In this section 'relevant detention and training order' means—

(a) a detention and training order under section 233,

(b) an order under section 211 of the Armed Forces Act 2006 (corresponding order under that Act), or

(c) an order under section 100 of the Powers of Criminal Courts (Sentencing) Act 2000 (detention and training order: offender convicted before the commencement of this Act).

The principles for imposing long-term detention now enacted in s 250 were originally set out by Lane LCJ in *R v Fairhurst* (1986) 8 Cr App R (S) 346. These principles were later expressly endorsed by Bingham LCJ in *R v Mills* [1998] 1 WLR 363. Below is a summary of the principles outlined in these two cases.

K4.2.1 *General principles*

Lord Bingham endorsed the approach that, on the one hand, there exists the desirability of keeping youths under the age of 18 out of long-term custody. On the other hand, it is necessary that serious offences committed by youths of this age should be met with sentences sufficiently substantial to provide both the appropriate punishment and also the necessary deterrent effect, and in certain cases to provide a measure of protection to the public. A balance has to be struck between these objectives. It is not necessary, in order to invoke the provisions of s 250, that the crime committed should be one of exceptional gravity, such as attempted murder, manslaughter, wounding with intent, armed robbery, or the like.

These observations should be considered in the light of the principles set out in the *Sentencing Children and Young People – Overarching Principles* definitive guideline. That makes clear that a custodial sentence must only be imposed as a measure of last resort and the court must bear in mind the negative effects that a custodial sentence can have on the welfare of a young defendant. Furthermore, unlike for adult offenders, deterrence is not a purpose of sentencing for those aged under 18 and the word does not appear in the guideline.

K4.2.2 *Offenders aged 15 to 17*

For those aged 15, 16, or 17, long-term detention under section 250 may be properly invoked where the crime committed is one within the scope of the section and is one that not only calls for a sentence of detention but detention for a longer period than 24 months. The court should not exceed the 24-month limit for a DTO without much careful thought; but if it concludes that a longer sentence, even if not a much longer sentence, is called for, then the court should impose whatever it considers the appropriate period of detention under s 250.

K4.2.3 *Offenders aged under 15*

Long-term detention will be the primary custodial option for the Crown Court in relation to offenders under 15, unless the offender is aged 12 to 14 and is deemed to be a persistent offender, in which case a DTO will also be available.

Where the seriousness of the offence warrants a sentence of over two years, there is no doubt that a sentence of long-term detention may be imposed. There are, however, conflicting lines of authority regarding the Crown Court's powers in relation to an offender aged under 15 years who cannot be deemed to be a persistent offender.

In *R v Gaskin* (1985) 7 Cr App R (S) 28, it was held that where no other custodial sentence was available because of the offender's age, a sentence of long-term detention (then under the CYPA 1933, s 53(2)) could be imposed for a period shorter than two years. This approach was later endorsed by Lord Bingham CJ in *Mills* and, after the introduction of DTOs, followed by the Court of Appeal in *R v S.J-R and D.G* [2001] 1 Cr App R (S) 109.

This line of authorities was not followed in the cases of *R (D) v Manchester City Youth Court* [2001] EWHC 860 (Admin) and *R (W) v Thetford Youth Court* [2002] EWHC 1252 (Admin). Judgments in both cases were delivered by Gage J. In *Thetford Youth Court*, having reviewed the above line of authorities, Gage J said (at a time when long-term detention was provided for by s 91 of the PCCSA 2000):

> There is no statutory restriction on a court, using its powers under section 91, passing a sentence of less than two years. But it seems to me that it will only be in very exceptional and restricted circumstances that it will be appropriate to do so, rather than making a detention and training order. The fact that an offender . . . does not qualify for a detention and training order because he is not a persistent offender does not seem to me such an exceptional circumstance as to justify the passing of a period of detention of less than two years under section 91 of the Act of 2000.My conclusion is that the authorities . . . do not alter my conclusions already expressed on the relationship between [the statutory provisions relating to long-term detention and detention and training orders] . . . I remain of the opinion that where an offence or offences are likely to attract a sentence of less than two years' custody the appropriate sentence will be a detention and training order. In the case of an offender under 15, who is not a persistent offender or a child under 12, the most likely sentence will be a non-custodial sentence. . . .However, I accept that there may be cases, where despite the fact that the offender is under 15, and no detention and training order can be made, the only appropriate sentence is a custodial sentence pursuant to section 91 and possibly for a period of less than two years. In expressing my views, as I did, in *D v Manchester City Youth Court*, my use of the expression 'very exceptional' may be more restrictive than was strictly necessary or justified . . . Perhaps it would be better to say that cases involving offenders under 15 for whom a detention and training order is not available will only rarely attract a period of detention under section 91; the more rarely if the offender is under 12.

This judgment of Gage J was expressly endorsed by Lord Woolf CJ and Sedley LJ in *R (W) v Southampton Youth Court* [2002] EWHC 1252 (Admin), at [28]–[30]. The reasoning of Gage J was, however, rejected by the Court of Appeal in *R v Thomas* [2004] EWCA Crim 2199, where Hooper LJ held that the Administrative Court decisions following on from the *Manchester City* case were not binding on the Court of Appeal and only, in fact, applied to the youth court decision regarding jurisdiction.

K4.2.4 *Sentencing for more than one grave crime together*

Where more than one offence is involved for which long-term detention is available, but the offences vary in seriousness, provided that at least one offence is sufficiently serious to merit long-term detention, detention sentences of under two years' duration, whether concurrent or consecutive, may properly be imposed in respect of the other offences.

K4.2.5 *Sentencing grave crimes together with non-grave crime*

Where there are two offences committed by a youth offender and one of them (A) carries a maximum sentence of 14 years and the other (B) carries a lower maximum, then generally speaking it is not proper to pass a sentence of long-term detention in respect of offence A which would not otherwise merit it in order to compensate for the fact that a 24-month DTO is grossly inadequate for offence B.

Where, however, it can be truly said that the defendant's behaviour giving rise to offence B is part and parcel of the events giving rise to offence A, such a sentence may properly be passed. See for example *R v Walsh* [1997] 2 Cr App R (S) 210.

The non-grave crime would also be an associated offence which could be taken into account when determining the seriousness of the grave crime. See for example *R v McKay* [2000] 1 Cr App R (S) 17.

K4.2.6 *Light at the end of the tunnel*

Even when dealing with serious offences, consideration should still be given to the youth of the offender. In *R v Storey* (1984) 6 Cr App R (S) 104, Mustill J gave general guidance which has been referred to in many subsequent appeal decisions:

> There is another principle to which effect must, in our opinion, be given. These are young men not of outstanding intellectual attainments, and perhaps not very gifted in imagination. It is important, when using the powers under the Act, that the court should not impose a sentence, which, the far end of it, would to young men like this seem completely out of sight.... The court must take care to select a duration for the order upon which the offender can fix his eye, so that he could buckle down to taking advantage of the structured environment [in detention], with a view to emerging from it in the foreseeable future improved by his study there.

K4.2.7 *Length of order*

The *Sentencing Children and Young People – Overarching Principles* definitive guideline is as applicable to the sentencing process of youths in the Crown Court as it is to those in the youth court. Its provisions need to be considered in detail. The extent to which a custodial sentence imposed on a youth may be considerably less than that applicable to an adult and the role of the adult guideline is set out in paras 6.45 and 6.46. The court must not, however, go straight to those paragraphs and must not ignore the important principles set out earlier in the guideline: *R v ZA* [2023] EWCA Crim 596.

K4.2.8 *Minimum sentences for firearms offences*

The SC, s 311 provides for a minimum sentence for possessing or minding a prohibited firearm. The minimum sentence applies where the offence was committed at a time when the offender was aged 16 or over. The minimum sentence for an offender aged 16 or 17 at the time of conviction is long-term detention under s 250 for three years. No reduction below the minimum is permitted for a guilty plea.

K4.2.9 *Remand time*

Time spent remanded in custody and time spent subject to a qualifying curfew on bail apply to long-term detention: CJA 2003, ss 240ZA and 240A; SC, s 325.

K4.2.10 *Interaction with detention and training order*

Where a court imposes a sentence of detention under s 250 (or s 252A) in the case of an offender who is subject to a DTO, the court may order the sentence of long-term detention to run consecutively to the DTO but only if the offender has not yet been released for supervision under the DTO. If the offender has been released, the s 250 sentence must run concurrently: SC, s 253.

K4.3 Special sentence of detention for terrorist offenders of particular concern

A person aged under 18 who is convicted of a specified terrorist offence after 30 April 2021 may be liable to a special sentence of detention for terrorist offenders of particular concern. Such a sentence is made up of a custodial term plus a further period of one year for which the offender is subject to a licence.

Section 252A of the SC provides:

Sentencing Code

252A Required special sentence of detention for terrorist offenders of particular concern

(1) Subsections (3) to (5) apply where—
  (a) a person aged under 18 is convicted of an offence listed in Part 1 of Schedule 13 (offences involving or connected with terrorism),
  (b) the offence was committed on or after the day on which section 22 of the Counter-Terrorism and Sentencing Act 2021 came into force,
  (c) the court does not impose either of the following for the offence (or for an offence associated with it)—
    (i) a sentence of detention for life under section 250, or
    (ii) an extended sentence of detention under section 254, and
  (d) the court would, apart from this section, impose a custodial sentence (see, in particular, section 230(2)).

(2) In determining for the purposes of subsection (1)(d) whether it would impose a custodial sentence, the court must disregard any restriction on its power to impose such a sentence by reference to the age of the offender.

(3) The court must impose a sentence of detention under this section.

(4) The term of the sentence must be equal to the aggregate of—
  (a) the appropriate custodial term, and
  (b) a further period of 1 year for which the offender is to be subject to a licence,

  and must not exceed the maximum term of imprisonment with which the offence is punishable in the case of a person aged 21 or over.

(5) For the purposes of subsection (4), the 'appropriate custodial term' is the term that, in the opinion of the court, ensures that the sentence is appropriate.

(6) Where an offence is found to have been committed over a period of 2 or more days, or at some time during a period of 2 or more days, it must be taken for the purposes of subsection (1) to have been committed on the last of those days.

Conviction for one of the specified terrorism offences does not automatically mean that a special sentence of detention will be imposed. The sentence only applies if the court considers that the offence is so serious that neither a fine alone nor a community sentence can be justified: ss 252A(1)(d) and 230(2). There is no age restriction; the sentence can be imposed on a defendant as young as 10 and on young defendants who are not persistent offenders: s 252(2).

Where a custodial sentence of less than two years' detention is merited, this sentence is available in the youth court.

K4.4 Extended sentence of detention

Sections 254 to 257 of the SC provide for extended sentences for offenders aged under 18 when convicted. An extended sentence of detention is a sentence of detention the term of which is equal to the aggregate of:

- the appropriate custodial term, and
- a further period (the extension period) for which the offender is to be subject to a licence: s 254.

K4.4.1 *Availability*

An extended sentence of detention is available where a court is dealing with an offender aged under 18 when convicted for an offence if:

- The offence is a specified violent/sexual/terrorism offence listed in the SC, Sch 18,
- The offence is one for which long term detention under ss 250 or 252A is available,
- The court is of the opinion that there is a significant risk to members of the public of serious harm occasioned by the commission by the offender of further specified offences (the assessment of dangerousness),
- The court is not required to impose a sentence of detention for life, and
- If the court were to impose an extended sentence, the term that it would specify as the appropriate custodial term would be at least 4 years: s 255(1).

K4.4.2 *The assessment of dangerousness*

The SC, s 308 provides that the court:

- must take into account all such information that is available to it about the nature and circumstances of the offence;
- may take into account all the information that is available to it about the nature and circumstances of any other offences of

which the offender has been convicted by a court anywhere in the world;
- may take into account any information which is before it about any pattern of behaviour of which any of the offences forms part; and
- may take into account any information about the offender which is before it.

The general guidance provided by the Court of Appeal in relation to the original legislation is still of assistance. In *R v Lang* [2005] EWCA Crim 2864, the court said:

- 'Significant risk' is more than the possibility of occurrence.
- Significant risk must be shown in relation to two matters: first, the commission of further specified, but not necessarily serious, offences; and secondly, the causing thereby of serious harm to a member of the public.
- Assessment of risk should include the offending history—the kind of offences, their circumstances, and the sentence imposed.
- The defendant's attitude to offending and supervision are also relevant.
- When sentencing young offenders, it is necessary to bear in mind that, within a shorter time than adults, they might change and develop. This and their level of maturity might be highly pertinent when assessing what their future conduct might be and whether it might give rise to significant risk of serious harm.
- In relation to a particularly young offender, an indeterminate sentence might be inappropriate even where a serious offence has been committed and there was a significant risk of serious harm from further offences.

K4.4.3 *Term of extended sentence*

The SC, s 256 provides:

Sentencing Code

256 Term of extended sentence of detention under section 254

(1) This section applies where a court is determining—
  (a) the appropriate custodial term, and
  (b) the extension period,

  of an extended sentence of detention under section 254 to be imposed on an offender in respect of an offence.

(2) The appropriate custodial term is the term of detention that would be imposed in respect of the offence in compliance with section 231(2) (length of discretionary custodial sentences: general provision) if the court did not impose an extended sentence.

(3) The extension period must be a period of such length as the court considers necessary for the purpose of protecting members of the public from serious harm occasioned by the commission by the offender of further specified offences.
This is subject to subsections (4) and (5).
(4) The extension period must—
(a) be at least 1 year, and
(b) not exceed—
(i) 5 years in the case of a specified violent offence (unless sub-paragraph (iii) applies);
(ii) 8 years in the case of a specified sexual offence or a specified terrorism offence (unless sub-paragraph (iii) applies);
(iii) 10 years in the case of a serious terrorism offence for which the sentence is imposed on or after the day on which section 16 of the Counter-Terrorism and Sentencing Act 2021 comes into force.
See section 306(2) for the meanings of 'specified violent offence', 'specified sexual offence', 'specified terrorism offence' and 'serious terrorism offence'.
(5) The term of the extended sentence of detention under section 254 must not exceed the maximum term of imprisonment with which the offence is punishable in the case of a person aged 21 or over.

A person sentenced to extended detention is liable to be detained in a place and under conditions determined by, or by a person authorized for the purpose by, the Secretary of State: s 261.

An offender sentenced to extended detention will generally be released on licence when they have served two-thirds of the custodial term. If the custodial term is ten years or more, the offender may have to apply to the Parole Board before release. The detailed provisions are set out in the CJA 2003, s 246A.

K4.5 **Detention for life**

The SC, s 258 provides:

Sentencing Code

258 Required sentence of detention for life for offence carrying life sentence

(1) This section applies where—
(a) a person aged under 18 is convicted of a Schedule 19 offence (see section 307),
(b) the court considers that the seriousness of—
(i) the offence, or
(ii) the offence and one or more offences associated with it,
is such as to justify the imposition of a sentence of detention for life, and

(c) the court is of the opinion that there is a significant risk to members of the public of serious harm occasioned by the commission by the offender of further specified offences (see sections 306(1) and 308).

(2) The court must impose a sentence of detention for life under section 250.

(3) The pre-sentence report requirements (see section 30) apply to the court in relation to forming the opinion mentioned in subsection (1)(c).

(4) An offence the sentence for which is imposed under this section is not to be regarded as an offence the sentence for which is fixed by law.

When the court finds that the defendant satisfies the criteria for dangerousness, a life sentence should be reserved for those cases where the culpability of the offender is particularly high or the offence itself particularly grave: *R v Kehoe* [2008] EWCA Crim 819.

When imposing detention for life, the SC, ss 321 and 323 require the court to set a minimum term which must be served in custody before the offender can be released at the direction of the Parole Board. This minimum term shall be such as the court considers appropriate taking into account:

- the seriousness of the offence, or the combination of the offence and one or more offences associated with it; and
- time spent on remand or subject to a qualifying curfew.

A person sentenced to detention for life is liable to be detained in such place, and under such conditions, as may be determined by the Secretary of State or by such other person as may be authorized by them for the purpose: SC, s 260. Release at the expiry of the minimum term is subject to the Crime (Sentences) Act 1997, s 28.

K4.6 Detention during His Majesty's pleasure

This is the mandatory sentence for a person convicted of a murder committed when they were under the age of 18.

The SC, s 259 provides:

Sentencing Code

259 Offenders who commit murder etc when under 18: duty to detain at Her Majesty's pleasure

(1) This section applies where—

(a) a court is dealing with a person convicted of—

(i) murder, or

(ii) any other offence the sentence for which is fixed by law as life imprisonment, and

(b) the person appears to the court to have been aged under 18 at the time the offence was committed.

(2) The court must sentence the offender to be detained during Her Majesty's pleasure.

(3) Subsection (2) applies notwithstanding anything in this or any other Act.

Section 10 of the Interpretation Act 1978 requires reference to 'Her Majesty' to be construed as a reference to 'His Majesty' as the Sovereign for the time being.

When detaining an offender under s 259, the judge must set a minimum term.

A person sentenced to be detained under s 259 shall be liable to be detained in such place and under such conditions as the Secretary of State may direct or arrange with any person: s 260.

K5 Appeal Cases

K5.1 Case management

When the Crown Court is dealing with a youth appellant, regard should be had to part 6.4 of the CPDs. The case may involve the hearing of evidence. Particular consideration should be given to modification of the court procedure to enable effective participation. See **I1–I3**.

Part 34 of the Crim PR deals with appeals to the Crown Court.

K5.2 Rights of appeal

The following decisions of the youth court which are subject to rights of appeal to the Crown Court are noted:

- Conviction and sentence: MCA 1980, s 108(1).
- Breach of conditional discharge: MCA 1980, s 108(2).
- Order to pay costs: MCA 1980, s 108(1) and (3)(c).
- Remand in custody: Senior Courts Act 1981, s 81(1)(g).
- Conditions attached to bail: CJA 2003, s 16.
- Grant of bail (prosecutor's appeal): Bail (Amendment) Act 1993, s 1.
- Decision or refusal to extend custody time limit: Prosecution of Offences Act 1985, s 22(7).
- Financial order against parent: SC, s 380(5).
- Parenting order: SC, s 366(9).
- Parental bind over: SC, s 377(1).
- Hospital or guardianship order: MHA 1983, s 45(1) and (2).

K5.3 Powers on appeal

In the course of hearing any appeal, the Crown Court may:

- Correct any error or mistake in the order or judgment incorporating the decision subject to appeal: Senior Courts Act 1981, s 48(1).
- Confirm, reverse, or vary any part of the decision: s 48(2).
- Remit the matter with its opinion to the lower court: s 48(2).
- Make such order as the court thinks just and, by such order, exercise any power which the lower court might have exercised: s 48(2).

Blackstone's Handbook of Youths in the Criminal Courts. Mark Ashford, Gareth Branston, and Naomi Redhouse, Oxford University Press.
 DOI: 10.1093/oso/9780198913146.003.0061

On an appeal against conviction or sentence, the Crown Court may order punishment which is more severe than that awarded by the lower court: s 48(4).

K5.4 Reporting restrictions

When the Crown Court is acting in its appellate role, reporting restrictions under the CYPA 1933, s 49 apply as if the court was sitting as a youth court.

Children and Young Persons Act 1933

49 Restrictions on reports of proceedings in which children or young persons are concerned

(1) No matter relating to any child or young person concerned in proceedings to which this section applies shall while he is under the age of 18 be included in any publication if it is likely to lead members of the public to identify him as someone concerned in the proceedings.

(2) The proceedings to which this section applies are—

(a) proceedings in a youth court;

(b) proceedings on appeal from a youth court (including proceedings by way of case stated);

(c) proceedings in a magistrates' court under Schedule 7 to the Sentencing Code (proceedings for breach, revocation or amendment of youth rehabilitation orders);

(d) proceedings on appeal from a magistrates' court arising out of any proceedings mentioned in paragraph (c) (including proceedings by way of case stated).

. . .

(10) In any proceedings under Schedule 7 to the Sentencing Code (proceedings for breach, revocation or amendment of youth rehabilitation orders) before a magistrates' court other than a youth court or on appeal from such a court it shall be the duty of the magistrates' court or the appellate court to announce in the course of the proceedings that this section applies to the proceedings; and if the court fails to do so this section shall not apply to the proceedings.

Reporting restrictions under the YJCEA 1999, s 49 cannot continue after the young person attains the age of 18: *T v DPP* [2003] EWHC 2408 (Admin).

Part L
Attaining 18

L1 Cautions

Youth cautions and youth conditional cautions may only be administered to a person under the age of 18. If the offender attains 18 before the final decision on disposal is made, then an adult caution or adult conditional caution should be administered.

Blackstone's Handbook of Youths in the Criminal Courts. Mark Ashford, Gareth Branston, and Naomi Redhouse, Oxford University Press.
 DOI: 10.1093/oso/9780198913146.003.0062

L2 **Before First Appearance**

If a youth attains 18 before the first court appearance, the youth court has no jurisdiction to deal with the case: *R v Amersham Juvenile Court, ex parte Wilson* [1981] 2 All ER 315.

If a youth is going to have their 18th birthday before a first appearance, they should be bailed or requisitioned to the adult magistrates' court.

If a youth fails to attend the first appearance and attains 18 before they appear or are brought before the court, the youth court will have no jurisdiction to deal with the case. There is no power to remit the case to an adult magistrates' court; proceedings will have to be restarted in the adult magistrates' court: *R v Uxbridge Youth Court, ex parte Howard* [1998] EWHC (Admin) 341.

Blackstone's Handbook of Youths in the Criminal Courts. Mark Ashford, Gareth Branston, and Naomi Redhouse, Oxford University Press.
 DOI: 10.1093/oso/9780198913146.003.0063

L3 **After the First Court Hearing**

Once a defendant has appeared before it, the youth court does not lose jurisdiction to deal with the case simply because the defendant attains 18, as long as the youth court has dealt with plea and allocation. If plea and allocation have not yet been dealt with, in the case of an either-way offence, the defendant who attains the age of 18 will now have the right to elect jury trial: *Re Daley* [1983] 1AC 327; *R v West London Justices, ex parte Siley-Winditt* [2000] Crim LR 926. Where a defendant first appeared aged 17 in the youth court, but proceedings were adjourned and allocation was only dealt with after their 18th birthday, an indictable-only offence should have been sent forthwith to the Crown Court; a guilty plea could not be accepted and there could be no committal for sentence: *R v Ford* [2018] EWCA Crim 1751.

Any new charges laid after the defendant has attained 18 must be in the adult court, even if the new charge arises out of the same facts as charges currently before the youth court: *R v Chelsea Justices ex parte DPP* [1963] 3 All ER 657.

Blackstone's Handbook of Youths in the Criminal Courts. Mark Ashford, Gareth Branston, and Naomi Redhouse, Oxford University Press.
 DOI: 10.1093/oso/9780198913146.003.0064

L4 Remand to Youth Detention Accommodation

Where the defendant turns 18 during a remand to youth detention accommodation, they will remain in the youth detention accommodation until they are released or returned to court. A local authority will not be liable for the cost of any time remanded to the local authority accommodation after the defendant has attained 18.

If the case is adjourned again after the defendant has attained 18, any refusal of bail will not be subject to the LASPO 2012, s 91 provisions and the remand will be to a remand centre or prison.

Blackstone's Handbook of Youths in the Criminal Courts. Mark Ashford, Gareth Branston, and Naomi Redhouse, Oxford University Press.
 DOI: 10.1093/oso/9780198913146.003.0065

L5 Remittal to Adult Magistrates' Court for Trial

Crime and Disorder Act 1998

47 Powers of youth courts

(1) Where a person who appears or is brought before a youth court charged with an offence subsequently attains the age of 18, the youth court may, at any time—

(a) before the start of the trial;

. . .

remit the person for trial or, as the case may be, for sentence to a magistrates' court (other than a youth court).

In this subsection 'the start of the trial' shall be construed in accordance with section 22(11B) of the 1985 Act.

(2) Where a person is remitted under subsection (1) above—

(a) he shall have no right of appeal against the order of remission;

(b) the remitting court shall adjourn proceedings in relation to the offence; and

(c) subsections (3) and (4) below shall apply.

(3) The following, namely—

(a) section 128 of the 1980 Act; and

(b) all other enactments (whenever passed) relating to remand or the granting of bail in criminal proceedings,

shall have effect in relation to the remitting court's power or duty to remand the person on the adjournment as if any reference to the court to or before which the person remanded is to be brought or appear after remand were a reference to the court to which he is being remitted ('the other court').

(4) The other court may deal with the case in any way in which it would have power to deal with it if all proceedings relating to the offence which took place before the remitting court had taken place before the other court.

Although s 47 does not explicitly distinguish between categories of offences, it cannot be used for indictable-only offences as the adult magistrates' court would have no sentencing powers in relation to such an offence: *R (Denny) v Acton Youth Court* [2004] EWHC 948 (Admin); [2004] 2 All ER 961.

Blackstone's Handbook of Youths in the Criminal Courts. Mark Ashford, Gareth Branston, and Naomi Redhouse, Oxford University Press.
 DOI: 10.1093/oso/9780198913146.003.0066

L6 Sentence

The relevant age for sentence is the age on the date of conviction (whether by guilty plea or conviction after trial) (see **J1.1**).

If the offender was 17 on the date of conviction, the court has the range of sentences set out at **J19**. If the offender has attained 18 before conviction, the youth court may still proceed to sentence (see **L6.2** below).

Where an offender crosses a significant age threshold between the date of the commission of the offence and the date of conviction, the starting point for determining the length of sentence is the sentence that they would have been likely to receive if they had been sentenced at the date of the offence: *R v Ghafoor* [2002] EWCA Crim 1857, [2003] 1 Cr App R (S) 428 (see **J1.2**).

L6.1 Purpose of sentencing

For offenders under the age of 18 on the date of conviction, there are no statutory purposes of sentencing as there are for adults. The court retains the duties to have regard to the principal aim of the youth justice system (to prevent offending by persons aged under 18) and to the welfare of the youth defendant: SC, s 58 (see **F1**).

If an offender has attained 18 by the date of conviction, the adult purposes of sentencing will apply. The SC, s 57 provides:

Sentencing Code

57 Purposes of sentencing: adults

(1) This section applies where—
  (a) a court is dealing with an offender for an offence, and
  (b) the offender is aged 18 or over when convicted.

(2) The court must have regard to the following purposes of sentencing—
  (a) the punishment of offenders,
  (b) the reduction of crime (including its reduction by deterrence),
  (c) the reform and rehabilitation of offenders,
  (d) the protection of the public, and
  (e) the making of reparation by offenders to persons affected by their offences.

(3) Subsection (1) does not apply—
  (a) to an offence in relation to which a mandatory sentence requirement applies (see section 399), or

Blackstone's Handbook of Youths in the Criminal Courts. Mark Ashford, Gareth Branston, and Naomi Redhouse, Oxford University Press.
 DOI: 10.1093/oso/9780198913146.003.0067

(b) in relation to making any of the following under Part 3 of the Mental Health Act 1983—
   (i) a hospital order (with or without a restriction order),
   (ii) an interim hospital order,
   (iii) a hospital direction, or
   (iv) a limitation direction.

L6.2 Available sentences

The sentences available to any court dealing with an offender who has attained 18 (but not 21) by the date of conviction are:

- Discharge (absolute or conditional);
- Fine;
- Community order;
- Detention in a YOI;
- Suspended detention in a YOI.

L6.2.1 *Community order*

When the offender has attained 18 before conviction, the appropriate community sentence is a community order under the SC, s 200 rather than a YRO under s 173. When imposing requirements on the offender as part of the community order, a court should balance the requirements, or combination of requirements, with the offender's personal circumstances, and avoid conflict with work, schooling, or religious beliefs.

The available requirements are contained in the SC, ss 200–220 and Sch 9. They are:

- unpaid work (40 to 300 hours, to be completed within 12 months);
- rehabilitation activity;
- programme;
- prohibited activity;
- curfew (two to 20 hours a day, not more than 112 hours in seven days, for up to two years; requires electronic compliance monitoring);
- exclusion (normally requires electronic compliance monitoring);
- residence;
- foreign travel prohibition (for up to 12 months);
- mental health treatment;
- drug rehabilitation treatment;
- drug testing;
- alcohol treatment;

- alcohol abstinence and monitoring (up to 120 days);
- electronic compliance monitoring;
- electronic whereabouts monitoring.

L6.2.2 *Detention in a young offender institution*

The usual custodial sentence for an offender who has attained the age of 18 but is under the age of 21 on the date of conviction is detention in a YOI under the SC, s 262.

The minimum term of the order is 21 days: s 263(2). This applies to the sentence passed for each offence and not just to the total aggregate sentence: *R v Dover Youth Court ex parte K* [1998] 4 All ER 24. When imposing detention in a YOI upon an offender who attained 18 between the date of the offence and the date of conviction, the starting point is the sentence that the defendant would have been likely to have received if they had been sentenced at the date of the commission of the offence: *R v Ghafoor* [2002] EWCA Crim 1857; [2003] 1 Cr App R (S) 84. The court should therefore have regard to the terms permitted for a DTO (which would have had a maximum term of 24 months) (see *R v Jones* [2003] EWCA Crim 1609, [2004] 1 Cr App R (S) 18, though this case was decided at a time when DTOs were permitted only for fixed terms of four, six, eight, ten, 12, 18, or 24 months).

L6.2.3 *Suspended detention in a young offender institution*

A term of detention in a YOI of no more than two years may be suspended: SC, ss 264 and 286. When a suspended sentence order is made, the community requirements listed in **L6.2.1** may be imposed.

L6.3 Committal for sentence

When an offender has attained 18 before being convicted of an *offence triable either way* in the case of an adult, the youth court or adult magistrates' court may commit the offender to the Crown Court for sentence under the SC, s 14 if the court is of the opinion that the offence or the combination of the offence and one or more offences associated with it was so serious that the Crown Court should have the power to deal with the offender in any way it could deal with the offender if the offender had been convicted on indictment.

Where an offender has attained 18 before being convicted of an *indictable-only* offence, committal for sentence under the SC, s 14 is not available.

L6.4 Remittal to adult court for sentence

The SC, s 27 provides:

Sentencing Code

27 Power of youth court to remit offender who attains age of 18 to magistrates' court other than youth court for sentence

(1) Subsection (2) applies where a person who appears or is brought before a youth court charged with an offence subsequently reaches the age of 18.

(2) The youth court may, at any time after conviction and before sentence, remit the offender for sentence to a magistrates' court other than a youth court ('the adult court').

(3) Where an offender is remitted under subsection (2), the adult court may deal with the offender in any way in which it could deal with the offender if it had convicted the offender of the offence.

(4) Where an offender is remitted under subsection (2), section 25(4) (duty of adult magistrates' court to remit young offenders to youth court for sentence) does not apply to the adult court.

A youth court should never remit under s 27 an offence which is indictable only in the case of an adult: *R (Denny) v Acton Youth Court* [2004] EWHC 94 (Admin), [2004] 2 All ER 961.

Remitting to the adult magistrates' court under s 27 does not mean that the receiving court will have any extra powers of sentence but it can be a useful power if the offender already has other matters for sentence in the adult court.

L6.5 Discretion to ignore fact offender has attained 18

The CYPA 1963, s 29 provides:

Children and Young Persons Act 1963

29 Provisions as to persons between the ages of 17 and 18

(1) Where proceedings in respect of a young person are begun for an offence and he attains the age of eighteen before the conclusion of the proceedings, the court may deal with the case and make any order which it could have made if he had not attained that age.

For the purposes of s 29, proceedings have not commenced until the defendant appears or is brought before the court: *R v Uxbridge Youth Court ex parte Howard* (1998) 162 JP 327.

In general, YOTs will not want to supervise offenders who have attained 18, so this provision will be rarely used. In some areas, YOTs are willing to work with offenders who have turned 18 on referral orders and YROs. The use of the provision to impose a DTO on an offender who had attained 18 before conviction was upheld in the case of *Aldis v DPP* [2002] EWHC 403 (Admin); [2002] 2 Cr App R (S) 88. In that case, the defendant was 17 when the youth court accepted jurisdiction in relation to a charge of wounding with intent. Invoking s 29, the magistrates sentenced him to an 18-month DTO after he had turn 18 years old. The sentence was upheld by the Administrative Court. It must have been plain to everyone that the possibility of a two-year DTO was a factor, if not the crucial factor, in the magistrates' decision to try the case summarily.

L7 Reporting Restrictions in Youth Court

The provisions of the CYPA 1933, s 49 no longer apply if the defendant attains 18 during the proceedings: *T v DPP* [2003] EWHC 2408 (Admin).

Blackstone's Handbook of Youths in the Criminal Courts. Mark Ashford, Gareth Branston, and Naomi Redhouse, Oxford University Press.
 DOI: 10.1093/oso/9780198913146.003.0068

L8 Breach Proceedings

The appropriate court to deal with breach of an order will depend on the nature of the sentence originally imposed.

L8.1 Conditional discharge

An adult offender convicted of a new offence committed during the period of a conditional discharge made by a youth court may be re-sentenced for the original offence by the convicting adult magistrates' court or Crown Court or, if no action is taken by that court, the youth court which gave the original sentence may summons the offender for the breach to be dealt with: CYPA 1933, s 48(2).

L8.2 Referral order

The breach proceedings must be dealt with by the adult magistrates' court if the offender has attained 18 by the first court hearing: SC, s 108(1). If the order is revoked, the court may re-sentence the offender by dealing with them in any way which they could have been dealt with for that offence by the court which made the order (assuming that a referral order is not available): SC, Sch 4, para 7(4) (see **J12.12.1**).

L8.3 Reparation order

Reparation orders have been repealed by the PCSCA 2022, s 162.

L8.4 Youth rehabilitation order

The breach proceedings must be dealt with by the adult magistrates' court if the offender has attained 18 by the first court hearing: SC, Sch 7, para 5(4). For the court's powers on breach see **J24.10**.

L8.5 Detention and training order

Proceedings for breach of the supervision requirements can only be dealt with in the youth court, even when the offender has attained 18: SC, Sch 12, para 2(3). For the court's powers on breach see **J5.8**.

Blackstone's Handbook of Youths in the Criminal Courts. Mark Ashford, Gareth Branston, and Naomi Redhouse, Oxford University Press.
 DOI: 10.1093/oso/9780198913146.003.0069

L9 Applying to Amend or Revoke a Sentence

L9.1 Referral order

If the panel wishes to refer an offender who has attained the age of 18 back to court to request early revocation under the SC, s 102(2) or at the request of the offender, the appropriate court is the adult magistrates' court acting in the local justice area in which it appears to the panel that the offender resides or will reside: SC, s 108(1). For the court's powers see **J12.12.2**.

If the panel wishes to refer an offender who has attained 18 back to court to extend the period of the order under the SC, Sch 4, para 12, the appropriate court is again the adult magistrates' court acting in the local justice area in which it appears to the panel that the offender resides or will reside: SC, s 108(1). For the court's powers see **J12.12.3**.

L9.2 Reparation order

Reparation orders have been repealed by the PCSCA 2022, s 162.

L9.3 Youth rehabilitation order

Applications to revoke or amend a YRO (subject to magistrates' court supervision) in the case of an offender who has attained the age of 18 by the date of the first court hearing must be made to the adult magistrates' court: SC, Sch 7, para 12(2). For the powers of the court when dealing with such an application see **F34.11** for revocation of the order and **F34.12** for amendment of the order.

Blackstone's Handbook of Youths in the Criminal Courts. Mark Ashford, Gareth Branston, and Naomi Redhouse, Oxford University Press.
 DOI: 10.1093/oso/9780198913146.003.0070

L10 Sexual Offences Notification Requirements

When determining whether an offender is subject to the notification requirements, the relevant age is the age on the date of the offence (see **J21.1**).

If the offender is subject to notification requirements, the reduced applicable period does not apply if the offender has attained 18 by the date of conviction (see **J21.2**).

Blackstone's Handbook of Youths in the Criminal Courts. Mark Ashford, Gareth Branston, and Naomi Redhouse, Oxford University Press.
 DOI: 10.1093/oso/9780198913146.003.0071

L11 Rehabilitation of Offenders Act 1974

The relevant age is the age on the date of conviction. The reduced rehabilitation periods do not apply if the offender has attained 18 by the date of conviction.

Blackstone's Handbook of Youths in the Criminal Courts. Mark Ashford, Gareth Branston, and Naomi Redhouse, Oxford University Press.
 DOI: 10.1093/oso/9780198913146.003.0072

Part M
Parents and Guardians

M1 Definition of Parent/Guardian

M1.1 Parent

There is no definition of who is a 'parent' but it is likely to include a person with parental responsibility under the Children Act 1989. Section 17 of the CYPA 1933 provides that 'any person who has parental responsibility for him (within the meaning of the Children Act 1989); or is otherwise legally liable to maintain him' is presumed to have responsibility for a child or young person.

M1.2 Guardian

The CYPA 1933, s 107(1) provides:

Children and Young Persons Act 1933

107 Interpretation

(1) In this Act, unless the context otherwise requires . . .
'Guardian', in relation to a child or young person, includes any person who, in the opinion of the court having cognisance of any case in relation to the child or young person or in which the child or young person is concerned, has for the time being the care of the child or young person.

Blackstone's Handbook of Youths in the Criminal Courts. Mark Ashford, Gareth Branston, and Naomi Redhouse, Oxford University Press.
 DOI: 10.1093/oso/9780198913146.003.0073

M2 Requiring Attendance at Court

The CYPA 1933, s 34A provides:

Children and Young Persons Act 1933

34A Attendance at court of parent or guardian

(1) Where a child or young person is charged with an offence or is for any other reason brought before a court, the court—
  (a) may in any case; and
  (b) shall in the case of a child or a young person who is under the age of sixteen years,

 require a person who is a parent or guardian of his to attend at the court during all the stages of the proceedings, unless and to the extent that the court is satisfied that it would be unreasonable to require such attendance, having regard to the circumstances of the case.

(2) In relation to a child or young person for whom a local authority have parental responsibility and who—
  (a) is in their care; or
  (b) is provided with accommodation by them in the exercise of any functions (in particular those under the Children Act 1989) which are social services functions within the meaning of the Local Authority Social Services Act 1970 or the Social Services and Well-being (Wales) Act 2014,

 the reference in subsection (1) above to a person who is a parent or guardian of his shall be construed as a reference to that authority or, where he is allowed to live with such a person, as including such a reference.

 In this subsection 'local authority' and 'parental responsibility' have the same meanings as in the Children Act 1989.

The Crim PR, rule 7.4(8) sets out two options:

Criminal Procedure Rules

7.4 Summons, warrant and requisition

(8) Where a summons or requisition is served on a defendant under 18—
  (a) the prosecutor or court officer who serves it must serve a copy on a parent or guardian of the defendant as well, and
  (b) if the court requires the parent or guardian to attend, the copy may impose that requirement or a separate summons or requisition may be issued for that purpose.

Blackstone's Handbook of Youths in the Criminal Courts. Mark Ashford, Gareth Branston, and Naomi Redhouse, Oxford University Press.
 DOI: 10.1093/oso/9780198913146.003.0074

The *Sentencing Children and Young People – Overarching Principles* definitive guideline provides the following guidance:

3.1 For any child or young person aged under 16 appearing before court there is a statutory requirement that parents/guardians attend during all stages of proceedings, unless the court is satisfied that this would be unreasonable having regard to the circumstances of the case. The court may also enforce this requirement for a young person aged 16 and above if it deems it desirable to do so.

3.2 Although this requirement can cause a delay in the case before the court it is important it is adhered to. If a court does find exception to proceed in the absence of a responsible adult then extra care must be taken to ensure the outcomes are clearly communicated to and understood by the child or young person.

M3 Responsibility for Financial Order

Different considerations apply to parents and guardians as opposed to local authorities with parental responsibility.

M3.1 Parents and guardians

Sections 42(4) (surcharge), 128(2) (fine), 140(2) (compensation), and 381 (costs), in combination with s 380 of the SC, provide the court with the duty and power to order a financial order to be paid by a parent or guardian instead of the offender themselves. Section 380(1) provides that, where the offender is aged under 16 years, the court **must** order the parent or guardian to pay the fine, costs, surcharge, and compensation if ordered unless:

- the parent/guardian cannot be found; or
- it would be unreasonable to make an order for payment having regard to the circumstances of the case.

Where the defendant is aged 16 or 17 years, the court **may** order the parent or guardian to pay the fine, costs, surcharge, and compensation if ordered unless:

- the parent/guardian cannot be found; or
- it would be unreasonable to make an order for payment having regard to the circumstances of the case.

Before making a financial order against a parent or guardian, that person must be given the opportunity of being heard: s 380(3). Also, the court may require details of their financial circumstances: s 35(4). If there is no cooperation with this inquiry, the court may make such determination as it thinks fit: s 382(1).

The question of when it is 'unreasonable' to make a financial order against a parent or guardian has been considered by the courts.

- A compensation order payable by a mother who 'had done what she could to keep her son from criminal ways' was quashed. She was also of limited means and the order meant that it would have taken her more than two years to pay: *R v Sheffield Crown Court ex parte Clarkson* [1986] Cr App R (S) 454.
- The parent of a child accommodated by the local authority under s 20 of the Children Act 1989 was not reasonably to be ordered to pay a financial penalty: *TA v DPP* [1997] 1 Cr App R (S) 1, [1996] Crim LR 606, QBD.

Blackstone's Handbook of Youths in the Criminal Courts. Mark Ashford, Gareth Branston, and Naomi Redhouse, Oxford University Press.
 DOI: 10.1093/oso/9780198913146.003.0075

- The policy underlying the legislation meant that it was in the public interest that the financial order be recovered from the parent unless there were special circumstances which made that inappropriate: *R(M) v Inner London Crown Court* [2003] EWHC 301 (Admin).
- In *R v JB* [2004] EWCA Crim 14, there seems to be an assumption that in the absence of parental fault it would be unreasonable to order the parent to pay.

M3.2 Local authorities

Where an offender for whom a local authority has parental responsibility is in the care of that local authority, any reference to parent or guardian is to be read as a reference to that authority: SC, s 404(1) and (2). Thus, the local authority will be responsible for the payment of any financial order. An order remanding a young person to the care of the local authority does not confer parental responsibility on the local authority. Parental responsibility is only acquired with a full care order: *North Yorkshire County Council v Selby Youth Court* [1994] 1All ER 991, QBD.

The question of when it is 'unreasonable' to make a financial order against a local authority has been considered by the courts.

- A local authority that had done everything it reasonably and properly could to protect the public from the criminal behaviour of a young person in its care could not be expected to assume responsibility for financial orders: *D and R v DPP* [1995] 16 Cr App R (S) 1040, [1995] Crim LR 748.
- A causal link between the authority's lack of care and the offending needs to be established before the court should order payment of the financial penalty by the authority: *Bedfordshire County Council v DPP* [1996] 1 Cr App R (S) 322; [1995] Crim LR 962.
- A company contracted by the local authority to look after the young person could not be ordered to pay a financial order: *Marlowe Child and Family Services Ltd v DPP* [1998] Crim LR 594 (see J7).

M4 **Parental Bind Over**

Since the introduction of parenting orders, the imposition of parental bind overs has declined. The making of a bind over requires consideration of its terms and the consent of the person being bound over.

The SC, ss 376 to 377 provide:

Sentencing Code

376 Binding over of parent or guardian

(1) This section applies where—
  (a) a person aged under 18 is convicted of an offence, and
  (b) a court is sentencing the offender for the offence.

(2) The court has the following powers—
  (a) the court may, with the consent of the offender's parent or guardian, order the parent or guardian to enter into a recognizance to take proper care of the offender and exercise proper control over the offender, and
  (b) if—
    (i) the parent or guardian refuses consent, and
    (ii) the court considers the refusal unreasonable,

  the court may order the parent or guardian to pay a fine not exceeding £1,000.

(3) For the purposes of this section—
  (a) taking 'care' of a person includes giving the person protection and guidance, and
  (b) 'control' includes discipline.

(4) If the offender is aged under 16 when sentenced, the court must—
  (a) exercise its powers under subsection (2), if satisfied, having regard to the circumstances of the case, that doing so would be desirable in the interests of preventing the offender from committing further offences, or
  (b) state in open court that it is not so satisfied, and why not.

(5) Subsections (2) and (4) are subject to section 37(8) of the Mental Health Act 1983 (order under this section not to be made where hospital or guardianship order is made) and to—
  (a) section 89(4)(b), and
  (b) paragraph 16(2) of Schedule 4,

  (restrictions on the powers of a court making or extending a referral order).

(6) If the court makes a youth rehabilitation order, a recognizance under this section may include a provision that the offender's parent or guardian ensure that the offender complies with the requirements of that order.

Blackstone's Handbook of Youths in the Criminal Courts. Mark Ashford, Gareth Branston, and Naomi Redhouse, Oxford University Press.
 DOI: 10.1093/oso/9780198913146.003.0076

(7) The period of a recognizance under this section—
   (a) may not be more 3 years, and
   (b) must end before the offender reaches the age of 18.
(8) A recognizance under this section may not be for an amount of more than £1,000.
(9) In fixing the amount of a recognizance under this section, the court must take into account, in particular, the means of the parent or guardian so far as they appear or are known to the court (whether doing so has the effect of increasing or reducing the amount).
(10) Section 120 of the Magistrates' Courts Act 1980 (forfeiture of recognizances) applies in relation to a recognizance under this section as it applies in relation to a recognizance to keep the peace.
(11) A fine imposed under subsection (2)(b) is to be treated, for the purposes of any enactment, as being a sum adjudged to be paid by a conviction.
(12) Section 404 (certain references to parent or guardian to be read as references to local authority) does not apply to this section.

377 Binding over of parent or guardian: appeals, variations and revocations

(1) A parent or guardian may appeal to the Crown Court against an order under section 376 made by a magistrates' court.
(2) A parent or guardian may appeal to the Court of Appeal against an order under section 376 made by the Crown Court as if—
   (a) the parent or guardian had been convicted on indictment, and
   (b) the order were a sentence passed on the conviction of the parent or guardian.
(3) A court may vary or discharge an order made by it under section 376 if, on the application of the parent or guardian, it appears to the court, having regard to any change in the circumstances since the order was made, to be in the interests of justice to do so.

The Sentencing Children and Young People – Overarching Principles definitive guideline gives the following assistance:

3.3 In addition to this responsibility there are also orders that can be imposed on parents. If the child or young person is aged under 16 then the court has a duty to make a parental bind over or impose a parenting order, if it would be desirable in the interest of preventing the commission of further offences. There is a discretionary power to make these orders where the young person is aged 16 or 17. If the court chooses not to impose a parental bind over or parenting order it must state its reasons for not doing so in open court. In most circumstances a parenting order is likely to be more appropriate than a parental bind over.

3.4 A court cannot make a bind over alongside a referral order. If the court makes a referral order the duty on the court to impose a parenting order in respect of a child or young person under 16 years old is replaced by a discretion.

Where a bind over is not made, the court must explain in open court its reasons.

Where the court makes a referral order, it cannot impose a parental bind over: SC, s 89(4).

The parent who is made subject to a bind over has the right of appeal to the Crown Court from the youth court or adult magistrates' court and to the Court of Appeal from the Crown Court.

M5 **Parenting Order**

A parenting order may be made upon conviction by any criminal court—youth court, adult magistrates' court, or Crown Court: SC, s 366(1).

A parenting order may also be made where a criminal court makes a CBO or SHPO: CDA 1998, s 8(1)(b). A youth court may make a parenting order where a parent or guardian has failed to attend meetings of the youth offender panel under a referral order: SC, s 368 (see **M6**). A parenting order is also available in respect of certain attendance offences under the Education Act 1996: SC, s 369. A local authority with parental responsibility for an offender cannot be made subject to a parenting order: SC, s 371.

The SC, ss 365 and 366 provide:

Sentencing Code

365 Parenting order

(1) A parenting order under this Chapter is an order which requires the person in respect of whom it is made ('the parent')—
  (a) to comply, for a period of not more than 12 months, with requirements specified in the order, and
  (b) to attend, for a concurrent period of not more than 3 months, such counselling or guidance programme as may be specified in directions given by the responsible officer (see section 372).

(2) But a parenting order need not include a requirement under subsection (1)(b) if a parenting order (whether under this Chapter or any other enactment) has been made in respect of the parent on any previous occasion.

(3) If the parenting order provides this in accordance with section 366(7), 368(5) or 369(5), a counselling or guidance programme specified under subsection (1)(b) may be or include a residential course.

366 Parenting order where offender is under 18

(1) A parenting order under this section is available to a court by or before which an offender aged under 18 is convicted of an offence.
This is subject to section 370.

(2) Subsections (3) and (4) apply where a parenting order under this section is available.

(3) If the offender is aged under 16 at the time of conviction, the court must—
  (a) make a parenting order under this section in respect of a parent or guardian of the offender if it is satisfied that the order would be desirable in the interests of preventing the commission of any further offence by the offender, or
  (b) state in open court that it is not so satisfied, and why not.

Blackstone's Handbook of Youths in the Criminal Courts. Mark Ashford, Gareth Branston, and Naomi Redhouse, Oxford University Press.
 DOI: 10.1093/oso/9780198913146.003.0077

But this does not apply if the court makes a referral order in respect of the offender.

(4) If the offender is aged 16 or 17 at the time of conviction, the court may make a parenting order under this section in respect of a parent or guardian of the offender if it is satisfied that the order would be desirable in the interests of preventing the commission of any further offence by the offender.

(5) Subsections (6) and (7) apply where a court makes a parenting order under this section in respect of a parent or guardian of an offender.

(6) The requirements that the court may specify in the order under section 365(1)(a) are requirements that it considers desirable in the interests of preventing the commission of any further offence by the offender.

(7) If the order contains a requirement under section 365(1)(b) and the court is satisfied that—

(a) the attendance of the parent or guardian at a residential course is likely to be more effective than that person's attendance at a non-residential course in preventing the commission of any further offence by the offender, and

(b) any interference with family life which is likely to result from the parent's or guardian's attendance at a residential course is proportionate in all the circumstances,

the court may provide in the order that a counselling or guidance programme which the parent or guardian is required to attend by virtue of the requirement may be or include a residential course.

(8) Before making a parenting order under this section in respect of a parent or guardian of an offender aged under 16, the court must obtain and consider information about—

(a) the offender's family circumstances, and

(b) the likely effect of the order on those circumstances.

(9) Where a parenting order is made under this section, the person in respect of whom it is made has the same right of appeal against it as if—

(a) that person had committed the offence mentioned in subsection (1), and

(b) the order were a sentence passed on that person for the offence.

A parenting order is an order requiring a parent or guardian to comply with specified requirements, for up to 12 months, that the court considers desirable in the interests of preventing the commission of any further offence by the offender.

Where an offender is aged under 16 years, the court must make a parenting order if satisfied that the order would be desirable in the interests of preventing the commission of further offences. If the court is not so satisfied, it must state this in open court and give reasons.

Where an offender is aged 16 or 17 years, the court has a discretionary power to make an order.

Before making an order, the court must obtain and consider information about the offender's family circumstances and the likely effect of the order on those circumstances.

Where the court is considering making both a referral order and a parenting order, this information shall be in a report by an appropriate officer: s 367.

Before making an order, the court must explain to the parent the effect of the order and of the requirements proposed to be included in it, the consequences of failure to comply, and the power of the court to review the order on the application of the parent or responsible officer: s 372(3).

M5.1 Terms of the order

The order will last for up to 12 months and must include a requirement to attend a counselling or guidance programme for a period not exceeding three months. It may be a residential course if it is likely to be more effective than a non-residential course and the likely interference with family life is proportionate.

The requirements should not interfere with religious, educational, or employment commitments.

M5.2 Breach

It is an offence for a person, in respect of whom a parenting order is made, to fail to comply with any requirement included in the order or specified in directions given by the responsible officer: s 375(1). Such an offence is punishable on summary conviction with a fine not exceeding level 3: s 375(2).

M5.3 Variation, discharge, and appeal

The responsible officer or parent may apply to the court which made the order to vary or discharge the order: s 374.

Appeal against an order made in the youth or adult magistrates' courts is to the Crown Court or to the Court of Appeal if the order is made in the Crown Court.

M5.4 Parenting order not on conviction

A court may make a parenting order where it is making a CBO or SHPO: CDA 1998, s 8(1)(b); SC, ss 342 and 355. The court may make the order if satisfied that it would be desirable in the interests of preventing any repetition of the kind of behaviour which led to the CBO/SHPO being made: CDA 1998, s 8(2) and (6).

The terms and requirements are similar to those for a parenting order following conviction: ss 8(4), (7), (7A), and 9(4). The court must explain the effect prior to making an order: s 9(3). Failure to comply is a summary offence punishable with a fine not exceeding level 3: s 9(7).

Where the court is making a CBO for a defendant aged under 16, the making of a parenting order is mandatory if the relevant condition is fulfilled, namely that it is desirable in the interests of preventing any repetition of the behaviour: s 9(1B)(a).

M6 Referral Order: Requiring Attendance at Panel

The SC, s 90 provides:

Sentencing Code

90 Order requiring parents etc to attend meetings

(1) This section applies where a court makes a referral order.

(2) The court—

(a) may make an order requiring—

(i) the appropriate person, or

(ii) if there are two or more appropriate persons, one or more of them, to attend the meetings of the youth offender panel, and

(b) must do so if the offender is aged under 16 when the referral order is made.

(3) If the offender is—

(a) a looked-after child, and

(b) aged under 16 when the referral order is made,

the person or persons required under subsection (2) to attend those meetings must include at least one representative of the responsible authority.

(4) But an order under subsection (2) must not require a person to attend those meetings—

(a) if the court is satisfied that it would be unreasonable to do so, or

(b) to an extent which the court is satisfied would be unreasonable.

(5) For the purposes of this section, each of the following is an appropriate person in relation to an offender—

(a) if the offender is a looked-after child—

(i) a representative of the responsible authority, and

(ii) each person who is a parent or guardian of the offender with whom the offender is allowed to live;

(b) otherwise, each person who is a parent or guardian of the offender.

(6) In this section—

'looked-after child' means a child who is (within the meaning of the Children Act 1989 or the Social Services and Well-being (Wales) Act 2014 (anaw 4)) looked after by a local authority, and

'responsible authority', in relation to a looked-after child, means the authority by which the child is looked after.

(7) The court must forthwith send a copy of an order under subsection (2)—

(a) to each person required by the order to attend meetings of the panel, and

Blackstone's Handbook of Youths in the Criminal Courts. Mark Ashford, Gareth Branston, and Naomi Redhouse, Oxford University Press.
 DOI: 10.1093/oso/9780198913146.003.0078

> (b) to any responsible authority whose representative is required by the order to attend meetings of the panel,
>
> unless the person was present, or the authority was represented, in court when the order was made.

Where a parent, who has been required to do so, does not attend meetings of the referral order panel, the panel can refer the parent to the youth court for consideration of the making of a parenting order.

The SC, ss 93 and 368 provide:

> ## Sentencing Code
>
> **93 Failure of parent or guardian to comply with order under section 90**
>
> (1) If—
>
> (a) a parent or guardian of an offender fails to comply with an order under section 90 (orders requiring parents etc to attend meetings), and
>
> (b) the offender is aged under 18 at the time of the failure,
>
> the youth offender panel may refer the parent or guardian to a youth court acting in the local justice area in which it appears to the panel that the offender resides or will reside.
>
> (2) To make the referral, the panel must send a report to the youth court explaining why the parent or guardian is being referred to it.
>
> (3) A youth court which receives a report under subsection (2) must cause the parent or guardian to appear before it.
>
> (4) For that purpose, a justice acting in the local justice area in which the court acts may—
>
> (a) issue a summons requiring the parent to appear before that youth court at the place and time specified in it, or
>
> (b) if the report is substantiated on oath, issue a warrant for the parent's arrest which requires the parent to be brought before that court.
>
> (5) For the youth court's power to make a parenting order where the panel refers the parent or guardian under this section, see section 368 (parenting order where parent or guardian fails to attend meeting of panel).
>
> (6) Making a parenting order under that section does not affect the order under section 90.
>
> (7) Accordingly, section 63(1) to (4) of the Magistrates' Courts Act 1980 (power to deal with person for breach of order etc) applies in relation to an order under section 90 (in addition to this section and section 368).
>
> **368 Parenting order where parent or guardian of offender fails to attend meetings of youth offender panel**
>
> (1) A parenting order under this section is available to a youth court where—

(a) an offender has been referred to a youth offender panel (see section 83), and
(b) a parent or guardian of the offender is referred by the panel to the youth court under section 93 in respect of a failure to comply with an order under section 90 (order requiring attendance at meetings of panel).

This is subject to section 370.

(2) Where a parenting order under this section is available, the youth court may make such an order if it is satisfied that—
(a) the parent or guardian has failed without reasonable excuse to comply with the order under section 90, and
(b) the parenting order would be desirable in the interests of preventing the commission of any further offence by the offender.

(3) Subsections (4) and (5) apply where the court makes a parenting order in respect of a parent or guardian of an offender.

(4) The requirements that the court may specify under section 365(1)(a) in an order under this section are requirements that it considers desirable in the interests of preventing the commission of any further offence by the offender.

(5) If the order contains a requirement under section 365(1)(b) and the court is satisfied that—
(a) the attendance of the parent or guardian at a residential course is likely to be more effective than that person's attendance at a non-residential course in preventing the commission of any further offence by the offender, and
(b) any interference with family life which is likely to result from the parent's or guardian's attendance at a residential course is proportionate in all the circumstances,

the court may provide in the order that a counselling or guidance programme which the parent or guardian is required to attend by virtue of the requirement may be or include a residential course.

(6) Before making a parenting order under this section where the offender is aged under 16, the court must obtain and consider information about—
(a) the offender's family circumstances, and
(b) the likely effect of the order on those circumstances.

(7) Where a parenting order is made under this section, the person in respect of whom it is made may appeal against it to the Crown Court.

(8) On an appeal under subsection (7) the Crown Court—
(a) may make such orders as may be necessary to give effect to its determination of the appeal, and
(b) may also make such incidental or consequential orders as appear to it to be just.

(9) An order of the Crown Court made on an appeal under subsection (7) is to be treated for the purposes of section 374 as having been made by the youth court.

See **J12**.

Part N
Civil Jurisdiction of the Youth Court

N1 General

In the case of adults, injunctions for anti-social behaviour and gang violence are dealt with in the county court or High Court. Since 2015, the youth court has been given a civil jurisdiction to grant such injunctions against persons under 18.

N1.1 Legal aid

Funding for representing respondents in applications for these injunctions is available through the civil legal aid scheme, subject to the usual civil merits and means testing. The work is permitted as 'Associated Civil Work' under the Standard Crime Contract 2022.

Breaches of these injunctions are civil proceedings but are covered by criminal legal aid. The application is made on a CRM14 eForm. It is not means tested. The Legal Aid Agency (LAA) requires proof of the proceedings to be uploaded with the application. A schedule of breaches and the supporting statements from arresting police officers will normally be sufficient.

N1.2 Procedure

Civil proceedings in the youth court are governed by Part 2 of the MCA 1980 and the Magistrates' Court Rules 1981. Specific procedural rules have also been issued for both anti-social behaviour injunctions (ASBIs) and gang injunctions (for which see below).

The Crim PR do not apply to civil proceedings except for Part 31, which deals with Behaviour Orders. Neither ASBIs nor gang injunctions are covered by Part 31. The Civil Procedure Rules (Civ PR) will apply to these injunctions in the county court, but the youth court does not come under the scope of those rules: Civ PR, r 2.1(1).

Magistrates' Courts Act 1980

53 Procedure on hearing

(1) On the hearing of a complaint, the court shall, if the defendant appears, state to him the substance of the complaint.

(2) The court, after hearing the evidence and the parties, shall make the order for which the complaint is made or dismiss the complaint.

The MCA 1980 also makes provision for:

- A power to adjourn: s 54;
- The non-appearance of the defendant: s 55;

Blackstone's Handbook of Youths in the Criminal Courts. Mark Ashford, Gareth Branston, and Naomi Redhouse, Oxford University Press.
 DOI: 10.1093/oso/9780198913146.003.0079

- The non-appearance of the complainant: s 56;
- The non-appearance of both parties: s 57.

N1.3 Case management

Magistrates' Courts Rules 1981

3A Case management

(1) The court must actively manage the case. That includes—
  (a) the early identification of the real issues;
  (b) the early identification of the needs of witnesses;
  (c) achieving certainty as to what must be done, by whom and when, in particular by the early setting of a timetable for the progress of the case;
  (d) monitoring the progress of the case and compliance with directions;
  (e) ensuring that evidence, whether disputed or not, is presented in the shortest and clearest way;
  (f) discouraging delay, dealing with as many aspects of the case as possible on the same occasion and avoiding unnecessary hearings;
  (g) encouraging the participants to co-operate in the progression of the case; and
  (h) making use of technology, including live links.
(2) The court must actively manage the case by giving any direction appropriate to the needs of that case as early as possible.
(3) Each party must—
  (a) actively assist the court in managing the case without, or if necessary with, a direction; and
  (b) apply for a direction if needed to assist with the management of the case.

If the application is to be contested, the court will normally set a timetable for the filing and service of further witness statements by the parties. It is common for the direction regarding the filing of evidence to stipulate that a witness who fails to file and serve a witness statement shall not be able to give evidence without the leave of the court.

The statutory regime regarding unused material under the Criminal Procedure and Investigations Act 1996 (CPIA 1996) does not apply to civil proceedings. There is no specific provision for the disclosure of documents between the parties in proceedings before the youth court (cf. Civ PR, r 31 applicable in the county court). However, in the context of a closure order application before a magistrates' court, it was held that the police applicant should disclose documents which clearly and materially affected its case adversely or supported the defendant's case: *R (Cleary) v Highbury Corner Magistrates' Court*

[2006] EWHC 1869 (Admin). There would seem to be no reason why a youth court could not direct disclosure on similar terms in contested proceedings for an ASBI or gang injunction.

N1.4 Evidence

N1.4.1 *Hearsay*

The Civil Evidence Act 1995 applies to both applications for injunctions and breach proceedings.

Civil Evidence Act 1995

1 Admissibility of hearsay evidence

(1) In civil proceedings evidence shall not be excluded on the ground that it is hearsay.

(2) In this Act—

(a) 'hearsay' means a statement made otherwise than by a person while giving oral evidence in the proceedings which is tendered as evidence of the matters stated; and

(b) references to hearsay include hearsay of whatever degree.

(3) Nothing in this Act affects the admissibility of evidence admissible apart from this section.

(4) The provisions of sections 2 to 6 (safeguards and supplementary provisions relating to hearsay evidence) do not apply in relation to hearsay evidence admissible apart from this section, notwithstanding that it may also be admissible by virtue of this section.

2 Notice of proposal to adduce hearsay evidence

(1) A party proposing to adduce hearsay evidence in civil proceedings shall, subject to the following provisions of this section, give to the other party or parties to the proceedings—

(a) such notice (if any) of that fact, and

(b) on request, such particulars of or relating to the evidence,

as is reasonable and practicable in the circumstances for the purpose of enabling him or them to deal with any matters arising from its being hearsay.

(2) Provision may be made by rules of court—

(a) specifying classes of proceedings or evidence in relation to which subsection (1) does not apply, and

(b) as to the manner in which (including the time within which) the duties imposed by that subsection are to be complied with in the cases where it does apply.

(3) Subsection (1) may also be excluded by agreement of the parties; and compliance with the duty to give notice may in any case be waived by the person to whom notice is required to be given.

(4) A failure to comply with subsection (1), or with rules under subsection (2)(b), does not affect the admissibility of the evidence but may be taken into account by the court—

(a) in considering the exercise of its powers with respect to the course of proceedings and costs, and

(b) as a matter adversely affecting the weight to be given to the evidence in accordance with section 4.

. . .

4 Considerations relevant to weighing of hearsay evidence

(1) In estimating the weight (if any) to be given to hearsay evidence in civil proceedings the court shall have regard to any circumstances from which any inference can reasonably be drawn as to the reliability or otherwise of the evidence.

(2) Regard may be had, in particular, to the following—

(a) whether it would have been reasonable and practicable for the party by whom the evidence was adduced to have produced the maker of the original statement as a witness;

(b) whether the original statement was made contemporaneously with the occurrence or existence of the matters stated;

(c) whether the evidence involves multiple hearsay;

(d) whether any person involved had any motive to conceal or misrepresent matters;

(e) whether the original statement was an edited account, or was made in collaboration with another or for a particular purpose;

(f) whether the circumstances in which the evidence is adduced as hearsay are such as to suggest an attempt to prevent proper evaluation of its weight.

The relevant rules regarding hearsay evidence are contained in the Magistrates' Courts (Hearsay Evidence in Civil Proceedings) Rules 1999.

Magistrates' Courts (Hearsay Evidence in Civil Proceedings) Rules 1999

3 Hearsay notices

(1) Subject to paragraphs (2) and (3), a party who desires to give hearsay evidence at the hearing must, not less than 21 days before the date fixed for the hearing, serve a hearsay notice on every other party and file a copy in the court by serving it on the designated officer for the court.

(2) Subject to paragraph (3), the court may make a direction substituting a different period of time for the service of the hearsay notice under paragraph (1) on the application of a party to the proceedings.

(3) The court may make a direction under paragraph (2) of its own motion.

(4) A hearsay notice must—

(a) state that it is a hearsay notice;

(b) identify the proceedings in which the hearsay evidence is to be given;

(c) state that the party proposes to adduce hearsay evidence;

(d) identify the hearsay evidence;

(e) identify the person who made the statement which is to be given in evidence; and

(f) state why that person will not be called to give oral evidence.

(5) A single hearsay notice may deal with the hearsay evidence of more than one witness.

4 Power to call witness for cross-examination on hearsay evidence

(1) Where a party tenders as hearsay evidence a statement made by a person but does not propose to call the person who made the statement to give evidence, the court may, on application, allow another party to call and cross-examine the person who made the statement on its contents.

(2) An application under paragraph (1) must–
  (a) be served on the designated officer for the court with sufficient copies for all other parties;
  (b) unless the court otherwise directs, be made not later than 7 days after service of the hearsay notice; and
  (c) give reasons why the person who made the statement should be cross-examined on its contents.

(3) On receipt of an application under paragraph (1)—
  (a) the designated officer for the court must—
    (i) unless the court otherwise directs, allow sufficient time for the applicant to comply with paragraph (4); and
    (ii) fix the date, time and place of the hearing; and
  (b) the designated officer for the court must—
    (i) endorse the date, time and place of the hearing on the copies of the application filed by the applicant; and
    (ii) return the copies to the applicant forthwith.

(4) Subject to paragraphs (5) and (6), on receipt of the copies from the designated officer for the court under paragraph (3)(c), the applicant must serve a copy on every other party giving not less than 3 days' notice of the hearing of the application.

(5) The court may give directions as to the manner in which service under paragraph (4) is to be effected and may, subject to the designated officer's giving notice to the applicant, alter or dispense with the notice requirement under paragraph (4) if the court considers it is in the interests of justice to do so.

(6) The court may hear an application under paragraph (1) *ex parte* if it considers it is in the interests of justice to do so.

(7) Subject to paragraphs (5) and (6), where an application under paragraph (1) is made, the applicant must file with the court a statement at or before the hearing of the application that service of a copy of the application has been effected on all other parties and the statement must indicate the manner, date, time and address at which the document was served.

(8) The court must notify all parties of its decision on an application under paragraph (1).

5 Credibility and previous inconsistent statements

(1) If–
  (a) a party tenders as hearsay evidence a statement made by a person but does not call the person who made the statement to give oral evidence, and

(b) another party wishes to attack the credibility of the person who made the statement or allege that the person who made the statement made any other statement inconsistent with it,

that other party must notify the party tendering the hearsay evidence of his intention.

(2) Unless the court or the justices' clerk otherwise directs, a notice under paragraph (1) must be given not later than 7 days after service of the hearsay notice and, in addition to the requirements in paragraph (1), must be served on every other party and a copy filed in the court.

(3) If, on receipt of a notice under paragraph (1), the party referred to in paragraph (1)(a) calls the person who made the statement to be tendered as hearsay evidence to give oral evidence, he must, unless the court otherwise directs, notify the court and all other parties of his intention.

(4) Unless the court or the justices' clerk otherwise directs, a notice under paragraph (3) must be given not later than 7 days after the service of the notice under paragraph (1).

The use of hearsay evidence in gang injunction applications (and by extension ASBI applications) has been held to be compatible with the right to a fair trial in civil proceedings enshrined in ECHR art 6(1): *Chief Constable of Lancashire v Wilson* [2015] EWHC 2763 (QB).

Applicants should state, by convincing direct evidence, why it is not reasonable and practicable to produce the original maker of the statement as a witness and if the statement involves multiple hearsay. Furthermore, if the statement involves multiple hearsay, the route by which the original statement came to the attention of the person attesting to it should be identified as far as practicable: *Moat Housing Group Ltd v Harris* [2005] EWCA Civ 287 at [140]. Consideration should also be given to the availability of special measures for a witness who may be in fear.

N1.4.2 *Convictions*

By virtue of Civil Evidence Act 1968, s 11, in any civil proceedings, a previous conviction is generally admissible in evidence for the purpose of proving, where to do so is relevant to any issue in those proceedings, that a person committed the offence.

This general rule is, however, modified in the case of spent convictions. The Rehabilitation of Offenders Act 1974 makes provision for both cautions and convictions to become spent (for which see **J13**).

The Rehabilitation of Offenders Act 1974, s 4(1) provides:

Rehabilitation of Offenders Act 1974

4 Effect of rehabilitation

(1) Subject to sections 7 and 8 below a person who has become a rehabilitated person for the purposes of this Act in respect of a conviction shall be treated for all purposes in law as a person who has not committed or been charged with or prosecuted for or convicted of or sentenced for the offence or offences which were the subject of that conviction; and, notwithstanding the provisions of any other enactment or rule of law to the contrary, but subject as aforesaid—
  (a) no evidence shall be admissible in any proceedings before a judicial authority exercising its jurisdiction or functions in England and Wales to prove that any such person has committed or been charged with or prosecuted for or convicted of or sentenced for any offence which was the subject of a spent conviction; and
  (b) a person shall not, in any such proceedings, be asked, and, if asked, shall not be required to answer, any question relating to his past which cannot be answered without acknowledging or referring to a spent conviction or spent convictions or any circumstances ancillary thereto.

The effect of s 4 is excluded from various types of proceedings including criminal proceedings. It does, however, apply to civil proceedings, where the Rehabilitation of Offenders Act 1974, s 7(3) provides:

Rehabilitation of Offenders Act 1974

7 Limitations on rehabilitation under this Act, etc.

(3) If at any stage in any proceedings before a judicial authority in England and Wales . . . the authority is satisfied, in the light of any considerations which appear to it to be relevant (including any evidence which has been or may thereafter be put before it), that justice cannot be done in the case except by admitting or requiring evidence relating to a person's spent convictions or to circumstances ancillary thereto, that authority may admit or, as the case may be, require the evidence in question notwithstanding the provisions of subsection (1) of section 4 above, and may determine any issue to which the evidence relates in disregard, so far as necessary, of those provisions.

N1.5 Trial

The procedure for a civil complaint in the youth court is governed by the Magistrates' Courts Rules 1981, r 14.

Magistrates' Courts Rules 1981

14 Order of evidence and speeches: complaint

(1) On the hearing of a complaint, except where the court determines under section 53(3) of the Act of 1980 to make the order with the consent of the defendant without hearing evidence, the complainant shall call his evidence, and before doing so may address the court.

(2) At the conclusion of the evidence for the complainant the defendant may address the court, whether or not he afterwards calls evidence.

(3) At the conclusion of the evidence, if any, for the defence, the complainant may call evidence to rebut that evidence.

(4) At the conclusion of the evidence for the defence and the evidence, if any, in rebuttal, the defendant may address the court if he has not already done so.

(5) Either party may, with the leave of the court, address the court a second time, but where the court grants leave to one party it shall not refuse leave to the other.

(6) Where the defendant obtains leave to address the court for a second time his second address shall be made before the second address, if any, of the complainant.

N1.6 **Costs**

The Magistrates' Courts Act 1980, s 64(1) provides:

Magistrates' Courts Act 1980

64 Power to award costs and enforcement of costs

(1) On the hearing of a complaint, a magistrates' court shall have power in its discretion to make such order as to costs—
   (a) on making the order for which the complaint is made, to be paid by the defendant to the complainant;
   (b) on dismissing the complaint, to be paid by the complainant to the defendant,

as it thinks just and reasonable . . .

The LASPO 2012, s 26(1) sets out the general principle that costs ordered against a legally aided individual in civil proceedings must be reasonable, having regard to all the circumstances, including the financial resources and conduct of the parties in the proceedings (referred to as 'cost protection').

There is no power to order the payment of costs by a parent or guardian (the power to do so under the SC, s 380 only applying to orders made on conviction of an offence).

N2 **Anti-social Behaviour Injunction**

ASBIs are governed by Part 1 of the Anti-social Behaviour, Crime and Policing Act 2014 (ABCPA 2014). The Magistrates' Courts (Injunctions: Anti-Social Behaviour) Rules 2015 apply. The Home Office has issued statutory guidance—*Anti-social Behaviour Powers: Statutory guidance for frontline professionals* (revised March 2023).

N2.1 **Age (s 1(1))**

An ASBI may be made against any respondent who is aged 10 years or over.

N2.2 **Grounds for making an injunction (ss 1 and 2)**

The court may grant an ASBI against a person aged 10 or over if two conditions are met:

- The court is satisfied, on the balance of probabilities, that the respondent has engaged or threatens to engage in anti-social behaviour; and
- The court considers it just and convenient to grant the injunction for the purpose of preventing the respondent from engaging in anti-social behaviour.

Section 2 defines 'anti-social behaviour' as:

> (a) conduct that has caused, or is likely to cause, harassment, alarm or distress to any person,
> (b) conduct capable of causing nuisance or annoyance to a person in relation to that person's occupation of residential premises; or
> (c) conduct capable of causing housing-related nuisance to any person.

The definition in paragraph (b) only applies if the injunction is applied for by a housing provider, a local authority, or a chief officer of police.

'Housing-related' in paragraph (c) means directly or indirectly relating to the housing management functions of a housing provider or a local authority.

Blackstone's Handbook of Youths in the Criminal Courts. Mark Ashford, Gareth Branston, and Naomi Redhouse, Oxford University Press.
 DOI: 10.1093/oso/9780198913146.003.0080

N2.3 Requirement to consult youth offending team (s 14)

Except in the case of a without notice application, a person applying for an injunction must *before* doing so:
(a) consult the local YOT about the application, if the respondent will be aged under 18 when the application is made; and
(b) inform any other body or individual the applicant thinks appropriate of the application.

'Local YOT' means:
(a) the YOT in whose area it appears to the applicant that the respondent lives; or
(b) if it appears to the applicant that the respondent lives in more than one such area, whichever one or more of the relevant YOTs the applicant thinks it appropriate to consult.

The statutory guidance states (at p 33):

> Although the consultation requirement does not mean that the youth offending team can veto the application, it is important that applicants fully consider and take into account representations from the youth offending team as part of developing good partnership working in cases involving young people.

Other individuals or organizations to inform could include a youth charity working with the respondent or the local children social care department as the respondent may be a child in need or on a child protection plan.

N2.4 Making an application

The agencies authorized to apply for an ASBI are set out in s 5. Applications will usually be made by the police, a local authority, or a housing provider.

Applications against respondents who are under the age of 18 must be made to the youth court: s 1(8)(a). The application must be made by way of complaint in writing: r 2.

By rule 3, an application to a youth court must:
(a) state the name, address and date of birth of the respondent;
(b) state the name and address of a parent or guardian of the respondent;
(c) be supported by evidence of the matters of which the court must be satisfied for the first and second conditions under section 1 to be met;
(d) state the terms of the injunction applied for; and
(e) in the case of an application made on notice, include a statement that the requirement for consultation in section 14(1) has been complied with.

In the case of an application made on notice, a copy of the application must be served by the applicant on—
(a) the respondent personally; and
(b) the parent or guardian personally, or by posting it to or leaving it at that parent or guardian's address.

N2.5 **Interim injunction (s 7)**

Where the youth court adjourns the hearing of an application for an ASBI, it may grant an interim injunction under s 1 lasting until the final hearing of the application or until further order if it thinks it is just to do so.

An interim injunction made at a hearing of which the respondent was not given notice may not have the effect of requiring the respondent to participate in particular activities.

N2.6 **Application without notice (s 6)**

An application for an ASBI may be made without notice being given to the respondent. An application without notice must also state the reasons why it is necessary for the application to be made without notice having been given: r 3(2).

If an application is made without notice, the court must either:
(a) adjourn the proceedings and grant an interim injunction;
(b) adjourn the proceedings without granting an interim injunction; or
(c) dismiss the application.

By rule 4, an interim injunction which is made on an application made without notice:
(a) must be served on the respondent personally as soon as practicable; and
(b) will not take effect until it has been so served.

N2.7 **Length of order (s 1(6))**

In the case of an injunction granted before the respondent has reached the age of 18, the order must specify the period for which it has effect and it must be no more than 12 months.

N2.8 **Contents of injunction (ss 1 and 3)**

An injunction may, for the purpose of preventing the respondent from engaging in anti-social behaviour:
(a) prohibit the respondent from doing anything described in the injunction;

(b) require the respondent to do anything described in the injunction.

Prohibitions and requirements in any ASBI must, so far as practicable, be such as to avoid:
(a) any interference with the times, if any, at which the respondent normally works or attends school or any other educational establishment;
(b) any conflict with the requirements of any other court order or injunction to which the respondent may be subject.

An order which includes a requirement must specify the person who is to be responsible for supervising compliance with the requirement. The person may be an individual or an organization. Before including a requirement, the court must receive evidence about its suitability and enforceability from the individual or organization to be specified. Before including two or more requirements, the court must consider their compatibility with each other.

A respondent subject to a requirement included in an injunction must:
(a) keep in touch with the person or organization supervising the injunction requirement specified, in accordance with any instructions given from time to time;
(b) notify the person of any change of address.

These obligations have effect as requirements of the injunction.

Section 13 provides a power to exclude a person from their home in cases of violence or risk of harm. This power cannot be imposed on a respondent under the age of 18.

N2.9 **Power of arrest (s 4)**

A court granting an ASBI may attach a power of arrest to a prohibition or requirement of the order if the court thinks that:
(a) the anti-social behaviour in which the respondent has engaged or threatens to engage consists of or includes the use or threatened use of violence against other persons; or
(b) there is a significant risk of harm to other persons from the respondent.

If the court attaches a power of arrest, the injunction may specify a period for which the power is to have effect which is shorter than that of the prohibition or requirement to which it relates.

N2.10 Respondent attaining 18 during the proceedings (r 16)

Where a respondent attains the age of 18 after the commencement of proceedings under Part 1 of the ABCPA 2014, the proceedings must remain in a youth court (subject to a direction by the court).

The youth court may, at the request of the applicant or the respondent or of its own motion, direct that the proceedings be transferred to the High Court or county court, having had regard in particular to:

(a) the stage which the proceedings have reached;
(b) the circumstances of the applicant and the respondent and
(c) the need to ensure fairness between the applicant and the respondent.

The court may not make such a direction without a hearing, on notice to both the applicant and the respondent.

N2.11 Adult respondents in the youth court (s 18(2) and r 15)

The applicant may apply to the youth court to give permission for an ASBI application against a person over the age of 18 to be made to the youth court if:

- an application to the youth court has been made, or is to be made, for an ASBI against a person aged under 18; and
- the youth court thinks that it would be in the interests of justice for the applications to be heard together.

Rule 15 sets out the procedural requirements for such an application.

N2.12 Reporting restrictions (s 17)

The usual automatic reporting restrictions in the youth court imposed by the CYPA 1933, s 49 do not apply to ASBI applications or any subsequent breach proceedings. The court still has a discretion to impose reporting restrictions under the CYPA 1933, s 39 as these are civil proceedings.

N2.13 Special measures (s 16)

The special measures for witnesses under the YJCEA 1999 are available notwithstanding that the proceedings are civil.

N2.14 **Variation or discharge of injunction (s 8)**

The youth court which made the ASBI (or the county court if the respondent has attained 18) may vary or discharge an ASBI on the application of:
(a) the person who applied for the injunction; or
(b) the respondent.

The power to vary an injunction includes power:
(a) to include an additional prohibition or requirement in the injunction, or to extend the period for which a prohibition or requirement has effect;
(b) to attach a power of arrest, or to extend the period for which a power of arrest has effect.

It is the opinion of the authors that this power does not allow the length of the injunction to be extended beyond the maximum 12 months specified in s 1(6).

An application to vary or discharge must be made by way of complaint in writing: r 2. By rule 6, an application must:
(a) specify—
  (i) the reason why the person applying for variation or discharge believes the court should vary or discharge the injunction; and
  (ii) if the application is to vary the injunction, the variation which is sought; and
(b) where the application is made by the person on whose application the injunction was granted, include a statement that the requirement to consult with the relevant YOT has been complied with.

N2.15 **Appeal (s 15)**

An appeal lies to the Crown Court against a decision of a youth court made under Part 1 of the ABCPA 2014.

N3 Breach of Anti-social Behaviour Injunction

The powers of the court to deal with an alleged breach of the injunction are contained in ABCPA 2014, ss 9 to 12 and Sch 1 and 2.

N3.1 Arrest without warrant (s 9)

Where a power of arrest is attached to a provision of the ASBI, a constable may arrest the respondent without warrant if they have reasonable cause to suspect that the respondent is in breach of the provision: s 9(1). A constable who arrests a person under a power of arrest must inform the person who applied for the injunction: s 9(2).

A person arrested for breach must, within the period of 24 hours beginning with the time of arrest, be brought before a justice of the peace: s 9(3). In calculating when the period of 24 hours ends, Christmas Day, Good Friday, and any Sunday are to be disregarded: s 9(4).

Where the respondent has attained 18 since the youth court made the original order, they must be taken before a judge of the county court: s 9(3)(b)(ii).

N3.2 Warrant of arrest (s 10)

Where no power of arrest is attached to the order and the injunction applicant considers that that respondent is in breach of any of its provisions, the person may apply to a justice of the peace (judge of the county court if the respondent has now attained 18) for the issue of a warrant for the respondent's arrest.

N3.3 Appearing before the youth court for breach

If the matter is not disposed of straight away, there is a power to adjourn the proceedings and remand the person subject to the ASBI. The justice of the peace before whom a person is brought must remand the person to appear before the youth court that granted the injunction: s 9(6).

By rule 8(2) and (3) of The Magistrates' Courts (Injunctions: Anti-Social Behaviour) Rules 2015, if proceedings are adjourned and the arrested person is released—

(a) the matter must be dealt with (either by the same or another youth court) within 28 days of the date on which the arrested person appears in court; and

Blackstone's Handbook of Youths in the Criminal Courts. Mark Ashford, Gareth Branston, and Naomi Redhouse, Oxford University Press.
 DOI: 10.1093/oso/9780198913146.003.0081

(b) the arrested person must be given not less than two days' notice of the hearing.

N3.4 Remand of the defaulter

A person under 18 may only be remanded on bail (unless the court has reason to think that a medical report will be needed and the remand in custody is to enable a medical report to take place and a report to be made): Sch 1, paras 2(1) and 6(1). As the breach proceedings are civil, the BA 1976 does not apply. Bail conditions may only be imposed if they appear to the court to be necessary to secure that the person does not interfere with witnesses or otherwise obstruct the course of justice: Sch 1, para 9.

N3.5 Powers of court on breach of an injunction (Sch 2, para 1)

A youth court, if satisfied beyond reasonable doubt that a person under 18 is in breach of a provision of the ASBI to which they are subject, may impose:

- a supervision order; or
- a detention order.

Neither of these orders may be made by the court of its own motion. They can only be made on the application of the person who applied for the injunction.

In considering whether and how to exercise its powers to make either order, the court must consider any representations made by the YOT specified as responsible for supervising a requirement of the order or, if a YOT is not so specified, the local YOT within the meaning of s 14 (see **N2.3** above).

A detention order may not be imposed in respect of a person aged under 14: Sch 2, para 1(5). The court may not make a detention order unless it is satisfied that, in view of the severity or extent of the breach, no other power available to the court is appropriate: Sch 2, para 1(6).

N3.6 Applying for supervision order or detention order (Sch 2, para 1)

A person making an application for a supervision order or detention order must before doing so:

(a) consult any YOT specified as responsible for supervising requirements of the order or, if a YOT is not so specified, the local YOT within the meaning of s 14 (see **N2.3** above);

(b) inform any other body or individual the applicant thinks appropriate.

The application must be made by way of complaint in writing: r 2. By rule 10, the application must:

(a) be supported by evidence of the breach of any provisions of the injunction which is alleged; and
(b) include a statement that consultation with the relevant YOT has been undertaken.

N3.6.1 *Supervision order (Sch 2, paras 2–13)*

A supervision order imposes on the defaulter one or more of the following requirements:

- a supervision requirement (keeping appointments with a YOT worker for a specified period up to maximum of six months);
- an activity requirement (participation in specified activities for a specified number of days which in aggregate must not be less than 12 and not more than 24 days);
- a curfew requirement (for a specified period not less than two hours and not more than eight hours a night).

Before making a supervision order, the court must obtain and consider information about the defaulter's family circumstances and the likely effect of such an order on those circumstances. Before making a supervision order imposing two or more requirements, the court must consider their mutual compatibility.

The court must ensure, as far as practicable, that any requirement imposed by a supervision order is such as to avoid:

- any interference with the times, if any, at which the defaulter normally works or attends school or any other educational establishment, and
- any conflict with the requirements of any other court order or injunction to which the defaulter may be subject.

The court must specify the maximum period for the operation of any requirement in the order. This period may not exceed six months.

The order must also specify the YOT which will work with the defaulter. This must be the YOT in whose area it appears to the court that the respondent will reside during the period of the supervision order.

A court may only include an activity requirement in a supervision order if:

- it has consulted the YOT which is to be, or is, specified in the order;

- it is satisfied that it is feasible to secure compliance with the requirement or requirement as varied;
- it is satisfied that provision for the defaulter to participate in the activities proposed can be made under the arrangements for persons to participate in such activities which exist in the area of the YOT which is to be or is specified in the order; and
- in a case where the requirement or requirement as varied would involve the cooperation of a person other than the defaulter and the responsible officer, that person consents to its inclusion or variation.

The youth court, on application by the injunction applicant or the defaulter, may:

- vary the operative period;
- amend the area of residence; or
- revoke the order.

If the responsible officer considers that the defaulter has failed to comply with any requirement of the supervision order, the responsible officer must inform the injunction applicant.

On being informed by the responsible officer, the injunction applicant may apply to the appropriate court. Before making such an application, the injunction applicant must consult with the YOT specified in the order and any person consulted before the making of the original application.

Where an application is made by the injunction applicant and the court is satisfied beyond reasonable doubt that the defaulter has without reasonable excuse failed to comply with any requirement of the supervision order, the court may:

- revoke the supervision order and make a new one; or
- revoke the order and make a detention order.

These powers may not be exercised at any time after the defaulter reaches the age of 18.

N3.6.2 *Detention order (Sch 2, paras 14 and 15)*

A detention order is an order that the defaulter be detained for a specified period not exceeding three months beginning with the day after the day the order was made.

The court may not make a detention order unless it is satisfied, in view of the severity or extent of the breach, that no other power available to the court is appropriate: Sch 2, para 1(6).

Before making a detention order, the injunction applicant must consult the YOT previously consulted and any other person consulted before the original application.

The order may be served in a YOI, secure training centre, or secure accommodation. There is no provision for early release so a defaulter would serve the whole of the period specified in the order.

The injunction applicant or the defaulter may apply to the court to revoke the order. The court may revoke the order if it appears to be in the interests of justice to do so, having regard to circumstances which have arisen since the detention order was made.

N3.7 Breach of injunction when defaulter has attained 18

The proceedings for breach of the injunction will be dealt with in the county court. The court will have a power to remand in custody if the proceedings are adjourned and, if the breach is proved beyond reasonable doubt, the county court has the power to deal with the breach as a civil contempt of court punishable by up to two years in prison and/or an unlimited fine.

N4 Gang Injunction

Gang injunctions are governed by Part 4 (ss 34–50) of the Policing and Crime Act 2009. The Magistrates' Courts (Injunctions: Gang-related Violence) Rules 2015 apply. The Home Office has issued statutory guidance *Injunctions to Prevent Gang-Related Violence and Gang-Related Drug Dealing* (last updated May 2016).

N4.1 Age

A gang injunction may be made against any person who has attained the age of 14: s 34(1).

N4.2 Grounds for an injunction (s 34)

A court may grant a gang injunction against a respondent aged 14 or over if:

- the court is satisfied, on the balance of probabilities, that the respondent has engaged in, or has encouraged or assisted, gang-related violence or gang-related drug-dealing activity; and
- the court thinks it is necessary to grant the injunction for either or both of the following purposes—
  (a) to prevent the respondent from engaging in, or encouraging or assisting, gang-related violence or gang-related drug-dealing activity;
  (b) to protect the respondent from gang-related violence or gang-related drug-dealing activity.

Something is 'gang-related' if it occurs in the course of, or is otherwise related to, the activities of a group that:

(a) consists of at least three people; and
(b) has one or more characteristics that enable its members to be identified by others as a group.

'Drug-dealing activity' means:

(a) the unlawful production, supply, importation or exportation of a controlled drug; or
(b) the unlawful production, supply, importation, or exportation of a psychoactive substance.

The definition of 'violence' includes both a threat of violence and violence against property: ss 34(6) and 49(1).

It has been held that gang injunctions do not involve the determination of a criminal charge within the meaning of the ECHR,

Blackstone's Handbook of Youths in the Criminal Courts. Mark Ashford, Gareth Branston, and Naomi Redhouse, Oxford University Press.
 DOI: 10.1093/oso/9780198913146.003.0082

art 6 and therefore the civil standard of proof is not incompatible with the right to a fair trial: *Chief Constable of Lancashire v Wilson* [2015] EWHC 2763 (QB); *Jones v Birmingham City Council* [2018] EWCA Civ 1189.

N4.3 **Consultation (s 38)**

Before applying for a gang injunction, the applicant must consult:

- any local authority, and any chief police officer, that the applicant thinks it appropriate to consult, and
- where the respondent is under the age of 18 (and will be under that age when the application is made), the YOT in whose area it appears to the applicant that the respondent resides, and
- any other body or individual that the applicant thinks it appropriate to consult.

If it appears to the applicant that the respondent resides in the area of two or more YOTs, it must consult such of those teams as the applicant thinks appropriate.

N4.4 **Making an application (s 37)**

An application for a gang injunction may be made by any of the following:

(a) the chief officer of police for a police area;
(b) the chief constable of the British Transport Police; or
(c) a local authority.

Applications in relation to respondents under the age of 18 must be made in the youth court: s 49(1). The application must be made by way of complaint in writing (r 2).

By rule 3, an application for an injunction must:

(a) state the name, address, and date of birth of the respondent;
(b) state the name and address of a parent or guardian of the respondent;
(c) be supported by evidence of the matters of which the court must be satisfied for the first and second conditions under s 34 to be met;
(d) state the terms of the injunction applied for; and
(e) in the case of an application made on notice, include a statement that the consultation requirement has been complied with.

In the case of an application made on notice, a copy of the application must be served by the applicant on:

(a) the respondent personally; and
(b) the parent or guardian personally, or by posting it to or leaving it at that parent or guardian's address.

N4.5 Interim injunction (ss 40 and 41)

Where the application was made on notice and the court adjourns the application, an interim gang injunction may be made if the court thinks that it is just and convenient to do so.

An interim order made after an application on notice may include any provision the court could have made in relation to a full injunction (including a power of arrest).

Where an application was made without notice and the court adjourns the application, the youth court may make an interim injunction only if it thinks it is necessary to do so.

An interim order made after an application without notice may include any provision the court could have made in relation to a full injunction (including a power of arrest) except for a requirement to participate in particular activities.

By rule 4, an interim injunction which is made on an application made without notice:

(a) must be served on the respondent personally as soon as practicable; and
(b) will not take effect until it has been so served.

N4.6 Application without notice (s 39)

An application for a gang injunction may be made without the respondent being given notice. If an application without notice is made, the application must also state the reasons why it is necessary for the application to be made without notice having been given: r 3(2).

If an application without notice is made the court must either—

- dismiss the application, or
- adjourn the proceedings.

If the court adjourns the proceedings, the applicant must comply with the consultation requirement before the date of the first full hearing.

N4.7 Length of order (s 36(2))

The gang injunction may not include a prohibition or requirement that has effect after the end of the period of two years beginning with the day on which the injunction is granted ('the injunction date').

N4.8 Contents of injunctions (ss 35 and 36)

A gang injunction may include both prohibitions and requirements.

The prohibitions included in the injunction may, in particular, have the effect of prohibiting the respondent from:

- being in a particular place;
- being with particular persons in a particular place;
- being in charge of a particular species of animal in a particular place;
- wearing particular descriptions of articles of clothing in a particular place;
- using the internet to facilitate or encourage violence or drug-dealing activity.

The requirements included in the injunction may, in particular, have the effect of requiring the respondent to:

- notify the person who applied for the injunction of the respondent's address and of any change to that address;
- be at a particular place between particular times on particular days;
- present themselves to a particular person at a place where they are required to be between particular times on particular days;
- participate in particular activities between particular times on particular days.

A requirement to be at a particular place between particular times may not be such as to require the respondent to be at a particular place for more than eight hours in any day.

The prohibitions and requirements included in the injunction must, so far as practicable, be such as to avoid—

- any conflict with the respondent's religious beliefs, and
- any interference with the times, if any, at which the respondent normally works or attends any educational establishment.

N4.9 Power of arrest (s 36(6) and (7))

The court may attach a power of arrest in relation to—

- any prohibition in the injunction, or
- any requirement in the injunction, other than one which has the effect of requiring the respondent to participate in particular activities.

Unlike ASBIs, there is no statutory threshold for attaching a power of arrest.

If the court attaches a power of arrest, it may specify that the power is to have effect for a shorter period than the prohibition or requirement to which it relates.

N4.10 Respondent attaining 18 during proceedings (r 16)

Where a respondent attains the age of 18 after the commencement of proceedings, their case will remain in a youth court. The youth court may, at the request of the applicant or the respondent or of its own motion, direct that the proceedings be transferred to the High Court or county court, having had regard in particular to:

(a) the stage which the proceedings have reached;
(b) the circumstances of the applicant and the respondent; and
(c) the need to ensure fairness between the applicant and the respondent.

The court may not make a direction to transfer the case without a hearing, on notice to both the applicant and the respondent.

N4.11 Adult respondents in the youth court

Unlike ASBIs, there is no provision for adult co-respondents to be dealt with in the youth court.

N4.12 Reporting restrictions

The usual automatic reporting restrictions under the CYPA 1933, s 49 apply to an application for a gang injunction.

N4.13 Special measures

There is no statutory provision extending the special measures contained in Part 2 of the YJCEA 1999 to an application for a gang injunction (cf statutory extension to applications for ASBI).

N4.14 Review hearing (s 36(3)–(5))

A review hearing is a hearing held for the purpose of considering whether the gang injunction should be varied or discharged. The youth court may order the applicant and the respondent to attend one or more review hearings on a specified date or dates.

If any prohibition or requirement in the injunction is to have effect after the end of the period of one year beginning with the injunction date, the court must order the applicant and the respondent to attend a review hearing on a specified date within the last four weeks of the one year period (whether or not the court orders them to attend any other review hearings).

Where:

- the respondent is under the age of 18 on the injunction date, and

- any prohibition or requirement in the injunction is to have effect after the respondent reaches that age and for at least the period of four weeks beginning with the respondent's 18th birthday,

the court must order the applicant and the respondent to attend a review hearing on a specified date within that period.

N4.15 **Variation or discharge of injunctions (s 42)**

The youth court may vary or discharge an injunction if:

- a review hearing is held, or
- an application to vary or discharge the injunction is made.

An application to vary or discharge the injunction may be made by:

- the person who applied for the injunction;
- the respondent.

The power to vary an injunction includes power to:

- include an additional prohibition or requirement in the injunction;
- extend the period for which a prohibition or requirement in the injunction has effect;
- attach a power of arrest or extend the period for which a power of arrest attached to the injunction has effect.

An application to vary or discharge a gang injunction must be made by way of complaint in writing (r 2). By rule 6, an application which is not made at a review hearing must be made to either the court which made the injunction or any youth court for the local justice area in which the respondent currently resides. Such an application must specify:

(a) the reason why the person applying for variation or discharge believes the court should vary or discharge the injunction; and
(b) if the application is to vary the injunction, the variation which is sought.

N4.16 **Appeal (s 46B)**

An appeal lies to the Crown Court against a decision of a youth court made under Part 4 of the ABCPA 2014.

On appeal, the Crown Court may make:

- whatever orders are necessary to give effect to its determination of the appeal;
- whatever incidental or consequential order appear to it to be just.

N5 **Breach of Gang Injunction**

The powers of the court to deal with an alleged breach of a gang injunction are contained in the Policing and Crime Act 2009, ss 43–46A and Schs 5 and 5A.

N5.1 **Arrest without warrant (s 43)**

Where a power of arrest is attached to a provision of the gang injunction, a constable may arrest a person where the constable has reasonable cause to suspect to be in breach of that provision.

If a constable arrests a person for breach of the injunction, the constable must inform the person who applied for the injunction.

A person arrested for breach must be brought before a relevant judge within the period of 24 hours beginning with the time of the arrest. In calculating when the period of 24 hours ends, Christmas Day, Good Friday, and any Sunday are to be disregarded.

'Relevant judge', in relation to an injunction, means a judge of the court that granted the injunction, except that, where the respondent is now aged 18 or over and the injunction was made by a youth court, it means a judge of the county court. A judge in relation to a youth court means a person qualified to sit as a member of that court: s 49(1).

N5.2 **Warrant of arrest (s 44)**

If the injunction applicant considers that the respondent is in breach of any of its provisions, that person may apply to a relevant judge for the issue of a warrant for the arrest of the respondent.

A relevant judge may not issue a warrant unless the judge has reasonable grounds for believing that the respondent is in breach of any provision of the injunction.

N5.3 **Appearing before the youth court**

If the matter is not disposed of when the person is brought before the judge, the judge may remand the person: s 44(5).

By rule 8 of The Magistrates' Courts (Injunctions: Gang-related Violence) Rules 2015, if proceedings are adjourned and the arrested person is released:

(a) the matter must be dealt with (either by the same or another youth court) within 28 days of the date on which the arrested person appears in court; and

Blackstone's Handbook of Youths in the Criminal Courts. Mark Ashford, Gareth Branston, and Naomi Redhouse, Oxford University Press.
 DOI: 10.1093/oso/9780198913146.003.0083

(b) the arrested person must be given not less than two days' notice of the hearing.

N5.4 Remand of the defaulter (Sch 5)

With the exception of a remand for the purposes of a medical report, an alleged defaulter under the age of 18 may only be remanded on bail: Sch 5, para 2(1). The youth court may remand them:

(a) with a recognizance: para 2(2);
(b) with such requirements as appear to the court to be necessary to secure that the person does not interfere with witnesses or otherwise obstruct the course of justice: para 7.

N5.5 Powers of court on breach of an injunction (s 46A and Sch 5A, para 1)

Where the youth court is satisfied beyond reasonable doubt that a person is in breach of any provision of the gang injunction, it may impose:

(a) a supervision order;
(b) a detention order: Sch 5A, para 1(1) and (2).

Neither of these orders may be made by the court of its own motion. They can only be made on the application of the person who applied for the injunction: para 1(1)(b).

In considering whether and how to exercise its powers to make either order, the court must consider a report made to assist the court in that respect by the YOT in whose area it appears to the applicant that the defaulter resides: para 1(5).

The court may not make a detention order unless it is satisfied that, in view of the severity or extent of the breach, no other power available to the court is appropriate: para 1(6).

Neither order may be made against a person who has attained the age of 18: para 1(1)(aa).

N5.6 Applying for supervision order or detention order (Sch 5A, para 1)

A person making an application for a supervision order or detention order must, before doing so:

(a) consult the YOT in whose area it appears to the applicant that the defaulter resides; and
(b) any other person previously consulted.

An application must be by way of complaint in writing (r 2). By rule 10, the application must—

(a) be supported by evidence of the breach of any provisions of the injunction which is alleged; and
(b) include a statement that the required consultation with the relevant YOT has been undertaken.

N5.6.1 *Supervision order (Sch 5A, paras 2–13)*

A supervision order imposes on the defaulter one or more of the following requirements:

(a) a supervision requirement (keeping appointments with a YOT worker for a specified period up to maximum of six months);
(b) an activity requirement (participation in specified activities for a specified number of days which in aggregate must not be less than 12 and not more than 24 days);
(c) a curfew requirement (for a specified period not less than two hours and not more than eight hours a day).

Before making a supervision order, the court must obtain and consider information about the defaulter's family circumstances and the likely effect of such an order on those circumstances. Before making a supervision order imposing two or more requirements, the court must consider their mutual compatibility.

The court must ensure, as far as practicable, that any requirement imposed by a supervision order is such as to avoid:

(a) any conflict with the defaulter's religious beliefs;
(b) any interference with the times, if any, at which the defaulter normally works or attends school or any other educational establishment; and
(c) any conflict with the requirements of any other court order or injunction to which the defaulter may be subject.

The court must specify the maximum period for the operation of any requirement in the order. This period may not exceed six months.

The order must also specify the YOT which will work with the defaulter. This must be the YOT in whose area it appears to the court that the respondent will reside during the period of the supervision order.

A court may only include an activity requirement in a supervision order if—

(a) it has consulted the YOT which is to be, or is, specified in the order;
(b) it is satisfied that it is feasible to secure compliance with the requirement or requirement as varied;

(c) it is satisfied that provision for the defaulter to participate in the activities proposed can be made under the arrangements for persons to participate in such activities which exist in the area of the YOT which is to be or is specified in the order; and
(d) in a case where the requirement or requirement as varied would involve the co-operation of a person other than the defaulter and the responsible officer, that person consents to its inclusion or variation.

The youth court, on application by the injunction applicant or the defaulter, may:
(a) vary the operation period;
(b) amend the area of residence; or
(c) revoke the order.

If the responsible officer considers that the defaulter has failed to comply with any requirement of the supervision order, the responsible officer must inform the injunction applicant.

On being informed by the responsible officer, the injunction applicant may apply to the appropriate court. Before making such an application, the injunction applicant must consult with the YOT specified in the order and any person consulted before the making of the original application.

Where an application is made by the injunction applicant and the court is satisfied beyond reasonable doubt that the defaulter has, without reasonable excuse, failed to comply with any requirement of the supervision order, the court may:
(a) revoke the supervision order and make a new one; or
(b) revoke the order and make a detention order.

These powers may not be exercised at any time after the defaulter reaches the age of 18.

N5.6.2 *Detention order (Sch 5A, paras 14 and 15)*

A detention order is an order that the defaulter be detained for a specified period not exceeding three months beginning with the day after the day the order was made.

The court may not make a detention order unless it is satisfied, in view of the severity or extent of the breach, that no other power available to the court is appropriate: para 1(7).

Before making a detention order, the injunction applicant must consult the YOT previously consulted and any other person consulted before the original application.

The order may be served in a YOI, secure training centre, or secure accommodation. There is no provision for early release so a defaulter would serve the whole of the period specified in the order.

The injunction applicant or the defaulter may apply to the court to revoke the order. The court may revoke the order if it appears to be in the interests of justice to do so, having regard to circumstances which have arisen since the detention order was made.

N5.6.3 *Breach of injunction when defaulter has attained 18*

The proceedings for breach of the injunction will be dealt with in the county court. The court will have a power to remand in custody if the proceedings are adjourned and if the breach is proved beyond reasonable doubt the county court has the power to deal with the breach as a civil contempt of court punishable by up to two years in prison and/or an unlimited fine.

Appendix Y1

Sentencing Children and Young People: Overarching Principles

Guideline effective from: 1 June 2017

Guideline users should be aware that the Equal Treatment Bench Book covers important aspects of fair treatment and disparity of outcomes for different groups in the criminal justice system. It provides guidance which sentencers are encouraged to take into account wherever applicable, to ensure that there is fairness for all involved in court proceedings.

The Sentencing Council issues this definitive guideline in accordance with section 120 of the Coroners and Justice Act 2009. It applies to all children or young people, who are sentenced on or after 1 June 2017, regardless of the date of the offence.[1]

Section 59(1) of the Sentencing Code provides that:

> "Every court –
> (a) must, in sentencing an offender, follow any sentencing guidelines which are relevant to the offender's case, and
> (b) must, in exercising any other function relating to the sentencing of offenders, follow any sentencing guidelines which are relevant to the exercise of this function,
> unless the court is satisfied that it would be contrary to the interests of justice to do so."

Guidance for sentencing children and young people set out in the 2006 robbery guideline and the 2007 sexual offences guideline, both produced by the Sentencing Guidelines Council, are replaced by this guideline. See also:

- Sentencing children and young people: robbery
- Sentencing children and young people: sexual offences

Guilty plea section only

Section 73 of the Sentencing Code provides:

(1) This selmust take into account the following matters—

  (a) the stage in the proceedings for the offence at which the offender indicated the intention to plead guilty, and

[1] 'Offence' includes breach of an order where this constitutes a separate criminal offence but not breach of terms of a sentence or licence

(b) the circumstances in which the indication was given.

This section of the guideline applies regardless of the date of the offence to all children or young people where the first hearing is on or after 1 June 2017. It applies equally in youth courts, magistrates' courts and the Crown Court.

Section one: General approach

Sentencing principles

1.1 When sentencing children or young people (those aged under 18 at the date of the finding of guilt) a court must[2] have regard to:
- the principal aim of the youth justice system (to prevent offending by children and young people);[3] and
- the welfare of the child or young person.[4]

1.2 While the seriousness of the offence will be the starting point, the approach to sentencing should be individualistic and focused on the child or young person, as opposed to offence focused. For a child or young person the sentence should focus on rehabilitation where possible. A court should also consider the effect the sentence is likely to have on the child or young person (both positive and negative) as well as any underlying factors contributing to the offending behaviour.

1.3 Domestic and international laws dictate that a custodial sentence should always be a measure of last resort for children and young people and statute provides that a custodial sentence may only be imposed when the offence is so serious that no other sanction is appropriate (see section six for more information on custodial sentences).

1.4 It is important to avoid 'criminalising' children and young people unnecessarily; the primary purpose of the youth justice system is to encourage children and young people to take responsibility for their own actions and promote re-integration into society rather than to punish. Restorative justice disposals may be of particular value for children and young people as they can encourage them to take responsibility for their actions and understand the impact their offence may have had on others.

[2] This section does not apply when imposing a mandatory life sentence, when imposing a statutory minimum custodial sentence, when imposing detention for life under the dangerous offender provisions or when making certain orders under the Mental Health Act 1983

[3] s.37(1) Crime and Disorder Act 1998

[4] s.44(1) Children and Young Persons Act 1933

1.5 It is important to bear in mind any factors that may diminish the culpability of a child or young person. Children and young people are not fully developed and they have not attained full maturity. As such, this can impact on their decision making and risk taking behaviour. It is important to consider the extent to which the child or young person has been acting impulsively and whether their conduct has been affected by inexperience, emotional volatility or negative influences. They may not fully appreciate the effect their actions can have on other people and may not be capable of fully understanding the distress and pain they cause to the victims of their crimes. Children and young people are also likely to be susceptible to peer pressure and other external influences and changes taking place during adolescence can lead to experimentation, resulting in criminal behaviour. When considering a child or young person's age their emotional and developmental age is of at least equal importance to their chronological age (if not greater).

1.6 For these reasons, children and young people are likely to benefit from being given an opportunity to address their behaviour and may be receptive to changing their conduct. They should, if possible, be given the opportunity to learn from their mistakes without undue penalisation or stigma, especially as a court sanction might have a significant effect on the prospects and opportunities of the child or young person and hinder their re-integration into society.

1.7 Offending by a child or young person is often a phase which passes fairly rapidly and so the sentence should not result in the alienation of the child or young person from society if that can be avoided.

1.8 The impact of punishment is likely to be felt more heavily by a child or young person in comparison to an adult as any sentence will seem longer due to their young age. In addition penal interventions may interfere with a child or young person's education and this should be considered by a court at sentencing.

1.9 Any restriction on liberty must be commensurate with the seriousness of the offence. In considering the seriousness of any offence, the court must consider the child or young person's culpability in committing the offence and any harm which the offence caused, was intended to cause or might foreseeably have caused.[5]

[5] s.63 Sentencing Code

1.10 Section 57 of the Sentencing Code sets out the purposes of sentencing adults aged 18 or over on the date of conviction. There is no corresponding provision as to the purposes of sentencing children and young people but, as noted above at paragraph 1.1, section 58 of the Code makes clear that the court has the following duties when sentencing children or young people: to have regard to the principal aim of the youth justice system (which is to prevent offending), and to have regard to the welfare of the child or young person.

For more information on assessing the seriousness of the offence see section four.

Welfare

1.11 The statutory obligation to have regard to the welfare of a child or young person includes the obligation to secure proper provision for education and training,[6] to remove the child or young person from undesirable surroundings where appropriate[7] and the need to choose the best option for the child or young person taking account of the circumstances of the offence.

1.12 **In having regard to the welfare of the child or young person, a court should ensure that it is alert to:**

- **any mental health problems or learning difficulties/disabilities;**
- **any experiences of brain injury or traumatic life experience (including exposure to drug and alcohol abuse) and the developmental impact this may have had;**
- **any speech and language difficulties and the effect this may have on the ability of the child or young person (or any accompanying adult) to communicate with the court, to understand the sanction imposed or to fulfil the obligations resulting from that sanction;**
- **the vulnerability of children and young people to self harm, particularly within a custodial environment; and**
- **the effect on children and young people of experiences of loss and neglect and/or abuse.**

1.13 Factors regularly present in the background of children and young people that come before the court include deprived homes, poor parental employment records, low educational attainment, early experience of offending by other family members, experience of abuse and/or neglect, negative

[6] s.44 Children and Young Persons Act 1933
[7] ibid.

influences from peer associates and the misuse of drugs and/or alcohol.

1.14 The court should always seek to ensure that it has access to information about how best to identify and respond to these factors and, where necessary, that a proper assessment has taken place in order to enable the most appropriate sentence to be imposed.

1.15 The court should consider the reasons why, on some occasions, a child or young person may conduct themselves inappropriately in court (e.g. due to nervousness, a lack of understanding of the system, a belief that they will be discriminated against, peer pressure to behave in a certain way because of others present, a lack of maturity etc) and take this into account.

1.16 Evidence shows that looked after children and young people are over-represented in the criminal justice system.[8] When dealing with a child or young person who is looked after the court should also bear in mind the additional complex vulnerabilities that are likely to be present in their background. For example, looked after children and young people may have no or little contact with their family and/or friends, they may have special educational needs and/or emotional and behavioural problems, they may be heavily exposed to peers who have committed crime and they are likely to have accessed the care system as a result of abuse, neglect or parental absence due to bereavement, imprisonment or desertion. The court should also bear in mind that the level of parental-type support that a looked after child or young person receives throughout the criminal justice process may vary, and may be limited. For example, while parents are required to attend court hearings, this is not the case for social workers responsible for looked after children and young people. In some instances a looked after child or young person (including those placed in foster homes and independent accommodation, as well as in care homes) may be before the court for a low level offence that the police would not have been involved in, if it had occurred in an ordinary family setting.

1.17 For looked after children and young people who have committed an offence that crosses the custody threshold sentencers will need to consider any impact a custodial

[8] Department for Education (2014) Outcomes for Children Looked After by Local Authorities in England, as at 31 March 2014. Statistical First Release 49/2014. [accessed via: https://www.gov.uk/government/statistics/outcomes-for-children-looked-after-by-local-authorities]

sentence may have on their leaving care rights and whether this impact is proportionate to the seriousness of the offence. For other young people who are in the process of leaving care or have recently left care then sentencers should bear in mind any effect this often difficult transition may have had on the young person's behaviour.

1.18 There is also evidence to suggest that black and minority ethnic children and young people are over-represented in the youth justice system.[9] The factors contributing to this are complex. One factor is that a significant proportion of looked after children and young people are from a black and minority ethnic background.[10] A further factor may be the experience of such children and young people in terms of discrimination and negative experiences of authority. When having regard to the welfare of the child or young person to be sentenced, the particular factors which arise in the case of black and minority ethnic children and young people need to be taken into account.

1.19 The requirement to have regard to the welfare of a child or young person is subject to the obligation to impose only those restrictions on liberty that are commensurate with the seriousness of the offence; accordingly, a court should not impose greater restrictions because of other factors in the child or young person's life.

1.20 When considering a child or young person who may be particularly vulnerable, sentencers should consider which available disposal is best able to support the child or young person and which disposals could potentially exacerbate any underlying issues. This is particularly important when considering custodial sentences as there are concerns about the effect on vulnerable children and young people of being in closed conditions, with significant risks of self harm, including suicide.

1.21 The vulnerability factors that are often present in the background of children and young people should also be considered in light of the offending behaviour itself. Although they do not alone cause offending behaviour—there are many children and young people who have experienced these circumstances but do not commit crime—there is a correlation and any response to criminal activity amongst children

[9] https://www.gov.uk/government/uploads/system/uploads/attachment_data/file/568680/bame-disproportionality-in-the-cjs.pdf

[10] https://www.gov.uk/government/statistics/children-looked-after-in-england-including-adoption-2015-to-2016 (National table, figure B1)

and young people will need to recognise the presence of such factors in order to be effective.

These principles do not undermine the fact that the sentence should reflect the seriousness of the offence. See section four for further guidance on assessing the seriousness of an offence.

Section two: Allocation

(See also the allocation charts [below] when reading this section.)

2.1 **Subject to the exceptions noted below, cases involving children and young people should be tried in the youth court.** It is the court which is best designed to meet their specific needs. A trial in the Crown Court with the inevitably greater formality and greatly increased number of people involved (including a jury and the public) should be reserved for the most serious cases.[11] The welfare principles in this guideline apply to all cases, including those tried or sentenced in the Crown Court.

This section covers the exceptions to this requirement.[12]

2.2 A child or young person must always appear in the Crown Court for trial if:

- charged with homicide;
- charged with a firearms offence subject to a mandatory minimum sentence of three years (and is over 16 years of age at the time of the offence); or
- notice has been given to the court (under section 51B or 51C of the Crime and Disorder Act 1998) in a serious or complex fraud or child case.

Dangerousness

2.3 A case should be sent to the Crown Court for trial if the offence charged is a specified offence[13] **and** it seems to the court that if found guilty the child or young person would meet the criteria for a sentence under the dangerous offender provisions.

2.4 A sentence under the dangerous offender provisions can only be imposed if:

- the child or young person is found guilty of a specified violent or sexual offence; **and**

[11] *R on the application of H, A and O v Southampton Youth Court* [2004] EWHC 2912 Admin

[12] s.24 Magistrates' Courts Act 1980

[13] As listed in schedule 18 Sentencing Code

- the court is of the opinion that there is a significant risk to the public of serious harm caused by the child or young person committing further specified offences; **and**
- a custodial term of at least four years would be imposed for the offence.

2.5 A 'significant risk' is more than a mere possibility of occurrence. The assessment of dangerousness should take into account all the available information relating to the circumstances of the offence and **may** also take into account any information regarding previous patterns of behaviour relating to this offence and any other relevant information relating to the child or young person. In making this assessment it will be essential to obtain a pre-sentence report.

2.6 Children and young people may change and develop within a shorter time than adults and this factor, along with their level of maturity, may be highly relevant when assessing probable future conduct and whether it may cause a significant risk of serious harm.[14]

2.7 In anything but the most serious cases it may be impossible for the court to form a view as to whether the child or young person would meet the criteria of the dangerous offender provisions without greater knowledge of the circumstances of the offence and the child or young person. In those circumstances jurisdiction for the case should be retained in the youth court. If, following a guilty plea or a finding of guilt, the dangerousness criteria appear to be met then the child or young person should be committed **for sentence.**

Grave crimes

2.8 Where a child or young person is before the court for an offence to which section 250 Sentencing Code applies and the court considers that it ought to be possible to sentence them to more than two years' detention if found guilty of the offence, then they should be sent to the Crown Court. The test to be applied by the court is whether there is a **real prospect** that a sentence in excess of two years' detention will be imposed.

2.9 An offence comes within section 250 where:

- it is punishable with 14 years' imprisonment or more for an adult (but is not a sentence fixed by law);
- it is an offence of sexual assault, a child sex offence committed by a child or young person, sexual activity with a

[14] *R v Lang* [2005] EWCA Crim 2864, [2006] 1 WLR 2509

child family member or inciting a child family member to engage in sexual activity; or

- it is one of a number of specified offences in relation to firearms, ammunition and weapons which are subject to a minimum term but, in respect of which, a court has found exceptional circumstances justifying a lesser sentence.

2.10 Before deciding whether to send the case to the Crown Court or retain jurisdiction in the youth court, the court should hear submissions from the prosecution and defence. As there is now a power to commit grave crimes for sentence[15] the court should no longer take the prosecution case at its highest when deciding whether to retain jurisdiction.[16] In most cases it is likely to be impossible to decide whether there is a real prospect that a sentence in excess of two years' detention will be imposed without knowing more about the facts of the case and the circumstances of the child or young person. In those circumstances the youth court should retain jurisdiction and commit for sentence if it is of the view, having heard more about the facts and the circumstances of the child or young person, that its powers of sentence are insufficient.

Where the court decides that the case is suitable to be dealt with in the youth court it must warn the child or young person that all available sentencing options remain open and, if found guilty, the child or young person may be committed to the Crown Court for sentence.

Children and young people should only be sent for trial or committed for sentence to the Crown Court when charged with or found guilty of an offence of such gravity that a custodial sentence substantially exceeding two years is a realistic possibility. For children aged 10 or 11, and children/young people aged 12–14 who are not persistent offenders, the court should take into account the normal prohibition on imposing custodial sentences.

Charged alongside an adult

2.11 The proper venue for the trial of any child or young person is normally the youth court. Subject to statutory restrictions, that remains the case where a child or young person is jointly charged with an adult. If the adult is sent for trial to the Crown Court, the court should conclude that the child or young person must be tried separately in the youth court unless it is in the interests of justice for the child or young person and the adult to be tried jointly.

[15] s.16 Sentencing Code

[16] *R (DPP) v South Tyneside Youth Court* [2015] EWHC 1455 (Admin)

2.12 Examples of factors that should be considered when deciding whether to send the child or young person to the Crown Court (rather than having a trial in the youth court) include:

- whether separate trials will cause injustice to witnesses or to the case as a whole (consideration should be given to the provisions of sections 27 and 28 of the Youth Justice and Criminal Evidence Act 1999);
- the age of the child or young person; the younger the child or young person, the greater the desirability that the child or young person be tried in the youth court;
- the age gap between the child or young person and the adult; a substantial gap in age militates in favour of the child or young person being tried in the youth court;
- the lack of maturity of the child or young person;
- the relative culpability of the child or young person compared with the adult and whether the alleged role played by the child or young person was minor; and/or
- the lack of previous findings of guilt on the part of the child or young person.

2.13 The court should bear in mind that the youth court now has a general power to commit for sentence (as discussed at paragraph 2.9); in appropriate cases this will permit a sentence to be imposed by the same court on adults and children and young people who have been tried separately.

2.14 The court should follow the plea before venue procedure (see flowcharts) prior to considering whether it is in the interests of justice for the child or young person and the adult to be tried jointly.

Remittal from the Crown Court for sentence

2.15 If a child or young person is found guilty before the Crown Court of an offence other than homicide the court must remit the case to the youth court, unless it would be undesirable to do so.[17] In considering whether remittal is undesirable a court should balance the need for expertise in the sentencing of children and young people with the benefits of the sentence being imposed by the court which determined guilt.

2.16 Particular attention should be given to children and young people who are appearing before the Crown Court only because they have been charged with an adult offender; referral orders are generally not available in the Crown Court but may be the most appropriate sentence.

[17] s.25 Sentencing Code

Allocation flowcharts

These charts are intended to be a reference tool only; for full guidance, particularly for grave crimes, see section two above.

1. Child or young person charged alone or with other children and young people

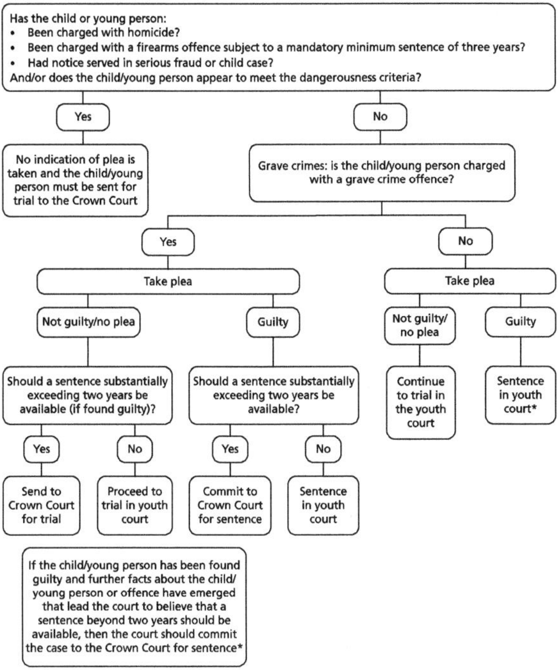

* If the dangerousness provisions appear to be satisfied the court must commit for sentence

2. Child or young person and adult charged as co-defendants where the adult is charged with an indictable only offence (or an offence where notice is given to the court under s.51B or s.51C Crime & Disorder Act 1998)

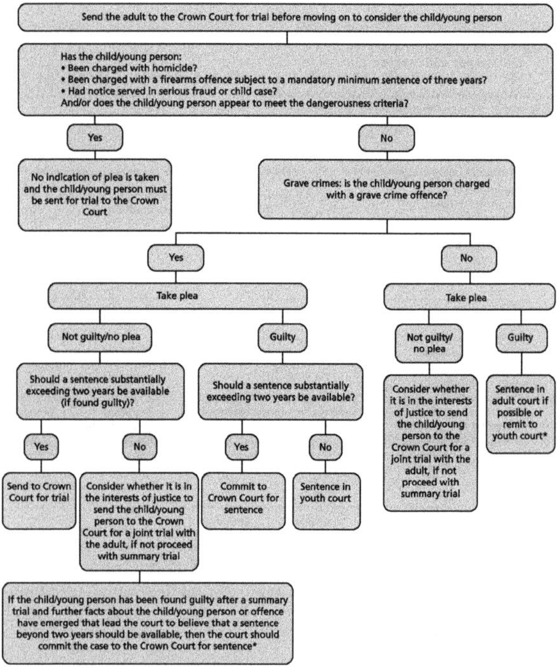

*If the dangerousness provisions appear to be satisfied the court must commit for sentence

3. Child or young person and adult charged as co-defendants where the adult is charged with either way offence

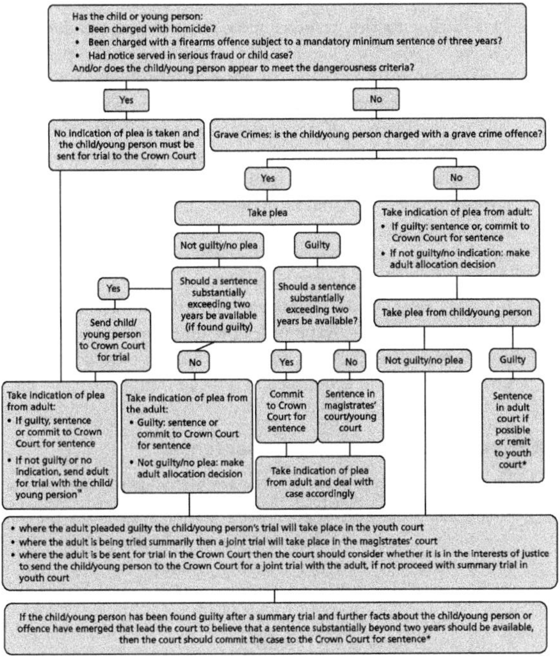

*If the dangerousness provisions appear to be satisfied the court must commit for sentence

Section three: Parental responsibilities

3.1 For any child or young person aged under 16 appearing before court there is a statutory requirement that parents/guardians attend during all stages of proceedings, unless the court is satisfied that this would be unreasonable having regard to the circumstances of the case.[18] The court may also enforce this requirement for a young person aged 16 and above if it deems it desirable to do so.

3.2 Although this requirement can cause a delay in the case before the court it is important it is adhered to. If a court does find exception to proceed in the absence of a responsible adult then

[18] s.34A Children and Young Persons Act 1933

extra care must be taken to ensure the outcomes are clearly communicated to and understood by the child or young person.

3.3 In addition to this responsibility there are also orders that can be imposed on parents. If the child or young person is aged under 16 then the court has a duty to make a **parental bind over** or impose a **parenting order**, if it would be desirable in the interest of preventing the commission of further offences.[19] There is a discretionary power to make these orders where the young person is aged 16 or 17. If the court chooses not to impose a parental bind over or parenting order it must state its reasons for not doing so in open court. In most circumstances a parenting order is likely to be more appropriate than a parental bind over.

3.4 A court cannot make a bind over alongside a referral order. If the court makes a referral order the duty on the court to impose a parenting order in respect of a child or young person under 16 years old is replaced by a discretion.[20]

Section four: Determining the sentence

4.1 In determining the sentence, the key elements to consider are:

- the principal aim of the youth justice system (to prevent re-offending by children and young people);
- the welfare of the child or young person;
- the age of the child or young person (chronological, developmental and emotional);
- the seriousness of the offence;
- the likelihood of further offences being committed; and
- the extent of harm likely to result from those further offences.

The seriousness of the offence

(This applies to all offences; when offence specific guidance for children and young people is available this should be referred to.)

4.2 The seriousness of the offence is the starting point for determining the appropriate sentence; the sentence imposed and any restriction on liberty must be commensurate with the seriousness of the offence.

4.3 The approach to sentencing children and young people should always be individualistic and the court should always have in

[19] s.376 & s.366 Sentencing Code
[20] s.366(3) Sentencing Code

mind the principal aims of the youth justice system.

4.4 In order to determine the seriousness of the offence the court should assess the culpability of the child or young person and the harm that was caused, intended to be caused or could foreseeably have been caused.

4.5 In assessing **culpability** the court will wish to consider the extent to which the offence was planned, the role of the child or young person (if the offence was committed as part of a group), the level of force that was used in the commission of the offence and the awareness that the child or young person had of their actions and its possible consequences. There is an expectation that in general a child or young person will be dealt with less severely than an adult offender. In part, this is because children and young people are unlikely to have the same experience and capacity as an adult to understand the effect of their actions on other people or to appreciate the pain and distress caused and because a child or young person may be less able to resist temptation, especially where peer pressure is exerted. Children and young people are inherently more vulnerable than adults due to their age and the court will need to consider any mental health problems and/or learning disabilities they may have, as well as their emotional and developmental age. Any external factors that may have affected the child or young person's behaviour should be taken into account.

4.6 In assessing **harm** the court should consider the level of physical and psychological harm caused to the victim, the degree of any loss caused to the victim and the extent of any damage caused to property. (This assessment should also include a consideration of any harm that was intended to be caused or could foreseeably have been caused in the committal of the offence.)

4.7 The court should also consider any aggravating or mitigating factors that may increase or reduce the overall seriousness of the offence. **If any of these factors are included in the definition of the committed offence they should not be taken into account when considering the relative seriousness of the offence before the court.**

Aggravating factors
Statutory aggravating factors:
Previous findings of guilt, having regard to a) the **nature** of the offence to which the finding of guilt relates and its **relevance** to the current offence; and b) the **time** that has elapsed since the finding of guilt
Offence committed whilst on bail
Offence motivated by, or demonstrating hostility based on any of the following characteristics or presumed characteristics of the victim: religion, race, disability, sexual orientation or transgender identity
Other aggravating factors (non-exhaustive):
Steps taken to prevent the victim reporting or obtaining assistance
Steps taken to prevent the victim from assisting or supporting the prosecution
Victim is particularly vulnerable due to factors including but not limited to age, mental or physical disability
Restraint, detention or additional degradation of the victim
Prolonged nature of offence
Attempts to conceal/dispose of evidence
Established evidence of community/wider impact
Failure to comply with current court orders
Attempt to conceal identity
Involvement of others through peer pressure, bullying, coercion or manipulation
Commission of offence whilst under the influence of alcohol or drugs
History of antagonising or bullying the victim
Deliberate humiliation of victim, including but not limited to filming of the offence, deliberately committing the offence before a group of peers with the intention of causing additional distress or circulating details/photos/videos etc of the offence on social media or within peer groups

Factors reducing seriousness or reflecting personal mitigation (non-exhaustive)
No previous findings of guilt **or** no relevant/recent findings of guilt
Remorse, particularly where evidenced by voluntary reparation to the victim
Good character and/or exemplary conduct

Unstable upbringing including but not limited to: • time spent looked after • lack of familial presence or support • disrupted experiences in accommodation or education • exposure to drug/alcohol abuse, familial criminal behaviour or domestic abuse • victim of neglect or abuse, or exposure to neglect or abuse of others • experiences of trauma or loss
Participated in offence due to bullying, peer pressure, coercion or manipulation
Limited understanding of effect on victim
Serious medical condition requiring urgent, intensive or long-term treatment
Communication or learning disabilities or mental health concerns
In education, work or training
Particularly young or immature child or young person (where it affects their responsibility)
Determination and/or demonstration of steps taken to address addiction or offending behaviour

Age and maturity of the child or young person

4.8 There is a statutory presumption that no child under the age of 10 can be guilty of an offence.[21]

4.9 With a child or young person, the consideration of age requires a different approach to that which would be adopted in relation to the age of an adult. Even within the category of child or young person the response of a court to an offence is likely to be very different depending on whether the child or young person is at the lower end of the age bracket, in the middle or towards the top end.

4.10 Although chronological age dictates in some instances what sentence can be imposed (see section six for more information) the developmental and emotional age of the child or young person should always be considered and it is of at least equal importance as their chronological age. It is important to consider whether the child or young person has the necessary maturity to appreciate fully the consequences of their conduct, the extent to which the child or young person has been acting on an impulsive basis and whether their conduct

[21] s.50 Children and Young Persons Act 1933

has been affected by inexperience, emotional volatility or negative influences.

Section five: Guilty plea

This section of the guideline applies regardless of the date of the offence to all children or young people where the **first hearing** is on or after 1 June 2017. It applies equally in youth courts, magistrates' courts and the Crown Court.

Key principles

5.1 The purpose of this section of the guideline is to encourage those who are going to plead guilty to do so as early in the court process as possible. Nothing in this section should be used to put pressure on a child or young person to plead guilty.

5.2 Although a guilty person is entitled not to admit the offence and to put the prosecution to proof of its case, an acceptance of guilt:

1. normally reduces the impact of the crime upon victims;
2. saves victims and witnesses from having to testify; and
3. is in the public interest in that it saves public time and money on investigations and trials.

5.3 A guilty plea produces greater benefits the earlier the plea is made. In order to maximise the above benefits and to provide an incentive to those who are guilty to indicate a guilty plea as early as possible, this section of the guideline makes a clear distinction between a reduction in the sentence available at the first stage of the proceedings and a reduction in the sentence available at a later stage of the proceedings.

5.4 The purpose of reducing the sentence for a guilty plea is to yield the benefits described above and the guilty plea should be considered by the court to be independent of the child or young person's mitigation.

- Factors such as admissions at interview, co-operation with the investigation and demonstrations of remorse should **not** be taken into account in determining the level of reduction. Rather, they should be considered separately and prior to any guilty plea reduction, as potential mitigating factors.
- The benefits apply regardless of the strength of the evidence against a child or young person. The strength of the evidence should **not** be taken into account when determining the level of reduction.
- This section applies only to the punitive elements of the

sentence and has no impact on ancillary orders including orders of disqualification from driving.

Approach

Stage 1: Determine the appropriate sentence for the offence(s) in accordance with any offence specific sentencing guideline or using this *Overarching Principles* guideline.
Stage 2: Determine the level of reduction for a guilty plea in accordance with this guideline.
Stage 3: State the amount of that reduction.
Stage 4: Apply the reduction to the appropriate sentence.
Stage 5: Follow any further steps in the offence specific guideline to determine the final sentence.

Nothing in this guideline affects the duty of the parties to progress cases (including the service of material) and identify any issues in dispute in compliance with the Criminal Procedure Rules and Criminal Practice Directions.

Determining the level of reduction

The maximum level of reduction for a guilty plea is one-third.

5.5 **Plea indicated at the first stage of the proceedings:** Where a guilty plea is indicated at the first stage of proceedings a reduction of **one-third** should be made (subject to the exceptions below). The first stage will normally be the first hearing in the magistrates' or youth court at which a plea is sought and recorded by the court.[22]

5.6 **Plea indicated after the first stage of proceedings—maximum one quarter—sliding scale of reduction thereafter:** After the first stage of the proceedings the maximum level of reduction is **one-quarter** (subject to the exceptions below).

5.7 The reduction should be decreased from **one-quarter** to a maximum of **one-tenth** on the first day of trial having regard to the time when the guilty plea is first indicated relative to the progress of the case and the trial date (subject to the exceptions below). The reduction should normally be decreased further, even to zero, if the guilty plea is entered during the course of the trial.

[22] In cases where (in accordance with the Criminal Procedure Rules) a child/young person is given the opportunity to enter a guilty plea without attending a court hearing, doing so within the required time limits will constitute a plea at the first stage of proceedings.

5.8 For the purposes of this guideline a trial will be deemed to have started when pre-recorded cross-examination has begun.

Applying the reduction

Detention and training orders

5.9 A detention and training order (DTO) must be for a term of at least 4 months but must not exceed 24 months. If the reduction in sentence for a guilty plea results in a sentence that falls below 4 months a non-custodial sentence should be imposed.

Imposing one type of sentence rather than another

5.10 The reduction in sentence for a guilty plea can be taken into account by imposing one type of sentence rather than another, for example:

- by reducing a custodial sentence to a community sentence; or
- by reducing a community sentence to a different means of disposal.

Alternatively the court could reduce the length or severity of any punitive requirements attached to a community sentence.

5.11 The court must always have regard to the principal aim of the youth justice system, which is to prevent offending by children and young people. It is, therefore, important that the court ensures that any sentence imposed is an effective disposal.

5.12 Where a court has imposed one sentence rather than another to reflect the guilty plea there should normally be no further reduction on account of the guilty plea. Where, however, the less severe type of sentence is justified by other factors, the appropriate reduction for the plea should be applied in the normal way.

More than one summary offence

5.13 When dealing with more than one summary offence, the aggregate sentence is limited to a maximum of six months. Allowing for a reduction for each guilty plea, consecutive sentences might result in the imposition of the maximum six month sentence. Where this is the case, the court **may** make a modest *additional* reduction to the *overall* sentence to reflect the benefits derived from the guilty plea.

Sentencing up to 24 months DTO for offences committed by children and young people

5.14 A DTO of up to 24 months may be imposed on a child or young person if the offence is one which, but for the plea, would have attracted a sentence of detention in excess of 24 months under section 250 of the Sentencing Code.

Exceptions

Referral order

5.15 As a referral order is a sentence that is only available upon pleading guilty there should be no further reduction of the sentence to reflect the guilty plea.

Further information, assistance or advice necessary before indicating plea

5.16 Where the sentencing court is satisfied that there were particular circumstances which significantly reduced the child or young person's ability to understand what was alleged, or otherwise made it unreasonable to expect the child or young person to indicate a guilty plea **sooner than was done**, a reduction of one-third should still be made. It may sometimes be appropriate to treat a child or young person as needing such information, assistance or advice, where it would not be needed in the case of an adult.

5.17 In considering whether this exception applies, sentencers should distinguish between cases in which it is necessary to receive advice and/or have sight of evidence in order to understand whether the child or young person is, in fact and law, guilty of the offence(s) charged, and cases in which a child or young person merely delays guilty plea(s) in order to assess the strength of the prosecution evidence and the prospects of a finding of guilt or acquittal.

Newton hearings and special reasons hearings

5.18 In circumstances where a child or young person's version of events is rejected at a Newton hearing[23] or special reasons

[23] A Newton hearing is held when a child/young person pleads guilty but disputes the case as put forward by the prosecution and the dispute would make a difference to the sentence. The judge will normally hear evidence from witnesses to decide which version of the disputed facts to base the sentence on.

hearing,[24] the reduction which would have been available at the stage of proceedings the plea was indicated should normally be halved. Where witnesses are called during such a hearing, it may be appropriate further to decrease the reduction.

Child or young person found guilty of a lesser or different offence

5.19 If a child or young person is found guilty of a lesser or different offence from that originally charged, and has earlier made an unequivocal indication of a guilty plea to this lesser or different offence to the prosecution and the court, the court should give the level of reduction that is appropriate to the stage in the proceedings at which this indication of plea (to the lesser or different offence) was made taking into account any other of these exceptions that apply. In the Crown Court where the offered plea is a permissible alternative on the indictment as charged, the child or young person will not be treated as having made an unequivocal indication unless the defendant has entered that plea.

Minimum sentence under section 51A of the Firearms Act 1968

5.20 There can be no reduction for a guilty plea if the effect of doing so would be to reduce the length of sentence below the required minimum term.

Appropriate custodial sentences for young persons aged at least 16 but under 18 when found guilty under the Prevention of Crime Act 1953 and Criminal Justice Act 1988

5.21 In circumstances where an appropriate custodial sentence of a DTO of at least four months falls to be imposed on a young person who is aged at least 16 but under 18, who has been found guilty under sections 1 or 1A of the Prevention of Crime Act 1953; or section 139, 139AA or 139A of the Criminal Justice Act 1988 (certain possession of knives or offensive weapon offences) the court may impose any sentence that it considers appropriate, having taken into consideration the general principles set out above.

[24] A special reasons hearing occurs when a child/young person is found guilty of an offence carrying a mandatory licence endorsement or disqualification from driving and seeks to persuade the court that there are extenuating circumstances relating to the offence that the court should take into account by reducing or avoiding endorsement or disqualification. This may involve calling witnesses to give evidence.

Mandatory life sentences for murder

5.22 Murder is the most serious criminal offence and the sentence prescribed is different from all other sentences. By law, the sentence for murder is detention for life and the child or young person will remain subject to the sentence for the rest of their life.

5.23 Given the special characteristic of the offence of murder and the unique statutory provision in Schedule 21 of the Sentencing Code [of starting points for the minimum term] to be served by a child or young person, careful consideration has to be given to the extent of any reduction for a guilty plea and to the need to ensure that the minimum term properly reflects the seriousness of the offence.

5.24 Whilst the general principles continue to apply (both that a guilty plea should be encouraged and that the extent of any reduction should reduce if the indication of plea is later than the first stage of the proceedings) the process of determining the level of reduction will be different.

Determining the level of reduction

5.25 In other circumstances:

- the court will weigh carefully the overall length of the minimum term taking into account other reductions for which the child or young person may be eligible so as to avoid a combination leading to an inappropriately short sentence;
- where it is appropriate to reduce the minimum term having regard to a plea of guilty, the reduction will not exceed one-sixth and will never exceed five years; and
- the maximum reduction of one-sixth or five years (whichever is less) should only be given when a guilty plea has been indicated at the first stage of the proceedings. Lesser reductions should be given for guilty pleas after that point, with a maximum of one-twentieth being given for a guilty plea on the day of trial.

The exceptions outlined at 5.16–5.18 apply to murder cases.

Section six: Available sentences

Crossing a significant age threshold between commission of offence and sentence

6.1 There will be occasions when an increase in the age of a child or young person will result in the maximum sentence on the date of the *finding of guilt* being greater than that available on the date on which the offence was *committed* (primarily turning 12, 15 or 18 years old).

6.2 In such situations the court should take as its starting point the sentence likely to have been imposed on the date at which the offence was committed. This includes young people who attain the age of 18 between the *commission* and *the finding of guilt of the offence*[25] but when this occurs the purpose of sentencing adult offenders[26] has to be taken into account, which is:

- the punishment of offenders;
- the reduction of crime (including its reduction by deterrence);
- the reform and rehabilitation of offenders;
- the protection of the public; and
- the making of reparation by offenders to persons affected by their offences.

6.3 When any significant age threshold is passed it will rarely be appropriate that a more severe sentence than the maximum that the court could have imposed at the time the offence was committed should be imposed. However, a sentence at or close to that maximum may be appropriate.

Persistent offenders

6.4 Some sentences can only be imposed on children and young people if they are deemed a persistent offender. A child or young person **must** be classed as such for one of the following to be imposed:

- a youth rehabilitation order (YRO) with intensive supervision and surveillance when aged under 15;
- a YRO with fostering when aged under 15; and
- a detention and training order (DTO) when aged 12–14.

6.5 The term persistent offender is not defined in statute but has been considered by the Court of Appeal. In general it is expected that the child or young person would have had previous contact with authority as a result of criminal behaviour. This includes previous findings of guilt as well as admissions of guilt such as restorative justice disposals and conditional cautions.

6.6 A child or young person who has committed one previous offence cannot reasonably be classed as a persistent offender,

[25] *R v Ghafoor* [2002] EWCA Crim 1857, [2003] 1 Cr App R (S) 428
[26] s.57 Sentencing Code

and a child or young person who has committed two or more previous offences should not necessarily be assumed to be one. To determine if the behaviour is persistent the nature of the previous offences and the lapse of time between the offences would need to be considered.[27]

6.7 If there have been three findings of guilt in the past 12 months for imprisonable offences of a comparable nature (or the child or young person has been made the subject of orders as detailed above in relation to an imprisonable offence) then the court could certainly justify classing the child or young person as a persistent offender.

6.8 When a child or young person is being sentenced in a single appearance for a series of separate, comparable offences committed over a short space of time then the court could justifiably consider the child or young person to be a persistent offender, despite the fact that there may be no previous findings of guilt.[28] In these cases the court should consider whether the child or young person has had prior opportunity to address their offending behaviour before imposing one of the optional sentences available for persistent offenders only; if the court determines that the child or young person has not had an opportunity to address their behaviour and believes that an alternative sentence has a reasonable prospect of preventing re-offending then this alternative sentence should be imposed.

6.9 The court may also wish to consider any evidence of a reduction in the level of offending when taking into account previous offending behaviour. Children and young people may be unlikely to desist from committing crime in a clear cut manner but there may be changes in patterns of criminal behaviour (e.g. committing fewer and/or less serious offences or there being longer lengths of time between offences) that indicate that the child or young person is attempting to desist from crime.

6.10 Even where a child or young person is found to be a persistent offender, a court is not obliged to impose one of the optional sentences. The approach should still be individualistic and all other considerations still apply. **Custodial sentences must be a last resort for all children and young people** and there is an expectation that they will be particularly rare for children and young people aged 14 or under.

[27] *R v M* [2008] EWCA Crim 3329
[28] *R v S* [2000] 1 Cr App R (S)18

Appendix Y1

Sentences available by age:

	Age of child or young person			
Sentence	**10–11**	**12–14**	**15–17**	**Rehabilitation period**
Absolute or conditional discharge (or reparation order if convicted before 28 June 2022)	✓	✓	✓	Absolute discharge and reparation: spent on day of sentence Conditional discharge: spent on last day of the period of discharge
Financial order	✓	✓	✓	Spent 6 months after the finding of guilt
Referral order	✓	✓	✓	Spent on day of completion
Youth rehabilitation order (YRO)	✓	✓	✓	Spent 6 months after the last day the order is to have effect
YRO with intensive supervision and surveillance or fostering	✓ For persistent offenders **only**	✓ For persistent offenders **only**	✓	Spent 6 months after the last day the order is to have effect
Detention and training order	x	✓ For persistent offenders **only**	✓	6 months or under: spent 18 months after the sentence is completed (including supervision period) More than 6 months: spent 24 months after the sentence is completed (including supervision period)

	Age of child or young person			
Sentence	**10–11**	**12–14**	**15–17**	**Rehabilitation period**
s.250 Sentencing Code detention (grave crime)	✓	✓	✓	More than 6 months – 30 months: spent 24 months after sentence completed (including licence period) More than 30 months – 48 months: spent 42 months after sentence completed (including licence period) More than 48 months: never spent
Extended sentence of detention*	✓	✓	✓	Never spent

* If found guilty of a specified violent or sexual offence and the court is of the opinion that there is a significant risk to the public of serious harm caused by the child or young person committing further specified offences.

6.11 Some sentences have longer rehabilitation periods than others, for example referral orders are spent on the last day on which the order is to have effect.[29] Sentences can also have varying impacts on the future of children and young people; for example absolute or conditional discharges are not deemed to be treated as convictions other than for the purposes of criminal proceedings[30] and therefore may have a lesser impact on the child or young person's future prospects than other sentences. The length of the rehabilitation periods and any likely effects on the child or young person's future prospects should be taken into account when considering if the sentence is commensurate to the seriousness of the offence.

[29] s.139 Legal Aid, Sentencing and Punishment of Offenders Act 2012
[30] s.82 Sentencing Code

Breaches and the commission of further offences during the period of an order

6.12 If a child or young person is found guilty of breaching an order, or commits a further offence during the period of an order, the court will have various options available depending upon the nature of the order (**see Appendix one**). The primary aim of the court should be to encourage compliance and seek to support the rehabilitation of the child or young person.

Absolute or conditional discharge and reparation orders

6.13 An absolute discharge is appropriate in the least serious cases when, despite a finding of guilt, the court considers that no punishment should be imposed.

6.14 A conditional discharge is appropriate when, despite a finding of guilt, the offence is not serious enough to warrant an immediate punishment. The fixed period of conditional discharge must not exceed three years. Unless exceptional circumstances are found, a conditional discharge cannot be imposed if the child or young person has received one of the following in the previous 24 months: two or more cautions; or a conditional caution followed by a caution.[31]

6.15 A reparation order is only available if the offender was **convicted of the offence before 28 June 2022**. It can require a child or young person to make reparation to the victim of the offence, where a victim wishes it, or to the community as a whole. Before making an order the court must consider a written report from a relevant authority, e.g. a youth offending team (YOT), and the order must be commensurate with the seriousness of the offence.

6.16 If the court has the power to make a reparation order but chooses not to do so, it must give its reasons.

Financial order

6.17 The court may impose a fine for any offence (unless the criteria for a mandatory referral order are met). In accordance with statutory requirements, where financial orders are being considered, priority must be given to compensation orders and, when an order for costs is to be made alongside a fine, the amount of the cost must not exceed the amount of the fine. If the child or young person is under 16 then the court has a duty to order parents or guardians to pay the fine; if

[31] s.66ZB Crime & Disorder Act 1998

the young person is 16 or over this duty is discretionary. In practice, many children and young people will have limited financial resources and the court will need to determine whether imposing a fine will be the most effective disposal.

6.18 A court should bear in mind that children and young people may have money that is specifically required for travel costs to school, college or apprenticeships and lunch expenses.

Referral orders

6.19 A referral order is the mandatory sentence in a youth court or magistrates' court for most children and young people who have committed an offence for the first time and have pleaded guilty to an imprisonable offence. Exceptions are for offences where a sentence is fixed by law or if the court deems a custodial sentence, an absolute or conditional discharge or a hospital order to be more appropriate.

6.20 A discretionary referral order can also be imposed for any offence where there has been a plea of guilty regardless of previous offending history. It should be remembered that they are not community orders and in general terms may be regarded as orders which fall between community disposals and fines. However, bearing in mind that the principal aim of the youth justice system is to prevent children and young people offending, second or subsequent referral orders should be considered in those cases where:

1. the offence is not serious enough for a YRO but the child or young person does appear to require some intervention OR
2. the offence is serious enough for a YRO but it is felt that a referral order would be the best way to prevent further offending (as an example, this may be because the child or young person has responded well in the past to such an order and the offence now before the court is dissimilar to that for which a referral order was previously imposed).

Referral orders are the main sentence for delivering restorative justice and all panel members are trained Restorative Conference Facilitators; as such they can be an effective sentence in encouraging children and young people to take responsibility for their actions and understand the effect their offence may have had on their victim.

6.21 In cases where children or young people have offended for the first time and have pleaded guilty to committing an offence which is on the cusp of the custody threshold, YOTs should be encouraged to convene a Youth Offender Panel prior to sentence (sometimes referred to as a 'pseudo-panel' or 'pre-panel') where the child or young person is asked to attend before a panel and agree an intensive contract. If that contract is placed before the sentencing youth court, the court can then decide whether it is sufficient to move below custody on this occasion. The proposed contract is not something the court can alter in any way; the court will still have to make a decision between referral order and custody but can do so on the basis that if it makes a referral order it can have confidence in what that will entail in the particular case.

6.22 The court determines the length of the order but a Referral Order Panel determines the requirements of the order.

Offence seriousness	Suggested length of referral order
Low	• 3–5 months
Medium	• 5–7 months
High	• 7–9 months
Very high	• 10–12 months

The YOT may propose certain requirements and the length of these requirements may not correspond to the above table; if the court feels these requirements will best achieve the aims of the youth justice system then they may still be imposed.

Youth rehabilitation orders (YRO)

6.23 A YRO is a community sentence within which a court may include one or more requirements designed to provide for punishment, protection of the public, reducing re-offending and reparation.

6.24 When imposing a YRO, the court must fix a period within which the requirements of the order are to be completed; this must not be more than three years from the date on which the order comes into effect.

6.25 The offence must be 'serious enough' in order to impose a YRO, but it does not need to be an imprisonable offence. Even if an offence is deemed 'serious enough' the court is not obliged to make a YRO.

6.26 The requirements included within the order (and the subsequent restriction on liberty) and the length of the order must be proportionate to the seriousness of the offence and suitable for the child or young person. The court should take care to ensure that the requirements imposed are not too onerous so as to make breach of the order almost inevitable.

6.27 The available requirements within a YRO are:

- activity requirement (maximum 90 days);
- supervision requirement;
- unpaid work requirement (between 40 and 240 hours);*
- programme requirement;
- attendance centre requirement (maximum 12 hours for children aged 10–13, between 12 and 24 hours for young people aged 14 or 15 and between 12 and 36 hours for young people aged 16 or over (all ages refer to age at date of the finding of guilt));
- prohibited activity requirement;
- curfew requirement
  - for an offence of which the offender was **convicted on or after 28 June 2022:** 2-20 hours in any 24 hours; maximum 112 hours in any period of 7 days beginning with the day of the week on which the requirement first takes effect; or
  - for an offence of which the offender was **convicted before 28 June 2022**: 2-16 hours in any 24 hours
- exclusion requirement (maximum 3 months);
- electronic monitoring requirement;
- residence requirement;*
- local authority residence requirement (maximum 6 months but not for any period after young person attains age of 18);
- fostering requirement (maximum 12 months but not for any period after young person attains age of 18);**
- mental health treatment requirement;
- drug treatment requirement (with or without drug testing);
- intoxicating substance requirement;
- education requirement; and
- intensive supervision and surveillance requirement.**

* These requirements are only available for young people aged 16 or 17 years old on the date of the finding of guilt.

** These requirements can only be imposed if the offence is an imprisonable one AND the custody threshold has been passed. For children and young people aged under 15 they must be deemed a persistent offender.

Many of the above requirements have additional restrictions.

Magistrates, always consult your legal adviser before imposing a YRO.

6.28 When determining the nature and extent of the requirements the court should primarily consider the likelihood of the child or young person re-offending and the risk of the child or young person causing serious harm. A higher risk of re-offending does not in itself justify a greater restriction on liberty than is warranted by the seriousness of the offence; any requirements should still be commensurate with the seriousness of the offence and regard must still be had for the welfare of the child or young person.

6.29 The YOT will assess this as part of their report and recommend an intervention level to the court for consideration. It is possible for the court to ask the YOT to consider a particular requirement.

	Child or Young person profile	**Requirements of order**[32]
Standard	Low likelihood of re-offending **and** a low risk of serious harm	Primarily seek to repair harm caused throu gh, for example: • reparation; • unpaid work; • supervision; and/or • attendance centre.
Enhanced	Medium likelihood of re-offending **or** a medium risk of serious harm	Seek to repair harm caused and to enable help or change through, for example: • supervision; • reparation; • requirement to address behaviour e.g. drug treatment, offending behaviour programme, education programme; and/or • a combination of the above.
Intensive	High likelihood of re-offending **or** a very high risk of serious harm	Seek to ensure the control of and enable help or change for the child or young person through, for example: • supervision; • reparation; • requirement to address behaviour; • requirement to monitor or restrict movement, e.g. prohibited activity, curfew, exclusion or electronic monitoring; and/or • a combination of the above.

[32] The examples provided here are not exclusive; the YOT will make recommendations based upon their assessment of the young offender which may vary from some of the examples given.

6.30 If a child or young person is assessed as presenting a high risk of re-offending or of causing serious harm but the offence that was committed is of relatively low seriousness then the appropriate requirements are likely to be primarily rehabilitative or for the protection of the public.

6.31 Likewise if a child or young person is assessed as presenting a low risk of re-offending or of causing serious harm but the offence was of relatively high seriousness then the appropriate requirements are likely to be primarily punitive.

Orders with intensive supervision and surveillance or with fostering

6.32 An intensive supervision and surveillance requirement and a fostering requirement are both community alternatives to custody.

6.33 The offence must be punishable by imprisonment, cross the custody threshold and a custodial sentence must be merited before one of these requirements can be imposed.

6.34 An order of this nature may only be imposed on a child or young person aged below 15 (at the time of the finding of guilt) if they are a persistent offender.

With intensive supervision and surveillance:

6.35 An order of this nature must include an extended activity requirement of between 90 and 180 days, a supervision requirement and a curfew requirement. Where appropriate, a YRO with intensive supervision and surveillance may also include additional requirements (other than a fostering requirement), although the order as a whole must comply with the obligation that the requirements must be those most suitable for the child or young person and that any restrictions on liberty are commensurate with the seriousness of the offence.

6.36 When imposing such an order, the court must ensure that the requirements are not so onerous as to make the likelihood of breach almost inevitable.

With fostering:

6.37 Where a fostering requirement is included within a YRO, it will require the child or young person to reside with a local authority foster parent for a specified period that must not exceed 12 months.

6.38 In order to impose this requirement the court must be satisfied that the behaviour which constituted the offence was due to a significant extent to the circumstances in which the child or young person was living, and that the imposition of fostering requirement would assist in the child or young person's rehabilitation. It is likely that other rights will be engaged (such as those under Article 8 of the European Convention on Human Rights)[33] and any interference with such rights must be proportionate.

6.39 The court must consult the child or young person's parent or guardian (unless impracticable) and the local authority before including this requirement. It can only be included if the child or young person was legally represented in court when consideration was being given to imposing such a requirement unless the child or young person, having had the opportunity to do so, did not apply for representation or that right was withdrawn because of the child or young person's conduct. **This requirement may be included only where the court has been notified that arrangements are available in the area of the relevant authority.**

6.40 A YRO with a fostering requirement must include a supervision requirement and can include other requirements when appropriate (except an intensive supervision and surveillance requirement). The order as a whole must comply with the obligation that the requirements must be those most suitable for the child or young person and that any restrictions on liberty are commensurate with the seriousness of the offence.

6.41 It is unlikely that the statutory criteria[34] will be met in many cases; where they are met and the court is considering making an order, care should be taken to ensure that there is a well developed plan for the care and support of the child or young person throughout the period of the order and following conclusion of the order. The court will need to be provided with sufficient information, including proposals for education and training during the order and plans for the child or young person on completion of the order.

Custodial sentences

A custodial sentence should always be used as a last resort. If offence specific guidelines for children and young people are available then the court should consult them in the first instance to assess whether custody is the most appropriate disposal.

[33] Right to respect for family and private life
[34] See paragraphs 5.28–5.30.

The available custodial sentences for children and young people are:

Youth Court	Crown Court
Detention and training order for at least 4 months but not more than 24 months	• Detention and training order (the same periods are available as in the youth court) • Long-term detention (under section 250 Sentencing Code) • Extended sentence of detention or detention for life (if dangerousness criteria are met) • Detention at His Majesty's pleasure (for offences of murder) • Required special sentence of detention for terrorist offenders of particular concern (under section 252A of the Sentencing Code)

6.42 Under both domestic and international law, a custodial sentence must only be imposed as a '**measure of last resort**'; statute provides that such a sentence may be imposed only where an offence is 'so serious that neither a fine alone nor a community sentence can be justified'.[35] If a custodial sentence is imposed, a court must state its reasons for being satisfied that the offence is so serious that no other sanction would be appropriate and, in particular, why a YRO with intensive supervision and surveillance or fostering could not be justified.

6.43 The term of a custodial sentence must be the shortest commensurate with the seriousness of the offence; any case that warrants a DTO of less than four months must result in a non-custodial sentence. The court should take account of the circumstances, age and maturity of the child or young person.

6.44 In determining whether an offence has crossed the custody threshold the court will need to assess the seriousness of the offence, in particular the level of harm that was caused, or was likely to have been caused, by the offence. The risk of serious harm in the future must also be assessed. The pre-sentence report will assess this criterion and must be considered before a custodial sentence is imposed. A custodial sentence is most likely to be unavoidable where it is necessary to protect the public from serious harm.

6.45 Only if the court is satisfied that the offence crosses the custody threshold, and that no other sentence is appropriate,

[35] s.230 Sentencing Code

the court may, as a preliminary consideration, consult the equivalent adult guideline in order to decide upon the appropriate length of the sentence.

6.46 When considering the relevant adult guideline, the court **may** feel it appropriate to apply a sentence broadly within the region of half to two thirds of the adult sentence for those aged 15–17 and allow a greater reduction for those aged under 15. This is only a rough guide and must not be applied mechanistically. In most cases when considering the appropriate reduction from the adult sentence the **emotional and developmental age and maturity of the child or young person is of at least equal importance as their chronological age.** This reduction should be applied before any reduction for a plea of guilty.

6.47 The individual factors relating to the offence and the child or young person are of the greatest importance and may present good reason to impose a sentence outside of this range. The court should bear in mind the negative effects a short custodial sentence can have; short sentences disrupt education and/or training and family relationships and support which are crucial stabilising factors to prevent re-offending.

6.48 There is an expectation that custodial sentences will be particularly rare for a child or young person aged 14 or under. If custody is imposed, it should be for a shorter length of time than that which a young person aged 15–17 would receive if found guilty of the same offence. For a child or young person aged 14 or under the sentence should normally be imposed in a youth court (except in cases of homicide or when the dangerous offender criteria are met).

6.49 The welfare of the child or young person must be considered when imposing any sentence but is especially important when a custodial sentence is being considered. A custodial sentence could have a significant effect on the prospects and opportunities of the child or young person and a child or young person is likely to be more susceptible than an adult to the contaminating influences that can be expected within a custodial setting. There is a high reconviction rate for children and young people that have had custodial sentences and there have been many studies profiling the effect on vulnerable children and young people, particularly the risk of self harm and suicide and so it is of utmost importance that custody is a last resort.

Detention and training order (DTO)

6.50 A court can only impose a DTO if the child or young person is legally represented unless they have refused to apply for legal aid or it has been withdrawn as a result of their conduct.

6.51 If it is determined that the offence is of such seriousness that a custodial sentence is unavoidable then the length of this sentence must be considered on an individual basis. The court must take into account the chronological age of the child or young person, as well as their maturity, emotional and developmental age and other relevant factors, such as their mental health or any learning disabilities.

6.52 A DTO cannot be imposed on any child under the age of 12 at the time of the finding of guilt and is only applicable to children aged 12–14 if they are deemed to be a persistent offender. (See section on persistent offenders [at paragraphs 6.4–6.10].)

6.53 For cases **sentenced on or after 28 June 2022**, any time spent on remand in custody to youth detention accommodation under section 91(4) of the Legal Aid, Sentencing and Punishment of Offenders Act 2012 will automatically be taken into account under section 240ZA of the Criminal Justice Act 2003 and does not need to be deducted from the length of the order. The court must consider whether to give credit for time spent on bail subject to a qualifying curfew in accordance with section 240A of the Criminal Justice Act 2003 and section 325 of the Sentencing Code.

A remand to local authority accommodation under section 91(3) of the 2012 Act is neither a remand in custody for the purposes of section 240ZA of the 2003 Act nor a remand on bail for the purposes of section 240A of the 2003 Act and section 325 of the Sentencing Code. Therefore, if the offender was subject to a qualifying curfew while remanded to local authority accommodation the relevant credit should be given by the court by reducing the sentence as if a direction under section 240A or 325 had been given.

Long-term detention

6.54 A child or young person may be sentenced by the Crown Court to long-term detention under section 250 Sentencing Code if found guilty of a grave crime and neither a community order nor a DTO is suitable.

6.55 These cases may be sent for trial to the Crown Court or committed for sentence only[36] (see section two for further information).

6.56 It is possible that, following a guilty plea, a two year detention order may be appropriate as opposed to a sentence of long term detention (under section 250 Sentencing Code), to account for the reduction.

Dangerous offenders

6.57 If a child or young person is found to be a dangerous offender they can be sentenced to **extended detention** or **detention for life.**

6.58 A sentence of extended detention may be imposed only where the appropriate custodial term would be 4 years or more. The extension period must not exceed 5 years in the case of a specified violent offence and 8 years in the case of a specified sexual offence. The term of the extended sentence of detention must not exceed the maximum term of imprisonment for an adult offender convicted of that offence.

6.59 A sentence of detention for life should be used as a last resort when an extended sentence is not able to provide the level of public protection that is necessary. In order to determine this, the court should consider the following factors in the order given:

- the seriousness of the offence;
- the child or young person's previous findings of guilt;
- the level of danger posed to the public and whether there is a reliable estimate of the length of time the child or young person will remain a danger; and
- the alternative sentences available.

The court is required to set a minimum term which must be served in custody before parole can be considered.

Detention at His Majesty's pleasure

6.60 This is the mandatory sentence for any child or young person found guilty of committing a murder. The starting point for the minimum term is set out in paragraphs 5A and 6 of Schedule 21 of the Sentencing Code.

[36] s.16 Sentencing Code

Appendix: Breach of orders

Breach of a conditional discharge

7.1 If a child or young person commits an offence during the period of conditional discharge then the court has the power to re-sentence the original offence. The child or young person should be dealt with on the basis of their age when convicted (if different from their current age) and the court can deal with the original offence(s) in any way which it could have if the child or young person had just been found guilty.

7.2 There is no requirement to re-sentence; if a court deems it appropriate to do so they can sentence the child or young person for the new offence and leave the conditional discharge in place. If the order was made by the Crown Court then the youth court can commit the child or young person in custody or release them on bail until they can be brought or appear before the Crown Court. The court shall also send to the Crown Court a memorandum of conviction.

7.3 If the offender is convicted of committing a new offence after attaining the age of 18 but during the period of a conditional discharge made by a youth court then they may be re-sentenced for the original offence by the convicting adult magistrates' court. If the adult magistrates' court decides to take no action then the youth court that imposed the conditional discharge may summon the offender for the breach to be dealt with.

Breach of a reparation order

7.4 If it is proved to the appropriate court that the child or young person has failed to comply with any requirement of a reparation order that is currently in force then the court can:

- order the child or young person to pay a fine not exceeding £1,000; or
- revoke the order and re-sentence the child or young person using the range of sentencing options that are currently available. However the sentence imposed must be one that could be imposed on a child or young person who was the age that the offender was when in fact convicted.

If re-sentencing the child or young person the court must take into account the extent to which the child or young person has complied with the requirements of this order.

7.5 If the order was made by the Crown Court then the youth court can commit the child or young person in custody or release them on bail until they can be brought or appear before the Crown Court.

7.6 The child or young person or a Youth Offending Team (YOT) officer can also apply for the order to be revoked or amended. There is no power to re-sentence in this situation as the child or young person has not been found to be in breach of requirements.

Breach of a referral order (referral back to court)

7.7 If a child or young person is found to have breached the conditions of their referral order the court can revoke the referral order and re-sentence the child or young person using the range of sentencing options (other than a referral order) that are currently available. However the sentence imposed must be one that could be imposed on a child or young person who was the age that the offender was when in fact convicted. If the court chooses not to revoke the referral order then it is possible to:

- allow the referral order to continue with the existing contract;
- extend the length of the referral order up to a maximum of 12 months (in total); or
- impose a fine up to a maximum of £2,500.

7.8 If an offender has attained the age of 18 by the first court hearing then breach proceedings must be dealt with by the adult magistrates' court.

Commission of further offences whilst on a referral order

7.9 The court has the power to extend a referral order in respect of additional or further offences. This applies to not only a first referral order but also to any subsequent referral orders. Any period of extension must not exceed the total 12 month limit for a referral order.

7.10 If the court chooses not to extend the existing referral order or impose a discharge they have the power to impose a new referral order (where the discretionary referral order conditions are satisfied) in respect of the new offences only. This order can remain or run alongside the new order or the court may direct that the contract under the new order is not to take effect until the earlier order is revoked or discharged. Alternatively, the court may impose an absolute or conditional discharge.

7.11 Where an order is revoked, if it appears to be in the interests of justice, the court may deal with the original offence(s) using the range of sentencing options (other than a referral order) that are currently available. However the sentence imposed must be one that could be imposed on a child or young person who was the age that the offender was when in fact convicted. Where the referral contract has taken effect, the court shall have regard to the extent of the child or young person's compliance with the terms of the contract.

Breach of a youth rehabilitation order (YRO)

7.12 Where a child or young person is in breach of a YRO the following options are available to the court:
- take no action and allow the order to continue in its original form;
- impose a fine (up to £2,500) (and allow the order to continue in its original form);
- amend the terms of the order; or
- revoke the order and re-sentence the child or young person.

7.13 If the terms of the order are amended the new requirements must be capable of being complied with before the expiry of the overall period. The court may impose any requirement that is currently available (provided the requirement is available to a child or young person who is the age that the offender was at the time in fact convicted) and this may be in addition to, or in substitution for, any requirements contained in the order. If the YRO did not contain an unpaid work requirement and the court includes such a requirement using this power, the minimum period of unpaid work is 20 hours; this will give greater flexibility when responding to less serious breaches or where there are significant other requirements to be complied with.

7.14 A court may not amend the terms of a YRO that did not include an extended activity requirement or a fostering requirement by inserting them at this stage; should these requirements be considered appropriate following breach, the child or young person must be re-sentenced and the original YRO revoked.

7.15 A court must ensure that it has sufficient information to enable it to understand why the order has been breached and should be satisfied that the YOT and other local authority services have taken all steps necessary to ensure that the child or young person has been given appropriate opportunity and the support necessary for compliance. This is particularly important if the court is considering imposing a custodial sentence as a result of the breach.

7.16 Where the failure arises primarily from non-compliance with reporting or other similar obligations and a sanction is necessary, the most appropriate response is likely to be the inclusion of (or increase in) a primarily punitive requirement such as the curfew requirement, unpaid work, the exclusion requirement and the prohibited activity requirement or the imposition of a fine. However, continuing failure to comply with the order is likely to lead to revocation of the order and re-sentencing for the original offence.

7.17 Where the child or young person has 'wilfully and persistently' failed to comply with the order, and the court proposes to sentence again for the offence(s) in respect of which the order was made, additional powers are available.

A child or young person will almost certainly be considered to have 'wilfully and persistently' breached a YRO where there have been three breaches that have demonstrated a lack of willingness to comply with the order that have resulted in an appearance before court.

7.18 The additional powers available to the court when re-sentencing a child or young person who has 'wilfully and persistently' breached their order are:

- the making of a YRO with intensive supervision and surveillance even though the offence is non-imprisonable;
- a custodial sentence if the YRO that is breached is one with an intensive supervision and surveillance requirement, which was imposed for an offence that was imprisonable; and
- the imposition of a DTO for four months for breach of a YRO with intensive supervision and surveillance which was imposed following wilful and persistent breach of an order made for a non-imprisonable offence.

The primary objective when sentencing for breach of a YRO is to ensure that the child or young person completes the requirements imposed by the court.

7.19 If an offender has attained the age of 18 by the first court hearing then breach proceedings must be dealt with by the adult magistrates' court. If the court chooses to revoke the order then its powers are limited to those available to the court at the time of the original sentence.

Commission of further offences during a YRO

7.20 If a child or young person commits an offence whilst subject to a YRO the court can impose any sentence for the new matter, but can only impose a new YRO if they revoke the existing order. Where the court revokes the original order they may re-sentence that matter at the same time as sentencing the new offence.

Breach of a detention and training order (DTO)

7.21 If a child or young person is found to have breached a supervision requirement after release from custody then the court may:

- impose a further period of custody of up to three months or the length of time from the date the breach was committed until the end of the order, **whichever is shorter;**
- impose a further period of supervision of up to three months or the length of time from the date the breach was committed until the end of the order, **whichever is shorter;**
- impose a fine of up to £1,000; or
- take no action.

Even if the offender has attained the age of 18 proceedings for breach of the supervision requirements must be dealt with in the youth court.

Commission of further offences during a DTO

7.22 If a child or young person is found guilty of a further imprisonable offence committed during the currency of the order then the court can impose a further period of detention. This period of detention cannot exceed the period between the date of the new offence and the date of when the original order would have expired.

7.23 This period can be served consecutively or concurrently with any sentence imposed for the new offence and this period should not be taken into account when determining the appropriate length of the sentence for the new offence.

Criminal Practice Directions 2023

5. TRIAL MANAGEMENT

5.15 Sexual offences in the Youth Court

5.15.1 This section applies to all cases involving the allocation of an allegation of a sexual offence capable of being committed to the Crown Court for a sentence of long-term detention under s.250 Sentencing Code or included in s.249(1) Sentencing Code i.e. offences punishable in the case of a person aged 21 or over with imprisonment for 14 years or more; sexual assault; child sex offences committed by children or young person, sexual activity with a child family member; inciting a child family member to engage in sexual activity, irrespective of the gravity of the allegation, the age and/or antecedent history of the defendant.

5.15.2 This section does not alter the test that the Youth Court must apply when determining whether a case should be sent to the Crown Court for a potential sentence pursuant to s.250 Sentencing Code.

5.15.3 These cases can only be dealt with by an authorised DJ(MC).

Procedure

5.15.4 The determination of venue in the Youth Court is governed by s.24A MCA 1980 and s.51A Crime and Disorder Act 1998, which provide that the youth must be tried summarily unless charged with such a grave crime that long term detention is a realistic possibility, or that one of the other exceptions to this presumption arises.

5.15.5 Such cases should be listed before an authorised DJ(MC), by live link if necessary, to make the allocation decision. The prosecution should notify the court in advance to ensure listing before an authorised DJ(MC). If jurisdiction is retained and the allegation involves actual, or attempted, penetrative activity, the case must be tried by an authorised DJ(MC). In all other cases, the authorised DJ(MC) must consider whether the case is so serious and/or complex that it must be tried by an authorised DJ(MC), or whether the case can be heard by any DJ(MC) or Youth Court Bench.

5.15.6 If it is not practicable for an authorised DJ(MC) to determine venue, any DJ(MC) or any Youth Court Bench may consider that issue. If jurisdiction is retained, appropriate directions may be given but the case papers, including a detailed case summary and a note of any representations made by the parties, must be sent to an authorised DJ(MC) to consider. As soon as possible the authorised DJ(MC) must decide whether the case must be tried by an authorised DJ(MC) or whether the case is suitable to be heard by any DJ(MC) or Youth Court Bench; however, if the case involves actual, or alleged, penetrative activity, the trial must be heard by an authorised DJ(MC).

5.15.7 If the case must be tried by an authorised DJ(MC), all further procedural hearings should, so far as practicable, be heard by an authorised DJ(MC).

Cases remitted for sentence

5.15.8 All cases remitted for sentence for a sexual offence from the Crown Court to the Youth Court should be listed for sentence before an authorised DJ(MC).

Arrangements for an authorised DJ(MC) to be appointed

5.15.9 Where a case is to be tried by an authorised DJ(MC) but no such Judge is available, the Bench Legal Adviser should contact the Chief Magistrate's Office for an authorised DJ(MC) to be assigned.

Index